Taking
LIVES

Taking

LIVES

Genocide and State Power

Fifth Edition, Revised

IRVING LOUIS HOROWITZ

TRANSACTION PUBLISHERS
New Brunswick (United States of America)
London (United Kingdom)

Copyright © 2002 by Transaction Publishers, New Brunswick, New Jersey.

All rights reserved under International and Pan-American Copyright Conventions. No part of this book may be reproduced or transmitted in any form or by any means, electronic or mechanical, including photocopy, recording, or any information storage and retrieval system, without prior permission in writing from the publisher. All inquiries should be addressed to Transaction Publishers, Rutgers—The State University, 35 Berrue Circle, Piscataway, New Jersey 08854-8042.

This book is printed on acid-free paper that meets the American National Standard for Permanence of Paper for Printed Library Materials.

Library of Congress Catalog Number: 2001035167
ISBN: 0-7658-0094-2 (cloth); 0-7658-0880-3 (paper)
Printed in the United States of America

Library of Congress Cataloging-in-Publication Data

Horowitz, Irving Louis.
    Taking Lives : genocide and state power / Irving Louis Horowitz,—5th ed., rev.
        p. cm.
    Includes bibliographical references and index.
    ISBN 0-7658-0094-2 (cloth: alk. paper) — ISBN 0-7658-0880-3
    (paper : alk. paper)
    1. Genocide. 2. Mass murder. 3. State-sponsored terrorism. I. Title

K5302 .H67 2001
304.6'63—dc21   2001035167

Contents

Foreword

ANSELM L. STRAUSS   ix

Preface to the Fifth Edition   xi

Part I: Present as History

  1 New Beginnings   3
  2 Defining Genocide   13
  3 Counting Bodies   29
  4 Collectivizing Death   49
  5 Individualizing Life   67

Part II: Past as Prologue

  6 Democracy, Autocracy, and Terrorism   89
  7 Human Rights and Personal Responsibilities   111
  8 Bureaucracy and State Power   129
  9 Nationalism and Genocidal Systems   153
 10 Totalitarianism as a Penal Colony   181

Part III: Future as Memory

11 Memory as History   211
12 Banality of State Power   229
13 A Natural History of the Holocaust   255
14 Jewish Survival in a Post-Holocaust World   273

Part IV: Toward a General Theory of State-Sponsored Crime

15 Functional and Existential Visions of Genocide   297
16 Exclusivity and Inclusivity of Collective Death   319
17 Surviving the Genocidal State   341

Part V: Studying Genocide

18 Life, Death, and Sociology   359
19 Researching Genocide   367
20 Gauging Genocide   389

Notes   407
Index   441

To my friend
Milton R. Konvitz

Foreword

IN THIS REMARKABLE, CAREFULLY REASONED BUT PASSION-
ATELY ARGUED BOOK, Irving Louis Horowitz challenges our
thinking on several of the most important contemporary issues
— not merely those faced by social scientists, but those deeply
significant for humans around the globe. Taking as his test-case
issue the terrifying phenomenon of genocide, which he links
in an entirely convincing argument with the rise of the nation-
state, Horowitz challenges social scientists to grapple with
both that all too prevalent phenomenon and that linkage with
governments which now have the technological means to
eradicate whole peoples within their own borders. I would
agree with him that the major social science positions fail us
badly in understanding those excruciatingly painful human
issues.

The nation-state that gives us genocide ought to make us
question the nation-state itself; this questioning is at the center
of Horowitz's inquiry as he raises unforgettable questions
about state power and collectivism, bureaucracy, terrorism
(the best discussion of terrorism that I have seen), and the fate
of human rights, individualism, and humanism.

Something of this basic position is suggested by a key
sentence near the end of *Taking Lives*, where Horowitz argues
both against extreme statism and the social scientists who
further it with schemes of "development," vulgar economism,
manpower considerations, and other related intellectual concerns: "System building urges us not to worry about how many
peoples' lives are taken, but to worry about the nature of the
social system. I am arguing the reverse: that we worry less

about the nature of the social system and more about how many lives are taken (whether by genocide, incarceration, war, or sacrifices demanded in the name of development) by each system, state or nation."

Horowitz's handling of the historical issues central to his argument owes much to traditions that knowledgeable readers will recognize, but the framing and range of questions and discussion are entirely his own. I would predict this book will long be read not in the hackneyed sense of "a social science classic," but because it will continue to state the case so brilliantly and persuasively for a human and creative democratic society, no matter how difficult it may be to attain such a society under late twentieth and twenty-first century conditions. Horowitz reminds us that social scientists have moral and possibly critical roles to play in the continuing political struggle.

— Anselm L. Strauss
University of California., San Francisco

Preface to the Fifth Edition

Working in areas that connect living events with historic memory involves appreciation for the fact that a work committed to text is never quite finished. Better yet, it is always subject to modification, alteration and evolution. Of course, one can always write about events at so specific a level that changes needed are few and far between. But then the author and reader alike lose a sense of higher purpose. Such work becomes archival rather than academic in nature. At the other end of the scale, one can write about world historic cataclysms like genocide at so abstract a level that changes are not only superfluous, but become downright impediments to the idea of perfection. Then the work becomes metaphysical rather than social scientific in nature. Living in Robert K. Merton's "middle range" (happily I might add) thus entails running risks of imperfection and incompleteness. But it also invites the pleasant prospect of improving one's own understanding — and hopefully, those of my readers.

I would like to believe that *Taking Lives* fits the profile of a work in progress, one that has grown in value over the years because there is still so much to learn for author and audience alike. The intellectual engagement with the incredible subject of life *taking* is also a side bar entrance into life *enhancement* as well. Increasingly, the touchstone for me at least of a social science with a human rights face is both the quality of collective life and even more, the stark survival of the solitary person against extraordinary odds. This is the drama of political sociology, a field I am proud to have served for many years.

Throughout *Taking Lives* I emphasize the extraordinary opportunity afforded by studying the tragic debris of the twentieth century. We now come to the realization that the great mission of social science is to test in its variegated grandeur the forms by which life is taken from us by seemingly impersonal statist forces. The bureaucratic and administrative formations that start with a demand for order often end with a call for a messianic mission. Genocide is essentially a stratagem to maintain and extend totalitarian control while subverting the larger forces of a society that service life and seek to extend it physically and enrich it culturally.

I seem to have written on this theme my entire life. Like Moliere's foil in *Le Bourgeois Gentilhomme,* "Good Heavens! For more than forty years I have been speaking prose without knowing it." I was similarly unaware that from the time of *The Idea of War and Peace* in 1955 until the present, the engagement with ultimate questions encapsulated my sense of the purpose of social research. This quest is far removed from concerns with earlier traditions that isolated the study of civilizations from their consequences with specific persons. Quite the contrary, nothing is so personal and intimate as a human life. By the same token, nothing is any larger or more impersonal than the taking of human life en masse. Bringing both the universal and the particular into a shared view has been the task of *Taking Lives* from the first edition to the present edition.

The basic synthesis in my thinking was achieved with the fourth edition of *Taking Lives.* Without in any way wish to claim that this is the only or even the surest road to social scientific truth, it remains the path I have chosen, and one to which others seem to have gravitated. And nothing has taken place in the last decade to deflect me from that admittedly subjective judgment. Nonetheless, changes have taken place in the study of genocide and state power in recent years that are worthy of attention.

I have tried to summarize these changes in five new chapters of the final segment of this edition. The first, "Toward a Natural History of Holocaust Studies," was first prepared for a Temple University conference and published in *Human Rights Review*. The second, "Gauging Genocide", was written for a volume of papers on founders of the study of genocide titled *Pioneers of Genocide*, a rather disquieting topic for which to be celebrated. The third piece is on the "Survival of the Jewish People in the Post-Holocaust" prepared for a conference at Bar Ilan University in Israel that appeared under the title *Jewish Survival: The Identity Problem at the Close of the Twentieth Century*. The fourth paper is essentially an appraisal of Hannah Arendt's path breaking, if controversial work on genocide and legal theory. It is an amalgam derived from a variety of papers included in an *Encyclopedia of Genocide* and several journal reviews and essays appearing in *Partisan Review* and *Modern Age*. The final effort is an amalgam of several review essays that first appeared in *Congress Monthly* and *Judaism*. It is an effort to review and explain contemporary German academic rationalizations for the Holocaust. That it reveals more about German scholarly concerns than Jewish quotidian destinies should surprise few. The order of these five new chapters has been shuffled to maximize a sense of continuity. But only modest cosmetic surgery has been performed on them, again with the goal of making for a better integration in the book.

Having a scaffold is one thing, filling it with substance is quite another. Over the past decade I have written a number of smaller works that bear on the larger themes of the book. They range from an evaluation of the extraordinary work of Daniel J. Elazar on the *Covenant Tradition in Politics*, to a variety of review essays ranging from American Jewish history to European contacts of Jews and Christians in the Medieval and early Renaissance epochs. But because I felt that these shorter works were tangential to the major theme and structure of *Taking Lives*, they are not herein included. In short, I have worked hard to keep abreast of new developments in the study of state power and arbitrary and impersonal murder. Working hard to develop the African Studies list at Transaction has deepened and broadened my sense of the horrors of contemporary varieties of genocide, and no less, their massive scope to people given too little attention by the presumably civilized world.

There are a number of people who have provided great support to me in the course of this life long odyssey. And while they may not always share my assumptions of how genocide connects up with the politics and sociology of our time, I would nonetheless like to express to them my professional appreciation and personal regard. Daniel Mahoney of Assumption College, Ernest Krausz of Bar Ilan University, Charles Moskos of Northwestern University, the late Daniel Elazar of Temple University, the late Anselm Strauss of the University of California, Eli Ginzberg of Columbia University, Milton Konvitz of Cornell University, all saw earlier drafts.

I must take special note of the design and formatting of this edition. It was performed with loving care by my colleague and outstanding scholar in his own right, Nathaniel John Pallone. There was no commplace assumption too small that he did not question, and no formulation too grandiose that he did not improve upon by injecting a note of modesty in the right place. I never felt intellectually alone in his warm presence. On a practical level, the editorial assistance I received from Laurence Mintz, our senior editor at Transaction, and Andrew McIntosh, my assistant, has spared me more mistakes and shortfalls than I care to remember. Beyond any capacity for repayment, I owe my deepest gratitude to Mary E. Curtis for her editorial advice and emotional support throughout. Each of these chapters was improved as a result of her steadying influence.

— Irving Louis Horowitz
Princeton, New Jersey
April 15, 2001

Part I

PRESENT AS HISTORY

1

New Beginnings

Is it utopian to suggest that the more fully and widely the implications [of genocide] are faced, the better the chance of recognizing and limiting, perhaps even of forestalling, similar aberrations in the future?

— *Norman Cohn*[1]

THERE ARE ESSENTIALLY TWO STRATEGIES THAT AUTHORS ADOPT IN DEALING with their earlier work. Perhaps the most common is to let that work stand for what it was and is — warts and all. The reasoning is that it is vanity to tamper with what one first presents to a professional public; and anyhow, changes ex post facto simply muddle whatever clarity there was in a work offered to an earlier generation. This might be called a monolithic approach to one's past efforts. An alternative approach is to argue that a book, article, or monograph is inevitably imperfect and hence subject to the iron law of decay and irrelevance, or at least less relevance. In this scenario, the author's task is not to hide past warts but to remove them in light of present researches and experiences. That this may lead to further changes in the future is implied in such a view. This might be called the evolutionary, or to be less charitable, error laden approach to one's past efforts.

My own strong preference is for the second approach. Indeed, I hold that the ultimate vanity is to think that writings aimed for a contemporary audience have the same value as a Bible. It might be argued that even the Hebrew and Christian Testaments were revised and refurbished over time — not only in style but also in details. As long as an author lives, then the books that he or she writes are also alive; or at least, they ought to be. A book is a multilayered dialogue: between author and reader; between author and other writers on the subject; and not least, between the past and present of the author.

In the case of genocide and state power, the tremendous increase in the volume of studies now available in contrast to twenty years ago would in itself justify a serious reexamination of the subject. For during these two decades, we have seen the development of massive encyclopedias and bibliographies on genocide and the Holocaust in particular; the emergence of more than a hundred national and local resource centers for the production and dissemination of educational materials; new publications such as *Holocaust and Genocide Studies*, *History and Memory*, and *Dimensions: A Journal of Holocaust Studies;* film and television specials depicting the Holocaust such as *Schindler's List;* and most recently, major museums documenting the Holocaust and other genocides of the twentieth century.

Such a tremendous outpouring of effort and achievement makes the task of producing a new edition of an older book both simpler and more complex at the same time. One can take for granted a level of awareness on the part of the reader that was not the case in an earlier period. At the same time, the need to factor in such developments in one's own efforts is a daunting task. Under the circumstances, I hasten to note that what has been altered and augmented from the fourth to the fifth edition of *Taking Lives* is not the broad outlines or general theory of what was first presented more than twenty years ago under quite different circumstances; but rather circumstances in which we now find ourselves. The reconfiguration of global political and military forces under the weight of the collapse of European communism has a great impact on how genocide itself is now understood. This factor, coupled with the explosion of information on genocide as such, has permitted a far greater in-depth treatment of the subject than was possible even a brief two decades ago.

More strongly than ever, I believe that the best way to deal with the awful truths of genocide is through an analysis of state power and social systems, rather than through analyses such as the earlier psychiatric or biographic accounts of the perpetrator and the victim of genocide. Indeed, over the years I have become concerned that genocide not be turned into the sentimentality of victimology. It is not that personal and behavioral levels are irrelevant — they most certainly do factor into any accounting; rather, it is that the task of the social scientist is to apply a specific, grounded, objective, and heuristic analysis. It is not my wish to preempt the work style of others nor to claim undue primacy of discovery; such vain efforts would be contemptible given the colossal sobriety of the subject matter; worse, they would be impossible given the continuing assaults on human dignity that take place with a frightening regularity through the final decade of the twentieth century.

But one does need to reflect on these new currents of analysis and to factor them into one's own frame of reference. For example, earlier editions of *Taking Lives* gave scant attention to issues of individual life taking, such as guided death under medical sponsorship or supervision. This is not for lack of interest or for lack of a position on the matter of eugenics. Rather, the new conditions allow for implementation of what was earlier viewed as only abstract and theoretical. This much we owe to the single-minded impetus of Dr. Jack Kevorkian and his followers.

My essential view is that society should be extremely cautious in invoking a "Kevorkian standard" with respect to assisted suicide. There are three elements to be considered: first that bodily pain may indicate the need for possible treatment to cure illness and not simply something unwarranted, somthing simply to be curbed; second, that a "Kevorkian standard" presumes that the termination of life is somehow a favor to the suffering patient; and finally, that this approach to personal suffering can so easily slip over into visions of euthanasia as the means to everything from population management to ethnic cleansing. In short, the rights and obligations of states to its citizens are entirely relevant — but these are essentially to protect and prolong, rather than take and destroy, human life.

I would be falsely modest to claim that the work done by others on genocide and state power — duly noted in this new edition — have simply made my efforts irrelevant or superseded my line of analysis. I do not believe that to be the case. I do view my own general scaffolding of the problem of genocide correct as it was initially offered and revised during the late 1970s. The political and social contexts in which policies sanctioning genocide are developed have been and remain central. For the question of life taking is no less an issue of power, of those who command the resources and organizations that make possible the arbitrary termination of human existence in mass and in individual cases. Still, I also feel keenly the need to enter into dialogue with newer approaches and methods of research and to determine for myself what is relevant and what is superfluous or even erroneous in these alternative ways of examining crimes against humanity at colossal levels. The reader in turn can determine for himself or herself the soundness of that which is presented anew in this edition.

It is a commonplace saying that an author spends a lifetime writing the same book — under a series of different titles. This may not always be the case. Sometimes the same author divides his time and energies writing two books on different themes during one lifetime. In any event, looking back upon four decades of writing in the social sciences, it is plain to me that the subject of life and death has been a constant companion, if not a steady compunction.

In the mid-1950s I emphasized problems of war and peace, especially the variety of twentieth-century doctrines on the subject. *The Idea of War and Peace in Contemporary Social and Philosophical Theory* came out at a time when Europe and the United States were recovering from World War II. The West was very much in the throes of worries about nuclear devices. Sad to say, the heavy emphasis of positivism in the postwar era tended to reject analysis of such worldly matters; positivism preferred to think of science as a linguistic entity apart from the technologies that it made possible.

By the mid-1960s, the situation had altered dramatically. The entrance of the United States in the Vietnam War had a bracing impact on social theory. Confronting unconventional forms of struggle led to a sharp rise in models of conflict that were based on game theory, in decision theory that was rooted in policy-related interests, and in a belief that technology, far from being irrelevant, actually preempted science in any broad sense of framing hypotheses and discovering regularities in the way the world works. In this climate, I produced *The War Game,* which was in tune with the spirit of the decade; but alas, I turned out to be seriously out of tune with the war-game technocrats who determined policy in the major powers.

The next decade, the 1970s, was noteworthy for a growing pessimism, a deepening sense not only that war was a pandemic feature of the twentieth century but that even in the absence of a nuclear holocaust, peace remained remote. Low-intensity conflicts, international terrorism, holocausts in Cambodia, Nigeria, and on a smaller scale throughout the Third World, changed the consideration of conflict from the transparent issues related to war and peace to the essential issues of death-making and life-giving forces in the structure of societies and states. It was in this context that I wrote the first edition of *Taking Lives* (initially called *Genocide and State*

Power, which was incorporated into the subtitle of later editions).

Clearly, few developments took place in the 1980s to create a hopeful climate on the theory or practice of the arbitrary termination of lives. For while by the close of the decade the Communist system had largely dissolved, at least in Europe, democracy did not break out all over the totalitarian world. Instead, we had the specter of mini-wars based on ethnic factors, nationalist rivalries, and tribal claims. No single area of the world and no single race could lay claim to uniquely expressing the well of resentment or bitterness in the new political configuration. At least we learned that the end of one variety of totalitarianism did not signify the beginning of the new millennium.

Perhaps it is a personal admission rather than a public fact, but I sense a growing sense of weariness with pacific solutions to complex problems. For while world war may be more remote than it has ever been since the defeat of fascism and the defeat of communism, world peace is also more remote than civilized peoples and nations would have hoped or imagined. The displacement of class by race, or international ambitions by nationalist claims, hardly qualifies the present moment as resolving problems of the century or, for that matter, of the millennium.

My work during the 1980s in part focused on this fragmentation, not just with several new editions of *Taking Lives* but also with smaller efforts to understand what had taken place in Cuba, in Armenia, and in the world of the Jews. At the same time, the situation in the 1990s compels us to reconsider categories long discarded by many social scientists. I have in mind especially notions of civilization and culture — big categories covering large chunks of the world that show marked patterns of similarity across national, ethnic, and parochial rivalries.

Along with changing patterns of emphasis grounded in individual decades is the steady, unrelenting rise of awareness that the first half of the century — especially the era of Hitler and the Holocaust-represented a defining moment in the history of the human race and not just a transitional phenomenon that one could bury in the rubble of a Berlin bunker. *Taking Lives* in each of its editions attempted to take stock of contemporary events, but increasingly, with each passing edition, an awareness grew that deep tragedies are sparked by long waves of social disintegration and state intervention.

More than a decade has passed between the publication of the third, augmented edition and of this new fourth edition of *Taking Lives*. During that time a great deal has happened — if not to improve the state of the human condition as such, then certainly to improve the state of our understanding of processes and structures that, far from being ad hoc comings and goings, represented pandemic networks embracing many people and systems. This new edition includes four new chapters and some modest supplements to the eleven chapters in the third edition. I have tried to avoid repeating what others have recently accomplished and to emphasize those areas that remain very much in need of further examination.

I have never felt a greater sense of solidarity among a large network of scholars drawn from the social and historical sciences and now joined once again by philosophical and ethical enquiry of the most serious sort. That eases my tasks greatly. I do not need to repeat what others have done, except to indicate in a new chapter some of the trends and tendencies that have emerged in the present period.

But the rise of professionalism in genocide studies, or if one prefers the older formulation, war and peace studies, creates problems of its own. One must avoid a clinical response to the massive death and destruction of innocent people. Professionalism necessitates a certain surgical approach — the way physicians approach an AIDS epidemic or an outbreak of cholera — but it should not become a method for isolating the expert from the public. This is easier said than done. The risks of abstracted empiricism remain a steady reminder that academic life often removes us from the feeling of pain and suffering that accompanies mass death.

At the same time, professionalism also carries the seeds of politicization — of the assumption that the study of state power is the same as the condemnation of sovereignty as such, or worse, the notion that every struggle in the world is between my rights and their wrongs. Again, this is easier to say than do. In the midst of the battle, the capacity to distinguish genocide from mere conflict — a civil war, a tribal conflict, a difference between groups that involves low-level violence and few deaths but grief of all other sorts — is a huge challenge, one not always well met or managed by the researchers in the truly dismal science of genocide.

And finally, there is a need to maintain a sense of the subject — to avoid subdividing it into ecocide, politicide, regicide, or all other forms of nasty and brutish human behavior. To do this, however tempting and however easy it is to demonstrate cleverness by reference to Hobbes' *Leviathan*, is especially dangerous for researchers on the theme of death. The master tendency of the century — the arbitrary and willful taking of massive numbers of innocent lives by states and tyrants, deserves to retain a special place of dishonor in the affairs of our century.

I cannot rightly say how well I have understood, much less synthesized, a vast literature, or how ably I have avoided traps and pitfalls described in these brief remarks. It is for the reader to assess my success in this agonizing enterprise. But at least the reader will have a sense of the guideposts that will enable such a determination to be made with fairness and, above all, in a way that does not minimize the tasks ahead or the tragedies left behind us in the wake of this most glorious and catastrophic century of our millennium.

I count it as a blessing that *Taking Lives* has generated continuous and strong readership over time. It is a further blessing that I am able to see my blend of new and old appear in print as a result of the extraordinary efforts of my colleagues at Transaction. Much of my life has been spent studying places and peoples like Armenia and Armenians, Cuba and Cubans, and Israel and Jews. In doing so, I have come to understand that important ideas do not so much depend on the size as on the soul of the nation and people under examination. In consequence, insight and outlook are neither diminished nor enhanced by the size of the field; only by the quality of the values and interests of the writer or scholar.

Taking Lives remains no less close to my heart than head. Given autobiographical — that is, who I am, what I am, and why I am — as well as analytical elements, this could hardly be otherwise. Writing at its best is a private, painful experience rendered meaningful by its public outreach. And when the subject is nothing short of the arbitrary termination of innocent lives by a collectivity called the state, the size of the chore is magnified. So I can only close this chapter by reminding one and all of what I noted at the close of the original edition of *Taking Lives:* The last laugh is always had by the living, by the survivors. They carry the culture and the tradition that denies to the dark destroyers any quarter, any victory, any joy, and any future. And so, far from viewing my work in this area as a grim necessity, I prefer to think of it as an ironic reply to such necessities.

2

Defining Genocide

If a crime unknown before, such as genocide, suddenly makes its appearance, justice itself demands a judgment according to a new law.

— Hannah Arendt[1]

THE TWENTIETH CENTURY GERMAN SOCIAL PHILOSOPHER ERNST BLOCH HAS APTLY written: "We paint images of what lies ahead, and insulate ourselves into what may come after us. But no upward glance can fail to brush against death which makes all things pale."[2] Even with a considerable new and controversial literature on the processing of death at an individual medical level, we still do not possess a corresponding political sociology that properly encompasses the phenomenon of death. Social psychologists have provided insights into the meaning of death[3] and into its personal consequences.[4] But we know precious little about how to account for differences between social systems and state organs that employ mass murder to maintain themselves and those that eschew or resist the ultimate strategy of enforcing the social order by the sacrifice of lives.

What is required is the large-scale movement beyond structures to processes, from systems to humans, not simply to bring people back into sociology or because of considerations derived from humanitarian concerns, but because of basic scientific concerns, namely, connecting theories employed to explain the world with what the world itself deems important at any given time. At this point in social science evolution, the tendency to seek explanations in terms of organization, structure, and system is common to most major tendencies of sociology, from functionalism to interactionism. Social science at a macro level tends to be satisfied with descriptive statements about trends and stages. As a result, the tendency is to infer functional similarities from presumed organizational prerequisites. This trend weakens the validity of scientific measurement and the quality of sociological theory by making such measurement a response to norms that simply may not be operational.

The concept of genocide is admittedly empirically ubiquitous and politically troublesome. Formal definitions are either too broad to invite action or too narrow to require any; political definitions invariably mean what *other* nations do to subject populations, never what one's own does to its subjects or citizens. Genocide is not simply a sporadic or random event such as the Katyn Forest Massacre, in which 15,000 Polish troops were liquidated by the Red Army during World War II.[5] In addition to its systematic character, genocide must be conducted with the approval of, if not direct intervention by, the state apparatus. Genocide is mass destruction of a special sort, one that reflects some sort of political support base within a given ruling class or national group. This contrasts sharply with vigilantism, which represents the maintenance of order without law, or some kind of mass participation without corresponding state support.[6] Genocide is also quite distinct from tyrannicide — the time-honored tradition of seeking redress against a tyrannical ruler — in which murder is perceived not as a crime but as a liberating act.[7]

While definitions vary, there now is nonetheless a broad consensus as to the definition of genocide. The recent work of Frank Chalk and Kurt Jonassohn is especially valuable in this regard. They speak of "genocide as a form of one-sided mass killing in which a state or other authority intends to destroy a group, as that group and membership in it are defined by the perpetrator." Realizing that this definition offers a necessary but not sufficient explanation, Chalk and Jonassohn provide a brief typology in which genocides are classified according to their motive, that is, "1. to eliminate a real or potential threat; 2. to spread terror among real or potential enemies; 3. to acquire economic wealth; or 4. to implement a belief, a theory, or an ideology."[8] Of course, in real-world terms, these four properties tend to coalesce.

Even these are not absolute categories. There is a slim line between systematic and sporadic destruction. Sporadic destruction may take more lives over time than systematic annihilation. Similarly, vigilante politics often has the tacit support of at least a portion of the state mechanism. For example, the vigilante practices of the Ku Klux Klan had the assistance of legislative assemblies and the courts in southern states between 1865 and 1920. Nevertheless, the distinction between genocide and vigilantism is significant and of more than academic consequence, for we are dealing with political structures, not just social events.

The concept of genocide in historical terms, while one of the best defined in the lexicon of modern times, offers little assurance of inhibiting such political behavior. Traditionally, genocide simply meant any attempt to destroy, in whole or in part, any one of a number of various groups. The General Assembly of the United Nations, in response to the horrors of World War II, declared in its Resolution of 11 December 1946 that genocide "is a crime under international law, contrary to the support and designs of the United Nations, and condemned by the civilized world." Genocide received further analysis by the United Nations Economic and Social Council, which appointed a special committee that approved a convention on the subject.[9] This convention was discussed and finally approved on 9 December 1948 by a unanimous vote of the fifty-six participants. The crux of the matter is contained in Article 2, which stipulates:

> In the present Convention, genocide means any of the following acts committed with intent to destroy, in whole or in part, a national, ethnical, racial, or religious group, as such: (a) Killing members of the group; (b) Causing serious bodily or mental harm to members of the group; (c) Deliberately inflicting on the group conditions of life calculated to bring about its physical destruction in whole or in part; (d) Imposing measures intended to prevent births within the group; (e) Forcibly transferring children of the group to another group.[10]

These essentially legal definitions have had the effect of stimulating intense present-day sociological interest in the subject of genocide. We shall consider only some of the more interesting and suggestive of these social generalizations.

One sociological approach to genocide is to link it to victimology, that is, to a study of those who suffer at the hands of criminals — political as well as sociological. In the work of Drapkin, Viano, Dadrian, and their followers, there is a profound imbalance: they study criminology without a corresponding examination of victimology. Specialty areas such as penology or criminal rehabilitation on such a theory deserve a corresponding framework for the rehabilitation of the innocent — those individuals or families dismembered as a result of criminal behavior. Dadrian fully understands that while all genocidal acts are criminal, not all forms of "victimology" refer to the victims of genocide. Still, there is a strong hint that genocide as mass murder deserves an empathic appreciation of those who are the mass victims of such practices; including the study of proper forms of restitution and rehabilitation of those who so suffer.[11]

The difficulties in this paradigm are important. First, it has been argued that many, perhaps most, "victims" of criminal behavior are knowing or willing participants. And by extension it has been argued that even racial genocide could not have happened without the willing or knowing participation of those so victimized. Whatever the merits of this argument, it is clear that before any firm "science" of victimology can be erected on foundations other than the conventional one of criminology, it will be necessary to distinguish the precise character and background of victims and criminal perpetrators. One gets the impression that the proposal for a science of victimology is addressed to those special subsets of people caught in the crossfire of criminal, deviant, or Stalinist elements and that Dadrian's concerns are less with a new science than with a proper sense of respect for the sufferings and outrages inflicted on innocent third parties. In this regard, the victims of genocide, whether Armenian or Jewish, appear as precisely a collective representation of such a victimology.

Second, to make the problem of genocide part of a new science of victimology tends to weaken the claims of genocide on its sociological and historical specificity; that is, genocide becomes one among a variety of forms whereby innocents are victimized by a society that does not properly control its criminal elements. This tendency to distinguish the so-called criminal element from the political factor has a serious built-in problem. In the case of genocide, it is precisely the transformation of the criminal into the political, the fusion of deviance to a special form of marginality, that gives this phenomenon its special poignancy and meaning. While there are some obvious appeals to making the study of genocide part of a larger "scientific" examination of victims and their behavior, it carries the danger of falsifying the terms of discourse by rendering the historical record irrelevant and fragmented into quasi-scientific variables.

One way of formulating the question of genocide is in terms of extrajudicial execution. As outlined by Edy Kaufman, this has come to encompass assassination not only for the manifest purpose of transferring political power but, increasingly, to retain such political power. Essential as a tool of genocide, the extrajudicial execution became a formula by which governments disposed of hundreds, thousands, and even hundreds of thousands of political enemies. Kaufman's main area of interest has been Latin America, where this formula probably has its highest utility; nations like Brazil, Uruguay, and Guatemala employ extrajudicial execution extensively. Whether it can be extended to a general law of political behavior is hard to say. One would have to incorporate a theory of totalitarianism to universalize such a framework — and that itself has become an arguable premise.[12]

The advantage of using extrajudicial execution as a category equivalent to genocide is that it enables one to render the genocidal concept in precise numerical terms. Kaufman's work represents a useful catalogue of assassinations not legally sanctioned in Asia, Africa, and Latin America. The difficulty with this approach to genocide becomes apparent when one recognizes that most forms of political assassination are not extrajudicial but, rather, quite judicial. Sanctions for genocide are strengthened, and the prohibition against genocide is lifted once the state embarks on such a course of action. As a result, in nations with undisputed high levels of genocidal practice — such as Cambodia — the line between the legal and extralegal vanishes. It is precisely in countries such as Uruguay, where strong legalistic traditions exist, that the law remains a factor in preventing genocide from becoming entrenched and widespread. It is not that the concept of extrajudicial execution is without merit. It is rather that it is so overly formalistic as to make more rather than less difficult the task of creating a useful framework and general model.

One recent and interesting study of ethnic tensions in Central Europe was conducted by Feliks Gross. What makes it so relevant to a study of genocide is Gross's belief that genocide, like other systems of state rule, has its own natural history. This approach derives in part from Gross's earlier work (and that of others) on the natural history of the revolutionary process, and it represents an extension of this concept to the field of genocide. He claims that the stages in the evolution of genocide, at least in the Julian Region (between Italy and Yugoslavia) of Europe, went something as follows:

▸ *First,* the "good" neighborhood in the Julian Region lasted from 1867 until almost 1920.

▸ *Second,* after 1920 and especially after 1922 there followed the oppression of the Slavic minority.

▸ *Third,* in 1943 the oppression changed into genocide of the Jewish population and cruel persecutions and executions of ideological and ethnic dissidents.

▸ *Fourth,* a short respite occurred and lasted a few insecure hours, perhaps a day or so at the end of April 1945.

▸ *Fifth,* next followed forty days of persecutions and massacres, recorded in the history books as liberation.[13]

But oddly enough, the *sixth* stage for Gross — the movement from oppression to genocide and massacre — is the reduction of tensions and the liquidation of old hostilities. His claim is that genocide is a function of political tensions between nation-states and that genocide characterized not only the period of domination by Nazi Germany but the interval of Yugoslavian control that followed, since both were authoritarian. Genocide was eliminated only at the point when the authoritarian system was forced to move back, and in what Gross calls political megasystems as well as subsystems. Ethnic and civil issues fused and tensions were reduced once a relative detente was reached between the Italian and Yugoslav governments. A new ideology advancing a concept of linkages between two neighboring states came into being, and the age of genocide in this area of the Julian Region was ended. Clearly, subsequent events indicate that this too is but a stage in organized life-taking from above.

Still, by placing ethnic issues in the forefront, Gross was able to see the importance of life and death questions and hence to characterize states as racist or tribal, intolerant or benevolent, universal or pluralistic, or subordinate and hierarchical. Another important point raised by Gross's work, which has been

neglected, is the often incomplete character of genocidal practices. The natural history technique allows for an appreciation
of the fact that even genocidal systems are not eternal and
have built-in limits and weaknesses.

The shortcomings in the natural history approach are also
manifest. Gross's typology is purely descriptive rather than
analytic, and there is no evidence to indicate that the natural
history outlined in one area will be equally true in others. For
example, Central Europe was an area where parties had great
influence on public policy making. But what about genocide
in areas where party processes are virtually nonexistent?

Another problem lies in seeing the issue of genocide solely
in ethnic terms and hence closing out the possibility of genocide as a reflection of other variables, such as race in the exact
anthropological sense and class in the exact economic-devel-
opmental sense. Ultimately, the weakness of Gross's approach
is that genocide is seen as simply a fifth or sixth stage in a
national process without an appreciation of its policy-making
ramifications: its utilization by leaders of nation-states. Still,
these criticisms registered, the attempt to create a taxonomy
of genocide is itself deserving of more than casual attention,
since at least it comes directly to terms with the life and death
framework rather than structural and functional prerequisites.

Long before the United Nations defined genocide, Raphael
Lemkin, in his work *Axis Rule in Occupied Europe*, gave a
succinct account of genocide as an entity effected through a
synchronized attack on different aspects of life of the captive
peoples: in the political field (by destroying institutions of
self-government and imposing a German pattern of administration, and through colonization by Germans); in the social
field (by disrupting the social cohesion of the nation involved
and killing or removing elements such as the intelligentsia,
which provide spiritual leadership); in the cultural field (by
prohibiting or destroying cultural institutions and cultural
activities [and] by substituting vocational education for education in the liberal arts, in order to prevent humanistic think-

ing); in the economic field (by shifting the wealth to Germans); in the biological field (by a policy of depopulation and by promoting procreation by Germans in the occupied countries); in the field of physical existence (by introducing a starvation rationing system for non-Germans and by mass killings, mainly of Jews, Poles, Slovenes, and Russians); in the religious field (by interfering with the activities of the Church, which in many countries provides not only spiritual but also national leadership); in the field of morality (by attempts to create an atmosphere of moral debasement through promoting pornographic publications and motion pictures, and the excessive consumption of alcohol).[14]

This extract is of critical importance, since it represents the first effort at a scientific statement on what was taking place. It also makes possible gradations of meaning in the concept of mass murder. The distinction between genocide and the Holocaust is the difference between denationalization of selected groups among those out of favor, and the total physical annihilation of members of a community, people, or nation. While there was a justified fear that after the Jews had been liquidated, all other ostracized groups — such as the Gypsies, Poles, and Romanians — would suffer the same fate, there was no systematic policy to that effect. Genocide is a national policy having adherents throughout the world, whereas the Holocaust was a specific practice of the Nazis that entailed the total murder of an entire population.[15] As bizarre as it may seem, it is the difference between defining people as subhuman but required as economic slaves and as not human at all, not even fit to serve in a slave capacity. It is perhaps the hallmark of the present age that a distinction between genocide as a general practice of state power and the Holocaust as a specific practice of Nazi power has to be made.

George Mosse put the matter in its starkest form: "The Holocaust transformed racial theory into practice." It is extremely important to realize that even genocidal systems have theoretical moorings. In the case of modern genocide such as the Hitler system, the biological mooring was central. Again, paraphrasing Mosse, racism made an unholy alliance with virtues such as cleanliness, honesty, moral earnestness, hard work, and family life. And these characteristics were presumed to be absent in the Jewish people as a "race."[16] Because of the wide penetration of racism, we are directed toward the cultural destruction of the Jewish people, the anthropological dismemberment of black people, the destruction of deviants, delinquents, the mentally retarded, or what have you. The genocidal society managed to garner adherents, even massive followings-not in the name of genocide, never in the name of genocide but through ideas held to be highly ethical: usually the virtues of both Christians and the middle class. In a telling passage, Mosse notes that racism so infected Christianity that in the end no real battle between racism and Christianity ever took place. As a result, there was no mass resistance to genocidal solutions.

There was no coalescence of opposition either. Since the blacks for the most part were outside of Hitler's reach, there was no rude awakening to the fact that all racism, whether aimed at blacks or Jews, was cut of the same cloth. Worse, this lack of awareness made possible a much more coalescent system than would otherwise have occurred. On religious and racial grounds alike, there was a greater degree of division among opponents of the genocidal society than among its supporters. This ultimately has been the strength of totalitarian systems generally: the state's single-minded interest in the absolute control of the movement and beliefs of large numbers of people.

In addition to legal definitions and historical taxonomies of genocide, there are structural dimensions. Two points must be subsumed under such a structuralist heading: First, genocide represents a systematic effort over time to liquidate a national population, usually a minority; second, it functions as a fundamental political policy to assure conformity and participation by the citizenry. There are exceptions to each point. Sometimes, as in the apartheid policy of South Africa, a minority practices forms of genocide on a majority. Also, there are many cases in which the overt statements of a government only vaguely reflect its covert actions, for instance, the case of Soviet policy toward its national minorities.

A formal distinction between genocide and assassination is also required. Genocide is herein defined as *a structural and systematic destruction of innocent people by a state bureaucratic apparatus,* whereas assassination designates random and sporadic efforts of people without power to illegally seize power and liquidate paramount central figures in a given regime as a means to that goal.[17] Assassination, like genocide, may take the lives of innocent third parties, but its primary focus is aimed toward the symbolic, and hence selective, liquidation of powerful enemies. The distinction between genocide and assassination is roughly analogous to that between force as the prerogative of state power and violence as the instrument of those excluded from state power. All linguistic devices have built-in limitations, and the fine lines of intellect may be crossed to satisfy the exigencies of immediate practice. Yet this distinction between genocide and assassination does permit a rule-of-thumb separation between death at the hands of the state, the behemoth, and death at the hands of the individual, the anarch.

Still, one must recognize exceptional forms of genocide, those that are not directly linked to state power. The assassination-suicide incident that took place under the sponsorship of the Reverend Jim Jones in his People's Temple of the Disciples of Christ in Guyana is perhaps the most recent and bizarre such instance. The death by poisoning of 910 members of this cult in 1978 took place in a climate that simulated totalitarian state power: a total institution, an environment closed to information from outside sources, absolute reliance on the leader for counsel and support and a corresponding sense of total dependence on the sealed environment for all forms of existence, to the point where existence outside the total institution (or the simulated state) became unthinkable.

In this instance, once again social life outstrips sociological categories. We have a concept of suicide, but essentially as a private and individuated, not a social and collectivized, event. We have a concept of infanticide, but again as something connected with highly refined and unusual ritual, not as a clinical and routinized act of engineered genocide. We have a concept of totalitarianism, but generally as a system of government rather than as a subsystem of religious organization. Genocide can thus be an episodic and even sporadic event. It does not have to be, as it was in the case of the Nazis, systematic and sustained. This is small consolation to those seeking precise correlations between totalitarian systems and human destruction. But it would be a huge error to conceive of genocide as a peculiar or bizarre entity rather than as part and parcel of the totalitarian temptation.

A special type of genocidal practice is employed against foreign rather than domestic populations. One of the fundamental characteristics of nineteenth-century European imperialism was its systematic destruction of communities outside the "mother country."[18] The decimation of Zulu tribesmen by British troops, the Dutch-run slave trade, and the virtual depopulation of the Congo by Belgians typify this form of colonial genocide. It would be simple to say that such events are merely a consequence of international strife and the division of spoils and that they thus do not qualify as genocidal practice.

Those engaging in genocide nearly always define the people to be purged and liquidated as alien or enemy populations. This is so even in the liquidation of ancient Indian civilizations by relatively recent white arrivals.[19] Whether they are aliens from within or without is an ideological quibble that disguises the fact of systematic mass extermination by a state power against a relatively powerless group or sector. The conduct of classic colonialism was invariably linked with genocide. It is the hypocritical heritage of European nations that they proclaimed concepts of democracy and liberty for their own populations while systematically destroying others. This was the heritage of nineteenth-century "civilized" existence. This bequest of the past became the norm of the twentieth century.

Although concern for problems of genocide fitted into the thinking of the United Nations at its inception, the series of proclamations designed to halt the spread of genocide, approved and even ratified, remained largely unenforced. The emergence of the Cold War after World War II, and its attendant polarization of all conflicts along a Communist-anti-Communist cost-benefit scale, led to a decline of attention to that very feature of the twentieth century that presumably differentiated it from all other centuries: the national, ethnic, racial, and religious violations of the rights of people. As a result, the genocidal norm outlasted any organizational efforts to displace it. As Leon Gordenker inquired:

> Who made the destruction of the 300,000 or so Indonesian communists after the attempted coup d'etat in 1965 a matter for the United Nations? Who saw the deprivation of the rights of Asians in Uganda as an outrage? Who labelled as genocidal the slaughter of baHutu tribesmen — 80,000 or so of them — by the waTutsi elite of Burundi? How much attention was given to the horrors of the civil war in Nigeria? Who has tried to ease the emergence of Angola by protecting the humanity of all involved? Who talks of the operations of the secret political police whose knock at dawn is a common sound in dictatorships of the right and left that occupy most of the world? Well, not the principal organs of the United Nations which for the moment have other priorities in the human rights field. Still, with the end of the Cold War, the United Nations and attendant organizations have repositioned themselves to pay attention precisely to such features. The struggle and attempted settlement of the ethnic and civil wars raging in former Yugoslavia indicate this profound shift in sentiment if not settlement.[20]

Quite beyond the process of labeling social systems and then determining whether any assistance should be rendered is the yet more recent pattern of intense rivalry between odious regimes. Genocidal systems have no more necessary affinity for each other than do other social systems. Thus, for example, the invasion and conquest of Cambodia by Vietnam represented, internally at least, a movement from a genocidal system to an incarceration system. The most authentic claim about Vietnam is that at the end of 1978 approximately 800,000 prisoners were distributed throughout the country, evenly divided between North and South Vietnam.[21] The placement of the internment camps, the conditions of the prisoners, and the forms of punishment are all adequately described in the current literature. But this system has now been extended to a nation where conservative estimates place the number of people liquidated at roughly 2 million out of a population of approximately 8 million. In the grim war of twentieth-century geopolitics, on a scale of living values at least, one might say that Cambodia has improved its situation!

Whatever examples of contemporary genocides we refer to, it is evident that the issue is less the existence of the phenomenon of mass slaughter than the reasons these take place. For the most part, the literature quite properly addresses those forms of totalitarian rule that permit the killing of people with impunity. Another dimension, too little appreciated, is that the victim people often represent an alternative social arrangement. Mark Levene nicely indicates how this foreign policy element played out in Turkish-Armenian relations: "The Armenians were eventually singled out for extermination by the post-1908 Committee of Union and Progress in power because they were perceived as a threat, not so much in terms of a threat to succession, almost an impossibility given their dispersion and the demographic realities of eastern Anatolia, but more strikingly, because they represented in political, social, economic, and cultural terms an alternative path which the empire might have taken."[22]

A multidimensional definition of genocide, rather than a unilinear, moralistic definition painted in black and white, is the surest safeguard against impoverished analysis.

This is not a claim to the legitimacy or legality of such forms of invasion or breakdown of territorial sovereignty, nor is it to enter a dispute concerning the proxy-like status of conflicts between national powers great and small. For with national entities of all sizes and shapes, the question of the internal regimes or of the proxy powers must itself be considered part of the grim tragedies of the present era. The fact that societies can be described as genocidal in their essence does not necessarily change foreign policy equations. The question of genocide is once again returned to the nation-state, to competition between sovereigns as much as to efforts to prevent opposition to a sovereign from within. If candor is to prevail, statesmen and scholars alike would have to admit that the umbilical cord between genocidal practice and state power has never been stronger. But the converse is also true: Popular resentment for and legal resistance to such practices have also become sharper and clearer. In such a context, the type of clinical analysis provided by the social scientific framework, will help in understanding the sources of the arbitrary taking of life by the machinery of state power, and with decent public participation, offer analytical tools for combating mayhem.

3

Counting Bodies

The problem is power. The solution is democracy. The course of action is to foster freedom.

— R. J. Rummel[1]

THERE HAS BEEN SUCH A PROLIFERATION OF TERMS RELATING TO THE ARBITRARY termination of life — including the resurrection of old words like "regicide" and the manufacture of new terms like "politicide" and "democide" — that the growing public awareness of genocide threatens to be sidetracked in this cascade of academic nuances concerning unnatural deaths. My purpose here is, first, to concentrate on the centrality of genocide in understanding the violence of the century; second, to explain how genocide is a function of political decision making; and third, to critically review the idea that modernity in itself serves as the source of genocide.

Simply put, a social scientific vantage point must try to understand and analyze genocide as a distinct social phenomenon rather than as a reaction to economy or technology. For this purpose, genocide must be clearly distinguished from other forms of the destruction of human beings, such as natural disasters, random killings, warfare, and symbolic or cultural assaults. The collective nature of genocide, in which the victim is "punished" for being part of some particular group, tribe, race, or religion, sets it apart from other social evils. The act of genocide contradicts traditional Western norms and approaches to law and morals, which emphasize individual responsibility for actions and, hence specific forms of punishments for transgressions.

In Chapter 9, I will outline a typology of state systems: from the libertarian at one end to the genocidal at the other end, with a range of negotiated order that includes guilt, shame, and toleration as essential social psychological characteristics.[2] In this edition, my aim is more precisely on developing a typology of repressive state systems that permit the taking of lives in circumstances that range from the highly selective, as with capital punishment, to the highly inclusive, as with genocide. It is also an effort to appreciate that even within the idea of genocide, profound differences in approaches to the issue of state terror need examination. This is not to dismiss the need for either sound methodology or operational typology. It is to locate both in a broader, more meaningful context.

In the bitter, so-called scientific study of state-sponsored terror or the mass destruction of human beings, few factors have been as compelling or as contentious as raw numbers. The evidence for the presence of genocide rests, after all, on the body counts of unknown victims whose remains attest to the tragedy in which they participated, usually unwillingly and often unknowingly. The study of genocide is an exercise in counting bodies; the assessment that follows also constitutes a footnote to my earlier work.

In raw numerical terms, the source of the killing in this century tells the story: Governments have been directly responsible for the deaths of roughly 120 million people, while war (both international and civil) accounts for 35 million deaths. In other words, in the last ninety-five years, over three-and-a-half times as many people have been killed by their own governments as by opposing states.[3]

A further breakdown reveals that of the 120 million killed by their own governments, over 95 million have been in Communist states and another 20 million in non-Communist authoritarian states. What we are dealing with is not some sideshow in this century but, increasingly, the main event, perhaps the only event, given the increasingly high risk of conventional warfare in this post-nuclear environment.

The importance of body counts is at least as well recognized by perpetrators of systematic acts of destruction as by those victims seeking moral restitution and historical recognition. Thus in every major genocide, the government authorities responsible have contested the numbers of victims involved, seeking to minimize their monstrous acts. While there may be something grisly about determining the qualitative worth of a genocide by the quantitative figures involved, the need to convert such data into a meaningful theoretical construct that helps us appreciate the grim potentials of state-sponsored murder is manifest.

I should like to examine the current theoretical interest in state-sponsored mayhem and indicate how known information on the number of people killed can affect such larger considerations.[4] I shall restrict myself to the following paired concepts:

- ▶ (1) natural forms of catastrophe as distinct from socially sanctioned murder;
- ▶ (2) systematic slaughter versus accidental or random killing;
- ▶ (3) genocide as distinct from warfare;
- ▶ (4) state-sanctioned murder in contrast to extralegal terror; and
- ▶ (5) actual body counts as distinct from symbolic wounds or cultural assaults.

I am engaging neither in Manichaeism nor in contrasting good and evil. Rather, my purpose here is to explore significant distinctions in the authority of states.

These five constructs by no means exhaust the ways of looking at genocidal data, but taken as a cluster they provide general theoretical guidelines for addressing and ultimately resolving long-standing concerns in the evolution of social research. This may appear to be a rather meager recompense for the punishment absorbed by millions. But insofar as social research can provide a basis for early warning signals and help prevent future mayhem and murder, this is at least a useful starting place.[5]

There remain serious obstacles to incorporating the study of genocide as part of the core rather than the periphery of research in political sociology. Qualitative problems cannot readily be ignored. For example, how does one distinguish between state-sponsored terror; quasi-state-sponsored terror through private armies, like the Ton Ton Macoutes in Haiti or Hamas in Lebanon; and antistate forms of terrorist activities such as that practiced two decades ago by the Bader-Meinhoff Gang in Germany, the Red Brigades of Italy and Japan, and countless other groups and individuals? Literally thousands of groups currently operate outside the law and in accordance with moral codes that seek nothing less than the radical transformation of civilization or, failing that goal, its destruction.[6]

Terrorism is a technique available to all and seemingly used by all. There are Armenian groups in opposition to Turkish groups; anti-Communist alliances against radical-dominated guerrillas; Afghan collectives and Jewish brigades; pro-Chinese versus pro-Vietnamese factions within Communist groups; and religious and secular revolutionary groups within the Arab world. Unlike genocidal conditions, terrorism often involves a strange balance of extragovernmental forces, a balance that prevents "final solutions." Terrorism becomes a basic norm, no less than a form of political combat using military power and extralegal means.

Having acknowledged this, the very plurality of terrorist clusters ensures a strange democracy of random violence. At the very least, this pluralism of extremes makes improbable the easy triumph of any single group and denies any one individual the possibility of mobilizing a state for genocidal destruction. This distinguishes the present epoch from the pre-World War II period, in which there was a concentration of weapons, as well as of conspiracies, in comparatively few hands.[7]

On the other hand, terrorism is sometimes defended as a protection of the present, of the state as such. Emissaries of Turkey, for example, constantly adduce this argument when they reject the claim that the Armenians were simply danger-ous secessionists. Another difficulty is that lumping together all people numerically fails to distinguish between those who are truly victims of genocidal massacre and those who are killed as an adjunct of a wartime effort, as the official Nigerian position holds is the case with the victims of the civil wars with Biafra of the 1960s, or, for that matter, the as the ex-Soviet Union held was the case for the victims of its war against Afghanistan in the 1980s.

Simply providing raw quantitative data does not resolve outstanding qualitative problems. However, the statistical study of genocide does make possible the resolution of some long-standing issues in the distinction between democracy and dictatorship, issues that have long awaited an objective indica-tor so that this distinction can become a *useful heuristic device* in the research and policy communities.

Perhaps it is wise to think of the special properties no less than general characteristics about this newest entry into the policy science of society. To ignore the specifities of genocide, of the study of organized murder, is to make of it a quotidian event. Genocide may best be viewed in terms of paired oppo-sites, or at least contrasting nuances.

This may be the best way to incorporate the horrors of the twentieth century into the common vernacular of social sci-ence and hence to transform the study of mass murder by state power into an early warning system against just such disas-trous events. Indeed, this search for anticipatory responses to genocide may be the most important element in the current stage of analyses.

DISTINGUISHING THE NATURAL FROM THE SOCIAL

The first and perhaps all too obvious point to make in the study of genocide is that it differs in kind and nature from the study of natural disasters such as plagues. The spread of the bubonic plague in Europe in the fourteenth and fifteenth centuries was catastrophic by any standard of measurement. It is believed that between 1346 and 1350 the disease ended the population rise that had characterized later medieval society. Within this four-year period, Europe lost roughly 20 million lives to the "Great Dying" or "The Pestilence," which was carried through bites from fleas on rodents throughout Europe and Asia.

The causes of the plague remained unknown until nearly the beginning of the twentieth century. Various explanations were offered. These focused on punishment for sins and transgressions, but the natural or pathogenic sources of the plague had a binding effect on the population, leading to a realization that larger, mysterious forces were allied against the human race as a whole and hence had to be dealt with in some sort of uniform manner. Travelers were quarantined, strangers were ostracized, and passengers were diverted to other shores. But the natural or supernatural basis of the plague did not generate struggles between peoples.

In the case of genocide, and again at the risk of laboring the obvious, the source of mass death is known to be social, that is, it is the liquidation of human beings by other humans. As a result, the divisive consequence of genocide contrasts markedly with the unifying character of the waves of bubonic plague. In the concentration camps, who would perish was diabolically juxtaposed against who would live. Genocide was selective and systematic rather than individual and random. The human objects selected for perdition were chosen "anthropologically," as the Nazis liked to say: on the basis of religion, ethnicity, race, or other ascribed features. This is a radically different and very much a twentieth-century invention, in contrast to natural disasters, which are not so much inventions as series of unplanned catastrophes.

Before leaving the theme of the distinction between the natural and the social, it is important to remind ourselves of the continuities of life. This theme, so brilliantly and beautifully articulated by the late Loren Eiseley,[8] has sometimes degenerated into a mystic pantheism that is self-defeating. But in its purest form, it is an awareness that all life has a common basis and common origins and hence is worthy of our respect. Earlier arguments about the levels of life and their worth or about whether the human species is the fulfillment of other forms of life, as Charles Darwin held, have now shifted. In this sense, the emergence of sociobiology is a powerful instrument for sensitizing the human race about its continuities with the natural environment. But this appeal to evolutionism remains only a caveat. Discontinuities between the biological and the sociological remain the bedrock for distinguishing between natural disasters and artificial creations, that is humanly willed, genocides.

DISTINGUISHING THE HOLOCAUST FROM GENOCIDES

One of the most nettlesome and contentious issues involves claimants for Holocaust status.[9] Why should this be an issue to begin with? Perhaps the answer lies in the awareness that, even within categories of genocide, there are *gradations of horror*. Each victimized group wishes to claim the ultimate honor for itself. A review of the situation of Poland under German occupation should shed some light on the distinction between genocide and the Holocaust.

Between 1939 and 1945, some 3 million non-Jewish Poles, about 10 percent of the population, were murdered by the Nazis. During this same period 3 million Jews living in Poland were also annihilated, about 90-95 percent of the Jewish population in the nation. The fact that both groups lost 3 million people disguises the fact that the Polish nation and 90 percent of Poles survived the war. The Jewish community of Poland was eradicated. And the small number of Jews who did survive Nazism did not survive the subsequent waves of Communist repression in that country.

The late Lucy Dawidowicz has commented on this unique example of a Holocaust and a genocide taking place at the same time within one land.[10] She put the issues squarely:

> However much the Poles suffered under the German occupation-and they suffered gravely — their situation was not comparable to that of the Jewish communities of Europe. The Jews were a national minority of 3 million within Poland; the Poles the majority of over 30 million. The Jews, before they were murdered, were locked inside ghettos and deprived of their freedom of movement; the Poles were allowed a minimum of local self — government and mobility within their places of residence. The Jews were being systematically starved; the Poles were undernourished. The Jews were altogether denied medical care and medicines. The Jews had no military supplies; the underground Polish Home Army had considerable reserves of material.

In short, the Germans doomed the Poles to bondage and slavery; they condemned the Jews to annihilation.[11] This was not a decision triggered by a new technology but, rather, an inherited hatred of the outsider, the alien, the cosmopolitan, the corrupter of mythology. In the Nazi Holocaust we had the definite presence of racist, annihilating behavior, which was directed specifically against the Jews. Any comparable pariah status was absent even in such diabolical and widespread genocides as those launched against the Armenian people.

Armenian analysts have drawn a distinction between an effort to exterminate, as conducted against the Jews, with a "pronounced effort to mingle Armenian blood with the gene pool of the new homogenized Turkish nation."[12] Such Turkish actions and the later Nazi effort to integrate the Aryan-looking Poles into the Greater German hegemony reflect traditional dominant-class efforts to convert portions of the infidels and heathens, and the use of selective killing as a mode of intimidation and persuasion.

Both the Armenian and Polish cases were terrible tragedies. But the fact that there was little racism in the ideology that authorized and legitimized the liquidation of large portions of both peoples raises anew the need for an analysis that will permit us to condemn all forms of torture and torment while carefully distinguishing the Holocaust from genocide, and even widespread pogroms and selective assaults upon a minority group by a majority system from the collective destruction of a whole people, otherwise known as genocide. These are hardly open and shut issues. For while race as such may not have been manifestly involved in either the Nazi German or Ottoman Turk responses, religion surely was. The declaration of war on the Jews as a religious group was roughly matched by the earlier war of the Muslims against the Christian Armenians. We may take our cue from George Steiner, who pointed out that "all too plainly, the issues defy the ordering of commons sense. They seem to be just on the other side of reason. They are extraterritorial to analytic debate."[13]

We have a paired set of continuums; or again as Steiner may have interpolated, a dialectic without resolution. History does not proceed in a straight line from genocide to civility, from state-sponsored murder to limits on the state by its citizens. Instead, we have circumstances, in even the most highly developed nations, when the distinction must be made between the collective (total) murder of a population and a selective (partial) murder of a subject population. Grim though this distinction may be, the failure to make it would result in a reprehensible misrepresentation of history and a profound error in the social analysis of the sources of genocide.

DISTINGUISHING GENOCIDE FROM WARFARE

Increasingly, a consensus is developing that genocide is to warfare what suicide is to murder; that is, genocide is a self-inflicted wound by the state upon its own subjects, whereas warfare is the defense of the state against external incursions or, when offensive, the attempt to eliminate external enemies or to seize an advantage by their defeat. Admittedly, there are conditions during which such tidy distinctions cannot be easily rendered, as in tribal warfare in Yugoslavia or Burundi. But operationally this remains a useful distinction, for it permits important analytic distinctions and also judicial decision making in the post-genocidal determinations of wrongdoing.

Another way of formulating this issue is to see genocide as an advanced form of state terrorism, a premeditated use of force by elites within a society to maintain or extend their power over a target group within the same state which is perceived as a threat. Those states with long histories of internal repression tend to be the same ones that have exhibited patterns of genocide in modern times. Czarist Russian traditions of repression were continued and refined rather than terminated under Stalinist rule in the Soviet Union; the same can be said, to a lesser degree, of the changeover, otherwise structurally deep, from the Ottoman Empire to the Turkish Republic.

Wars are made by nations and peoples upon other nations and peoples. Democratic and libertarian states, no less than repressive or totalitarian states, make war as an instrument of foreign policy. Indeed, wars have been fought between democratic and authoritarian states throughout the twentieth century; wars are common to all sorts of social systems. Genocide, on the other hand, is the operational handmaiden of a particular social system, the totalitarian system.

Civil conflicts often create moral ambiguities for outsiders. Struggles endemic to a single nation sometimes take on such extraordinary proportions that charges and claims of genocide are raised. Here we may confine ourselves to the Nigerian civil war, in which the internal struggle between the Hausa and Ibo peoples spilled over into genocidal patterns. Some have estimated that 3 million people died in this struggle and have blamed the indifference of the advanced nations and the hypocrisy of the United Nations.[14] But the fact remains that a civil war was transformed into a systematic effort to destroy a people. (One might place the autogenocide that took place in Cambodia under Khmer Rouge domination in a similar category of national horror in the name of national liberation.) Soon after the fall of Biafra in 1970, a modest relief effort began. What the relief workers found represents the outer limits of warfare and the initial stages of a genocide: Of an estimated 5.8 million Ibos, 970,000 suffered from edema, marasmus, or kwashiorkor. Nearly one-third of Biafra's children showed signs of severe malnutrition, and these were the lucky ones. It was too late for the estimated 1 million Ibos who had died, in part as a result of the Nigerian government's blockade of humanitarian relief during the war. The situation in Rwanda between the Hutu and Tutsi peoples is not yet in the body count stage, but it is quite clear that the human carnage equals, if not surpasses, that of the Nigerian civil war.[15] Indeed, that particular civil war reveals the breakdown of even the least notion of safe havens. The churches, which in past massacres served as respites from madness, were enmeshed in the forces conducting the murder-often with the aid of priests from the warring tribes.

The rules of war in advanced nations become muddled when war is carried on without rules in the less-developed nations. Indeed, the level of social and economic development of a nation extends to how it conducts conflicts: When a society has firm and clear rules of combat, then the civilian-military distinctions are much sharper than in areas of the world where such standards for conflict do not obtain.

DISTINGUISHING STATE-SPONSORED MURDER FROM ALL OTHER FORMS OF STATE-SPONSORED VIOLENCE

Perhaps the most troublesome category confronting the analyst of genocide is those forms of state-sponsored mayhem that fall short of collective murder, but not by much. Deportation is such an instance. A claim frequently made by students of the Armenian genocide is that the Turkish mass deportation of Armenians from their cultural and geographic roots constituted a protracted form of genocide, since Armenians, so dislodged, could not re-create their society or culture in a generationally meaningful way.[16] The difficulty with this Hobbesian argument is that however nasty, brutish, and difficult such a life became, there was no actual physical dismemberment. This difference is critical: The Turkish beys, like the czarist counts, were cruel and malevolent beyond words, but the Armenians survived as a people, as did the Jews of pre-Communist Russia.

A more dramatic example is the recent experience of the Kurds, a people whom Turkey, Iran, Iraq, and Syria have all unsuccessfully tried to assimilate. In the 1990s, the Iraqis have probably been the most savage: Some 300,000 Kurds have been forcibly deported from their mountainous regions and resettled in the deserts of the south.[17] This Arabization policy extended to the division of contiguous Kurdish lands and finally to the outright destruction of Kurdish villages. When this failed to disperse the Kurds as a people, 3,500 out of 5,000 Kurdish villages were destroyed, and chemical weapons were used against the people. It is estimated that 100,000 Kurds have perished, and 500,000 have been relocated.

The level of atrocity against Kurds is systematic and brutal, involving the loss of a great many lives, the forceful assimilation of people into new regions, as well as widespread wanton destruction and dislocation. In the face of such overwhelming tragedy and evidence of destruction, the United Nations failed even to pass a resolution on the illegitimacy of chemical warfare. And yet, without passing moral judgment on who suffers more, the living or the dead, the fact remains that the Kurdish people have survived as a people. The question of "amnesty" for the Kurds may be vile and hypocritical on the part of Iraq, but the fact that it has been offered shows the absence of a genocidal program to totally annihilate a thriving people.

One scholar of African genocide has recently introduced the notion of "selective genocide," looking specifically at the treatment of the Hutus by the Tutsi people in Burundi.[18] In 1972, long before the 1992-1993 round of killing, it was estimated that 100,000 Hutus had been killed in retribution for their effort to seize power from the Tutsi-dominated government. And again in 1988, when a local struggle between Tutsi and Hutu villagers erupted into a wide-ranging struggle to oust a mayor, the Burundi army moved in, shooting every Hutu in sight. Estimates of the number of Hutus killed range from 5,000 to 20,000 victims; another 40,000 fled to neighboring Rwanda; again there was colossal silence from world bodies of law and order. The inevitable round of retaliations took place in 1992-1993. Hutu hit squads, estimated at between 40,000 and 50,000 men, are estimated to have massacred anywhere from five to ten times that number of Tutsi peoples.

But calling this mutual assault on Hutu and Tutsi peoples a genocide is as problematic as is using the term "genocide" for the massacre of the Kurdish people. Despite the brutality and the savagery involved, both the Hutu and Tutsi peoples survive, and the dominant regime categorically denies any systematic effort at total destruction of a whole people. In this sense, the use of such terms as "selective genocide," like the notion of cultural genocide, is essentially an emotive effort to lay claim to the special character of mass murder, perhaps to heighten the sense of the horrors these often neglected peoples have experienced.

It may seem terribly harsh to make surgical distinctions between varieties of death and varieties of cruelty. But that is precisely the challenge that social research must confront in the study of genocide. Such careful distinctions are made not for the purpose of choosing between forms of evil but in order to evaluate what consequences these evils bring about. As Goethe said, in the real world, the choices that one makes are not so much between good and evil as between forms of evil. And the study of such forms shows what separates death, the ultimate punishment allowing no rectification or correction, from all other forms of victimization, where, in theory at least, recovery if not redemption is possible.

There will be honest differences of opinion and continuing debate on such concepts as gradations of genocide as well as the distinction of genocide from other forms of statist assault on human dignity and tranquillity. But out of the ashes of such debates and discussions an honest social science can emerge, one with the power of quantitative analysis on one hand and the force of moral judgment on the other. This, at any rate, is the promise of the widespread study of genocide now underway in many lands and in many contexts.[19] One can take only small comfort in the fact that social theory is developing such concepts as the measurement of deaths vis-à-vis forms of mayhem. But this does not negate the responsibility of the social sciences to join forces in order to combine the best of the value-free traditions of study with the value-linked approaches to policy on genocide.

ACTUAL AND SYMBOLIC GENOCIDE

For those who would instruct others on the meaning of the Holocaust and genocide in general, there is a need to avoid cheapening this whole tragic theme by spreading its meaning to include cultural deprivation or the punishment of select individuals, even if they symbolically represent whole populations.

The lynching of blacks during the Reconstruction period was terrible. But at its worst epidemic proportions just prior to World War I, it could be measured in hundreds per annum. The bulk of the black population was suppressed and discriminated against, but it was not summarily liquidated. In this very fact there is an essential distinction to be made between a democratic United States and a totalitarian Nazi Germany.

Likewise, one must distinguish between such things as exile and death. The various boat lifts that sent 125,000 Cubans and perhaps a third that number of Haitians to U.S. shores in the 1980s were tragic episodes in the history of Cuba and Haiti, but they were not disastrous in the lives of Cubans and Haitians. This uneasy moral distinction between suffering and death is significant for its post-exile consequences. Likewise, although the Koreans were used as slave labor and systematically deprived of their culture throughout the Japanese occupation of 1910-1945, this too was a reversible process and ultimately a failed policy. And here we must make sharp distinctions within less-than-democratic regimes, no less than between systems of political rule.

The point is hard to accept in emotional terms, but it is all the more significant in empirical terms: Actual genocides involve real deaths. These deaths are not reversible by posthumous rehabilitation, party edict, or collective assumptions of guilt. They are finite, *final* events. So-called symbolic or cultural genocide, whether experienced by the Irish, the blacks, or the Koreans, is reversible. However, the very attention that the issue of genocide inspires aims precisely to reverse trends of neglect or cultural suppression.

That said, it would be dangerous and a disservice to the sobriety of this topic to melt the specific notion of genocide into a general discourse on human failings. To do so is to convert into pestilence and decimation all the tragic injuries human beings heap on each other. In short, to condemn the modern epoch or modernity as such is no more reasonable than to charge atomic power with the causes of World War II. To heap scorn on the world in which we reside is to trivialize and sentimentalize the subject of genocide.

Most forms of exploitation and decimation are tragic but also finite, subject over time to moral correction. It is the irreversibility of state murder that gives the subject of genocide its unique and awesome dimension. Paradoxically, the study of genocide gives to the social sciences a tool for the analysis of whole societies, one that puts the social sciences back in touch with common sense, not to mention with the common people whom they so often claim to serve.

THE COLLECTIVE AND THE INDIVIDUAL

A key distinguishing quality of genocide is its collective nature. This is a source of anguish when it comes to attributing responsibility. Unlike criminal behavior and punishment of criminals, genocide does not involve individuals who are acting on their own initiative and who may be punished. For genocide carries the force of law no less than the power of the state. The valiant efforts of the Nuremberg trials notwithstanding, confusion and ambiguity on the subject of genocide remain because human liquidation is done in the name of state authority and with legal sanction. Hence the executioners are in part relieved of any feeling of transgression or guilt by the official character and collective nature of genocide.[20] "Punishment" for belonging to the wrong group is carried out by impersonal forces, extending from special militia to engineering corps.

The inability to identify specific individuals who carry out such crimes and who are punishable for such crimes is a basic characteristic of genocidal environments. An additional problem is the often encountered failure to identify individual victims, which makes escape from punishment as well as from moral judgment possible. In democratic societies, collective guilt is not a concept readily admitted. Indeed, individual punishment for specific crimes is the very essence of liberal environments. The complex legal issues that genocide raises make it clear that punishment of war criminals is not the same as attributing responsibility for mass murder. The difference between national leaders, middle-echelon bureaucrats, technicians carrying out instructions, and general populations that are compliant points to the need for an area of law that has yet to come into its own nearly half a century after the Holocaust.

In Raul Hilberg's study of how the German railway system was mobilized to transport Jews to their deaths, it is apparent that the entire technical apparatus of railroad workers, office managers, and individual civilians riding the trains had to be aware of the trains' human cargo.[21] How does one go about punishing all those involved in the transport of human cargo to their ultimate deaths? The massive character of this operation makes the issue of numbers of transgressors just as central a concern as the issue of the number of victims. It is also a concern without simple resolution.

Western law is based upon individual punishment for specific deeds. Western morals are equally built upon individually internalized codes of conduct. It may be an oversimplification, but one of the most interesting aspects (if one may dare use such a phrase) of the study of genocide is to discover how it is that some people can transgress the law and escape not only punishment but even feelings of guilt for what they have done. How individual behavior translates into collective behavior, into the administration no less than the execution of sanctioned murder, is the focus for the advanced social and psychological study of genocide in this century.

In this essential unity of human behavior, I am reminded of Jane Goodall's reflections on the historic treatment of the chimpanzee, the primate more like humans in genetic terms than any other in the animal kingdom. In discussing the human beings who are responsible for chimps used in experimental settings, she wrote:

> They are victims of a system that was set up long before the cognitive abilities and emotional needs of chimpanzees were understood. Newly-employed staff members, equipped with a normal measure of compassion, may well be sickened by what they see. And in fact, many of them do quit their jobs, unable to endure the suffering they see inflicted on the animals, and feeling powerless to help. But others stay on and gradually come to accept the cruelty, believing that it is an inevitable part of the struggle to reduce human suffering.[22]

Similarly, acts of genocide can be undertaken in the belief that to do so, to remove enemies of the state, is to purify the society. The engineering of death is a continuum, just as is life itself. Zygmunt Bauman captures this in a moving fashion. "[Auschwitz] was a mundane extension of the modern factory system. Rather than producing goods, the raw material was human beings and the end product was death, so many units per day marked carefully on the manager's production charts. The chimneys, the very symbol of the modern factory system, poured forth acrid smoke produced by burning human flesh. The brilliantly organized railroad grid of modern Europe carried a new kind of raw material to the factories."[23] Perpetrators of death see themselves as engaged not in personal evil but in collective good. That is the final irony left by the Nazi doctors working on their Jewish victims. Even when personal doubts do arise, they are readily rationalized by the belief that their actions bestow vast technological benefits upon those elites who still live.

We do not need to enter a debate over vivisection to understand the linkage of all living creatures. Nor for that matter need we labor the ambiguities and artifacts of modernity to understand the connection between life giving and life taking. The disjunction between means and ends, between the utilization of cruelty, torture, mayhem, and murder for apparently noble ends of a supposedly good society, is at the root of the arbitrary taking of human life. The branches, or means, are many, some of which have been discussed here. But the root, the end, is singular. We need to take the measure of life and the documentation of death as a research end unto itself. By so doing, we can spare ourselves metaphorical extractions and pet theories that only confuse the issue of life giving and life taking while reducing both to a series of empty platitudes.

If we observe proper rules of evidence and avoid exaggerated claims of emotion, then we may well be within sight of a fundamental understanding of human behavior that has been the goal of social research since its inception. That we have had to endure a century of genocide to locate the wellsprings of an integrated, general theory is a tragic and admittedly terrible price to pay for knowledge.[24] But perhaps that is also the lesson of social life: The struggle for knowledge takes place in the crucible of savage acts. The struggle for the preservation and extension of life teaches us that the good is not always the pleasant or the pacific. The study of genocide is a painful confirmation of such an axiom. Out of the ashes of despair may come the hope of a better social science, and perhaps a better society as well. After all, the chimney and smoke stack have given way to a far more environmentally pleasant industrial order. Whether this betokens a more humane social order remains to be determined.

4

Collectivizing Death

Show me a Leni Riefenstahl film of the Olympics or a Mikhail Sholokhov novel about the idyllic life on a kolkhoz and I'll show you the Auschwitzes and the Kolymas looming behind them.

— Stanislaw Baranczak[1]

THE PRACTICE OF GENOCIDE HAS CONTINUOUSLY IN-CREASED AS THE twentieth century has progressed. For concerned citizens as well as social scientists, the unresolved question is whether the increase is an accident of human nature or a result of fundamental changes in the social system or the moral order. Put another way: Can we look forward to more of the same in the next century, or is what has taken place in a variety of places and systems an aberration of this century?

Before one attempts to respond to this question, it is necessary to rule out at least a few hypotheses that have become fashionable in recent years. Those I would reject include the notion that modern society itself is the "cause" of genocide. This is simply a contemporary version of the late-nineteenth-century notion that industrialism causes warfare. Quite apart from the intellectual difficulties of this position is the practical problem that accepting it would require not only that one suspend moral judgment of individual actions but also that one also reject the scientific and technical forces that have yielded so many perceived benefits to so many people in this century.

Such primitive thinking about science and technology simply confuses the *uses* to which modernity is put with the *causes* of massacre. One might just as well declare that everything good derives from modernity, that all security and sense of well-being that permits ordinary people to live like kings and queens of the past are a function solely of steadily advancing technology. In fact, for most of the eighteenth and nineteenth centuries such theories were widely held. But historical optimism no more advances our study of the causes of genocide than does the pessimism scattered across the present academic landscape.

It should be obvious that science has potential for good or evil. It allows for new and improved visions of physical and biological space that can be turned to advantage or disadvantage. Experimentation can help us discover new ways to solve medical ailments, and, as we know from the behavior of the Nazi and Japanese physicians, it can also be used in bizarre, nightmarish forms of human torture and destruction that have become an end in themselves.

The notion that science or modernity is somehow responsible for society's successes or failures derives from the long history of utopias and dystopias. In Tommaso Campanella's *City of the Sun*, the good life is a function of eugenics: All reproduction and mating is government controlled.[2] It was easy enough in this century for Aldous Huxley, in *Brave New World*,[3] and George Orwell, in *1984*,[4] to expose the dark side of such equations of state control with the perfect society. Beneath the search for earthly perfection lurks an incapacity to live with imperfection. The technocratic vision that drove utopian beliefs also fueled the statism that drove totalitarianism to its desperate genocidal measures.

I would further rule out teleological arguments of human destiny as explanations for the modern penchant toward genocide. Such arguments assert that the human world as such has predetermined limits and that when excesses or transgressions exceed these boundaries, destructive events occur — like the plagues of the fourteenth century or the genocides of the twentieth century. In other words, these are Providential interventions that, by design, redress such excesses. The engineering of mass murder is a far cry from the natural occurrence of diseases like bubonic plague, of whose causes the humans of the time had scant information or knowledge.

Classical Kantian philosophy rebukes such thinking. But a further difficulty with presuming that genocide is a strict consequence of natural causes is that genocides, unlike plagues, are selective rather than universal in their assault on the human race. Genocidal behavior is highly purposive and directive. Such acts of massive murder on a grand scale can almost never be described as purely randomized behavior.

A further difficulty with the teleological argument is that one would have to demonstrate that the twentieth century is somehow more wicked than were previous ages or contains more people who transgress than did previous ages. One is left with a circular reasoning: We know that God's will has been at work only by the consequences of genocides as such. Such predeterminism includes not so much a discourse on Providence as a surrender to mythology. It is little more than a citation or recitation of terrible things that happen in the world, followed by an assurance that this is all a function of Providential Will.

Curiously, once we get beyond the argument from modernity at one end and the argument from teleology at the other, there are very few discussions about the causes of genocide beyond the historical — or what I would call the middle-range-level. Thus we have a number of explanations of genocide predicated upon the uneven distribution of power, upon the unleashing of bestiality in wartime, or upon the continuation of religious and ethnic hatreds over the centuries.

These arguments certainly are in one form or another valid as ex post facto *descriptions*. That is to say, within the narrow limits of, say, Armenian-Turkish relations or Hutu animus against Tutsis or Christian animosity toward Jews or a myriad of other intergroup struggles, such commentary serves to make somewhat comprehensible specific genocidal patterns of behavior. Unfortunately, as *explanations* they carry scant predictive value. We can describe all sorts of conditions of uneven distribution of power or long-lived racial and ethnic enmities that have not resulted in genocide.

Such arguments are also unsatisfactory in some larger sense, because we have an abundance of counterevidence: of Christian-Jewish cooperation, Serbian-Croatian coexistence, and even long periods in which Armenians were able to survive in relative security under a variety of Turkish regimes under the Ottoman Empire. One is led to assume that new conditions may have emerged that change simple animus between peoples to situations ripe for mass murder by a dominant human force against a weaker force.

This leads us into either another sort of search, an intense exploration of minutiae in search of specific acts and behaviors that become the seeds or sources of specific acts of genocide. For the most part, social science and historical science have chosen the latter course of action — and with telling impact. Still, a nagging doubt remains. Something more is needed to explain the genocides that have claimed many millions of human lives in this century. I should like to take a different approach and explore changes in the technological and moral orders that have become widespread and afford the basis of new forms of theorizing about the causes of genocide.

Essentially, the moral order can be examined (at least for my purposes) in terms of two poles: the Augustinian and the Rousseauian. More specifically, one can argue that in St. Augustine's *City of God*, although human beings live in a state of social and political institutions and hence far from a condition of grace (or if you will, touched to some degree by original sin), they always have the capacity to be redeemed through God's healing powers. In St. Augustine's thought, we live in a world of sinners (with the exception of a very few saints) living in anxiety and imperfection and yet with the constant aware-ness that, through public confession, personal salvation is real.[5]

But far more important than the notion of original sin or the limitations of the hope of perfection on earth is the Aug-ustinian aspiration to heaven. As Christoph Schonborn wrote in a brilliant exposition on "The Hope of Heaven, the Hope of Earth": "The separation of secular and spiritual authority has become something we take for granted. In fact, we owe this distinction, as well as the acknowledgment of the freedom of conscience that is linked to it, to Christianity's fundamental conviction that no man belongs wholly to the state, the nation, or 'collective,' but can and may belong wholly only to him who is his Creator and his goal."[6] This modern restatement of the Augustinian position is clearly relevant to our effort to under-stand the problem of genocide. For if the arbitrary taking of life is the prerogative of the state, then the foundations of Christianity itself must crumble as the earth under our feet must turn to quicksand.

The Rousseauian pole, as expressed in the *Social Contract* and even more clearly in the *Discourses on Inequality*, offers a direct challenge to this Judeo-Christian tradition.[7] Rousseau argues that human beings in their natural state are unspoiled, that it is advancing society that pollutes and corrupts the human race (note the similarity to the argument that the source of genocide is modernity). Hence, Rousseau reasons, human beings are touched by original goodness; the savage knows little of evil, whereas the civilized man lives constantly at the edge of evil. And as this civilized person does and thinks evil to society and self, he is aided and abetted by Christianity itself. Redemption is through expression rather than confes-sion.

These are simplified versions of doctrinal and philosophical issues that have occupied many minds over many centuries. My aim here, however, is not to refine these theories but to explain the causes of genocide. This classic polarity between St. Augustine and Rousseau gives us a way into basic theory and perhaps even a mode of discourse that can help curb genocide, the scourge of our age. (It must be left to experts on Islamic, Buddhist, and Shinto faiths to see how such "Eurocentric" concerns require modification for other genocides.)

The Hebrew scriptural tradition gives great emphasis to law and history. Indeed, Moses the lawgiver epitomizes this aspect of Hebrew tradition. National salvation, if not individual salvation, depends upon the internalization of law. It does not matter whether there is an empirical demonstration that eating certain foods is bad for one's health, nor is the law empirically confounded if there seem to be conditions under which killing or maiming are acceptable forms of behavior. Rather, the Mosaic emphasis on the law reflects the sanctity of life in the Jewish tradition. And that sanctity extends from the birth to the death of every individual.[8]

One must assume that Moses the lawgiver was wise enough to know full well that commitments to rituals and behaviors can be easily confounded, in that exceptions can be made at any point along the way of history. By eliminating human choice and posing situations in terms of categorical imperatives or natural laws, a people can be mobilized and civilized at one and the same time. One must take as prima facie evidence of the wisdom of this assessment the very survival of the Jewish people through six thousand years and through a period of unparalleled adversity marked by the Holocaust. In the absence of such commitment to the law with respect to the claims of leaders to control all facets of human existence, lacking a sense of rights and responsibilities of a people upon a piece of earth, many tribes and peoples have vanished, some even without trace or name. So one must confess that the notion of original goodness does not necessarily yield historical longevity. However much one bemoans the loss of many ancient peoples, and however one might wish to argue that external forces were the cause of such dissolution, the brutal fact is that they are no longer with us.

Whether the cause of the dissolution of a people is inner lack of resolve or outer forms of pressure, we do know that the struggle for biological, social, and cultural survival is a serious end unto itself-even in the absence of genocide. The state of nature cannot be declared a state of grace if only because the history of humanity is strewn with so many lost peoples, never mind lost causes. Beyond that, to speak of a state of nature is to imagine a condition in which all human beings lacked conscience-precisely that instrument that separates the natural from the social.

What, then, has our discussion led to thus far? I would say it places us squarely in a world in which moral obligation vanishes in the face of utilitarian rights, or even whims. But moral conditions change far more slowly than do technological orders. A reductionist utilitarianism sees obligations in purely instrumental terms: I do something for the Third Reich because the Third Reich protects my status and position. And my assertion is that this collectivization of moral obligation opens a Pandora's box of human mayhem.

This is not to say that every person operating from the pleasure principle is a potential killer or that every person who accepts a nonutilitarian concept of moral law is a potential saint or pacifist. It is to say that when an entire social order is predicated on obligations only to a collective power, or only to a charismatic leader, we are in danger and that likewise, when people have personal proclivity to rights without obligations, the potential for genocide is far higher than when moral obligations and personal responsibilities of the sort one finds in both the Hebrew and Christian traditions are present.

The argument that one finds good Jews and Christian who also kill quite misses the point. In the case of Christians, killing is highly individual. Putting a heathen or a sinner to death involves potential for repentance or remission of sin. Now such an approach may be difficult for the modern mind to accept, but individual obligation is itself a problem for the so-called modern mind. The dramaturgy of death is highly evocative in the Judeo-Christian faiths. Expulsion of a person from the faith or a community of believers is preceded by great doctrinal discourses. And the execution of a supposed heretic or witch is specifically targeted to a particular person, in the presumed hope that this act of killing will forewarn the community of believers not to transgress the moral order that constitutes faith in God.

This may not be an entirely pleasant reading of the Jewish or the Christian tradition, nor is it intended to offer a refined version palatable to the late twentieth century. It does, however, place death in a context in which an individual is punished for specific acts, a tradition that has passed over into civil and criminal codes in every civilized nation in the West. This allows us to come to grips with the causes of genocide, namely, the breakdown precisely of such stringencies — sometimes in the name of licentious behavior, other times in the name of replacing Providence with Leviathan.

Totalitarian states exhibit not just the classic characteristics of absolute states but new characteristics derived from one or another variety of scientism, that is, the ideology of science pressed into the service of human and social transformation. Thus the Nazi notion of a master race has a strong dose of an outmoded anthropology and a discredited biological organicism; and the Communist emphasis on "a new man" is also indebted to a distorted vision of physiological psychology, as well as to the conversion of history into a philosophy of history.

One of the very first researchers to understand the unitary character of totalitarism, whatever its multidimensional forms, was Wilhelm Reich. His sociological psychology can hardly be improved upon even now. "An ethos based on the misery of masses and demanding such great sacrifices and discipline that only a few are capable of measuring up to it, and an ethos that is so severe and continues to be so severe that even those who support it cannot keep the pace, may have an elevating effect;

but it will never solve a single objective problem of the social community."[9]

In seeking out the causes of the genocidal state, one cannot easily overlook how easily classic religious models have been replaced with presumably contemporary social scientific models. This is not to elevate the former at the expense of the latter. However, it was far easier to utilize slogans derived from social science than references to the Talmud and the Bible — popular sources of belief that motivated ordinary people. For the classic tradition dealt in virtues, while the contemporary counterculture deals in values, relativized with the aid of pseudo-scientific formulas.

It is instructive to heed the words of Gertrude Himmelfarb, who in her work *The De-Moralization of Society: From Victorian Virtues to Modern Values*[10] points out that it was not until the present century that morality became so thoroughly relativized that virtues ceased to be "virtues" and became "values." She goes on to add that "this transmutation is the great philosophical revolution of our time, comparable to the late-seventeenth-century revolt of modern science against classical philosophy."[10] She goes on to note how this created a cultural milieu that made deviant, illegitimate, and criminal acts acceptable. But of course, by extension, this same transmutation, understood so well and uniquely by Friedrich Nietzsche, also made possible medical experimentation on innocents and mass executions of peoples as a whole.

It might well turn out that even the "vices" of past ages are more impressive and worthy than the "values" of the present century. That is to say, even were we to admit that the search for an appropriate set of "virtues" for the fin de siècle through which we are living is more than we have a right to expect, the "vices" inherited from a more austere, primitive period ought to be reflected upon. Let me be specific on this point. In *The Travels of Olearius in Seventeenth Century Russia,* we come upon this intriguing notion of crime and punishment:

If someone is accused of robbery and convicted, he is put to torture all the same [to determine] if he has stolen something besides. If he admits nothing more, and this is the first offence, he is beaten with the knout all along the road from the Kremlin to the Great Square. Here the executioner cuts off one of his ears, and he is put into a dungeon for two years. If he is caught a second time, then, in the manner described above, he has the other ear cut off and is installed in his previous lodging, where he remains until other birds of the kind are found, whereupon they are all sent to Siberia. One who commits a murder not in self-defense, but with premeditation is thrown into prison, where he must repent under severe conditions for six weeks. Then he is given communion and decapitated.[11]

If we go to an earlier period yet in Western Europe, and recall the linkages of sociability with theatricality offered by Michel Foucault in *Discipline and Punish*, we see a similar notion of cruel punishment; what we moderns would rightly consider as vice rather than virtue. Here is a partial description of the disposal of a condemned fellow, Damiens the regicidist, in the account left behind by the officer of the watch:

The sulfur was lit, but the flame was so poor that only the top skin of the hand was burnt, and that only slightly. Then the executioner, his sleeves rolled up, took the steel pincers, which had been especially made for the occasion, and which were about a foot and a half long, and pulled first at the calf of the right leg, then at the thigh, and from there two fleshy parts of the right arm; then at the breasts. Though a strong and sturdy fellow, this executioner found it so difficult to tear away the pieces of the flesh that he set about the same spot two or three times, twisting the pincers as he did so, and what he took away formed at each part a wound about the size of a six pound crown piece.

After these tearings with the pincers, Damiens, who cried out profusely, though without swearing, raised his head and looked at himself; the same executioner dipped an iron spoon in the pot containing the boiling potion, which he poured liberally over each wound. Then the ropes that were to be harnessed to the horses were attached with cords to the patient's body; the horses were then harnessed and placed alongside the arms and legs, one at each limb.

Monsieur Le Breton, the clerk of the court, went up to the patient several times and asked him if he had anything to say. He said he had not; at each torment, he cried out, as the damned in hell are supposed to cry out, "Pardon, my God! Pardon, Lord." Despite all this pain, he raised his head from time to time and looked at himself boldly. The cords had been tied so tightly by the men who pulled the ends that they caused him indescribable pain. Monsieur Le Breton went up to him again and asked him if he had anything to say; he said no. Several confessors went up to him and spoke to him at length; he willingly kissed the crucifix that was held out to him; he opened his lips and repeated: "Pardon, Lord."

The horses tugged hard, each pulling straight on a limb, each horse held by an executioner. After a quarter of an hour, the same ceremony was repeated and finally, after several attempts, the direction of the horses had to be changed, thus: those at the arms were made to pull toward the head, those at the thighs towards the arms, which broke the arms at the joints. This was repeated several times without success. He raised his head and looked at himself. Two more horses had to be added to those harnessed to the thighs, which made six horses in all. Without success.

Finally, the executioner, Samson, said to Monsieur Le Breton that there was no way or hope of succeeding, and told him to ask their Lordships if they wished him to have the prisoner cut into pieces. Monsieur Le Breton, who had come down from the town, ordered that renewed efforts be made, and this was done; but the horses gave up and one of those harnessed to the thighs fell to the ground. The confessors returned and spoke to him again. He said to them (I heard him): "Kiss me, gentlemen." The parish priest of St. Paul's did not dare to, so Monsieur de Marsilly slipped under the rope holding the left arm and kissed him on the forehead. The executioners gathered around and Damiens told them not to swear, to carry out their task and that he did not think ill of them; he begged them to pray to God for him, and asked the parish priest of St. Paul's to pray for him at the first mass.

After two or three attempts, the executioner Samson and he who had used the pincers each drew out a knife from his pocket and cut the body at the thighs instead of severing the legs at the joints; the four horses have a tug and carried off the two thighs after them; namely, that of the right side first, the other following; then the same was done to the arms, the shoulders, the arm-pits and the four limbs; the flesh had to be cut almost to the bone, the horses pulling hard carried off the right arm first and the other afterwards.

When the four limbs had been pulled away, the confessors came to speak to him; but his executioner told them that he was dead, though the truth was that I saw the man move, his lower jaw moving from side to side as if he were talking. One of the executioners even said shortly afterwards that when they had lifted the trunk to throw it on the stake, he was still alive. The four limbs were untied from the ropes and thrown on the stake set up in the enclosure in line with the scaffold, then the trunk and the rest were covered with logs and faggots, and fire was put to the straw mixed with this wood. In accordance with the decree, the whole was reduced to ashes. The last piece to be found in the embers was still burning at half-past ten in the evening. The pieces of flesh and the trunk had taken about four hours to burn.[12]

My aim is not to shock or to make a claim that this is a higher Christian humanism. Indeed, poor Damiens was tortured for nearly eighteen hours in the vain hope that he would repent of his sins. That he failed to do so only ensured his final monstrous demise; but at no loss to his humanity.

Whether we take the fourteenth- or seventeenth-century examples cited above, the point is that crime and punishment was connected to, indeed rooted in, specific acts of moral transgression. Barbaric though punishment meted out in the pretechnological era may have been, it was part of a moral drama of sin and redemption. The absence of instruments for the conduct of mass, collective death served to reinforce this powerful sense of moral individuation.

Precisely the transformation from individual punishment to institutional destruction of great numbers characterizes the shift from the pregenocidal to the genocidal period in human history. This genocidal period has two stages: In the first, an early technology of death is available that is best described as killing with a wide range of weapons, from hatchets and knives to automatic machine guns and bombs. Thus if we look at a range of nations in which massive numbers of people have died, from the Turkish prototype early in the century to Cambodia, Serbia, and Rwanda in the present epoch, we see a correlation of social disintegration with the collectivization of death under conditions of limited technological capacity. One would have to say that the moral depravity of killer regimes are not all that different; rather, it is the technological capacities that distinguish backward from advanced regimes. It is not that Turks were kinder to Armenians than Nazis were to Jews. It is that the capacity for extermination grows exponentially under advanced technological orders and regimes.

Advanced technology of the sort brought to a fine point by the National Socialist regime makes possible the transformation of the problem of death from a personal or even mechanical problem to an engineering situation; that is, how many bodies can effectively be murdered in the least amount of time with the lowest costs to the murderers? In this way, ethics are reduced to policy making, and technology of large numbers replaces the search for any sort of redemption of the individual lost soul; not to mention retribution for the perpetrators of specific genocidal crimes.

Without inviting ridicule for hoping for the bizarre, perhaps a reduction in genocide can best be effected by a return to individuated notion of punishment, or better yet, to the de-collectivization of killing. It is unpleasant to assume that human beings in social contexts are incapable of exercising constraint and moral behavior. But by making that assumption we at least move away from a sort of vapid and empty pacifism that assumes an outright confrontation of good and evil in abstract terms-terms that do not reckon with the draconian beast that lurks in the angelic man.

If the issue of numbers, of the quantity of people murdered, is a critical variant to the study of state propensities to take lives, so too is the issue of numbers significant at the level of personal responsibility. Perhaps the thorniest, and certainly most widely used defense of the perpetrators of genocide is that they were "only following orders." From the Nuremberg war crimes trials of 1946 to the Serbian war crime trials in the Hague in 1996, the same excuses are introduced.

The argument made is simple: if the police officer or soldier given instructions to round up and kill people were to disobey, then that officer or soldier's own life would be at high risk. The argument further holds that resistance would be futile, since others would step forward to carry out the bidding of the executioner state. To be sure, this argument is employed not only with respect to genocide but a wide panoply of orders issued from a command position of absolute authority.

This rationale has a variety of shortcomings: First, some individuals do indeed resist carrying out odious orders, and hence a distinction must still be made between those who and do not carry out high crimes. Second, it is no less a presumption that the state will retaliate against the "conscientious objector" as it is that the state will back away in the face of wide numbers of objectors. This is clearly the empirical basis of Gandhism in the struggle for an India without colonialism. Third, there is a mathematics of morality. If one person is asked to round up or execute hundreds or even thousands of other people, it is entirely reasonable and it would appear legal, to put on a scale the life of that single genocidist over and against the lives of thousands destroyed.

This slight legal digression is not intended to trivialize moral dilemmas that arise in the course of life-taking. Quite the contrary, it is to note that those who argue that they were only following orders are guilty precisely of an oversimplified model of human behavior, one that does not require legal codification or any limitations on behavior other than self-preservation — in short, barbarism.

In the absence of any religious sensibility or moral responsibility, we have a situation in which biologism and historicism have run amok, disguised as moral forces rooted in the utilitarian tradition. We also have genocidists using more abstract rationales: in Nazi Germany, everything from tales of medieval knighthood to nineteenth-century phrenology to prove the racial superiority of Aryans; and in the now-defunct Soviet Union all manner of beliefs from tales of Russian nationalism to Lamarckian doctrines of environmental control of genetic distributions. The nationalisms that spawn genocide are not a pleasant subject to contemplate, but clearly they are central to the performance of genocide. They are perhaps best summarized as a situation in which politics takes place in a vacuum, in an environment lacking political culture. We emphasize too greatly the reduction of the victim to nonhuman or animal status; but the converse of this, the elevation of the killers to a status of superhuman, needs far greater attention than we have given it.

Once genocide is seen as a consequence of interaction between victim and victimizer, or subordinate and superordinate sets of relationships, the focus itself becomes concretized. One must ask, Which victims? and What victimizers? The conditions and cultures of each side need to be examined. But more than that, the interconnections of moral and technological orders may themselves generate a series of responses. A fascinating element in this interplay is displayed in *Schindler's List;* specifically, how the social organization within the death camps served to unleash mayhem.[13] The concentration camps were a source of power unto themselves, a set of legal regulations created ad hoc, a minisociety devoted to death that may have been initially inspired by a racist ideology but that, once unleashed, gathered force and momentum by itself.

Thus the issue of causation is linked to proximate no less than general human conditions. In such a microcosm, individual proclivities and backgrounds become extremely important. The genocidist, no less than his victim, is reduced to highly specific psychological characteristics. These may be the most difficult elements in forging a causal network leading from mocking to killing large numbers of innocents.

This chapter has been an effort to explain the causes of genocide in the specific relations exposed by a stagnant moral climate and a rapidly changing technological order; it is not necessarily a defense of either the Hebrew or Christian faiths. There are simply too many illustrations of organized religion's passivity and even tacit support for genocidal practices to adopt an entirely sanguine attitude about them. Too many of the same prayers are sent aloft in praise of victims and victimizers alike. Why in the twentieth century and why with particular brutality societies engage in genocide may not be questions that can be answered in the same way for different societies, or even for different killing fields within the same society.

There are anomalies: If we take the ten major categories of William J. Bennett's *The Book of Virtues*,[14] we find that Germany is and has long been a nation with strong positive values in at least seven of them: work, self-discipline, responsibility, courage, perseverance, loyalty, and faith. True enough, the German character may be weak on compassion, friendship, and honesty, but this hardly explains the rise of a genocidal state authority.

By the same token, Russia has long been recognized as a nation long and strong on friendship, courage, and loyalty. But unless one is prepared to claim that a nation must be dedicated to all ten aspects of "moral stories" to avoid the excesses of political power, such a litany can scarcely explain the rise of Leninism-Stalinism. Indeed, Russia is a nation with a tradition of sporadic violence but hardly with much capacity for the systematic destruction of millions.

Cambodia is certainly not a place where one would have expected mass murder to become a norm. Just how many people are consigned to the "killing fields" is therefore a function of the special relationship between moral belief and technological cunning. The linkage of culture to violence is not new. But working backward — from the genocidal state to the culture that underwrites such a system — has merits as a way to address the riddle of the causes of genocide.

It might be argued that what is offered here is less a distinction between good and evil than a distinction between lesser and greater evils mediated by lower and higher orders of technology. More bluntly, the classic religions have been guilty of excesses that need no further repetition here. But in starting from presumptions of the evil propensities of human beings, and by stating a catalogue of virtues necessary for curbing those propensities, the far worse evils of genocide that have dotted the processes of secularization can at least be addressed. Clearly, it is far easier to develop a rationale for moral education than to argue the case for zero-growth technology. And in a universe of imperfect beings, the choice between mild forms of repression and even unpleasant forms of fanaticism, on the one hand, and total annihilation in the name of emancipation, on the other, should be self-evident to all people of science and religion alike. Virtue is by no means quiescence in the face of total evil. Nor is forthright resistance to ultimate forms of tyranny properly to be considered as vice. Beyond pleasant moral categories is the need to defend individual life — our lives and those of others — with the same dedication and ferocity that has become characteristic of the death makers. The forms of such self-defense may vary with time and technology. The content of such actions is nothing other than individual and moral survival in an unfinished human universe.

5

Individualizing Life

The fact that a man is a man is more important than the fact that he believes what he believes. Nothing is quite that simple: I know it. But when circumstances grow unbearably complex, it is natural that we should grope about for a very simple credo. And so, after all, we tell ourselves, man's real quiddity is that he is a human being, not that he is a Zionist, a Communist, a Socialist, a Jew, a Pole, or, for that matter a Nazi. But any man who cannot recognize this basic maxim is an agent of Anti-Humanity, and his purpose, whether conscious or not, is the wiping out of mankind.

— John Hersey[1]

ONCE UPON A TIME, INDIVIDUALISM WAS A DOCTRINE THAT COULD READILY BE DISMISSED as archaic, idiosyncratic, and simply out of phase with the modern fashion. Even those who wanted to make a place for the individual were compelled to talk apologetically about the new individualism as a kind of hybrid of social welfare economy and the old laisser faire individualism. Henry Steele Commager reminded us that "the phenomenon of socialization was a logical expression of the American temperament in the new century. It reflected that decline of the importance of individualism and that growing awareness of social responsibility that could be noted similarly in law, education, business, and legislation."[2] With the triumph of the United States as a world power after World War I and with the rapid emergence of communism, fascism, and Nazism as alternative empire systems soon thereafter, the banishment of the individual seemed complete. Everywhere in Western society good citizens shriveled at the charge of individualism, especially if it was prefaced by the word "bourgeois." There seemed no place to hide before the onslaught of the collective: the collective conscience, the collective will, and collective plan. In the eyes of a rhetorical liberalism, individualism came to be viewed as an impediment to responsible and communitarian development, in effect, to social change itself. In one recent version of this theme, individualism has gone "too far encouraging narcissism. Egocentric, impulsive-ridden behavior has run amok."[3] To listen to most pundits of solidarism, individualism is one "ism" that seemed to violate the spirit of the century. The model of community development, even in the hands of its best practitioners, tended toward predetermined ends and was sanctioned by socialism, fascism, and welfarism.

Now that the twentieth century, for all ideological intents and organizational purposes, is behind us, it is rather these other "isms" that have become increasingly suspect. The old individualism failed because of the metaphysical presumptions that underlie Adam Smith's notion of the "hidden hand." Smith seemed to imply some kind of mystical ghost in the machine regulating the behavior of one and all to the greater good of society as a whole. But the new collectivism failed because of the "heavy boot": the widespread recognition that mechanisms to regulate behavior, like machines without ghosts, also worked imperfectly and that achieving the economic goals involved such stupendous costs in human life that even the most obdurate, dedicated servant of the gross national product (GNP) was compelled to wonder whether the hidden hand in its marketplace was not a trifle better than the heavy boot and the barbed wire.

It turned out that inherited doctrines of individualism and socialism were really not at stake. Rather, the ultimate showdown, stripped of all "isms," was between individuals and their right to self-definition and self-delineation, and states and the authority to destroy invested in them by virtue of their monopoly of power, both presumed and real. The essential litmus test became not one of social systems but of personal survival. How people died became a measure of how societies lived. As a result, genocide rather than welfare served to define the limits of state power. Continuities of living and dying, the inalienable rights of individuals in such a cycle, served to show how inalienable rights become subject to deterioration and ultimately dismissal by the state and the powers vested in it.

Michel Foucault's point in presenting his description of the disposition of the body of Damiens the regicide (which I have quoted at length in Chapter 4) is that in an earlier period, whatever the mode of torture, the body of the condemned was specifically singled out as the appropriate recipient of just retribution for a specific crime. As we moved into the utilitarian nineteenth century, forms of generalized punishment were enveloped by complete and austere institutions called prisons. Punishment was organized around the principle of incarceration; prison life created the framework of rationality and universality that no longer necessitated a direct assault on the body of the condemned. Docile bodies required no direct assault.

In an odd way, Foucault missed the point of his own illustrations. For it was not only the system of incarceration in total institutions that was at stake, but the erosion of an entire Judeo-Christian tradition of individual punishment for specific individual crimes. As crimes became massified, punishment too became massified in the form of scientific imprisonment systems. But at the same time, the possibility of heroic death was denied. The prison as a negotiated order created conditions for a contrite life. Survival through rehabilitation involved a tacit acceptance of the prison system as such. In this way the state did not simply move from a vicious to a benign system; rather, through the science of human engineering, citizens subject to the penalties of total institutions were denied their distinctiveness and instead were offered universalist norms of rehabilitation that conveniently included a belief in their own guilt as a precondition to prison life.

However awful in recounting, poor Damiens died a martyr's death. He was recalled and memorialized even by his own executioners. If his life was a mixed bag, his death was an unfettered example of heroism. Two hundred years later, the problem of death was not one of exact punishment for a well-defined wrongdoing but an engineering problem in efficient mass annihilation. Even death had become collectivized. At the trial of Adolf Eichmann, Peter Bamm, a German army physician, recited the magical technology of genocidal death. Hannah Arendt's summary of the engineering ethic reveals the moral impotence caused by this new technology:

> They were collected by "the others" [as he calls the S.S. mobile killing units, to distinguish them from ordinary soldiers] and were put into a sealed-off part of the former G.P.U. prison that abutted on the officer's lodgings, where Bamm's own unit was quartered. They were then made to board a mobile gas van, in which they died after a few minutes, whereupon the driver transported the corpses outside the city and unloaded them into tank ditches. We knew this. We did nothing. Anyone who had seriously protested or done anything against the killing unit would have been arrested within twenty four hours and would have disappeared. It belongs among the refinements of totalitarian governments in our century that they don't permit their opponents to die a great, dramatic martyr's death for their convictions. A good many of us might have accepted such a death. The totalitarian state lets its opponents disappear in silent anonymity. It is certain that anyone who had dared to suffer death rather than silently tolerate the crime would have sacrificed his life in vain. This is not to say that such a sacrifice would have been morally meaningless. It would only have been practically useless. None of us had a conviction so deeply rooted that we could have taken upon ourselves a practically useless sacrifice for the sake of a higher moral meaning.[4]

But if this new technology is morally impotent, it certainly does not lack for efficiency in the hands of state authorities. Both the level and types of death imposed on victims is a direct function of the sophistication of technology available to the victimizers. In states where only an intermediary technology is available, intermediary levels of genocide are practiced. Thus in a regime such as that of Idi Amin, which held power in Uganda between 1971 and 1979, the death system could be described as a halfway house between seventeenth-century France and twentieth-century Nazi Germany. The summary report filed by a former officer of the Gestapo-modeled State Research Bureau, Abraham Kisuule-Minge, gives strong evidence that genocide as a style is directly linked to technological availabilities and not developmental goals:

> Saturday was the cruelest day of all. In the morning he [Farouk Minawa, one of Amin's most trusted Nubian aides] would order prisoners brought to the reception area. With a wave of his hand, he would signal which were to die that night. At 7 p.m. precisely, the cars parked in the courtyard would be started to drown out the screams to come. Each prisoner was brought down and told to kneel before an officer in the yard. He was asked to explain why he had been brought in and was told he was being released. Then guards would leap from the darkness, loop a thick rope round the victim's neck and slowly strangle him. The *coup de grace* was a sledgehammer blow to the chest. It took about ten minutes to kill each prisoner. The bodies were piled in trucks and driven north for five hours to the Karuma Falls to be thrown to the crocodiles.[5]

This bizarre mix between the primitive and the modern, between state murder as individualistic and mechanical, helps to define the form of genocide, even if it does not precisely explain its causes. The essence of the modern death system is a deprivation of both individual accountability and individual transcendence in death. In a remarkable commentary on the reprint edition of Horace Bleackley's minor classic *State Executions Viewed Historically and Sociologically*, John Lofland provides a clinical framework for Foucault's type of narrative. He points out the essential distinction between "the open and concealed dramaturgy of state execution."

Open executions are characterized by long death waits and death trips; public death places; professional executioners with personal contact with the condemned; death techniques that are noisy, painful, scream-provoking, mutilating, struggle-inducing, odor-causing, and highly visible; public and prolonged corpse disposal; and finally, death that is announced by the suspension of institutional activities. Concealed executions are characterized by short death waits and death trips; private and enclosed death places; part-time executioners with impersonal and limited contact with the condemned; death techniques that are reliable, fast-acting, quiet, painless, nonmutilating, odorless, and concealed; quick and anonymous disposal of the corpse; and finally, death that involves no suspension of institutional activities. It is to Lofland's credit that he appreciates that however "raucous or crude historic executions may have been, they did provide the condemned with opportunity for dying with a display of courage and dignity utterly denied in modern executions."[6]

The issues of alternative death systems represent considerably more than half a trade-off in humanistic styles. The depersonalization of death is hardly a random event, or even a matter of simple strategic options. At its essence, the modern death system is linked to the emergence of genocide as a centerpiece of state power and the display of its monopoly of power. Orwell quite properly pointed out that one cannot have a worthy picture of the future unless an understanding of the losses occasioned by Christianity are also factored into the mix.

The conservative idea that Christianity stands as a bulwark against slaughter fails to reckon with the historical examples to the contrary. For its part, socialism only postpones a consideration of the role of the individual by urging the solution to basic material needs that begins and ends with the collective will. The modern state may be a useful technique to overcome the anarchy of the marketplace, but, unlike individualism, it is scarcely a statement of personal obligation or commitment to the private person.

> Western civilization, unlike some oriental civilizations, was founded partly on the belief in individual immortality. If one looks at the Christian religion from the outside, this belief appears far more important than the belief in God. The western conception of good and evil is very difficult to separate from it. There is little doubt that the modern cult of power worship is bound up with the modern man's feeling that life here and now is the only life there is. If death ends everything, it becomes much harder to believe that you can be in the right even if you are defeated. Statesmen, nations, theories, causes are judged almost inevitably by the test of material success. Supposing that one can separate the two phenomena, the decay of the belief in personal immortality has been as important as the rise of machine civilization. Machine civilization has terrible possibilities, but the other thing has terrible possibilities too, and it cannot be said that the Socialist movement has given much thought to them.[7]

Twentieth-century totalitarianisms created pioneering innovations in depriving death no less than life of meaning. One's guilt is collectivized and accrues to a class, race, or religion as a whole. Once this process is successfully concluded, the problem of innocence is also easily collectivized. Neither guilt nor innocence are any longer matters of individual conscience; rather, in a sense they accrue to a master race, the historically sanctioned party, or the purified race. Death is life's ontological opposite: It accrues to the degenerate religion, the backward race, and the oppressed class. It is indeed the essence of twentieth-century ideology to collectivize the spirit of guilt and innocence; therein lies the banality of evil.

In some measure, this collectivization process was ordained by the breakdown of the distinction between deviance and marginality, between social outcasts and political radicals. Hence a notion arose that the common danger stemmed from those who would be different, and the character of their transgression vanished. As a result, whatever the nature of the crime, it too became generalized and universalized.

The point I made in the essay on "Social Deviance and Political Marginality" has only been partially confirmed by time and events. The blend of criminality and politicality, although it defines the essential quality of the collective spirit of the age, does not quite explain the moral superiority of a life of politics over that of crime. The line between the social deviant and the political marginal is fading. It is rapidly becoming an obsolete distinction.

As this happens, political dissent by deviant means will become subject to the types of repression that have traditionally been a response to social deviance. This development compels social scientists to reconsider their definition of the entire range of social phenomena from deviance to politics.[8] The practical implication of this conflation between deviance and marginality is the enlistment of criminal elements in political extermination and execution. The body of literature on the quotidian conduct of Nazism and Communism reveal how central this process was in the conduct of both of these totalitarian regimes.

The distinction between the social and pathological on one side and the political and ideological on the other nonetheless persists in part because the criminal phenomenon accepts almost unqualifiedly the collective judgment of society. It internalizes its sense of guilt and believes in its wrongdoing and hence is reduced to working the system. Aleksandr Solzhenitsyn describes this distinction between common criminals and political prisoners, the "suckers" who retained their sense of personal worth, with stunning precision in *The Gulag Archipelago:*

> They had their own "original code" and their own original concept of honor. But it was not a question of their being patriots, as our bureaucrats and writers would have liked to have it, but of their being absolutely consistent materialists and consistent pirates.

And even though the dictatorship of the proletariat was so assiduous in courting them, they did not respect it even for one minute; they do not recognize the earthly institution of private property, and in this respect they really are hostile to the bourgeoisie and to those Communists who have dachas and automobiles. "Everything they come across on life's path they take as their own (if it is not too dangerous). Even when they have a surfeit of everything, they reach out to grab what belongs to others because any unstolen article makes a thief sick at heart.[9]

Political prisoners were not simply morally superior to common thieves; rather, they had not understood the twentieth century nearly as well. They had not understood the role of the collective in mass society, or, put another way, they understood it all too well and refused to go along with that program.

What was that program that so collectivized the Archipelago? Again to paraphrase Solzhenitsyn, it comprised ten points: constant fear, servitude, secrecy and mistrust, universal ignorance, squealing, betrayal as a form of existence, corruption (the lie as a form of existence), cruelty, generalized cruelty, and finally, slave psychology, the assumption that the executioner was right because he held the monopoly of power to execute. These propositions so characterize the collective spirit, and do so with such little regard to social system, place, or geography, that we must begin to take seriously the dangers of collectivism as a whole and the need for some kind of return to an individual framework as a base of all moral and political decision making.

In his collection of essays on the social situation of inmates, appropriately entitled *Asylums*, Erving Goffman makes the important points that the relationship between the totalitarian institution and democratic society may be far closer than one initially anticipates or expects and that our model forms of democracy have their own way of providing intimidation of the cruelest sorts. In this passage, Goffman is not aiming to destroy a belief in democracy, but to make it clear that assaults on the human spirit begin with a denial of the private person;

and this pre-eminence of privacy, under such strong assault throughout the century from technical and political quarters alike, is basic to a free society. "If the institution has a militant mission, as do some religious, military, and political units, then a partial reversal on the inside of external status arrangements can act as a constant reminder of the difference and enmity between the institution and its environing society. It should be noted that in thus suppressing externally valid differences the harshest total institution may be the most democratic; and in fact, the inmate's assurance of being treated no worse than any other of his fellows can be a source of support as well as deprivation."[10]

What this means — whether we are talking about concentration camps in Germany, slave labor camps of the Soviet Union, or mental asylums in the United States — is a system that presents itself under various labels but that ultimately reduces itself to a struggle between individuals and the state. Goffman shrewdly points out that getting out of an asylum involves a negotiation of the system and accommodation to its social order. To leave an asylum means to surrender, to presume one's own guilt or sickness, one's own weaknesses, one's own need for rehabilitation. It is only when that need is sufficiently felt that one can be "free" in the collective sense.

This is also the basis of Orwell's *1984*. Here too freedom means perfect slavery, not simply as a literary juxtaposition but as the necessary assumption that to have even a modest amount of freedom in the collective society is to assume a therapeutic position. And that entails manipulating the system rather than changing it. There must be something wrong with an individual in order for him or her to be cured. In such a system, resistance, even questioning of authority, whether that authority be psychiatric, legal, medical, or political, becomes the main danger to state power. What has to be extirpated, uprooted, is not a particular kind of individual resistance but the very idea of resistance.

An excellent report of a teacher of English who spent several years in Mao's China during the Red Guard Terror underscores the elimination of resistance through the annihilation of the individual as a meaningful category. Beneath the heavy-handed sarcasm is the feeling that the anarch individual comes upon the behemoth collective, and that with the new collectivisms we are once again in a Hobbesian world, but one that is technologically far more proficient than anything known in seventeenth-century England:

> All these things helped me finally see the connection: The freedom to have opinions, that is a Bourgeois freedom. And likewise the freedom to have information. The important freedom for a Socialist is the freedom to have correct opinions; that is, the freedom to repeat the Party Line. In other words, people who have opinions are class enemies. Throughout China now the system of "Socialist Courtyards" is in force. This brings Party leadership right to your door. Every three or four families has one person appointed to report to the local Party committee. On everything. The Chang boy is playing truant. The Wangs seem to quarrel a lot. Young Chen is sometimes out late at night. If the appointee doesn't make these reports, that is conspiracy. Counterrevolution. This is perhaps why China is so ardently against the Helsinki agreements. Nowhere in that document is there any mention of the essential human right: the right to Party leadership.[11]

The Chinese, whether as a result of ethnic homogeneity or a refined sense of internal history, are uniquely uninvolved in genocidal solutions to socioeconomic problems. Even their ability to create a society free of individualism has been placed in serious doubt. The need for real material development pushed through the weight of inherited rhetoric. And if China has not yet achieved a level of moral responsibility as a concomitant of personal behavior, it has at least made the first moves in that direction by recognizing the rights of material satisfaction as an individual as well as collective decision.

These remarks are not intended as a contribution to ongoing discussions on the merits or drawbacks of capital punishment. That issue has received ample, if inconclusive, coverage in nearly every advanced industrial nation; the same nations that turn strangely myopic when it comes to collective punishment. The genocidal practices of Paraguay, Uganda, or Cambodia can hardly elicit a proper quorum in the United Nations among the very nations that agonize breathlessly over capital punishment.

Caryl Chessman and Gary Gilmore, however different their crimes from each other's or from those committed by Damiens, have in common a strong sense of individuation, of being punished for an exact crime or series of crimes. In this peculiar sense, they illustrate the healthier agonies of a society. In demanding that the State of Utah carry out its capital punishment clause, Gilmore confronted the society with its legal system and the limits of its own moral foundations. In contrast, the essence of modern genocidal systems is that collective death makes it possible to avoid such issues.

The technological devices that permit collective death are also at work in creating a profound sense of total distance between victims and victimizers. The modern state, with its bureaucratic orientation, converts the problem of choice by making death a nonproblem of necessity. People must die because they represent symbolic evil: Jews in Poland, peasants in the Ukraine, Catholics in Northern Ireland, Indians in Uganda, blacks in South Africa. As a result, in the absence of moral choice, the state exempts or at least suspends judgment for the executioners. Killing becomes a matter of policy making rather than ethical decision. Thus the individual is reduced to the status of nonperson not simply as victim but, with equal profundity, as victimizer. In this way, the breakdown of individual responsibility opened the pathway toward collective guilt and punishment.

This assertion that the breakdown of individual responsibility opens wide the gates to collective repression should not be construed as a defense of capitalism or a critique of socialism. True enough, advocates of the former system of economy use a rhetoric of free enterprise and individual initiative, while devotees of socialism celebrate the virtues of social ownership of the means of production. But the character of the economy would appear relatively indifferent to the issue of genocide. There are as many societies presumably following capitalist models of development practicing such mass annihilation as those following socialist models of development.

Even if we ignore the obvious fact that the issue of capitalism and socialism has become more a problem in measuring the size and character of the public sector vis-à-vis the private sector and less a critical cutting point for measuring social systems, Brazil handles the problem of minority groups with at least as much vicious vigor as the former Soviet Union handled its unwanted Aryan minorities, or the United States its Indian problem. Those that cannot be entirely eliminated are reduced to enclave status. Such people are permitted a bare cultural survival without structural components for autonomy. The collective will of state power, rather than the presumed needs of economic growth, dictates and determines the character of punishment. In this way the battle is joined at its purest levels, between individuals and the small communities in which they huddle, and the state and its machinery of repression. Economic systems may account for levels of production or rates of growth, but these appear in history as strategic decisions that a state takes. Beyond strategy is the omnipotence of the state as such and the impulse to nullify the individual as sovereign entity.

When, for example, a society comes upon an issue so pervasive and yet personal as abortion, advocacy of socialism or capitalism hardly helps matters at decision-making levels. Whether abortion is a matter of a woman's right to her body or a medically sanctioned form of contraception; whether abortion is even a matter of life or death, given the special status of the fetus; whether poor people should have special access to federal funds for abortion purposes — these are issues disguising basic extensions of state power. For example, the Nazis constantly linked the "final solution" with "racial purification" at birth. What the state does is render moral determinations meaningless by providing a fait accompli. The state can argue that all fetuses are the property of the state and that therefore decisions about abortion are in the domain of federal or local directives. Or alternatively, the state can place at the disposal of communities a massive network of sponsored clinics that permit abortions to take place in an atmosphere free of guilt but also free of moral responsibility.

The key issue is not the disposition of laws governing abortions but the absolution from moral responsibility that federal intervention into personal morality so often represents. To pose the issue in terms of sanctioning abortions by untrained practitioners brandishing coat hangers versus abortions on demand by sophisticated medical personnel brandishing scalpels is to fudge the issue. Such a series of false antinomies disguises the collectivization of decision making within most advanced industrial systems. Both sides in the abortion debate, assuming that it can be resolved by law, take for granted the main danger: state power over personal morality.

Much of the rebellion against authoritarianism is also an assertion that individuals can manage their own affairs best; funds should be left in the hands of wage earners and taxpayers and kept away from the coffers of a federal or state treasury. Viewed in this way, demands for federal abortion clinics seem as wide of the mark as demands that abortions be prohibited as a violation of Providential guidelines. The collectivization of responsibility is the problem, not the "right to life" or "abortion on demand." Only when moral issues are restored to individual decision can concrete specific issues be meaningfully resolved in a civilized manner. Otherwise we face an endless series of false alternatives: issues fought without principles enunciated; equities gained while liberties are lost.

There is a continuity of the way people live and die with the way social systems conduct their affairs. It becomes especially instructive to examine the social processing of officially sanctioned death because in this area of universally shared agony we have presumed that we are more civilized than all past societies. But in the technical proficiencies in distancing killers from those killed, we stand exposed as the least civilized. We recoil in horror at medieval torture systems, at diabolical inventions that were supposed to symbolize fit punishment for thieves, plunderers, murderers, and assorted others. But their very individuation, their continued existence as figures in history, give them a standing denied to the collective martyrdom of the twentieth century. Engineering as an ideology is no moral match for religion. On the other hand, religion as an ideology is no match for engineering as a system ensuring mass death with personal sentiment.

As a general equation within a finite social system, more state authority means less individual capacity to survive, and a higher individual capacity to survive means less state authority. This point cannot be waffled by charges that this represents simply a return to an old-fashioned individualism or conservatism. Such ideological eyewash will no longer suffice. Too much suffering has transpired and too many norms have been transgressed to warrant a belief in the state as benefactor.

The state provides not simply its elites but its masses as well. The state not only provides decision making by experts at the top, but it generates mass mobilization at the bottom. Statements that appear as polarized expressions of social life are in fact a part of the same monolithic entity. The task of individual survival, indeed of individualism as such, is not simply to ferret out one polar expression of "anti-statism," but to seek out the personal worth of the individual as such. The dialectic of state power resides in its capacity to convert the person into a mass and an elite into a ruling class. The carrots the state offers below disguises the stick it holds above. The outcome of the struggle between the public and the private, the state and the person may well be in doubt, but at least lines of struggle have become clarified as the century draws to a close.

There is a need to be cautious about stretching this duality between individuals and the state into a Manichaean doctrine of contending principles in which goodness is identified with the person — or the more likely prospect of identifying liberty with individual caprice — and evil with the state. In strategic terms, demands for extending human rights, covenants intended to limit national excesses, and legislation stipulating root factors entering into deliberation of rights most often proceed through demands for state support. As a result, the state becomes both root problem and the core of any solution.

Paradoxically, there seems to be an intellectual consensus that in the long run, the state is culpable; but there is also a short-run belief that the state must aid in fostering human rights and even extending human potentials. Rather than attempt a surgical resolution of this evident dilemma, it should suffice for social science purposes to carefully disentangle the web of confusion surrounding such dramatic issues as individual liberties, human rights, and state powers. Demands for improvements must come to rest on a careful delineation of inconsistencies and inequities in present arrangements of structures. If this is a modest proposal for gigantic issues, so too is the foundation of this chapter: the social processing of death as a measure of the life-giving potential of any given society.

As I have already discussed in Chapter 3, there is a danger in broadening the concept of genocide so that it becomes symbolically all-embracing and hence meaningless. The difference between actual and symbolic genocide is not simply a matter for academic disputation; it has to do with the survival capacities of entire peoples. If we broaden our approach to include an entity called "cultural genocide," the results might be counterproductive.

A deflated, pessimistic, and ultimately confused concept of genocide deprives the very people who are presumably genocide victims of the capacity to resist and retaliate. For that reason, I have come to believe that a restrictive rather than an omnibus concept of genocide is the most operationally valid. To repeat: Genocide means the physical dismemberment and liquidation of people on large scales, an attempt by those who rule to achieve the total elimination of a subject people; genocide does not mean simply depriving people of their cultural heritage or of opportunities for education, welfare, or health, however hideous such deprivations might be. One must avoid liberal fantasizing about people who are victimized in ways short of genocide. Broadening the concept so that everyone somehow ends up a victim of genocide only leads to a tautological reasoning. Physical genocide is tragically large enough, in raw numerical terms, not to require a vision of symbolic genocide. Ideological mannerisms that add fuel to an already grotesque fire are counterproductive to practical efforts to limit or reverse genocidal patterns.

There is a growing realization that the shift in politics from an ideological to a personalistic basis is not simply another rhetorical form but a politics based on individuals in contrast to parties, officials, and leaderships. It is a Chilean living in exile in the United States, Orlando Letelier; it is a Brazilian journalist named Vladimir Herzog and a Russian physicist named Andrei Sakharov, who become the focus of attention by Amnesty International. Human rights as a movement are of, by, and for individuals. In such a context the body is a willing hostage to free expression. The theory of this movement is that every individual counts as one — no more and no less. Hence the death or torture or maltreatment of every individual is important, and not just part of a state's calculation of the human costs necessary to achieve abstractly predetermined levels of economic production. Undoubtedly, exaggeration, even mistakes of judgment, will be made by such a new politics of human rights. However, that such a movement even exists indicates that individualism has found a new source of energy, one predicated on the universal right to live rather than the sovereign requirements of state power.

Individualism has provided the question of genocide with renewed philosophical meaning. As the relationships of non-humans, robots, and infants to adult human beings become hotly debated, they raise a number of questions. Abortion comes into question: When does a fetus cease being a human vegetable and become an entity and then a personality? Mentation comes into question: What do the relationships between computers performing human tasks and doing so more rationally than most people can (for example, playing chess) do to explode the idea that humans are sacrosanct? The issue requires a volume unto itself, and has received a great deal of treatment.

At the philosophical level, justifications of homicide are similar to those for genocide. What emerges in the medical literature under euthanasia emerges in the political literature under racial purity. This is no simple matter. But perhaps one beginning at this philosophical level has to place the matter of genocide in the context of a means-ends continuum — what might be referred to as Kant's principle of personality: "that human beings are always to be treated as ends in themselves and never as means or instrumentalities." If this principle has significance, it does so by the assertion that the destruction of people can never be simply a matter of social convenience, nor can a personality be regarded as subhuman simply as a convenience or as a racial designation. This meaningful formulation is contained in a work by Philip E. Devine, *The Ethics of Homicide,* in which he points out:

> The principle of personality is both plausible in its own right and capable of making sense of many of our considered judgments about moral issues. The difficulty of arguing with those who do not share such intuitions on this point should not inhibit our acting upon such convictions, whether as individuals or as citizens. To allow philosophical skepticism concerning the first principles of ethics to paralyze action would be to surrender the practical sphere to immoralists and fanatics, neither of whom is likely to be

troubled about such issues. So far as ethics proper is concerned, this kind of reply will have to suffice.[12]

To raise the principle of personality is to argue the case for the restoration of individualism on a new basis. Specifically, it is to see matters of life taking and life giving as a one-by-one affair, and hence to reduce the likelihood of converting technology into a rationale for massive liquidation predicated on general theories of race, class or nation.

Part II

PAST AS PROLOGUE

6

Democracy, Autocracy, and Terrorism

The task of men of culture and faith is not to desert historical struggles nor to serve the cruel and inhuman elements in those struggles. It is rather to remain what they are, to help man against what is oppressing him, to favor freedom against the fatalities that close in upon it. That is the condition under which history really progresses, innovates—in a word, creates. In everything else it repeats itself, like a bleeding mouth that merely vomits forth a wild stammering.

— Albert Camus[1]

THE QUESTION OF TERROR, THE ORGANIZED OR SPORADIC EFFORT TO OVERTHROW existing systems, has in common with genocide its transcendent characteristics; the direct confrontation with matters of who shall live or die. The role of terror must be assessed and responded to by all social systems. Neither capitalism nor socialism, democracy nor totalitarianism, market economies nor collective economies can remain aloof from it. The state can monopolize the power to coerce, but it cannot prevent responses to such coercion. Maurice Merleau-Ponty said it well in noting that "the human world is an open or unfinished system, and the same radical contingency . . . threatens it with disorder and prevents us from despairing of it, providing only that one remembers its various machineries are actually men and tries to maintain and expand man's relations to man."[2]

Current attitudes toward the uses of terror range from a belief that it is the only possible means to bring about social change to a view of terror as the last refuge of scoundrels. Terrorists themselves are seen either as the only authentic heroes in a notably unheroic age or as petty criminals who coat their venal acts with an ideological gloss.

In such a polarized climate of opinion, attempts to introduce shadings into the analysis of terror invite instant rebuke from both an impatient Left and an outraged Right. Only "reformists" and "bleeding hearts" are apparently willing to challenge the common rhetoric. Yet Communist dictatorships, socialist democracies, and capitalist systems must all face the problems of terrorism. Skyjackings, assassinations, bombings, extortions, and sabotage do not stop at any national or regional borders. While different social systems react differently to terror, in accordance with their particular ideological premises, no society can be indifferent to the problems raised by terrorism.

For social scientists who have a civil libertarian viewpoint, any analysis of terrorism must consider not only the attacks on civil liberties by those acting in the name of terror but also the potential damage from those responding in defense of organized society. They must also consider the need for legitimate dissent if the world community of nations is not to become frozen into its present political positions, along with their economic and social inequities. By exploring how and why terrorism arises, who the terrorists are, and what the costs and benefits of antiterrorism are for civil liberties, we should bring more precision to the analysis of the various terrorist activities now facing world society.

The minute one attempts to profile the terrorist, considerable problems of definition arise that inhibit possible remedial action. Can the IRA (Irish Republican Army) operating in Northern Ireland really be compared to the PFLP (Popular Front for the Liberation of Palestine)? And if so, on what basis? The former has a large membership and the support of many, and it operates on a well-defined home terrain. The latter has an extremely small membership, with more covert than overt support in the Middle East. Yet there are similarities: The militant Palestinians believe that the destruction of Israel is a prerequisite for a general peace settlement, while the leaders of the IRA for the most part believe that the defeat of Protestant Northern Ireland and its reunification with the rest of Ireland are necessary for peace.

A large factor in ascertaining the differences between guerrilla warfare and terrorist activities is linked to the size of the movements, their organizational efficacy, and their geographic locale. And even when ideological predispositions are similar, one may still claim a difference between guerrilla organizations and terrorist operations.

The essential difference between the two just mentioned seems to be that the Irish Catholic militants are involved in an internal struggle for political control, whereas the Arab Palestinians are involved in an external struggle for geographic control. It is this gulf between national liberation efforts and international symbolic acts that seems most emphatically to distinguish guerrilla warfare from terrorist activity. Rather than emphasizing the points of similarity between terrorists and guerrillas, it would appear more worthwhile to draw a profile that makes plain the differences. This is not always easy; for example, the psychological characteristics that lead some to guerrilla movements may be similar, if not entirely identical, to the psychological characteristics of members of a terrorist group. Nonetheless, despite the difficulties, a tentative evaluation of the essential nature of the terrorist threat is required.

- ▸ A terrorist is a person engaged in politics who makes little if any distinction between strategy and tactics on the one hand and principles on the other. For him (and for the most part terrorism is a male activity), all politics is a matter of principle, and hence nothing beyond the decision to commit a revolutionary deed of death and personal commitment requires examination, planning, and forethought.

- ▸ A terrorist is a person prepared to surrender his own life for a cause he considers transcendent in value. A terrorist assumes not only that taking the lives of others will lead to desired political goals but that the loss of one's own life is a warranty that such a cause or political position is correct and obtainable.

- ▸ A terrorist is a person who possesses both a self-fulfilling prophetic element and a self-destructive element. The act of destroying another person or group of persons itself becomes the basis upon which future politics can be determined and decided, and the absence of terror is hence held to signify the absence of meaningful events. The self-destructive element is coincidental with the previous point, namely, that one's own death is the highest form of the politics of the deed: the only perfect expression of political correctness.

- ▸ A terrorist is a person for whom all events are volitional and none are determined. The terrorist, in contrast to the revolutionary, perceives the world pragmatically as a place to be shaped and reshaped in accord with the human will or the will of the immediate collective group. Beyond that, there is no historical or sociological force of a hidden or covert nature that can really alter human relationships, geographic boundaries, and so on.

- ▸ A terrorist is a person who is young, most often of middle-class family background, usually male, and economically marginal. Collectively, persons caught as terrorists, whether hijackers, assassins, or guerrillas, are remarkably similar: aged twenty to thirty-five, relatively well educated, with some college or university training but rarely of the uppermost achievement levels, and clearly not of peasant or working-class stock.

- ▸ A terrorist performs his duties as an avocation. That is to say, he may hold a position in the larger society quite unrelated to his terrorist actions. This anonymity provides an essential cover for his activities. It also makes the contest between police power and political terror far more problematic, since sophisticated weaponry is relatively useless without adequate methods of detection and prevention.

▸ The terrorist defines himself differently from the casual homicide in several crucial respects: he murders systematically rather than at random; he is symbolic rather than passionate — that is, he is concerned with scoring political points rather than responding to personal provocation; and his actions are usually well planned rather than spontaneous. Terrorism is thus primarily a sociological phenomenon, whereas homicide can more easily be interpreted in psychological terms. Terrorism essentially has a group nature rather than a personal nature.

▸ The terrorist by definition is a person who does not distinguish between coercion and terrorism because he lacks access to the coercive mechanisms of the state. The essential polarity is not between pacifism and terrorism, which is mechanistic. The essential choice that those responding to terror can make is either coercive mechanisms, which may range from the mild presence of police or the military in the body politic to imprisonment and limitation of the rights of opposition groups, or outright counterterrorism, which goes far beyond coercion since it violates the sanctity of life itself as an overriding perspective. The believer in coercion must also assume that the victims of coercion can be rehabilitated; the terrorist denies the possibility of rehabilitation for the victim.

▸ A terrorist is a person who, through the act of violence, advertises and dramatizes a wider discontent. The advertising function does more than make evident public displeasure with a regime. It provides instantaneous recognition of the person performing terrorist acts through mass communications. Terrorism becomes a fundamental way of defining heroism and leadership.

▸ A terrorist believes that the act of violence will encourage the uncommitted public to withdraw support from a regime or an institution and hence make wider revolutionary acts possible by weakening the resolve of the opposition. Practically, however, such acts often work to lend greater support to the regime by sealing up fissures and contradictions in the name of opposing a common enemy, the terrorist.

▶ A terrorist may direct his activities against the leadership of the opposition by assassinating presidents and political leaders; such terrorists usually tend to function alone and in the service of an often poorly defined ideology rather than a political movement. Other terrorists may direct their activities against the symbols of establishments and agencies; such terrorists are less concerned with the individuals against whom terror is performed than with the organizations and agencies of which they are a part. For example, the Munich massacre of Israeli athletes was directed at the State of Israel; the specific people eliminated were not an issue. This kind of terrorist is usually himself under a strict political regimen and is responsible to counterorganizations or guerrilla groupings that define and determine the extent and types of terrorism.

▶ A terrorist does not have a particularly well-defined ideological persuasion. He may work for the state or against the state, for an established order or in an effort to overthrow one. The level of his ideological formation is generally poor and half-digested, reflecting a greater concern for the act than for alternative systems that may flow from the act. It is important in a morphology of the terrorist not to confuse such rhetorical features with the generic nature of terror, which transcends personality and even social structural characteristics.[3]

THESE ITEMS STATED, WE MUST NOW TURN TO A CONSIDERATION OF THE GENERIC NATURE of terror and not just the biographic nature of the terrorist. The definition of someone as a terrorist is a labeling device. The act of homicide, or at rare times even terrorist suicide, cannot disguise the moral aspect of such definitions. What is usually referred to as terrorism is unsponsored and unsanctioned violence against the body or bodies of others. However, whether or not violence performed with official sanction against the leadership or the membership of other groups and institutions is nonterrorist in character, it is part of a continuous process of definition and redefinition in political life. And in the current ambiguous and even ubiquitous conditions, performing a terrorist act does not uniquely make one a terrorist, any more than random nonviolence alone defines the pacifist.

This raises the entire matter of legitimation and labeling, since terrorism is not uniquely an act but also a response to an act; and further, since terrorism is a set of punitive measures taken against those so defined, the problem of definition is compounded by the existence of subjective factors in the body politic — factors that in some measure help define and even determine the treatment, punishment, and reception of acts of political violence.

When terrorism is an "internal matter" and not a minigroup invasion of a nation by foreign citizens and alien subjects, the approach must be more sensitive to the ills in the society being addressed. The armed forces and police have a much easier time dealing with foreign nationals, such as the Japanese in the Lod Airport raid in Tel Aviv or Muslim extremists in the Munich Olympic encampment. The difficult chore comes in handling native populations. Here we must make a fundamental distinction between guerrillas and terrorists. The distinction must be made on the basis of whether the participants in assassination attempts, bombings of buildings, and so on are nationals or foreigners. In the case of the latter, true terrorists, it is possible to employ the police and the armed forces to defeat and destroy them. In the case of nationals or guerrillas, the aim of the state must always be to contain, restrain, and finally reconcile. This distinction between guerrillas and terrorists is significant not simply as a typology but in terms of operational responses to terror as distinct from national guerrilla movements, which frequently are a response to long-smoldering inequities.

In a special sense the question of terrorism, quite apart from the characteristics of the terrorists, is an "internal concern" of Marxism and the socialist tradition. Within Western liberal democratic thought, from John Locke to Montesquieu to John

Stuart Mill and John Dewey, there has never been any doubt that terrorism is largely counterproductive for real social change and that excessive use of terror to put down terrorism is even more counterproductive since it calls into question the legitimacy of the entire body politic. Of course, there have been bourgeois and populist traditions of romantic violence. Theories of the will emanated from the bowels of European irrational and mystical traditions. Yet overall, and especially in the Anglo-American framework, terror has been declared outside the purview of the legitimate exercise of protest and opposition.

The socialist and Marxist traditions are quite different. From the outset, Marx contested Pierre Proudhon, and Lenin argued with the Russian anarchists. In general the organizational tradition has been dominant. The argument against "spontaneity" rests at its core on a disbelief in the efficacy of violence; or as Lenin held, a rejection of the idea that a revolution can be reduced to an insurrection, or that an insurrection in turn can be reduced to a conspiracy.[4] Even the Chinese representative to the United Nations debated whether the discussion of terror should be on the agenda of the General Assembly and admitted to a parting of the ways with the Arabs on the question of the political payoffs of terrorist tactics.

The Chinese Communists, to the degree that they respond as Marxists, and also insofar as the whole Maoist notion of the revolution involves armed military struggle, react negatively to the current wave of "petit bourgeois violence" associated with religious fundamentalists. While long-range goals of different revolutionaries are similar, the orthodox socialist tradition continues to emphasize that military operations, performed in conjunction with the political support of masses, in contrast to the *foco* belief that one can implement a revolution through hit-and-run military operations, and a minimal show of popular support. The Chinese Maoist position, if anything, demanded even greater adherence to organizational constraint than did the Soviet Stalinist position, since Russian Bolshevism was based on party organization, whereas the Chinese party position was based on military organization. Both in the past and present, the orthodox Marxist vision has been one of high organization, disciplined assaults on class enemies, and a strong sense of leadership to reduce random acts in politics. A belief in history rather than in human volition dominates this tradition: Faith in violence is tempered by a belief that the laws of history are inexorable and that only the timing of such historical inevitabilities remains to be ironed out by human action.

A minor motif has run through the socialist-Marxist tradition. It extends from Georges Sorel's vision of the general strike that spontaneously brings down the system to Régis Debray and the theory of the *foco*. This motif is based upon the idea of the unattached group effecting revolutionary change.

The reason the debates within the Western world seem so much beside the point is that they assume that the existing order of things can somehow either survive or only be changed through parliamentary mechanisms. As a result, one finds a lumping together of quite distinctive phenomena, class conflict such as mass guerrilla warfare with minoritarian phenomena such as urban terror. They all seem to be linked as one of various pieces in the same red garment of rebellion, and hence much discussion on terrorism in the West is a surrogate for discussions on social change of any sort.

The new wave of terror is both menacing to those singled out for assault and novel in the random internationalization of victims as well as terrorists. The use of Japanese terrorists to perform essentially Arab actions is but the most refined aspect of this randomization of violence. The question of terror, however, is not going to be significantly altered by finely worded judicial statements calculated to appease the intended victims of random terror. It can be altered by a recognition within the socialist camp that gains of a substantial sort have been made without terror (for example, in Salvador Allende's Chile) and that the resort to terror may have become counter-productive to the maintenance and growth of socialism in the Third World. Of course, if there were a collapse of this phase (of what was once referred to as "legal socialism" in pre-Bol-shevik Russia), the question of terror might well create an East-West confrontation all over again. But this seems un-likely given the present era of good feelings between the big powers — East and West, Communist and capitalist, authori-tarian and democratic. And with so much at stake in terms of a broad-ranging Metternichean settlement now under way between the great powers, it is extremely doubtful that random terrorism will be countenanced in the Communist bloc nations any more than it is within the Western bloc. This international rapprochement of power, rather than the cries of anguish by the powerless, will probably lead to an early end to the current terrorist wave.

The definition of terrorism I employ is this: *the selective use of fear, subjugation, and intimidation to disrupt the normal operations of a society*. The power to inflict such injury is a bargaining power that in its very nature bypasses due process of law. It seeks an outcome by means other than a democratic or consensual formula. The act of terror — whoever performs it — violates civil liberties. All the cries about redressing injustices cannot disguise this fact.

Terrorism is based on a calculation of what its victims can and cannot tolerate. A threshold of pain replaces the articula-tion of shared values or the rationality produced by consensus politics. The act of terrorism — again without regard to who performs it — involves a substitution of pain for reason as the way to determine political and social issues.

A policy of terror also assumes the social system to be inherently and necessarily law-abiding. It presumes that the desire to return to rationality in the maintenance of a system will help those engaged in terror. In this sense, observance of civil liberties is also a normal state that the attacked society wants to get back to as soon as possible.

Terrorism as a policy is both antidemocratic and anti-civil libertarian because the terrorists' ultimatums are addressed to leadership elites rather than to the people. Because terrorism demands instantaneous decision making, it places great strain on conventional legal mechanisms, which require due process and a strong evidentiary base to take action. Thus the appeal for swift action shifts power in the attacked society to its elites.

Finally, terror violates the civil liberties of those who are nonparticipants or noncombatants. Terrorists usually have as their victims people who are innocent of any crime. Whatever else civil liberties involves, it rejects holding people who have committed no specific criminal acts responsible for the alleged acts of others. In this sense, terrorist acts violate the civil liberties of individuals and collectivities alike.

Increased incidents of terrorism, whether spontaneous or organized, inevitably invite countermeasures, from increased security checks, greater police surveillance, and improved search-and-seizure measures to changes in the basic legal code, such as the restoration of capital punishment. There are also ideological and organizational changes in the society affected. In place of criminology there emerges a new emphasis on victimology; alongside national organizations dedicated to civil liberties there arise organizations dedicated to maintaining civil order. The costliest aspect of terrorism is not the destruction of physical property and loss of life but — as terrorists intend — the weakening of the social and political fabric, that complex series of norms and laws upon which democratic conflict resolution ultimately rests.

The seeming inability of national and international legislative bodies to curb terrorism derives, at least to some extent, from an appreciation of the political costs involved. To be sure, when a particular society is attacked, the victim's demand for "action" usually follows. Yugoslavs who resist formal condemnation of Palestinian terrorists are outraged by U.S. passivity in the face of Croatian nationalist hijackings. Syrians who are quite willing to see citizens of Tel Aviv randomly blown up, publicly hang the same PLO (Palestinian Liberation Organization) representatives when their acts are committed in Damascus.

It is easier to stretch the notion of what civil society can tolerate than to establish inflexible legislation that would probably escalate levels of terrorism without leading to international tranquility. The idea of prohibitory legislation as a cure-all, or even a limiting element, against terrorist actions is itself dubious.

In the aftermath of urban disorders in the United States, President Lyndon Johnson established a major commission, the National Commission on the Causes and Prevention of Violence. The analyses of the historical and social causes for the disorders proceeded smoothly enough. The real problems arose at the policy level: what to do about preventing violence in the future. The issues were rather similar to those raised now by terrorism. Indeed, all acts of terrorism involve a necessary review of the risks that are entailed in preventing such terror over and against the risks to the social compact of citizens within a nation. My views expressed in the late 1960s seems quite applicable to the situation we find ourselves in in the late 1990s.

The destruction of the antiwar movement, whether in its abstract universalist or pacifist form, or in its nasty, brutish, or opportunistic forms would represent a far greater loss to the integrity of American democracy than any silence in the streets of our major cities or quiescence in the hubs of our major universities. Obedience is not tranquility. Seething heavily is not the same as breathing easily. The antiwar movement has caused destruction in government operations, increased the cost of domestic military preparedness, stimulated disaffiliation from major parties, and has been a general nuisance for an already burdened police force. But these are costs that can be borne by a society still capable of distinguishing between national concern and national celebration. Those who want law and order, of whom there are many, as well as those who want lawlessness and disorder, of whom there are a few, must weigh carefully the premium price to be paid in a punitive state in which a rage for order displaces a rationality of innovation. That price would be nothing short of a total militarization of the nation.

TO BE CLEAR ABOUT THE ISSUE, WE MUST RECOGNIZE THAT IT IS ENTIRELY POSSIBLE to achieve a society largely free from terrorism. Fascist systems manage to reduce terrorism by a series of devices: mass organizations in which membership is compulsory; block-by-block spying networks; mandatory police identification certificates; and clear delineations of "friends" and "enemies" of the regime. With the increased sophistication of computerization techniques, such mechanisms for social and personal control loom ever larger. The question remains not one of technique but of social policy: Does a citizenry wish to pay such a price for tranquility?

The acceptance of some terrorism, like some protest violence, is a sign of a society's acceptance of the costs of liberty. The potential for terror is also a reminder that the state's force has its counterforce. The hardware of the state is almost always greater, more pervasive, and more devastating than the disruptive possibilities available to terrorists. In short, we are faced not so much with issues of broad theory, but considerations of immediate danger to the body politic as such.

In this connection, one need only consider the activities of the CIA and the FBI intelligence operations involving hundreds of thousands of individuals and the expenditure of billions of dollars. They are carried out by a complex community of organizations whose functions interact and overlap. As the Senate committee assigned the task of investigating the CIA and FBI noted in its final report, "the very effort to deal with problems of terror, violence, and domestic intranquility, has led to this kind of incredible malaise within the legal system, whereby the entire country has been rendered under the control of a paralegal system, a paramilitary system, in terms of dealing effectively with threats of violence." One need only remember Watergate to see how counterterrorist activities can erode our civil liberties.

To make greater sense of the terrorism dilemma, we must discuss large-scale political events and their impact on us in terms of political processes. This means seeing how terrorism affects particular actors in the political dramaturgy. If we evaluate terrorism in terms of the number of people that have been killed by design or by accident, there is clearly no comparison to the genocidal behavior of Stalin in Russia or Hitler in Germany. The autocratic state has nearly unlimited power to terrorize entire communities, ethnic or racial groups, and, of course, religious networks. If terrorism is judged simply in terms of lives dispatched, the Nazi Holocaust — the genocidal benchmark of our century — outstrips the desultory performances engaged in by contemporary terrorists.

If we consider terrorism in terms of its disruption of local political systems or social organizations, again there is scarcely any comparison between what terrorists achieve and the disruption caused by a major automobile accident on an urban superhighway or the massive temporary breakdown occasioned by a power failure in a big city. But it is the symbolic effect of terrorism that represents its real impact. When persons are assassinated or kidnapped because of their national origins or religious affiliations, this threatens the entire structure of intergroup toleration and support. Because terrorism involves death and destruction by design, it is clearly different from the random character of highway accidents or technological breakdowns.

Terrorism is sometimes defended as a special method for speeding up social change. In the sense that terrorists believe their actions can shape the outcome of historical events, they reflect those outlooks in radical thought that stress the will of human actors to affect the outcome of social drama, as opposed to those theorists who conceive of political events as moving in fixed, inexorable patterns.

We have no satisfactory method of determining what history's timetable really is, or when the full potential for growth of an old social system has been realized and the next revolutionary step becomes possible, as Marx felt necessary. But we should avoid treating terrorism as a form of "madness" — psychological or political — on the unprovable assumption that terrorists cannot really change history. The plain fact is thet they do change history with far greater impact than their capacity to change social systems.

Take, as one example, the question of whether terrorism in the United States during recent decades should be regarded as successful. Measured in terms of overthrowing state authority, it failed. Yet consider how far a small number of terrorist acts have disrupted the normal character of the U.S. political system. For even when a terrorist act is committed by a presumably unaffiliated individual, that same individual often comes with an ideological baggage inherited from organized terrorist groups. Can one really deny that the assassination of John F. Kennedy, Robert Kennedy, and Martin Luther King, Jr., and the attempted assassinations of Governor George Wallace and Presidents Gerald Ford and Ronald Reagan, changed the structure and not just the style of U.S. presidential politics? The very nature of the political process was interfered with profoundly. The traumas involved in terrorist assassinations of a president, a candidate for the presidency, and the leading figure within the black liberation movement espousing nonviolence and the attempt on the life of a major figure in southern conservatism helped create the crises that led to Watergate.

The measurement of terrorism's success, therefore, is not only its ability to loosen that order in symbolic terms by weakening the legitimizing capacities of elected officials and casting doubt on our concept of the rights of a society and the obligations of a state. Take a situation well known to anyone

who travels: The act of boarding an airplane involves an acceptance of commonplace procedures that a few short years ago
would have been deemed direct violations of civil liberties. A
passenger has to have all his or her luggage examined and
person scanned or frisked. Then there is often a separate
waiting area to which only those with boarding passes can go,
so that the ordinary pattern of being greeted by or departing
from loved ones is often no longer permitted. In addition,
passengers can no longer place luggage in a locker room in
most major airports, bus stations, and rail terminals — the
consequence of one solitary airport bombing at La Guardia
Airport in 1975. Most people accept the frisking and new
baggage procedures as the necessary cost of a safe flight.
Nonetheless, one has a perfect right, even a duty, to raise
questions about these new social costs of travel.

Still another problem with current approaches to terrorism
is the presumption that terrorism demoralizes populations and
disintegrates societies. This is an oversimplified view. A successful response to terrorism may serve to bind people together in a common cause. The Israeli response to the
hijackings of 103 people from an Air France flight in June 1976
— the raid on Entebbe Airport in Uganda — served to galva-
nize and unify Israeli society as had no other event since the
Six-Day War of 1967. Sporadic acts of terror can thus mobilize
sentiments to strengthen the very system the terrorists aim to
destroy.

Resolutions or recommendations for controlling terrorist
activities, no matter from which quarter they emanate, are
scarcely going to be enacted if the leadership of a nation feels
that its interests are served by a particular form of terrorist
engagement. But certain frameworks can be devised in the
international community that might delegitimize, if not entirely curb, acts of terrorism.

Terrorism as a primary tactic will tend to be viewed negatively by "socialist" states as well as by "democratic" states. It
should be possible to draw up a bill of human rights under

United Nations sponsorship indicating a universal belief in the right of the citizen to life, including the rights of people to free international travel and communication. Such a bill, to have teeth, must be built into legislation concerning postal regulations and international rules for travel by sea and air. Random populations cannot become the objects of political actions without all norms of international association becoming dismantled and unhinged.

Insofar as possible, a statement of what measures a nation will employ in responding to terrorism should be outlined in advance, so that those engaging in terrorist activities of a specific or random variety will at least be aware of the consequences of their acts. At present, every situation involving terrorists, from kidnapping embassy officials to bombing department stores in crowded neighborhoods, becomes a dramatic confrontation treated sui generis, without a uniform standard of response.

Since the state is the repository of authority and of the mechanisms of coercion, it can not only refuse safety and comfort to terrorists but it can also punish the random use of violence. This it must do, for national polity and national survival depend in part on maintaining a monopoly of the means of violence. Indeed, when the state can no longer do so, its very survival becomes conjectural. The inability of the U.S. Congress to enact tough gun-control legislation may thus be viewed as a limitation of the state to control its citizenry; or to the contrary, an appreciation of how consonant the widespread availability of weapons may be with the conduct of democratic government.

Through such mechanisms as Interpol, a file and fact sheet should be maintained on terrorists who cross national boundaries. Just as those who cross state boundaries to perform illegal actions within a nation such as the United States are subject to heavy penalties, so too should terrorists who move across national boundaries be subject to this principle. In that way, legitimate national liberation movements will be able to sur-

vive and grow insofar as they reflect a national consensus or
dissensus, while the use of terrorism abroad, precisely because
of an absence of true national support, would be profoundly
curbed, if not entirely thwarted. The problem here is that
legislation that would reinstate the death penalty, for example,
might be considered retrogressive rather than ameliorative.

The lines of distinction between guerrillas and terrorists are
hard to establish, just as the definition of legitimate geopoliti-
cal boundaries may vary. For example, if the Cubans define
their activities as the liberation of Latin America as a whole,
can the incursion of Che Guevara into Bolivia be considered
a terrorist invasion of foreign terrain? The point here is that
the Cuban government, and not a small band of uncoordinated
terrorists, made this decision. Similarly, the Egyptian government urged the Palestinians to form a government in exile. This
suggestion was rejected for a long while, and in a sense, the
idea of national legitimacy and responsibility was repudiated.
But when such policies were altered, and the idea of a national
homeland for Palestinians, living alongside the Israelis, became policy, reliance upon terrorism as a method of political
pressure became profoundly weakened precisely as government legitimacy as a means for realizing national demands
were strengthened. The problem of terror is real and must be
faced — but as a balance of forces not a metaphysical imperative.

Terror is a disruption in the modern technological order.
The number of people involved can be exceedingly low and
the amount of damage created exceedingly high — that is the
nature of high-velocity military and weapons technology. But
in another, larger, societal sense, terrorism has always been
with us and always will be, as long as a monopoly of terror is
reserved for a small fraction of society called the state and as
long as people are divided into units called nations. Perhaps in
that sense, the very existence of terrorist groups is a warrant
to the health of a particular nation-state: If the nation-state
can survive terrorism, if in the face of personal tragedy it can

forge public solidarity, terrorist acts will be proven counter-productive. But if such terrorism forges links with the broad masses, if it articulates the feelings and beliefs of large numbers, and if the nation-states involved are indecisive and insecure in the face of such unsanctioned violence, then those states are doomed to perish; and here the purposes of terrorism will be proven quite productive.[5]

What must be said in conclusion is that terrorism can indeed be stamped out — or at least drastically limited — but that in doing so, society does not necessarily offer a demonstration of its health; it may offer a reflection of its weakness. If the capacity for totalitarianism is completely exhausted in an effort to combat random terrorism, the social costs and political consequences alike become so grave that the very foundations of the system become more menaced than they could possibly be by any set of random terrorist activities. Indeed, if it is correct to point out that such random terrorism has a highly mobilizing effect on the masses of the population, rallying that population to the political commonweal, then one might also reasonably infer that the total repression of terrorism could have a demobilizing, and even worse, a demoralizing effect on these same masses and could ultimately serve as a catalyst for a new round of social revolutionary actions that ironically serve the purpose of terrorists more nearly than they do the purpose of established authority. Such then is the dialectic of terrorism: Its existence may prove the health of a society, and its absence may be a demonstration of the stagnation of a society.

The conduct of genocide is most often determined by the state, but terrorist operations are performed by individuals. As a result, the translation of "state power" into "state punishment" becomes a matter of intense legal concern. Individual responsibility for specific acts is exceedingly difficult to negotiate. Hence the punishment for acts of genocide is usually far less exacting than the performance of terrorist acts. In his work on the Malmédy Massacre of 1944, in which troops of a Waffen

SS battle group murdered hundreds of U.S. prisoners of war and Belgian civilians, James Weingartner points out in his work on the Malmédy Massscre that punishment was muted, sentences commuted, and the legal situation left unclear because of the gulf between systems and people, leaders and gunmen.[6]

Arguments have raged for the past half century on individual culpability for genocidal acts. The ferocity of World War II, coupled as it was with the ongoing Holocaust behind the lines, made for an ambiguous analytical situation: Can an individual really be blamed for carrying out orders? And on the other side, is collective guilt transmissible to individuals serving the very state that denies such individual responsibility? In some measure, despite some preliminary efforts at closure on this in the previous chapter, the focus on punishment is a separate and discrete work — one that perhaps defies legal definitions and yet transcends universal propositions about good and evil.

It is more important to focus on the termination of genocide by states than upon forms of punishment. Little if any evidence exists that punishment is a deterrent to terrorism, and much evidence exists that it has no such deterrent value, especially in the context of a state that condones rather than condemns acts of genocide. The random terrorist activities of marginal groups in society are more readily identifiable and hence more easily punishable than are the systematic genocidal activities integral to continuance of state power. As a result, the issue of punishment too often has a minor meliorative worth that, just as often as not, permits genocidal state practices to go undetected, much less punished.

Social scientists today are being called upon increasingly to focus their skills on the terrorism problem.[7] Research is being conducted on possible future acts of terrorism, for example, the ability of small bands of terrorists to steal atomic weapons or fissionable materials and then hold the country for "ransom." Yet there are serious doubts that terrorists, even if successful in obtaining fissionable material, would have either the scientific or technological capability to produce atomic weapons. Furthermore, the anticipatory research being conducted on this subject may invite a tightening of counterterrorist techniques that would seriously threaten the vitality of individual rights and political protest for decades to come.

There is high risk in researching ways to prevent future occurrences. Not only does such research plumb events that have not happened, but researchers are led to develop structures of analysis that can be self-fulfilling. This can produce an antiterrorist industry under whose banner enormous erosion of civil liberties could be made to seem all too rational and enlightened to the general public.

Risk is an inherent part of the democratic system. To deny modes of behavior that are uncontrolled and experimental in nature is to freeze democracy at a certain moment in space and place; and hence to negate democracy as a process. To insist that new mechanisms have to be created to prevent terror may be more risky than accepting the possibility of certain terrorist acts or questioning the need for pursuing some developments, such as plutonium recycling, for which heavy antiterrorist measures would be inevitable. What needs distinguishing, especially in terms of civil liberties, is society's readiness to respond to an immediate and dangerous threat from its readiness to install built-in "protective" structures to anticipate every form of terrorist behavior.

The solution to the problem of terror is invariably beyond the framework of counterterror. Responses to terror must be accompanied by a strengthening of the social fabric as a whole and the economic order specifically. But strength cannot be reduced to a codeword for increased surveillance; it clearly entails real changes in the social system, including new weighting in the distribution of wealth, power, and status.

Social scientists asked to indulge their penchants for applied research and futurology ought to be extremely wary about joining the organized search to prescribe and enact antiterrorist programs. If they join in discussions about such matters, they should insist on taking a hard-nosed view of the

evidence as to how much terrorism actually has been committed, what its nature really is, and how much more of it a
democratic society can — indeed must — be willing to suffer
rather than slide into the conversion of democratic systems to
totalitarian ones.

The same conclusion applies to the general public and civil
libertarians. Whether put forward by political leaders or social
science experts, programs to forestall terrorism should be
examined closely to see what their costs are for individual
privacy, group protest, political competition, and social change.
There are more than a few wolves among those offering to help
guard the lamb from the tigers. Defending a strengthened
status quo against the advocates of garrison-state security
should be the battle position of all those who cherish a constitutional order.

Human Rights and

Personal Responsibilities

The kind of faith or obedience that is bought with bread is evil, and so is any constraint on man's conscience, in whatever form, even if the constraint is exercised for ostensibly good ends. Freedom is not to be confounded with goodness or happiness. Goodness festers if bred by constraint, and happiness turns into brutish contentment. Only when freely chosen do they acquire a human content.

— *Philip Rahv*[1]

AT FIRST GLANCE, IT MIGHT WELL APPEAR THAT HUMAN RIGHTS AND SOCIAL SCIENCE are perfectly harmonious, and that breakdowns of such a parallelism constitute some sort of aberration. The conduct of organized reason called science should issue into an expansion of human rights, and conversely, the unfettered exercise of human rights should allow for the expansion of social scientific research. While there is an obvious moral sentiment that leads us to wish for such a combination of human rights and social sciences, any sort of careful reflection makes clear that the two are quite distinct, occupying discrete realms of reality no less than ideology. Tragically perhaps, the connection between human rights and social science is less one of aesthetic balance than of creative tension.

Specifically, social science must examine the issue of human rights with the same critical dispassion and reserved cutting edge that it would apply to any political slogan or social myth. In particular, the notion of rights requires a compatible notion of obligations. To allow less than this is to substitute utopian aspirations for social experience: a fatal confusion that may itself lead more into human misery than human rights. As I have emphasized throughout, we need a minimalist, not maximalist approach to genocide; otherwise the concept is reduced to a catch-all for whatever ails whomever by exhausting the meaning of the word. Social scientists too have a bill of particular rights of their own: The first human right is that of criticism, the second human right is that of analysis, and the third human right is that of construction. Let me take up the subject of human rights in terms of these three notions: criticism, analysis, and construction.

Let us first criticize the human rights movement, insofar as it has political coherence, for its conceptual failure to take into account human obligations. To so criticize it is to take seriously the occasions and conditions under which rights are frequently in competition with each other and hence still require the exercise of social science for rendering analytic judgment. Finally, we need to indicate those mechanisms by which the human rights question can be monitored and evaluated to determine its centrality in social and political practice. This is admittedly a tall order for a brief chapter; but the attempt must at least be made if we are to get beyond the present state of political opportunism followed too frequently by empty moral bluster.

The widespread disregard, even disdain, for a concept of human obligation paralleling that of human rights has generated the sort of one-sided, interest-group politics that has tended to sacrifice the whole for the parts and all but destroyed a notion of international or national community in favor of regional, local, and even entirely personalized "issues." Single-interest politics, and its attendant special-issue lobbying efforts, have made the political process a jungle of impenetrable hazards. Any sort of political statement, on matters ranging from taxation to education to defense policy, becomes part of a concerted effort either to depose or impose the public official. A government of laws runs the risk of being reduced to one of lawyers; the force of institutional affiliations is eroded and transformed into a base force of personalities and influentials. To have an obligation to more than the bottom line or to perceive of obligations as anything beyond a payoff matrix becomes absurd in this perfect world of an exchange system in which one hand continually washes the other.

When the call for human rights becomes a demand for sameness, a hedonist calculus of statistical claims in which the least reward differential within a society becomes a cause célèbre and a reason for public outcry, then social science and human rights must part company. At such a point, the question of human rights becomes one of private avarice. Demands for statistical parity also raise serious questions as to whether a national structure can exist, whether creative powers can be acknowledged, or whether incentive and reward can be recognized. This transvaluation of human rights into perfect egalitarianism holds open the specter of "Robespierrism": In an ideology and a system in which democracy is secured through a totalitarian mechanism, such an approach to rights becomes all-absorbing and hence quickly dispenses with democracy in favor of massification.

With human rights, as with other public concerns, political events often dictate public discourse. Since the beginning of the United Nations in the mid-1940s, the question of human rights has remained in the province of UNESCO conferences; in the late 1970s it emerged, suddenly, as a central issue. Certainly, this new sense of concern cannot be explained on the basis of an intellectual breakthrough in the past thirty years. Rather, human rights have become a major instrument of U.S. foreign policy. It should be evident that the passion for human rights, however genuine, is a measured response to the interests of this (or any other) nation.

Yet one should not be cynical about the subject of human rights simply because the sense of concern appears so clearly tied to national interests and mandarin policies. Intellectuals, and social scientists in particular, have long inhabited a world where desultory issues locked away in library archives become dramatic events of considerable public consequences. The War on Poverty became a political invention long after the emergence of a literature on poverty, and even though that particular rhetorical war has passed into oblivion, the realities of poverty remain. No matter how the major collective issues of the century are placed on the agenda of public discourse, the best efforts of social scientists must be put forward, however cynical one might be with respect to the national origins or even the frivolous nature of such commitments.

Politics is a game of vulnerabilities, and the human rights issue is clearly one in which the "socialist" world has proven most vulnerable, just as the economic rights issue is where the "capitalist" world is most open to criticism. The very interplay of forces, the competition of world historic systems and empires, provides an opportunity for individuals and smaller collectivities to register marginal advantages over the systems they inhabit. Because of the practical potential of concerns for human rights, rather than because of an effort to capitalize on a policy quirk of this specific moment in time, social science can play a useful, albeit limited, role. The various social science disciplines have pioneered the transformation of the question of human rights from a series of indecisive philosophic propositions to a precise matter of measurable statistics and theorems.

The debate on human rights can be conceptualized at its most general level as a struggle between eighteenth-century libertarian persuasions and nineteenth-century egalitarian beliefs — that is, from a vision of human rights having to do with the right of individual justice before the law to a recognition of the rights of individuals to social security and equitable conditions of work and standards of living. Whether human rights are essentially a political or economic concern is not a secondary issue. However, the social sciences need not choose between politics and economics. They have enough on their hands in demanding a system of accountability for monitoring and evaluating both. Most recently, discussions of human rights have gotten beyond formal categories into substantial issues as to whether human rights implies a theory of justice involving impartiality, or a theory of behavior involving toleration of differences. However, these issues play out in the academic arena, it is most certainly the case that human rights must start with forms of settling disputes short of mayhem and massacre.

The social sciences have introduced an element of accountability not only into their disciplines but also into the policy systems and networks that social scientists find themselves in. As a result, the measurement of human rights has become the monumental contribution of social science. Big words are rightfully suspect, but concepts are doubly so. It therefore becomes a central act of faith to translate the abstract into the concrete. This is largely what economists, sociologists, psychologists, political scientists, and anthropologists have accomplished through the use of social indicators.

Rights — for example, the right to justice or formal education — are concepts easy enough to absorb within the framework of almost any social system. But when rights become carefully stipulated in terms of costs — when freedom of beliefs becomes translated into freedom to impart information and ideas without harassment, when social security is translated into old-age insurance, when rights to privacy are viewed as the right of every individual to communicate in secrecy, when rights to work involve protection of actual workers and involve the right to form and join trade unions and the right to strike, when social rights are translated into the rights of mothers and children to special care and protection, when rights to personal security involve measures to protect the safety of conscientious objectors, when rights to fair trials include protection against arbitrary arrest or detention — then the entire panoply of rights assumes an exact meaning that lifts them from the realm of sermon to one of seriousness.

The habitual interest in human rights in part reflects the absence of these rights. There is a great deal of concern on matters of cruel, inhuman, or degrading treatment because there is so much cruelty, inhumanity, and degradation present in world affairs. There is concern about the rights of self-determination because there are so many violations of those rights in the name of national integration. International law calls for the punishment of genocide because the twentieth century has seen the alarming development of mass homicide practiced for statist ends.

There is a colossal dichotomy between practices and principles. This split between reality and rhetoric gives the human rights issue its volatility. Yet the one enormous breakthrough that has evolved over the century is the sense of right and wrong. A common legacy of democratic and socialist politics, of marketing and planning systems, of libertarian and egalitarian ideologies, is the assumption that there is such a goal as human rights. When one recollects that it was only one hundred thirty years ago that slavery and serfdom were vital forces in human affairs and that wars were fought to protect chattel slavery as states' rights, then the extent and speed — at least conceptually — of our progress becomes evident.

The central characteristic of the twentieth century, what so profoundly demarcates it conceptually from previous centuries, is that a world in which obligations were taken for granted has been transformed into one where rights are presumed to be inalienable. Our institutions were largely concerned with theories of human obligation: what individuals and collectivities owe to their societies and to their states — an automatic presumption that one has an obligation to fight in wars whatever the purpose of the war, or the notion that economic failure is a mark of individual shortcoming rather than societal breakdown. The hallmark of the twentieth century and the achievements of the social sciences is to have made the question of human rights the central focus while placing the question of obligations on the shoulders of institutions rather than individuals.

There are risks in this transformation. One might well argue that the retreat has turned into a rout; that issues of the duties of individuals to the community or the limitations on human rights to ensure national survival have not received proper attention; that social research has so emphasized the minutiae of imbalances of every sort that even homicides are now blamed on violence on television. But such transmigrations carry within themselves potential for hyperbole, and there is little point in discarding the baby with the bath water.

The literature of the past was written in terms of dynasties, nations, and empires. As long as that was the case, the matter of human rights hardly counted. Only now, when these larger-than-life institutions — these dynasties, nations, and empires — are dissolving, can it be seen that the individual is the centerpiece of all human rights and that the expression of these rights must always remain the province of the free conscience of a free individual. In this very special sense, ours is the century in which individualism has emerged beyond the wildest imaginings of previous centuries. Paradoxically, it is also the century of the most barbaric collectivisms, which put into sharp and painful relief the subject of human rights by assuming the right of states to terminate individual life for political reasons. If the momentary strategy of the political system is such that the subject of human rights now is central, the principles of social research must convert those strategies into durable gains. How is this to be accomplished?

The most serious presumption about social science involvement in the human rights issue is the uncritical identification of one with the other. That is to say, an unstated commitment to the idea that clear human rights policies can and should emanate from social science information. One suspects that social science interest in human rights is not unlike past such involvements: the mandarin-like features of social scientists perceiving their interests to flow from political messages to the point where true meanings in social science are inextricably linked to political guidelines and attractive slogans. In the past, social scientists did not so much lead as follow political guidelines. Whether it be a presumed War on Poverty or a revolt against taxation, the social science community has had a strong proclivity to follow public officials rather than to provide self-motivated leadership.

The human rights issue has sadly tended to follow a similar "natural history" of political ideology. This is not to deny the reality of the human rights cause. Whatever operational guidelines are employed toward maximizing human equality and fairness among citizens and governments is worthy of support; so too are motherhood and apple pie. However, the presupposition that social scientists have the capacity to extract new meanings from the human rights cause or to manufacture innovative politics presumes that the social science community is privy to a normative structure not granted to ordinary mortals. This is clearly not the case.

At the mundane level of national policy, the call for human rights, like the New Deal, the Fair Deal, and the Great Society, represents a historical tendency on the part of the executive branch of the U.S. government to give distinction and individual character to each of its administrations. This seems especially true for the Democratic Party, which has traditionally seen the need of each administration to delineate itself in contrast to previous administrations. In part, this trend is a consequence of a breakdown of party loyalty as such in the United States and the substitution of political formulas based on mass communication in its stead. Under such circumstances, it is understandable that the political system does not wait for the social science community to establish national guidelines. Rather, the large political system expects support from the relatively small social science community, and it is willing to handsomely underwrite such support in the form of ongoing research grants and contracts.

What is interesting about the human rights issue, in contrast to previous executive political rallying cries, is its international dimension. In the past, most major slogans were confined to the national political system. Human rights issues are located in the international arena. Quite beyond the disintegration of party organization in the United States is the obvious fact that the United States, like every other major power, places its best moral foot forward whenever possible.

In the 1950s, the key was "modernization," a term easily enough defined as the maximization of consumer goods and human resources. In operational terms, modernization was strongly equated to transportation and communication, that is, to those areas in which the United States was a world leader. In the 1960s, with the growing apprehension that material abundance or modernization might actually be counterproductive to national goals because it leaves intact the uneven distribution and class characteristics of such impulses to consumerism, the key concept became egalitarianism, the drive toward equal distribution of world resources and goods.

But by the end of the 1960s, a new dilemma became apparent: As we were urging upon others egalitarianism as an international ideology, the virtual monopoly by the United States of material conditions of abundance in the West converted the drive for equality to a domestic rhetoric. The costs of international egalitarianism were not voluntarily borne by the richest nation on earth. There were other problems in driving the equity stick too hard: lower innovation, higher taxation, and the huge shift in moral specifications. Above all, egalitarianism came to mean that growth itself had a higher price than many environmentalists and social ecologists were willing to pay. When the growth curve leveled off and even began declining as a result of energy shortfalls and oil embar-

goes, the egalitarian slogans of the 1960s became increasingly
hard to support.

The key to the emphasis on explaining the turn toward
human rights, has been a Western policy presentation that
found it more amenable to convert demands for equity into
demands for liberty. It started with a feeling of declining U.S.
hegemony and corresponding growth in a shift in power to
Europe and Asia. The human rights issue, covertly for the most
part, celebrated the fact of high political and social freedom in
the West — just as the valorization of modernization in the
1950s celebrated the fact that the United States was a consumer society and the call for egalitarianism in the 1960s
highlighted the fact that there were large numbers of people
sharing in this largesse. The long and short of it is that the
human rights issue, like those political formulas of previous
decades, provides a sharp contrast to the socialist sector with
its prima facie constraints on human rights, from exacting high
punishment for low crimes to refusal to grant travel visas for
emigration purposes. Human rights, whether measured by
press standards, due process of law, freedom of worship, voluntary associations, multiple parties, or some other standard,
became the strong suit of the West even after the fall of
communism. Its displacement by a viral nationalism and tribal-
ism only enhanced the human rights approach as a model in
Western political theory.

THE PROBLEM OF BIG-POWER PRIORITIES

If one takes the evidence of the conduct of foreign policy
on any given day, never mind year, it is clear that general guide
lines give way to specific decision-making. The United States
can censure China for its gross violation of copyright protec-
tions and illegal reproduction of name brands, yet argue the
case for extending most favored nation status. Attitudes toward violations of human rights by smaller nations, say Haiti,
can and are met with far more severe responses and sanctions.
Powerful nations capable of purchasing new airplanes are

treated differently than nations incapable of making such purchases, but instead are recipients of loans and gifts. In short, human rights as a policy is far more difficult to implement than human rights as a set of theoretical premises. That a powerful state such as China can take lives with more impunity than can weak states points to an incongruity: it can take lives without fear of retaliation or retribution. This is hardly a new point. But it is one that needs to be reiterated at a juncture in which it is argued that human rights has somehow changed the power equations that nations live by.

THE PROBLEM OF POLITICAL-ECONOMIC RIVALRY

When one thinks of the human rights question in the context of international economic realities, it becomes apparent that there are limits to the implementation of any policy. Vacuums are filled, and economic vacuums are filled rapidly. While the United States denied certain loans to Brazil, again on the basis of presumed human rights violations, the Japanese and Italians were more than willing to fill this gap, providing a $700 million arrangement whereby Japanese and Italian capital was to help in the long-term financing of new steel projects in Brazil. In addition, three companies, Sidebras, Kawaski, and Finsider of Italy, provided terms that assisted in Brazilian capital needs on more favorable terms than had United States loans in the past.

The Problem of Indifference to Human Rights: There are countries that help each other for which human rights are not a particularly important constraint. For example, Pakistan, one of the more overt violators of the human rights of its masses, developed close links to the Muslim countries and to Iran, with the Iranians underwriting everything in Pakistan from highway construction to wheat importation. In this situation, not only was Iran helping Pakistan, but the orchestration of this pact was done through the Eurodollars provided by none other than the American Citibank corporation; the bank also helped set the rate of interest to be charged to Pakistan by Iran. These technicalities are replicated every day of the year.

As a result, it is impossible to speak of the implementation of a human rights policy as if it were a geometric axiom. It might well be that the politics of boycott are the ultimate expression of a policy of human rights. But this presupposes a monopoly of goods and services, which the United States does not now possess.

The Problem of Indirect Support for Human Rights Violators: One serious dilemma that constantly arises is the need for diplomatic, political, and military assistance pacts between big powers, which in turn filter such aid to other nations. For example, the United States may, on strictly military grounds, be compelled to effect hardware sales to say, Egypt and Israel, and find that some of such weapons ultimately come to be employed in supporting despotic powers such as Libya. This problem may arise for other governments too, of course: Egypt sold advanced MiG-23 fighters to China, the very nation that the Russians are least inclined to see such aircraft go to. What this suggests is that human rights considerations are of a multilateral, and not just a presumed bilateral, character. Aid and trade can be contained only in unusual circumstances, that is, when there is a threat to cancel future agreements of an urgent sort. Unless a nation is prepared to monitor the circuitous routing of its entire foreign sales and aid effort, it must accept as a fact the relatively secondary status of human rights as a central foreign policy plank.

The Problem of Which Humans, What Rights: A special dilemma that plagues politicians interested in the centrality of human rights is the choice of persons to be preserved and rights to be guarded. In a situation such as the Cambodian dispute with Vietnam, one in which an alleged two million Cambodians were subject to genocidal liquidation and almost a million Vietnamese languished in concentration camps, a choice between evils is often faced by appeals to larger political considerations. For example, diplomatic recognition of the People's Republic of China by the United States not only dampened criticism of China's internal human rights violations but also led to playing down the grotesque violations of human rights in Cambodia, for a long while a Chinese proxy state. It may also have led to heightened consciousness of human rights violations in Vietnam as a mechanism for dealing with the Soviet Union. In short, decisions are required in the treatment of nations that have little in common other than the harsh treatment of citizens by states.

The limits of foreign policy based upon human rights were painfully revealed in a mini (or proxy) war between Cambodia and Vietnam. The flagrant and clear-cut invasion of Cambodia by Vietnam — in 1978 and 1979 — compelled the United States, along with a majority of states, to invoke the principle of territorial sovereignty. Considerations of policy prevailed rather than a pragmatic acceptance of incarceration as a lesser evil than genocide and hence more in keeping with the spirit of a human rights posture. This is not adduced as evidence of any foreign policy inconsistency; quite the reverse, the decision in this particular instance was entirely appropriate and had the force of international law as its precedent. But such situations, occurring with alarming frequency, do point up the inevitable tensions between policy and principle, or more specifically, between a political requirement of statecraft and a moral requirement of world order.[2]

It is appropriate that the West, and the United States in particular, pay stricter attention to the primary and secondary forms of constraints and contradictions. The simple moralism that denied aid to both Nicaragua and Brazil because of human rights violations fails to account for the differential importance of the two nations in the maintenance of U.S. foreign policy. As a result, even if there is a basic human rights policy, implementation needs to be differentiated if it is to make any sense or if it is not simply to be ignored as a political spoof or bluff. A central task of social science is to make clear situational realities and contradictory tendencies within a policy network. Social scientists should not simply lend moral weight to these efforts without regard to empirical realities and world situations; rather, they should lend their practical weight to appropriate decision making.

The discussion concerning human rights, at least on a global perspective, has been linked to choices between political deprivation, presumably characteristic of the East (the Second World), and economic exploitation, presumably characteristic of the West (the First World). Aside from the reification and polarization involved, the problem is that the human rights issue is thrown back upon ideological grounds.

A fitting and proper role of social science in the human rights issue is to move beyond such broad abstractions and seek out concrete expressions of both the exercise and abridgement of human rights. In this regard, the human rights issue can be joined to a framework larger than itself and more politically significant. It can be fused to questions about social systems, political regimes, and economic frameworks. Human rights may not pre-empt state power, but they become a potent ideological and diplomatic tool in the conduct of foreign affairs.

One contribution that social science can make at this level is the expansion of social indicators; that is, the breakout and disaggregation of the human rights question. Instead, for example, of talking abstractly about the right to work, social scientists can talk concretely about conditions of work, protection of migrant workers, occupational work and safety measures, and social services for employees. Instead of talking about the right to life and liberty, social scientists can talk specifically about protection under the law, a right to a fair and open trial, security of a person who is incarcerated, rights of individuals to deviate from official standards of behavior. If we are talking about political rights, questions should be raised about conditions of voting, levels of participation, numbers of parties permitted to contend, electoral expenses, and the role of local vis-à-vis national government. Instead of talking about citizen's rights, social scientists can raise issues of the conditions of migration outside a nation, freedom of movement within a nation, rights of asylum, protection against deportation, and the character of national and ethnic affiliations. These are the sorts of distinctions that are increasingly being made by Amnesty International, Freedom House, and by select, specialized agencies of the United Nations.[3]

There are national varieties in presenting the issue of human rights, and these cannot easily be glossed over or eliminated. But a sophisticated series of social indicators, can provide some flesh, and not just flab, to the human rights issue. For example, several European nations now extend questions of the right to work to include free choice of employment, conditions of employment, protection against unemployment, equal pay for equal work, the right to favorable remuneration, and even the right to form trade unions. On the other hand, differences arise with respect to the right to strike. At this point, the social science community needs to achieve a stage beyond the aggregated national data of the United Nations and develop firm internationally recognized human rights goals to which all nations in the civilized world adhere, at least in terms of ideals to reach.

There will doubtless still be strong ideological components to the implementation of these goals based on whether a society has an "open" or "mixed" or "central" economic system, or whether it has a multiparty, single-party, or no-party political system. There will also be differences in terms of the character of punishment and restraint characteristic of a region or nation. But these items can themselves become an area of comparative investigation. That is to say, what nations under what circumstances are in violation of human rights when the same practices in other nations may be characterized as fully observant of such rights becomes a problem rather than a paradigm.[4]

Another facet beyond that of social indicators is the study of social norms. What are the norms expected from a nation in the field of human rights? Here certain items can be addressed.

▸ *First,* there should be annual country reports on social questions, just as there are annual country reports on economic questions, which thus focus attention on specific patterns of human rights violations or observances.

▸ *Second,* independent, nongovernmental organizations should be encouraged which can both monitor and pressure official reports in order to gain creditability and reliability.

▸ Third, social science is uniquely equipped to monitor and should monitor unusual conditions or emergency situations, such as famine, floods, and earthquakes, and in general should monitor victims in chronic misery and distress. In this way human rights reporting will not become mechanistic and ignore flash dangers.

▸ *Fourth*, an area that should be examined at this normative level is whether violations of human rights are being conducted officially or unofficially by governments, or whether governments use conduits to engage in human rights violations. This distinction too will prevent the monitoring of governments from becoming mechanical, ignoring the utilization of agencies perpetuating human rights violations.

▸ *Fifth*, insofar as possible, human rights reporting should be made uniform and should be monitored by the social scientific community so that agencies like the International Sociological Association or the International Political Science Association do more than meet every four years to exchange nationalistic platitudes and develop standing committees for monitoring, evaluating, and estimating human rights gains in any period of time.

These are complex as well as ambitious tasks. But at least they provide a central role for the social scientific community beyond servicing the state as mandarins. The social science community is responsible for both the construction of a better future and the criticism of present realities. It cannot subvert one for the other in the name of national unity; it can become neither a permanent positivist arm of state power nor a perpetual destructive critique of such power. In the dialectic of construction and criticism inheres the great strength of social science. The utilization of social science by each nation in the international community of nations will itself provide a bona fide measure of human rights. But this entails a serious recognition that the tasks of policy makers and social scientists, although intertwined, are by no means identical either in principle or in practice. Such an awareness of the durability of differences between social sectors and intellectual forces is itself a clear representation of the status of human rights in any given society.

8

Bureaucracy and State Power

Once it is fully established, bureaucracy is among those social structures which are the harder to destroy. Bureaucracy is the means of carrying "community action" over into rationally ordered "societal action." Therefore, as an instrument for "socializing" relations of power, bureaucracy has been and is a power instrument of the first order — for the one who controls the bureaucratic apparatus. . . . The consequences of bureaucracy depend therefore upon the direction which the powers using the apparatus give to it. And very frequently a crypto-plutocratic distribution of power has been the result.

— Max Weber[1]

IN EXAMINING POSTINDUSTRIAL SOCIETY AND THE FUTURE OF PUBLIC ADMINISTRATION, we would be well advised to follow the dictum of the theoretical physicist John Archibald Wheeler, who warns us that "no elementary phenomenon is a phenomenon until it is an observed phenomenon."[2] Rather than a postindustrial society, we actually observe a series of societies at relative plateaus of socioeconomic development and a variety of administrative networks responding to and influencing different levels of development. As long as we distinguish the empirical from the speculative, we may talk about postindustrialization as a generic type and the future of public administration as an extrapolation from its past and present.

The importance of the subject of the modern bureaucratic state is vouchsafed by the enormous destructive power it contains with respect to those who fall outside its scope. The state, in replacing the church in power, also displaced the church with respect to legitimacy. And mechanisms to prevent equal access — in places such as Hitler's Germany and Stalin's Russia — became an ability to stigmatize and finally eliminate a whole people. Jacob Katz reminded us that "as Jews kept a distance between themselves and the churches, they were in turn kept at arm's length from the institutions of the state and excluded from the ranks of its servants."[3] This huge gap between those who are represented and those who do the representing is the core of the problem of order in contemporary societies. Even if the issue of genocide is not obvious in such an administrative context, it lurks darkly off to the side.

The term "postindustrial society" has no recognizable denotive content. If it means a world in which knowledge replaces artifact as central, then the connection of knowledge to production, like the relationship of head work to hand work, is a matter for study and simply to be assumed. The character of mechanization has shifted, and the role of policy maker has enlarged; however, in itself this is not postindustrial but simply an evolution of the industrial order. We still inhabit a universe largely defined by preindustrial characteristics. The industrial sector remains far from universally characteristic of social systems.

The major axioms of postindustrial society are evident: Western societies are characterized by private property and the private control of investment decisions, but also by an industrial base whose primary logic is technological efficiency. Using such a division, we can identify different sequences of development. Along the axis of technology we have preindustrial, industrial, and postindustrial. There is a built-in contradiction between the principle of bureaucratization, based on hierarchy, and the principle of equality, based on participation. Bureaucracy compartmentalizes people into roles. Social tensions in Western democracy have been framed by contrary logics of bureaucratization and participation, undergirded by a change of scale in institutions leading to a profound shift in functions. The major principle of postindustrial society is the codification of theoretical knowledge, specifically new technological-scientific activities oriented around computers, telecommunications, optics, polymers, and electronics. Control of the means of information augments struggle over the means of production in such a society, and hence the character of work alters significantly. Work becomes a struggle between persons rather than against nature. In a postindustrial universe, society becomes a free choice by free people rather than a banding together against nature or an involuntary joining together in routinized relations imposed from outside.

The phrase "postindustrial society" is infelicitous. It is inherently transitional, arguing about a movement from before to after something called "industrial." It is ambiguous, since it refers to cultural norms in the most advanced nations and is subject to a variety of interpretations; few are operational and even fewer are consonant with each other. Societies do not emerge de novo; we are still trying to ascertain meanings to ascribe to industrialization. Much has happened since the end of World War II, above all the ability of mankind to "totalize" destruction, to engineer genocide, and to engage in atomic warfare. Authoritarianism is no longer confined to a single state apparatus: rather, it expands to the global decimation of peoples. Whether we use the phrase "postindustrial society" or some equivalent label is less important than arriving at a meaningful framework to handle life and death issues.

The term "postindustrial" is often employed as a hygienic way of saying "authoritarian" in an age of public-sector dominance; or at least, it suggests the ascendance of policy over politics. The postindustrial vision admits only of a "deeply pessimistic" view of society. Postindustrialism conjures up the image of engineered totalitarianism. "A technocratic society is not ennobling"; it lacks a "rooted moral belief system" and despite the "cockpit of decisions" it permits, the "cultural contradictions of society" are buried rather than expressed by this new postindustrial environment — or more simply, this totalitarian temptation. Implicit is a deep mistrust of bureaucratic administration, one shared by a host of ideological standpoints common to our age.[4] Whether such postulates add up to postindustrial society or to a neotechnocratic state with authoritarian tendencies is a choice of language and an amplification of different pessimisms. However, that the contours of social structure and social stratification have shifted dramatically is beyond contest.[5] Determining how public administration intersects and interfaces this new reality becomes central. Before doing so, the same yardstick of linguistic rigor must be applied to the notion of public administration as to the notion of postindustrial society; a not inconsequential task in a field of strong sentiments and polarized frameworks.

The most essential fact about public administration is that it came into existence prior to any theory. Whether things, people, or ideas are administered, administrators clearly preceded any general theory. Public administration emerged in a context of justification and of celebration rather than of general theory, that is, in the context of making "something happen in the public interest." It has an inevitable bias toward the practical, toward getting things done; an uneasiness, even a discontent, with frustrating questions that in their breadth and scope may prove to be incapacitating.[6] The private woe of public administrators has been theory writ large. Their preference has been for middle-range theories, and if those are unavailable, for no theory at all. This is the first time that practical people have lived a full and useful life without always knowing what they are doing.

The relationship of public administration to economics, sociology, political science, and psychology speaks of an insecure search for broader meaning. As administration is distinguished from its parts (forms of administration at different levels covering different subject areas), it simply is no longer possible to make do with makeshift definitions. How does one train a public administrator involved in the Department of Commerce over and against one involved in Health, Education, and Welfare? How does one train public administrators who operate at city levels in contradistinction to those who operate at national levels? These are but the most obvious questions.

General theory emerges in pedagogic contexts when the need to know becomes overriding. Determining entry level skills becomes more exacting in an era of affirmative action. There are questions of the relationship between those who administrate through political appointment and those who administrate through civil service appointment. These issues emerge in the literature on administration, but in a context of search for a simplified paradigm of general theory, as if this alone could transform administration from craft to science.

If not a science, what is the art of public administration? Here the giant assumption, central to understanding government per se, is that administration is a function of state authority or authorities. One administrates things, peoples, and ideologies on behalf of an employer called the state. Therefore the linkage between administrator and state offers a direct link between administration and policies. The conventional nineteenth-century image of social classes manipulating bureaucracies to gain advantage is not accurate. Rather, it is an administrative machinery manipulating other sectors that becomes decisive: Labor forces decrease in size, but managerial sectors increase in power.

Public administration takes place in a context of policy inversion: a displacement of power from the economy to the polity, mediated by the monopoly of allocation and distribution of public funds. Public administration services not one class or sector but the state. The class interest of the middle administrator is the class of top administrators insofar as they are directly linked to forms of state power. Public administration is, therefore, inextricably linked to state power. To say that administrators are politically neutral is a naive statement of politics as an elite activity. To be neutral with respect to a party or an interest group is perfectly reasonable, even a prerequisite of sound administrative procedures. But for the administrator to be neutral to the existence of state power as such is a contradiction in terms. For the essential politics of the administrator is the survival, prolongation, and strengthening of the apparatus. This is administrative politics writ large, whatever disclaimers are made about political participation writ small, that is, as party loyalty or partisan activity.

The essential contest in class terms shapes up as one between elites and masses, or, expressed ideologically, as statism versus populism. Those who have a vested interest in the state and its organized activities must view with suspicion populist activities that would move against state power. On the other hand, those with populist concerns can no longer rest easy with old-fashioned formulations concerning class. The lesson of the current era is the confrontation of classes, sexes, races, and ethnic groups directly with state authority. The legal mechanisms and financial systems make possible broad layers of social change in attitudes and behavior precisely through reinforcing the ascribed features of the status system.

Administrators do not oppose change. Rather, they demand that changes occur legally, through a further enlargement and acceptance of the administrative apparatus. To the extent that the system as a whole can manage a reward-and-punishment framework that appeals to the state, to that extent does state power become enhanced and public administration enlarged. However, to the degree that the state cannot manage rational rewards and punishments or cannot orchestrate and mobilize the economy to do its bidding, it invites populist rebellion and popular opposition.

The postindustrial world resembles the postfeudal, monarchical era of Machiavelli and Thomas Hobbes more than it does entrepreneurial capitalism. Systems do not rise or fall on the basis of economic merit but on the grounds of political control. The reason a postindustrial world is so comfortable with Machiavelli and Hobbes is that the relationship of ruled to ruler has become, as in the preindustrial age, astonishingly simplified. Mediating institutions such as parties and pressure groups have less clout and less ability to deliver basic services than do state managers. In such a postindustrial climate, interest groups are reduced to fundamental conflict and competition. In the cosmic dialectic of postindustrial conflict, the manipulation of funds and forces rather than the administration of people becomes a rallying cry within administrative work, much as it did for the nineteenth-century utopians who argued for the withering away of state power.

A central aspect of this rationalization process is the need for the state to confront new Leviathans, ranging from multinational corporations to NASA-type space programs, which control budgets equal to conventional government expenditures. In substantive areas, public administration turns to the state as an essential monitoring and evaluating tool of potential threats to the commonwealth. The emergence of regional trade associations and national associations also requires a tighter framework for state decision making; everything from arranging sales to supervising contracts involves administrative servicing. While mediating agencies within a nation lose some of their potency, the need for state power grows as a response to external agencies.[7] The state must negotiate with a wide variety of foreign and domestic agencies and interest groups; public administration does not lack for new areas to conquer.

Much is taken for granted in public administration; even its size and scope remains obscure. As late as the mid-1930s, people were recruited for public-administration posts among a wide variety of professions and disciplines. But by the postwar period, public service had become a field unto itself. One

writer described this evolutionary process as the development
of a new mandarinate:

> Syracuse University started the first American school of public
> administration back in 1924, and the University of Southern
> California followed a few years later. But the idea has really come
> into its own during the 1970s. In 1972 the National Association of
> Schools of Public Administration boasted 101 affiliates; today it
> is up to 220. The number of students graduating from such schools
> each year doubled in the same period-up to 6,000 in 1977. That
> may be a trickle next to the floodtide of government bureaucra-
> cies (the federal Department of Energy alone employs 20,000
> people). But it is an increasingly influential and well regarded
> trickle. And with growth in the number of university-trained
> administrators has come insistence that there should be more.[8]

Administrative personnel include, first, those who service
the executive and legislative branches of government; second,
those involved with interest groups ranging from veterans and
homebuilders to the handicapped and police chiefs; third,
those who service regulatory and monitoring agencies; fourth,
those who manage the roughly five hundred separate grants-
in-aid programs sanctioned by congressional action; fifth, lob-
byists who support every program enacted or proposed in the
first four layers. The magnitude of the federal administration
is enormous.

As has been recently observed, the rising tide of administrative expertise stands in inverse proportion to the elector-
ate's sense of diminishing returns. "What is happening in
Washington is a fragmentation that feeds defensiveness. Almost every elected official in Washington from the President
on down is an independent, the end result of the steady decline
in the party system. The White House has put together a
different coalition for every issue, and frequently it is as de-
pendent on Republicans as Democrats to win a vote."[9] These
considerations pertain only to the federal bureaucracy located
in Washington, D.C., a metropolitan area of three million
people in which administration is the central occupational

role. Recent demographic estimates of state and local government administrators — excluding salaried managers and those working in private, nonpublic, administration — count nearly five million people working as public administrators, broadly defined. Between 1950 and 1980, public administration trebled in size. For example, in the census tables covering industrial distribution of employment in the tertiary sector, public administration nationwide jumped from 2,491,000 in 1950 to 4,202,000 in 1970.[10] Public administration represents a large segment of the labor force: a labor force that is well educated, increasingly subject to specialization of roles and functions, and quite willing to execute and interpret the will of state authority.

The postindustrial concept is organically related to public administration. Public administration's enlarged role is part of a changing pattern of class relationships. Max Weber's trepidations over the growth of bureaucracy were well founded.[11] Public sector activities have grown at a pace and in power far beyond older classes: The proletariat has declined as capital-intensive industry replaces manual labor; the peasant-farmer sector has shriveled in size as technology has improved food and agricultural production; the bourgeoisie as an owning group has been allowed to remain constant in numbers, but its decision-making ability has been reduced by the need for federal public-sector supports.

The growth in middle management in industry has become the corollary to growth in the public sector. Their decision-making function permits one to think of industry, no less than government, as a set of bureaucratic institutions or leaders with divergent ideas.[12] But if neither government nor industry offers a single rational actor, they do offer a picture of two central facets of advanced industrial society operating with profoundly different models of economic well-being. The contrast in economic philosophies between the public and private sector is well known. The critical contradictions between these two sectors prevent any new class of administrative workers from emerging despite similarities at the functional level.[13]

Public administrators function as a subclass of the public sector, and industry managers function as a subclass of the private sector. The character of class competition also changes dramatically in the postindustrial world. The familiar competition *within* the private sector between bourgeoisie and proletariat yields to the less familiar but more potent struggle *between* the administrative vanguards of the public sector and the private sector. The coterminous existence of older forms of class competition remain intact, but even these are mediated by new administrators and their authorities, interests, and regulations.

The Sherman Antitrust Act of the late nineteenth century introduced a tension between public and private sector economies that has not yet abated. It is precisely the tilt toward the public that permits one to characterize our epoch as postindustrial. Implied is a change not only from the production of goods to the production of services, or from the production of commodities to the production of ideas, but, more exactly, a shift in the locus of power and the force of numbers.[14] Public administration is properly perceived as a subclass functioning as an independent social force, representing public sector requirements in its great struggle to involve the private sector in the goals of equity and opportunity. The public administrator functions in the classic bureaucratic mold, as the representative of the presumed national interest over and against managers of industrial or economic interests. Whether public administration can do so without destroying the innovation, initiative, and inventiveness of an advanced society becomes the challenge of its claims to domination of the social order.[15]

As in other areas of applied research, the power of the U.S. style emerged with raw pragmatism that rests on a problem-solving context in which "means and ends are sometimes impossible to separate, where aspirations and objectives are in constant development, and where drastic simplification of the complexity of the real world is urgent."[16] Public administration in particular grew in a context of only a barely disguised animus for theorists, those for whom a "rational comprehensive" model has meaning. Public administration was celebrated as "the science of muddling through," and the only widely acknowledged problem was the swiftness of technological innovation so that there was an "absence of enough persons who are knowledgeable in computer use." The solution was better functional division of technology and more extensive training.[17]

To look back even a few decades is to observe a brave new world of public administration, in which technological breakthroughs are constant and solutions to thorny problems are registered through improved data control. Governance through data control reached its crescendo in the United States with the Vietnam War, the Watergate scandals, and a series of discovered deceptions at the legislative level. As the mechanics of administration became unmanageable, the science of muddling through led to a series of overseas defeats and domestic miscalculations. As a result, there was a dramatic contextual shift from Europe to the United States in the practical implementation of public administration.

The major theses of the radical 1960s were delineated and articulated in advanced texts and by major figures, but they were left unresolved. Little more could be expected when even the most advanced researchers proposed that public administration overcome its "crisis of identity by trying to act as a profession without actually being one."[18] The implications were clear: The main issues were turned from the social conditions of administration to the professional status of administration. As a review essay of the ten leading public administration texts points out: "Only one author devotes much space to posing the question of which groups and social class are best served by the administrative structure of the state."[19] As the emphasis inexorably shifted from issues of broad social meaning to narrow professional issues, mi-

cromethodology replaced theory construction; problems of
the measurement, evaluation, and even monitoring of programs and plans rapidly displaced more fundamental concerns. Under such circumstances, the source of new inspiration
in public administration inevitably shifted toward technique
and away from service.

The cutting edge of public administration theory shifted
from the United States directly after World War II, to Europe,
especially France, during the height of the Cold War epoch.
The reasons for this geographic change are socially complex,
ranging from the polarization of party politics to the rise of a
student movement which took on characteristics of a social
revolution, but the facts are clear.[20] The major divisions shifted
from those who thought about government in functional categories to those who saw government as a total system, that is,
in structural terms. The debate raged between ideologists who
preferred the language of bureaucracy because it reflected the
actual hierarchy of government, and technocrats who preferred public administration precisely because of its nonhier-
archical or functional characteristics. Those who urged a
general systems perspective were denounced by those wishing
to construct theory at the partial theory level. Some viewed
bureaucracy as generic; others saw administration as generic,
with public administration as one of its aspects. Finally, the
argument revolved about whether public administration is a
separate discipline or part of the social and political sciences.

The collapse of the 1968 student rebellion, along with the
marginzalization of communist and fascist-nationalist politics,
led to new approaches in how state power is manifested. The
higher functionaries, disturbed by the anarchism on the left
and the fascist potential on the right, began to examine the
premises of postindustrialism, looking at it as a question of
elitism versus populism rather than in 1930s terms of social
class or even 1960s terms of social function. In the hands of
public administrators, the state became the guardian of public

interest over and against private interest. Two schools of thought emerged.

One was led by Michel Crozier, who argued that the administrative apparatus had as its unique charge superseding social stagnation by making an institutional investment to render habits, negotiations, and systems of rules more complex, more open, more comprehensive, and more efficient.[21] The investment was not impeded by financial constraint or lack of political will but by the need for an intellectual change of course toward serious analysis, real understanding of change, and deeper personal involvement in institutions.

In contrast, Nicos Poulantzas, in a series of intriguing if dogmatically stated works, indicated that the decline of legislative power, the strengthening of the executive, and the political role currently assumed by the state administration now constitute the tripartite leitmotiv of political studies.[22] Ernest Mandel elaborated on this neo-Marxian theme by noting the heavy increase in the service sector and hence the expansion of administrative state power. Unlike Poulantzas, he feels that such a shift does not "lower the average organic composition of capital."[23] For the French intellectual Left, bureaucracy should mainly be viewed not as an impediment to inefficiency but as a response to structural deformities within private and entrepreneurial sectors. The economic role of the state, and not the need for efficiency or innovation, undergirds the expansion of public administration. In Poulantzas's view, administration becomes the terrain in which an "unstable equilibrium of compromises" between the power elites and the popular masses takes place and is elaborated.[24] His view is a far cry from the characterization of bureaucracy as serving a class function inherited from an earlier period in socialist history.

Behind the heavy theorizing was a shaken intelligentsia that tried to come to terms with state power as murderous power in both capitalist and communists contexts. Crozier is arguing the central role of administration in adjudicating the claims of interest groups and in bringing about innovations that otherwise would not be made by the private sector.[25] Poulantzas, for his part, has become profoundly antitotalitarian, centering his attack on the giganticism of state power. He concludes his work *State, Power, Socialism* with a vigorous and full-blown critique of Stalinism as an extension of Leninism.[26]

But it remains the case that the 1970s ended with the same sad indecisiveness as had the 1960s. Resolution of the issues on the basis of dependence versus the autonomy of public administration is but a more advanced form of the same theoretical bind characteristic of American thinking in the decades immediately following the Vietnam War. The reason for this is not too difficult to locate: Researchers like Crozier were essentially policy-oriented meliorists, interested in getting society going again; whereas theorists like Poulantzas and Mandel held no hope for moving forward through administrative efficiency as long as a market economy remained the essential motor for economic development. Curiously, none of these neo-Marxist types seemed to appreciate that the administrative bureaucracy had developed a life of its own, one made evident in the management of the more than ten thousand concentration camps operated by the Nazi regime during World War II.

The problem is partially the reification of administration itself. It makes little sense to argue an anticapitalist premise when state power grows even more forcefully in totalitarian planned economies. As shrewdly noted by Jean-Jacques Servan-Schreiber, the ability of the Soviet Union and its East European satellites to insure a minimal living wage to their entire population depended on maintaining a high degree of coercion.[27] When the capacity for coercion was restricted by over reaching, the totalitarian system itself came under attack and eventual collapse. What distinguishes the United States is not so much the administration of power, as the limits placed on such power by the legal and ethical codification of a democratic system. The problems of racial strife, sexual conflict, and ethnic group tensions are just as powerful in the United States as in Europe. What is different in the United States, and the Western democracies as a whole, is a sense of the administrator both as part of the larger state apparatus and as a relatively autonomous sector with its own interests. At a concrete level, the political goal of administration is only its own expansion and extension. But at a more generic level, its specific political aims are circumscribed by the larger forces of state and economy.

The concentration of administrative power is common to socioeconomic systems designated as postindustrial. One reason for employing the term "postindustrial" is that it avoids the reductionist tendency of identifying the concentration or curtailment of power with any one kind of economic environment or party apparatus. Differences between social systems and nations have not evaporated. They remain potent cultural forces. In any democratic culture, control is in the hands of the popular sectors. The struggle between such popular sectors and bureaucratic regimentation is real. Personality factors in leadership are common to all types of economic systems. Public administration, with its impersonal norms, comes into conflict with the political apparatus it presumably serves, with its continuing norms of personalism and charismatic authority.

The administrative apparatus, however close it might appear to the state apparatus, must remain responsive to the led no less than the leaders, to the broad stratum of people who are outside the decision-making process but who support it through their taxes and commitments. Public administration cannot be characterized as part of the state any more than it can be viewed as a buffer against that mechanism. They must both operate in a context that negotiates the machinery of power and the interests of the public while trying to control the budget.

This sort of conflict becomes an essential proprietary consideration in postindustrial environments, where older forms of conflict have collapsed. Polarization remains deeply embedded in advanced social structures, but it takes the form of efforts to dominate funds rather than classes. In consequence, postindustrial society is in some respects close to postfeudal society: It simplifies social relations just when technological forms of negotiating those relations become ever more complex.

The relationship between planners (the policy-making element in advanced states) and the financiers (middle-management bureaucrats or public administrators) becomes a most intriguing issue to monitor.[28] It can either evolve into an area of severe friction between those who make policy and set the nation on its long-range course and those who carry out policy and hence do not easily take to interference or sudden shifts of direction; or it can become a symbiotic relationship in which forces are joined to preserve and extend state power. Given the natural antipathies of those at the top of decision making versus those in middle management, one might well expect antagonism. Increasingly, these antipathies are held in check by decision making, which has itself become postindustrial in the special sense that data determine decisions. In this evolution, decision making has increasingly been removed from the political arena.

Certain characteristics of bureaucracy prevail over policy-making concerns in the art of governance. The growing professionalization of government work, whatever the type or level, moves to counter politicization. As a result, one should not anticipate the end of public ideologies so much as the decline of party politics. The essential danger is closure on political participation. The main issue is not how administrators function in postindustrial societies but how government administration — local, state, regional, and federal — begins with a theory of negotiating between policy makers and political officials but ends with assuming the reins of state power.

Politics becomes conflated to the defense of the presumed national interest. The defense of those interests against overseas transgressions becomes central. Hegel overwhelms Marx: The state, not the class, becomes the main organizing premise of modern societies. Public administration is uniquely situated to take full advantage of the new conditions of nationalism. Reared in a tradition of professionalization before politicization, organized to serve the needs of the state directly and not any one subset of special interests, and being directly tied to the process of governance without the encumbrances of electoral affairs, such a group becomes the basic sponsor of the national interest, the guardian of the state, and the definer of its specific survival capacities.

This implies growing conservatism within the public administration sector, not in traditional ideological terms, as a philosophical desire for community and order, but to preserve the state and its interests against military incursion from abroad and fiscal disintegration from within. Public administration creates a solid phalanx because mass politics has long since dissolved in the narcotizing impact of the communications media. The steady expansion of public administration, particularly at local, state, and regional levels (the federal level seems saturated at this point), also provides linkages between the administrative apparatus and further inhibits the emergence of any grassroots or local, state, or regional opposition. A certain equilibrium, longed for by federal administrators, becomes the norm. In the West, state power increases not as a function of ideology — as with fascism and communism — but as a believed consequence that public officials no best what is good and necessary for the much abused people.

The attempt to distinguish administration from politics is understandable, but it ultimately remains an exercise in futility. The bifurcated vision derives from a Western democratic belief that professionalism is somehow uniquely anti-political, or better, purely instrumental.[29] Gordon Tullock puts the issue properly:

> There is no way this sort of ultimate policy formation by low ranking personnel can be avoided; it will arise on occasion in all organizations, no matter how efficiently these are organized. . . .
> Not only the initial decisions, but all subsequent decision, may be

made by men operating at the lower reaches of the hierarchy. The sovereign neither ratifies nor disapproves of these decisions either because the chain of command is so clogged that he does not hear of the issues at all, or because he is lazy or because he fears that any decision on his part will, in turn, annoy his own superior in the hierarchy. In such an organization as this, the lower ranks, after perhaps vainly trying to get the higher officials to take action, may be forced to make decisions. Out of a series of such events, a sort of organizational policy may develop by precedent, and the higher officials may never have to make any choices of significance at all.[30]

In a period of computer driven technology, administrative decisions by fiat become more frequent. The danger in this equation between expertise and administration is that vox populi gets left out of the reckoning. However, the demos as the ultimate repository of power compels elected officials to take responsibility for decision making. Opposition to this enlarged federal administrative apparatus comes from a re-vived populism — from opposition to government and its services that will undoubtedly cut across traditional left and right lines.

In state after state there are motions and bills to limits federal impingements on private records, reduce property taxes, and in general, weaken federal controls in areas such as education. One can no more convert this populism into a left or right impulse than one can identify government administrative actions as left or right. The shape of things to come is already plain: a struggle between the state and its organized participants, on the one hand, and the people, with its interest groups, tax clout, and ultimately, sheer numerical force, on the other.

And as we have witnessed in the firebombing of federal buildings and large commercial edifices, violence, such as sabo-tage and terror, is more likely in a depoliticized context than in a highly centralized one. Politics is an essential cement of moral authority, since it alone guarantees a sense of participation and control over matters of state power. But in the antiseptic climate of top-down rules and regulations, where party identification is low and political allegiance shaky, the legitimacy of the state can be severely threatened. In such a context the administrative machinery of government may be seen as the government itself. Popular actions will become less symbolic and increasingly oriented toward direct action. Getting things done is achieved by threatening bureaucrats with the dire consequences of a given interest group. Hence the web of government, that delicately laced network of authority and legitimacy, can easily become unhinged in a brave new world of bureaucratic determinism.

Postindustrial technology has been unevenly absorbed. Line managers have been afraid of the new technology, while those staff who procure it have emphasized the efficiency of machines rather than the effectiveness of programs. As one report indicated, "The impact of computers on the federal government's operations and procedures is pervasive," and federal expenditures for computer-based information systems have grown to the point that the essential contours of the relationship between the public right to know and the private right not to tell has become the essential pivot of the postindustrial world.[31]

In the immediate future, much more effort will be devoted to developing a symbiosis between electronic information systems and administrative tasks, involving the modeling of complex systems as much as simply processing routine data. Forecasting and assessment of technology are linked to greater use of advanced computer systems. Until now, public administrators have focused on short-term uses of advanced technology. In the next round, long-term planning is likely to prevail. The danger is that complex decision making will become the responsibility of machines rather than of human political actors. Here is an area of maximum potential danger for future public-sector policy making.

The "good" or "evil" potential of technology is moot, but we must not forget that public administrators not only react to a postindustrial technology but have long been involved in guiding it. The military and nuclear areas are particularly vulnerable. "The direction of technology involves two kinds of activity which, in a sense, act against each other yet are also opposite sides of the same coin. We refer to the activities of promoting and controlling technology, the former referring to the encouragement of technology and the latter to its regulation."[32] Because of the enormous costs in research and development and the consequent impact on profitability, the role of technology is not simply external to public administration; rather, it is organic to it in an advanced postindustrial setting. Technology becomes integral to decision making.

Administration is a service as well as a system. Advanced societies evolve toward increases in this service sector. But over and against this inexorable tidal wave of paperwork over hardware production, of allocation over innovation, and of decision making in lieu of mass politics stands the specter of new public managerships, a new class that loses intimate contact with ordinary events and plain people and so jeopardizes the political system as a whole. Even if bureaucratic administration is impervious to internal assault, its removal from the taproots of incentive and innovation make any society susceptible to destruction from without.[33] The need to consider public administration as a servant or at least an agency for developing incentive, and not a master of government, is the alpha and omega of democratic life and also ensures the future of public administration as an entity apart from special or private interests.

It is dangerous to conceive of postindustrial technology as necessarily feeding the fires of administrative domination. Mindless slogans and irrational specializations tend to thwart any sense of citizen participation. But certain developments, like cybernetic systems design, can facilitate radical, technological, and social decentralization. The distinction drawn by

Manfred Stanley between technology and technicism is useful, since the aims of education, whether of an administrative or political sort, are serviced by redesign of social research methods, the institutionalization of linguistic accountability, and the critique of irrational specialization.[34] The pace of technological innovation and the size of bureaucratic administration have both quickened. On the stable presumption that historical clocks cannot be turned back, the need to harness the former and counterbalance the latter becomes a major task of democratic culture. The democratic culture must itself be sensitized to new patterns of administration.

There will still be opposition between branches of government in a technological context. The executive branch will still mobilize its bureaucrats to disprove the claims of legislatively appointed bureaucrats. But such conflict among administrators should become less significant as the tasks of governance become more complex. The entire arsenal of populist politics will be required to offset the advantages of bureaucracy. Electoral politics are episodic, sporadic, and ideological in character. Administration is continuous, fluid, and rationalistic. If the two sides need each other, in a more proximate sense, such a need is tempered by realization that different constituencies, functional prerequisites, and ultimately different visions of law and order are involved.

Holding this dialectical chain intact, maintaining unity through opposition, becomes an essential task for constitutional law and a pivotal function of the modern judiciary. Democracy has been, and will continue to be, affected by the rise of public administration in a postindustrial society in which state power grows and in which the relationship between politics and economics is inverted, with politics becoming the base and economics the superstructure.[35] Democracy will also be attacked for its inefficiencies. That is the essential meaning of totalitarian postindustrialism: The adjudication of the innate tensions of mass demands and organizational rules becomes the essential role of public administration in a democratic community.

Democracy is decreasingly definable as a specific system and increasingly definable as a process of mutual setting forth of interests that can be adjudicated and negotiated in an orderly and maximally noninjurious way.[36]

To the extent that such an admittedly rarified definition of democracy has meaning, conflicts between public administration and mass politics should be viewed only as a late-twentieth-, or possibly a twenty-first, -century possibility. As old conflicts between judicial, legislative, and executive branches of government decrease in importance through increase in the technology of scientific decision making, a clustering effect may occur in which the process of government that takes lives is pitted against the process of being left alone. The private sector will come to mean those areas of individual performance left intact, without genocidal incursions, rather than a portion of the economy left under entrepreneurial control.

A new system of checks and balances might evolve in accord with emerging characteristics of the political process as a whole. The basis for such programmed differentiation of tasks and distinction in goals may not be spelled out constitutionally except as a series of mandates permitting administrative functions to operate in a pluralistic context. The specific functions of various branches of government will appear more rational in a context of opposition, or at least functional differentiation of administrative bureaucratic tasks. At one level, this is the politics of the last word: The executive head who spends twenty hours on the budget, not the administrators who spend thousands of hours preparing the budget, has the final say interpreting the annual message. The congressman or originator, purveyor, and mediator of preferences must vote on legislation even though bureaucrats and managers may inundate a legislator with evidence that a bill is too costly or not operational.

Major movements of our time revolve around the size and strength of the bureaucratic state. The task becomes one of making that state responsible, increasing its efficiency while decreasing its omnipotence. Insofar as blockage to further political development is administration itself, either through tax pressure or through withholding of political legitimacy, and insofar as the blockage to further development is the narcissistic propensity of the popular will, one can expect political elites to assert their own claims over popular forces.

Whatever the nature of the economic system, our epoch bears witness to a constant expansion in state power, growth in bureaucratic norms, and an increase in administrative domination and disposition of people. The economic system a nation lives under has become less important than the fact of state growth and its allocative mechanisms. We have seen new forms of popular rebellion having little to do with class membership and crossing traditional social boundaries. Advanced technology helps ensure a simplified society — not necessarily a more pleasant one but certainly a society more direct in its conflicts of choice and interests.

The new technology offers potentials for both dictatorship and democracy. The outcomes are in doubt not because of the feebleness of social research but due to the willfulness of human actors. Before the torrent of populism, the wall of every known elitism threatens to crumble. But populism itself comes to provide a new form of irrational solidarity. The owl of Minerva gazes upon different social forces and relations than in the past yet bears witness to the endless search for the utopia underwriting the dystopia.

It is thus a cruel choice that we must confront: the destruction of liberty as a result of a postindustrial system or a possible destruction of life as a result of the populist rebellion against such a system. Whatever the path taken, the risks are great — and hence the need for a nation governed by laws, not men, remains a primary requirement of the age.

It might be objected that we have moved far from discussing genocide and the Holocaust. I think not. If the fate of victims of ultimate decimation is determined by impersonal forces of state power, the character of that power, no less than the exclusion of these groups from such instruments must be understood. The destruction of European Jewry may have had the tacit approval of large, amorphous masses and mendacious business interests, but was carried out by representatives of the state, by special units of the armed forces, police, and the judiciary system as such. Hence, the struggle for control of, and participation in, the act of governance is the surest safeguard against acts of murder as such. And that struggle is itself what is known as the democratic organization of society.

9

Nationalism and

Genocidal Systems

A civilization is a struggle to keep self-control, and in this it is like some great tragic person, some Niobe who must display an almost superhuman will or the cry will not touch our sympathy. The loss of control over thought comes toward the end; first a sinking in upon the moral being, then the last surrender, the irrational cry, revelation — the scream of Juno's peacock.

— William Butler Yeats[1]

THERE ARE AT LEAST EIGHT BASIC TYPES OF SOCIETIES THAT CAN BE DEFINED ON A measurement scale of life and death. I place these broad types within a framework of political regimes rather than of cultural systems. It is not that anthropology has been incorrect in its emphasis on the importance of culture, tradition, and language. Without the work of anthropologists, the social sciences would be even more bereft of a theoretical frame of reference than they are at present. However, the cultural framework, most particularly in its present deconstructionist phase, has proven unable to move beyond psychological categories of guilt or shame or to achieve more than a critical posture that envisions the life and death systems in terms of paralleling the life and death of individuals. The classical tradition in anthropology, at least until the contemporary period when political anthropology became a recognized field,[2] was unable to show how state authority, bureaucratic networks, and nationalist claims generated their own forms of genocidal patterns. For the internalization of guilt or shame to be effective, there must be a set of external, and usually political, restraints on behavior. The potency of guilt societies or shame societies not only entails forms of conservatism and consensus but also, as has recently been pointed out, is at the heart of the revolutionary processes in many newer societies.[3]

The following definitions of societal types should thus be viewed as political guidelines with near infinite shadings and not as rigid psychological types such as those laid out in Spranger's *Types of Men*.[4] Social systems provide a continuum; it is only when one examines the poles of this continuum that the extent of the differences in human organization becomes apparent. Beyond that, we are faced with the grim truth that any given nation may exhibit all eight patterns if one looks at a sufficient length of its history. In short, a great deal depends on the primary and secondary definitions of a society rather than the existence of any one type and the absence of all other types.

▸ There are the *genocidal societies,* in which the state arbitrarily takes the lives of citizens for deviant or dissident behavior. Since this work is dedicated to a full exploration of this subject, an extended definition is not required. But it must be emphasized that the distinction between genocidal and all other types of societies is qualitative: The genocidal society is the only form of rule that takes lives systematically.

▸ There are *deportation* or *incarceration societies,* in which the state either removes individuals from the larger body politic or in some way prevents their interaction with the commonwealth in general.

▸ One finds *torture societies,* in which people, defined as enemies of the state, are victimized short of death, returned to the societies from which they came, and left in these societies as living evidence of the high risk of deviance or dissidence.

▸ Then there are the *harassment societies,* in which deviants are constantly being picked up, searched, seized, or held in violation of laws that are usually remote from the actual crimes the state feels these individuals have committed. Since laws can be invoked against almost any behavior, the possibility of harassment of individuals through legal channels is infinite.

These four types of societies have in common the physical discomfiture and dislocation of deviant, dissident individuals, brought about by means of everything from simple harassment for nonpayment of taxes, for example, to direct liquidation of the person. In order to avoid the undue softening of categories, it is important to appreciate that patterns of genocide involve physical actions, and not just symbolic threats. To be sure, there are four other types of social systems that employ what might be called symbolic or noncoercive methods for gaining allegiance and adherence.

▸ In *traditional shame societies*, participation in the collective will is generated through instilling the individual with a sense of disapproval from outside sources and ensured by the isolation suffered as a result of nonparticipation in the normative system.

▸ Then there are *guilt societies*, closely akin to shame societies but in which a sense of wrongdoing is internalized in the individual, causing persons of all persuasions to respond to normative standards.

▸ In many Western societies we observe *tolerant systems,* where norms are well articulated and understood but where deviance and dissidence are permitted to go unpunished; they are not celebrated, but they are not destroyed either. These can be described as a series of pluralisms operating within a larger legal monism.

▸ Finally, there are *permissive societies*, in which norms are questioned and in which community definitions are transformed as needed rather than enduring as state definitions of what constitutes normative behavior. The decision-making process is itself subject to change. Such systematic alterations do not entail a loss of status or position within the society.

While at least the last seven of these eight types of societies overlap in their general avoidance of taking lives, they are distinct enough to merit differentiation and understanding on their own terms. Each of these types of societies can be found in capitalist, socialist, or mixed welfare forms of economy. It would be gratuitous, in light of actual historical experience, to claim that the movement from capitalism to socialism requires or involves a movement from less punitive to more permissive or less permissive to more punitive societies. The reverse is more often the case.

To attempt a correlation between economic systems and personal safety is a snare and delusion inviting spurious sorts of measures and variables. That such correlations are attempted is a tribute to the reductionist impulse, to the ideas that forms of economic arrangement in and of themeselves, improve the lot of ordinary human beings. Communist societies claiming international socialist economies are no less brutal, and are arguably more so, than are fascist societies claiming national socialist economies. And both varieties of totalitarianism proved more brutal than the regimes they overthrew.

Capitalism and socialism are not strictly economic systems. They yield all sorts of mixed political and ideological persuasions. Thus if we isolate but one item — the number of parties operating in a given social system — we find a similar lack of correlation between types of polity and forms of rule. While it would appear to be the case that single-party states reveal far higher levels of coercion than do multiparty states, the single-party apparatus of Mexico or Israel (with all due tolerance for the formal existence of smaller, satellite parties in these two nations) operate more democratically than the multiparty apparatus in Nigeria, Peru, or Indonesia. In any event, the purpose of this chapter is not to examine the relationship between democratic processes and political parties. Rather, it is to develop first a typology and then an explanation for state-perpetrated violence that distinguishes genocidal societies from other types of domination and authority.

To Turkey we owe two developments that were to have a profound impact on the course of the twentieth century: the harnessing of traditional regimes to nationalist causes and the continuation of genocidal policies even as traditional regimes are overturned — as it was in Turkey by the Kemalist Revolution. This revolutionary regime functioned as a prototype for Third World patterns of development half a century later. Both in practice and in concept, Turkey initiated a revolution from above under military bureaucratic sponsorship that took that agrarian society to the threshold of the twentieth century.[5] Equally important, and far more ominous, was the final legacy of the Ottoman Empire. From the start of the century until the empire's demise in 1918, it developed a policy of genocide on a scale unparalleled in any earlier epoch. The destruction of the Armenians was an event whose magnitude was matched only by the silence of the "civilized world" too absorbed in its own horrors of World War I to realize the qualitative uniqueness involved in the mass extermination of the Armenian peoples.

In 1915 the leaders of the Turkish Empire put into action a plan to remove and exterminate its Armenian population of approximately 1,800,000 persons. The Turks were not particular about the methods they employed to this end: of at least a million and a half Armenians forced to leave their homes, supposedly to be deported, fully one third were murdered before ever reaching their destinations. Descriptions of this massacre clearly indicate an attempt to deliberately, systematically exterminate all or most of the group.[6]

The genocide committed against the Armenian people illustrates how different facets of state authority, and even overlapping state authorities as such, serve to generate an appropriate ideology to perform the necessary nationalist dirty work. The Turkish overseers began the destruction of the Armenian minority in the name of the Ottoman Empire. The Young Turks continued the process in the name of Turkish nationalism. The Kemalists completed this process in the name of social development and hegemonic integration.[7] Vahakn Dadrian explains the intimacies of this process: Both the old Ittihadist chieftains and the new Kemalists "needed each other, and hence, used each other in the name of patriotism, with Kemal being more circumspect lest his open avowal of wanting to dissociate himself and his movement from former Itthadists might be belied. Moreover there was the problem of the ballast of old loyalties. In consideration of this fact, Kemal was willing to avail himself of old Itthadists up to a point, and under strict conditions that they make a choice between him and such erstwhile Itthadist leaders as Enver and Talat — in terms of a binding and exclusive loyalty. The symbiotic relationship served its purpose for the duration of the insurgency and beyond it."[8]

Without delving too deeply into modern Turkish history, it is clear that the pragmatic coalitions between old and new forms of state power had a disastrous impact on the Armenians. Between 1893 and 1923 roughly 1.8 million Armenians were liquidated, while another million were exiled, without a single political or military elite within the state assuming responsibility for the termination of the slaughter, or for that matter, granting the Armenians national autonomy or territorial rights. This is not to equate the final stages of the Ottoman Empire with the first stages of the Kemalist Republic, only to point out that any effort to establish a precise correlation between a type of state system and the character of response to national minorities is dangerously mechanical and reductionist.[9]

The fate of the Armenians is the essential prototype of genocide in the twentieth century. Identifying the Armenians was simple enough: They were identified by tax collectors, public officials, and neighbors within the Ottoman Empire.

After that, a process took place where first they were segregated by gender; second they were required to surrender all weapons; third, Armenian men went into the armed forces in special units called "labor battalions"; fourth, the elites or prominent members of the Armenian community were arrested and secretly murdered, leaving the others numbed by terror; fifth, the remaining males in each village were summoned by the town to report immediately and were then slain out of town; sixth, women and children were prepared for deportation, driven into the desert by soldiers, and then slain out of town.

Without wishing to engage in an ideological refinement, that is, whether the genocide perpetrated against the Armenian people was or was not of Holocaust proportions, the fact remains that this people provided a major benchmark for events of the century. The disposition of this people dispels the common illusion that genocide is simply a function of economic development. In the Armenian case, a backward Ottoman Turkish Empire initiated the first major mass destruction and expulsion of a people. It was followed by the Kemalist regime, which made common cause with the Soviet Union to liquidate a nascent Armenian Republic that had been recognized as an independent republic by the Paris Peace Conference following the conclusion of World War I. The Armenian question represented a fusion of national, religious, and cultural issues. If the genocidal outcome was "incomplete" in the case of the Armenian people, it was less a consequence of Turkish mercy than of Turkish lack of systematic administrative techniques of engineered death.

Explanations offered for the genocidal treatment of Armenians provide crucial elements in any explanation of premeditated mass murder carried out by the state. The summary prepared by Dadrian clearly delineates these elements:

> Acute interferences with mainly political, military, and economic goal-directed activities gave rise to anger, or aggressive tendencies. The Armenians were perceived as the available source of

much of this frustration, and hostile attitudes against them were amplified. The process of scapegoating added to these hostilities and angers, which could not be directed toward the actual frustrater, i.e., the opposing Allies. Social and cultural inhibitions which might have directed anger into channels other than aggression were minimal or absent. Hostility became so intense and restraint so weak as to allow aggressive behavior of the most violent nature to occur, thanks to the original decision of the Turkish government.[10]

Such social-psychological features as external threat, opposing beliefs, competition for scarce goods, and frustration-aggression-scapegoating syndromes are often present in social systems without triggering genocide. These characteristics are often extant during wartime conditions. In this regard, analysts of genocide come upon a gigantic ambiguity: the difficulty in distinguishing the selective mayhem caused by conventional warfare and the collective isolation of a people or ethnic group for liquidation, incarceration, or torture. In comparing the Armenian and Jewish cases, we can develop a significant typology that reduces, if not entirely resolves, such ambiguity.

▸ *Primary Importance Common Features*. Acts of genocide were designed and executed during the exigencies of so-called world wars. In both instances, the principal instruments for the conception, design, and execution of the holocausts were political parties (Young Turks and Nazis) that invested themselves with monolithic power and literally took over the functions of their respective states.

▸ *Secondary Importance Common Features*. The war ministries and the selected organs and outfits of the affiliated military structures were subverted and utilized for the manifold purposes of genocide. Economic considerations involving official as well as some personal designs of enrichment at the expense of the relatively better-off members of the victim group played a key role. In both cases, the victim groups were minorities whose overall vulnerability was matched by the degree of ease with which the dominant groups implemented their schemes of extermination.

▶ *Tertiary Importance Common Features.* Cultural, religious, and in a sense racial, differences separated the victim groups from the perpetrator groups — notwithstanding the incidence of certain patterns of assimilation and even amalgamation through which multitudes from both groups felt, and were, identified with one another. Many Ottoman Armenians and German Jews felt politically and socially, if not culturally, identified with the respective dominant groups. The bureaucratic machinery had a crucial role in the administration and supervision of genocidal violence. Sanctions, both negative and positive, were the operationally controlling factor in both cases through which military and civilian personnel, from the highest to the lowest echelons of the administrative setup, were demoted or promoted, punished or rewarded, threatened or cajoled on the basis of their attitudes and performances vis-à-vis the processes of genocide.[11]

Whether a "symbolic interactionist" perspective really flows from available evidence remains somewhat doubtful.[12] Rather, it seems to move the discussion of genocide away from its promising roots in political economy into a softer theoretical plane of social psychology. The search for metaphor would better take us into the realm of social biology, or more simply, neo-Darwinian survivalist perspectives. Metaphorical reasoning, however attractive and clever, still leaves intact a study of the specifics of genocide; more poignantly, of how genocide serves as an ultimate test of the stratification of a society and the prevention of any realization of equities among different races, religions, tribes, and nationalities. For we must still try to demonstrate that genocide is endemic to the social structure. And genocide must serve as a basic measuring device for creating a new typology of social and political systems, rather than being viewed as a response to mass contagion or elitist charisma.

However, the emergence of victimology, as a response to criminology, raises as many problems as it resolves. Studies in genocide address themselves to those who are victimized by official representatives of the state. On the other hand, if the emphasis on victims is randomized, that is, without concern for sources or ranges of violence, a serious dilemma emerges: a breakdown of the notion of criminal rehabilitation at the expense of assistance to the victims. This may also entail abandonment of the notion of meliorative behavior in the political and social systems. The pitfall of victimology as a "science" is its tendency to produce an overly conservative outcome. Victimology tends to emphasize victims as if they existed independently of another entity called the criminal. Victimology, in its very outrage, omits from consideration a hundred years of social science research that has placed questions of crime and punishment, victims and criminals, in a larger political and sociological perspective. Victimology is an important tendency in social research, but it is a one-sided, emotive substitute for a theory of power and its distribution. Analysts should be wary of any overreaction to genocidal problems, of seeing every form of deviant behavior as an insult to the dignity of the potential victim. An "institutional" victimization approach to a social problem carries with it the further dilemma that the identity of the victim is no more self-evident than is locating the criminal.[13] Moreover, in creating a feeling that every member of an ethnic or national group is a victim, victimology leaves unanswered the nature of the victimizer.

How then does one respond to those who engage in genocide? What juridical options and alternatives are available to punish its practitioners? Strategies have ranged from the Nuremberg trial of Nazi leaders to the Japanese war criminal trials, trials which sought to enunciate and codify limits to state or official violence. But when all is said and done, such legal codification reduces itself to a much more simplified theory than we like to admit: We punish those who lose rather than those who engage in genocide. While victors have a healthy, spirited reaction to those who participate in mass murder, they are selective about criminal prosecution, based on the degree of loss and gain of those who engaged in these acts. It is hard to distinguish between the persecution of Armenians by Turks and the persecution of American Indians by European settlers of the Western frontier. Yet in this case there is a world of difference in the way popular classes and intellectual elites handle the question of punishment, or even the way in which these problems are framed. There are serious ontological issues in this area of genocide: Are we punishing criminals or those who made the mistake of losing massive military engagements?

As in all high-level generalizations, one must account for sharp variations in political systems. At one extreme is the weak state that underwrites mass violence and genocide in order to foster its own survival. The most pronounced and unique illustration of this is Colombia throughout the twentieth century. Here we have a nation characterized by *la violencia* that demonstrates how weak state authority can yet manage to foster its interests without alleviating mass destruction.[14] The importance of this case is transcendent: The issues of genocidal societies cannot be reduced to a simplistic formula that juxtaposes the anarch with the behemoth and that presumes that the liquidation of state authority is equivalent to ushering in an age of respect for human rights.

William Stokes refers to the Colombian state syndrome as *machetismo*. He notes that Colombia has been in a condition of violence that geographically includes almost the entire country, and worse, temporally includes almost the entire century. "When no one caudillo can peacefully subjugate existing opposition, when one or more challengers claim supreme power, *machetismo* becomes a costly and time consuming methodology for establishing authority. Among seventy nationwide examples of *machetismo* in Colombia in the nineteenth century, one conflict alone took approximately 80,000 lives, and the struggle which covered the years 1899 to 1903 took about 100,000 lives."[15] Colombia is an example of a state that, although exhibiting weak central authority, yet manages, by that very factor, to institutionalize and stabilize a genocidal system.

Since we are concerned with establishing the genocidal social system as a basic category of social life, the Colombian case is just as significant as the Turkish case; indeed no less, extended over time. In most cases of recorded genocide, the ruling class, party, or regime established itself as supreme and exclusive. But in Colombia an *entente* took place between two aristocratic and patrician institutions that succeeded in maintaining oligarchic domination even in the twilight of their actual economic power. Darcy Ribeiro traces the morphology of dictatorial state authority during the twentieth century. Genocidal societies have in common a "homogenization period" in which real opposition, usually liberal in character, is systematically decimated. "Figures based on statistics of recent years show that in 1960 Colombia had a rate of death by homicide of 33.8 per 100,000 inhabitants, whereas that of the United States, by no means a tranquil nation, was 4.5, and Peru 2.2."[17] Ribeiro plainly states that the entire social structure came to operate "as the generator of lawless forms of conduct on the individual or the family plane, forms that constitute the regular modes of maintaining the overall regime, or in other words, the very function of the institutions."

> The eruption of violence in Colombia en masse — with its 300,000 officially admitted murders and surely more than 1,000,000 wounded, exiled, robbed, crippled in one decade — occurs when the overall order represented by the regulative institutions of national scope (government, church, justice, army, police, parties, press) becomes confused with local order in the exacerbation of partisan hatred, everything becoming fused and swallowed up in the same generalized dysfunction.[18]

Let us take Uganda as a third example of a genocidal society. The following report on differences between Tanzania and Uganda sums up what a genocidal society looks like, when one considers that the estimated 80-90,000 people who died at the hands of the Amin government represent a considerable slice

of the population. General Idi Amin seized power in an overthrow of the Milton Obote government in 1971. Prior to the
demise of Amin's regime in 1979, the International Commission of Jurists published an extended report of offenses against
human rights in Amin's Uganda, with some horrifying details
of the persecution and murder of individuals and of whole
communities within this African state. A low estimate is that
50,000 people who were considered "enemies" of the regime
were murdered and that another 50,000 were forced into exile.
A relative of Amin, who was Uganda's foreign minister in
1971-1972 and who then sought exile himself, estimated that
80-90,000 people died at the hands of Amin's government.[19]

A 1978 estimate provided by Amnesty International placed
the upper limits of the number of Ugandans killed by the Amin
regime at 300,000 or more. The report noted that the people
killed were drawn from all social classes, various religious
groups (but especially Catholics), and occupational segments
such as teachers, lawyers, and doctors. The final tortured twist
in the Amin regime was to set up a "Ugandan Human Rights
Committee" comprised of the same security organizations and
personnel accused of responsibility for the genocidal practices
to start with.[20]

The full measure of how a genocidal society operates becomes clear by examining such data. Until the fall of Idi Amin
in 1979, Uganda was also a deportation society, having exiled
40,000 Indians within a four-week period of time, against their
will. What is especially noteworthy about viewing Uganda
primarily as a genocidal society is that one does not become
encumbered with lengthy discussions about communism or
fascism and comparative governments of Europe and Africa.
Defining Amin's economic system becomes a secondary intellectual task. Ethnocentricities prevent us from viewing Nazi
Germany or Stalinist Russia in terms similarly unencumbered
by ideological definitions.

One should not assume that genocide is unique to movements that claim revolutionary outlooks. It is equally the case

that reactionary systems can practice genocide on revolutionary movements. The case of Malaysia between 1948 and 1956
is indicative of the extermination not simply of an internal
political movement but of a political movement deemed to
represent a national minority, in this case Chinese. In the
Malaysian situation, the linkage between genocide and ethnocide was apparent. The guerrilla forces never numbered more
than 8,000 men, who were eventually defeated by a force of
40,000 British and 45,000 Malaysian home guards. This huge
overkill was based on a profoundly erroneous persuasion that
the Chinese minority was interested in setting up a Chinese
hegemony. As a result, a genocidal policy was followed that
took an estimated 5,000-20,000 lives.[21]

Nor, in the quarter century after the massacre, did the
Malaysian attitudes toward the Chinese abate. In 1979 the
government of Malaysia, in the teeth of worldwide opposition,
initiated the practice of putting to sea and to certain death the
76,000 Vietnamese refugees (most of Chinese ethnic extrac-
tion) who landed between 1976 and 1979 from the Vietnam
mainland. In further issuing a prohibition against any such
further landing and a "shoot on sight" order, the Malaysian
state took upon itself the task of determining, once again,
which peoples would live and which would die — blaming the
victims in the process. It is noteworthy how during the course
of this century the unthinkable act of genocide has passed over
into the realm of the commonplace.

Nor can there be any extrinsic justification, such as the
reputed acceleration of rates of industrial growth. When societies are economically backward, the consequence of a high
assassination and/or expulsion rate has been to intensify backwardness and stagnation. Uganda, even more than Malaysia,
is a prime example of this tendency. The rates of industrial
expansion and consumer purchasing power both fell off badly
in the final three years of the Amin regime.[22] This is not to
deny that when industrially advanced societies turn into genocidal states, they tend to maintain their high levels of economic

productivity. Terror can produce at least short-run upswings in economic growth rates. This was the case of Germany under Hitler and the Soviet Union under Stalin in the 1930s. But there certainly is no "iron law" in which human extermination can be coupled with social development.

Attempts have also been made to extend the concept of genocide to include cultural repression. For example, questions have been raised about the position of black people in contemporary America. Questions have been urgently raised as to whether punitive sterilization, breakdowns in advanced obstetrical care, tubal ligations, and hysterectomies do not constitute new elements in genocide.[23] The difficulty with assumptions about genocidal characteristics of family planning and medical care is the ubiquitous nature of the data. The steady increase in the black population since the end of World War II — even beyond the population increase in the general society — the decrease in occupational differentiations, and crude birth and death statistics would indicate that although the punitive treatment of American blacks continues, such differences are selective; and, above all, do not have federal support.[24]

The ubiquity of the concept of genocide is nowhere better illustrated than in the treatment of black American citizens by their government. In the antebellum South, the killing of portions of the black population for the purpose of exploiting the remainder represented a systematic policy. Less certain is the designation of genocide as a national rather than sectional policy in pre-Civil War contexts; and even less warranted is the assumption that every form of vigilante behavior in the post-Civil War context represents genocidal policy. Certainly from 1865 through 1945 one could detect a systematic, state-sponsored pattern of legal persecution, economic inequality, and police harassment against black people. Beyond that, health, welfare, and educational differentials have constituted a monumental assault by the white on the black population.[25] As late as 1950 these differential policies toward black and white accounted for roughly 32,000 more deaths among blacks than whites, despite the aggregate difference in numbers of black and white citizens. There can be no question that racial discrimination endured by American blacks is unparalleled in U.S. history. What can be questioned is how systematic or structural such practices are at present, compared to earlier epochs.

If we are left only with the legal definition of genocide, all manner of empirical problems arise. For example, in speaking of deliberately inflicted measures or forcible transferring of populations, the question inevitably arises: Who carries out such deliberate and forcible actions? In the case of the United States, there seemed to be a pattern of vigilantism rather than genocidal practices by the state for the purpose of maintaining social order. The range of additional attitudes by the state toward its black citizens extended from a long line of federal legislation to diminished racial animus and racial integration, to an assumption that legislation simply would not work and that "benign neglect" under such circumstances would be better than forced integration. This relationship between the U.S. government and its black citizens is a complex issue made more so by considerable sectional differences and psychological attitudes. Yet it would be both dangerous and hyperbolic to equate the U.S. treatment of its black citizens with the German Nazi treatment of its Jewish citizens. The demographic information we have concerning crude birthrates and the expanding size of the black population would move to counter such a mistaken equation. We are not engaged in active apologetics for the brutality of hostile white power structures toward their black communities, but this must nonetheless be distinguished from the sort of systematic extermination associated with the concept of genocide.

There is a thin line, then, between systematic and sporadic destruction. There are even times in which sporadic destruction might take more lives than systematic annihilation, especially in tribal contexts, where legal limits to genocide do not exist; or at least are not enforced. Vigilante politics in advanced contexts is another instance of high genocide with low controls. Such state sponsored violence often has the tacit support of at least a portion of population. Nevertheless, the distinction between sporadic and systematic destruction of human life is of practical significance, and of more than academic consequence. It is a distinction which points to trends over time, and also compels an examination of the role of resistance to genocide among different peoples.

The end of an era when formal declarations of warfare were made also signifies the beginning of a new era in which the line between war and genocide becomes profoundly blurred. Consider the undeclared war in Vietnam: its mortifying levels of deaths through air attacks, including napalm bombings and the wide use of chemical defoliants have led serious critics of that war to argue that it was a case of genocide.[26] Others, however, believe that the Vietnam conflict was not a matter of genocide since the killings were not systematic but simply a result of the enemy not accepting the terms of an honorable settlement.[27] The distinction between internal and foreign peoples who are being killed helps little, since it must be confessed that in all genocidal practices, the perpetrators of mass violence define those destroyed as outsiders. What legitimately can be asserted in such cases is that the widespread use of mass violence by state authorities against one portion of a population clearly has spillover potentials for another part of humanity, sometimes thousands of miles away. This in itself might serve as a deterrent to any further legitimization of a genocidal state.

Peoples subject to genocide have been faced with their strategic requirements for negotiating their own survival. Black resistance to lynchings, hangings, and vigilantism in general served as a major obstacle to successfully carrying out genocidal policies, just as in the antebellum South the totality of intimidation weakened such resistance by limiting the social organization of the black community. The literature on the Holocaust is filled with similar choices and decisions. The

Warsaw Ghetto is perhaps the classic model of Jewish acquiescence being replaced by Jewish resistance once the choices
were starkly narrowed to unambiguous life-and-death concerns. But clearly, whereas the American black community's
struggle for survival had the potential to be victorious, the
same was not the case in the liquidation of the European
Jewish communities under Nazism; nor for that matter, for the
Tutsi communities in present-day Rwanda.[28] There is, in short,
no a priori assurance that either acquiescence or resistance
will guarantee survival within the confines of a genocidal
regime. The choice of resistance strategies is a constant problem that must be faced not only by those aiming at the death
of the minority population but by those negotiating the survival of that population as well. In this regard, the definition
of the genocidal enemy as external, as was done in the Vietnam
conflict, may assist in the liberation effort.

A major category left unresolved by such an interior or
national model is the function of genocide due to imperial
aggression or foreign intervention. Here we have the contradiction of fine, upstanding European and American cultures
being responsible for the liquidation of masses of native populations. There is the destruction of the Zulu people by the
British; the decimation and virtual elimination of many Indian
tribes by early European settlers in the American continent;
and the impoverishment of the indigenous people in the former Belgian Congo. These are forms of genocide against foreign peoples rather than nationals.

A central tendency in all genocidal societies is to initially
create juridical-legal separations between citizens and aliens,
elites and masses, dominant and backward races, and so forth.
This serves as a pretext for genocide and also as a precondition
to the implementation of genocidal policies. We are dealing
with an oblique problem that has many ramifications: attempting definitions of social systems, not on economic grounds
alone, nor any of the other customary variables of polity,
military, and society, but rather on mortality data. American

Indians and African Zulus, many of whom sought pacific solutions, were defiled and denied even the remote participation of their numbers in any dominant imperial framework. Again, we have the seeds of a study unto itself. Yet the role of classic imperialism as a critical element in creating the conditions for modern mass genocide cannot be ignored.

Cuba following the Castro revolution is an illustration of the deportation-incarceration society. Without minimizing the enormity of its social reformation, the fact remains that more than one million Cubans were sent, or went voluntarily, into exile out of a total population of less than ten million. One can argue that deportation is an incredibly humane form of treatment compared to assassination, and that, of course, is true. It can also be argued that it is more humane to use incarceration than incineration,[29] although Cuba had its share of the latter as well. After 37 years of dictatorship, there remain an estimated 5,000 political prisoners languishing in Cuban jails. The point is not humanity but forms of punishment, and how the state removes deviants and dissidents from its midst. It is exceedingly important to emphasize the difference between assassination and incarceration societies. It is the most fundamental distinction of all since those either deported or incarcerated often live to tell the story; and in the case of Cuba, to confront their tormentors. This is not to deny that deportation and incarceration are fundamentally non-democratic methods of dealing with and eliminating enemies of the state; but the distinction does serve to illustrate differences between relatively benign totalitarian regimes and manifestly vicious genocidal systems.

Easier to identify as a pure deportation society than Cuba, is France under Napoleon III in the mid-nineteenth century. After the coup d'état of 1851, Louis Bonaparte inaugurated a system of military dictatorship that entailed expropriation, exile, and acts calculated to restore an empire. No differentiation was made between deviants, criminals, and dangerous political elements. A "mixed commission" made up of civil and military authorities passed sentence without concern for evidence, procedure, or appeal. The convicted would be deported to Guiana or Lambassa. In nineteenth-century terms, the numbers were impressive. By the middle of March 1842, over 26,000 persons had been arrested, of whom 6,500 were acquitted and somewhat more than 5,000 sentenced to police surveillance. Of the 15,000 actually punished, nearly two-thirds were sentenced to deportation to Algeria, while the rest were either handed over to other tribunals — *against* common law — or expelled from France.[30] Despite the severity of punishment, expulsion was viewed as the ultimate punishment rather than the outright physical elimination of "undesirable elements."

Some societies, like Brazil and Argentina under previous military rule, had no capacity to remove or deport enemies of the state. They thus became torture societies, in which police and other agencies of the state minimize opposition and maximize obedience through human disfigurement.[31] The numbers tortured are of course important. In countries like Brazil, Argentina, or Chile under Pinochet, the numbers reached into the tens of thousands. One must once again distinguish torture from both assassination or incarceration. For the most part, those tortured quickly return to the larger society. One might argue that the purpose of a torture society is to reinfiltrate these people into the larger society as a mechanism of contagion and mass fear. But such people sometimes become change agents for revolution.

When referring to such Latin American nations as classic torture societies, I specifically have in mind the treatment by state authorities of its urban white citizenry. Like the nineteenth-century United States in relation to its Indian minorities, the twentieth-century Brazilian state has adopted entirely genocidal standards in relation to its Indian minorities. And this race-based genocide is itself a basic stratification system within nondemocratic regimes.

The huge losses sustained by the Indian tribes of Brazil in past decades were catalogued. Of 19,000 Munducurus believed to have existed in the thirties, only 1,200 were left. The strength of the Guaranis had been reduced from 5,000 to 300. There were 400 Carajas left out of 4,000. Of the Cintas Largas, who had been attacked from the air and driven into the mountains, possibly 500 had survived out of 10,000. The proud and noble nation of the Kadiweus — the Indian Cavaliers — had shrunk to a pitiful scrounging band of about 200. A few hundred only remained of the formidable Chavantes, who prowled in the background of Peter Fleming's Brazilian journey, but they had been reduced to mission fodder — the same melancholy fate that had overtaken the Bororos, who helped to change Lévi-Strauss's views on the nature of human evolution. Many tribes were not represented by a single family, a few by one or two individuals. Some, like the Tapaiunas — in this case from a gift of sugar laced with arsenic — had disappeared altogether. It is estimated that between 50,000 and 100,000 Indians survive today. Without active intervention, the Indian population of Brazil seems doomed to extinction in the name of developmentalism.[32]

There are harassment societies where those in opposition to the state are not physically mistreated so much as legally abused. The range of societies performing such harassment extends from large states like the United States to much smaller societies in Western Europe that likewise engage in mass forms of harassment to guarantee political allegiance. Here the purpose is to harness the legal mechanism to the aims of the state so that all forms of harassment appear to be for real rather than political crimes, and hence punishment becomes a nonpolitical response to political opposition. The fundamental characteristic of the shame society is the idea of rehabilitation: Errors against the state are responded to by making the individual criminal feel a sense of shame, and hence the need for reformation. China comes to mind as the best example of that kind of system. Both military and civilian authorities are oriented toward the aim that everyone can be rehabilitated, and this rehabilitation is best defined by self-recognition (shame) and the internalization of guilt. In practice, the gulf between shame and guilt societies may be quite narrow.

One reason that torture societies have increased in potency as well as numbers is the growing sophistication of the medical and biological sciences. The same techniques employed by a doctor to reduce pain can also be employed by the torturer to intensify pain short of killing. In some states, such as Iran under the high point of the Shah's power or Greece under the rule of its military junta, such an abusive extension of science became a method of governing. While antitorture legislation advocated by organizations like the International Commission of Jurists has floundered, the exposé of torture societies and their techniques did have the effect of profoundly reducing the use of overt torture among states like the aforementioned Iran and Greece during the last stages of their repressive regimes.

Vigilante groups are a powerful deterrent to crime. Militia patrols tend to deal out rough justice to offenders on the spot instead of bringing them before civil authorities. This usually takes the form of a beating for crimes of theft or pilfering. The militia is also expected to take part in propaganda work and to change the thinking of bad elements.

A recent (official) report from Tientsin talked of militia units "organizing, arming, and propagandizing the masses and rebuffing the wrecking activities of a handful of class enemies." The People's Militia appears to do quite an effective job of law-and-order maintenance. Its main drawback is that a paramilitary organization of this sort can sometimes grow too powerful. "The first task of the militia is to back up the People's Liberation Army in time of war. Urban units in large cities are trained in sophisticated techniques of warfare, including antiaircraft defense, rocketry, antitank exercises, and tunnel warfare. The second function of the militia, however, is to assist the public security forces in maintaining law and order, and militiamen and women on patrol with rifles and fixed bayonets are a familiar sight."[33]

Guilt societies are less concerned with psychological manifestations than with the sociological recognition of wrongdoing. The guilt society rests on authorities implanting a clear recognition that there is such a thing as deviance from norms, that those who perform deviant acts are guilty by virtue of that fact alone, and that those who are normative are innocent by virtue of obedience to those norms. Guilt societies rest on the authoritative justification of normative behavior; on the assumption by deviants as well as punishers of the soundness of the social order or public property.

Although we have characterized China as a shame-guilt society, the imposition of such a shame-guilt axis is not without its own form of coercion. A 1978 report issued by Amnesty International made it quite plain that between 1949 and 1975 at least, China could be characterized as a nation of legally sanctioned coercion through a relatively high imprisonment system.[34] The trial system was either closed to the public, or in more serious cases, consisted of mass public trials that represented little other than big meetings to announce sentence. The penalty system involved supervised labor, rehabilitation through labor, and control over movement in lesser cases. While the death penalty was not invoked frequently, it did exist. More frequent were detention centers, labor groups, and punishment by long working hours, withdrawing of food, the absence of medical treatment, and harsh discipline within the prison confines.

There is a process of amnesty taking place in which people arrested and incarcerated for years have been rehabilitated, sometimes tragically after death rather than in life. But this does point out a theme I have emphasized throughout the work: that a vast gulf exists between genocidal societies and others that rest upon shame-guilt, or even imprisonment. It is nothing other than a gulf of life and death itself written on the faces of people.

Perhaps the classic model of the tolerant society is Great Britain, where norms, rituals, and rites are fully understood and appreciated but minority views are also found in great abundance. What characterizes these societies is firm allegiance to normative behavior and nondeviant behavior, while the normal apparatus of the state remains nonpunitive. It is left to the citizenry to apply proper social pressure to obtain obedience to the law. In the tolerant society, the practice of intimidation is carried on informally rather than formally, normatively rather than legally. The hegemonic character of island societies, like Great Britain or Japan, help to explain this moral basis of social order.

Finally, there are the permissive societies. They are identified by their open-ended responses to the question of what constitutes moral law or normative behavior. The permissive society not only tolerates deviance and dissidence but also understands that the role of the state is nothing other than the orchestration of a series of dissident and deviant acts without appreciation or understanding of what constitutes the perfect norm. Every permissive society has its legal limits, but even these tend to be stretched on behalf of the perpetrator no less than the victims of crimes, so that the legal system is involved in a series of plea bargains. The accused are not only presumed innocent, but also guilt is relatively shared by all concerned in the criminal process.

Where the United States might fit in such a modeling device is a subject for an entire volume. The brief discussion on its treatment of Indian peoples indicates similarities and continuities with nations elsewhere. Yet there is a special feature: The United States illustrates all eight elements in this typology, from the conduct of genocide toward its black population in the nineteenth century to permissive liberalism toward a variety of interest groups and deviant forces in the late twentieth century.

One might argue that any typology that cannot adequately settle accounts for the United States (and as we have already noted, countries like Brazil) is not worth much; that we are better off utilizing old-fashioned categories such as capitalism and democracy.

Such a typology as herein outlined does provide a new basis for comparison of the United States with other societies. True enough, to be left with an eight-part modeling device as an explanation of the United States raises proper questions as to the operational worth of the model as such. On the other hand, the mix between these eight items becomes crucial in the case of Western democratic states. Beyond that, the very inability to place such nations as the United States or Brazil in any one (or two) frames of the model itself indicates the complexities of advanced nations, not a need to return to an oversimplified model based on entirely mechanistic variables. The issue of the United States and other Western liberal societies can better be resolved once some clear-cut measures are established for those other countries, and they are in the disastrous majority, which reveal strong tendencies to fit into one or another of these frames.

Why should this be the case? If George Mosse is correct that genocide is deeply embedded in the cultural milieu of Central Europe, and there is a tragic amount of evidence to support this contention, then we can better appreciate how such a concept migrated to the New World. In a most unusual thesis on the mythology of the American frontier, Richard Slotkin suggests that "the Europeans who settled the New World possessed at the time of their arrival a mythology derived from the cultural history of their home countries and responsive to the psychological and social needs of their old culture."[35] While much of the language of this approach is shrouded in Jungian archetypes, the conclusions drawn by Slotkin stand apart from such theories: "This racial-cultural conflict pointed up and intensified the emotional difficulties attendant on the colonists' attempt to adjust to life in the wilderness. The picture was complicated for them by the political and religious demands made on them by those who remained in Europe, as well as by the colonists' own need to affirm-for themselves and for the home folks-that they had not deserted European civilization for American savagery."

While this helps to explain the genocidal attitudes of colonists toward Indians, it does not explain why such attitudes were not translated into genocidal practice against blacks. For in addition to Jungian archetypes of regeneration through violence, American colonists also exhibited Lockean constitutional persuasions fused with a French utilitarian culture, in which every person was to count as one-no more or less. From the outset, the "three-fifths" doctrine, by which black slaves could be differently punished, came upon hard times. The basis of American values was that individuals rather than collectivities are judged and either punished or rewarded. That is why the myth of genocide in America remained just that, and never had widespread public support. But given the realization of the Holocaust in bastions of advanced European culture, one must take small comfort in purely judicial constraints on genocide.

The problem of applying the model to concrete cases notwithstanding, we at least have a nonreductionist sketch of types of societies in terms of a life-and-death continuum. Almost every society has all eight types present in one admixture or another. It becomes an analytic task to determine the essential characterization of the system and the point where quantity is transformed into quality: at what point the numbers of people involved in sanctions by the state begin to define the character of that state.

Beyond an appreciation of types of societies that promote or oppose genocidal practices is the final realization that "types" of people are extremely resistant to their own elimination:

▸ The black population of the United States is larger in numbers and percentages than at any time in its two-hundred-year history.

▶ Despite the utter decimation of European Jewry at the hands of the Third Reich, the total present-day Jewish population is equal to, if not greater than, it was start of World War II.

▶ Even the American Indian population of the United States more than doubled between the census reports issued in 1960 and again in 1990.

Without becoming self-satisfied or counseling benign neglect about genocidal practices, it is nonetheless a fact that the growth of organized resistance to destruction of one's group or person should not be minimized, even in this age of maximum state power.

10

Totalitarianism as a Penal Colony

Not even the dead are spared when the living become lost and grow evil.

— Milovan Djilas[1]

IF THE CENTURY CAN BE POLITICALLY SUMMARIZED IN A WORD, ONE WOULD BE HARD-PRESSED to find a more appropriate term than collectivism. The necessity for getting products to the market and policies into practice seem to speak of the need to move beyond the individualist ideals of the British and U.S. empirical traditions. But beyond politics as such is the need to define the century in systemic terms, or in terms that which go beyond the political in any conventional sense. In doing so the most appropriate word to be developed is "totalitarianism." For in its completeness, the potentials for taking lives is multiplied beyond anything known in previous epochs.

A few elementary points are in order, foremost of which is that while there are many collectivist societies in the twentieth century, covering a range from fascism to communism, there have been few, if any, that have upheld the principles of democratic governance. This has been the unspeakable blemish that has converted ecstasy into agony for devotees of democratic socialism — a fusion easier to erect in theory than to observe in practice.

As a result, and without obscuring the differences between communism and fascism at one end of the libertarian scale and communism and social democracy at the other, it is fitting and natural to focus on the former Soviet Union as a prototype in this discussion of totalitarianism and state power. Soviet communism was the self-proclaimed model of collectivism. It continues to claim adherents, and its memory has fueled powerful ideological beliefs and political processes that have survived its demise as a system in one nation. Unlike fascism, even in defeat communism has been able to command sympathy from an admittedly amorphous Left within democratic societies. This makes it eminently feasible to focus on the great masterpiece that has emerged out of the ashes of twentieth-century Communist history and legacy: *The Gulag Archipelago*. In the analysis Solzhenitsyn therein provided, personal testimony is added to the shank of modern totalitarianism. As he noted in his Nobel statement:

> This twentieth century of ours has proved to be crueler than its predecessors, and its horrors have not been exhausted with the end of its first half. The same old atavistic urges — greed, envy, unrestrained passion, and mutual hostility — readily picking up respectable pseudonyms like class, race, mass, or trade union struggle, claw at and tear apart our world. A primitive rejection of all compromise is given the status of a theoretical principle and is regarded as the high virtue which accompanies doctrinal purity. This attitude creates millions of victims in ceaseless civil wars, it drones into our souls that there exist no lasting concepts of good and justice valid for all mankind, that all such concepts are fluid and ever-hanging. . . . Less and less restrained by the confines of long-established legality, violence strides brazenly and triumphantly through the world, unconcerned that its futility has already been demonstrated and proven many times in history. It is not even brute force alone that is victorious, but also its clamorous

justification: the world is being flooded by the brazen conviction that force can do all and righteousness — nothing.[2]

The first volume of *The Gulag Archipelago* is a classic statement of social reality. It is widely acknowledged as the foremost contribution to the literature on power and power-lessness, and it will continue to contribute to that literature long after the biography of the author ceases to be a point of contention or argumentation. A sure measure of a classic is that any one specialist is unable either to encapsulate or for that matter emasculate its contents. From this flows a second measure of high quality: the desire it arouses in every field and specialist to interpret the book's contents from a particular professional vantage point. In a work such as this, ubiquity and grandeur go together.[3]

Since *The Gulag Archipelago* is a work of autobiography as well as of biography, ethnography, sociology and history, it is impossible not to comment on Solzhenitsyn, although the efforts to lionize as well as to dismiss this extraordinary man are really quite independent of this latest publication. Yet *The Gulag Archipelago* also stands apart from the personal career of a single individual, even its author. The work is more than the sum of the 277 other contributions to the volume, many made by persons Solzhenitsyn has kept anonymous. While it can be considered as all one piece with his other works, *One Day in the Life of Ivan Denisovich, The Cancer Ward,* and *The First Circle*, this volume is singular. *The Gulag Archipelago* itself is only two-sevenths of a work, only two parts of what the author intends as an "experiment" in literary investigation. Those who argued that the book has exaggerations or mistakes have long since been set to rout by the publication of the other five-sevenths, or the second and third volumes. *The Gulag Archipelago* is not simply a trilogy on Soviet slave labor camps; rather, it is a narrative on everything from twentieth-century Russian history to the course of European dictatorship. But above all, it an allegory on the trained capacity of dictatorship to eat its own, to destroy diversity and individuality in the name of collectivity, or at least the organic ideal of preserving the state at all costs.

Solzhenitsyn is a writer. It would be a mistake to call him a sociologist, or for that matter, a novelist. He conveys experiences, he recites the truths of an entire society. He captures the essence of civilization in the degeneration of one individual's behavior toward another. On the other hand, in the tradition of literary realism, his individuals typify and represent an archetype within society as a whole. Beyond that, Solzhenitsyn is a product of two clashing systems of culture: Marxist-Leninist sociopolitical theory and Russian literary tradition. His intellectual vision is thus fused with a sense of politics characteristic of Soviet Marxism as a whole and with a capacity for irony and a certain pessimism characteristic of Russian literature, particularly its nineteenth-century classic period. He knows nothing of formal social science techniques, probably could not care less about ethnographic safeguards, and is not interested in characterizing a society from the point of view of a general theory of totalitarian political systems, the history of an organization called the Communist Party, or the fate of individuals within the penal colony formerly known as the USSR.

In *The Gulag,* Solzhenitsyn takes for granted that the Soviet Union as such was a total institution, a network of integrated agencies of coercion dedicated to the survival and promulgation of maximum state power over minimally empowered human beings no matter what the extent of the carnage. Few have been privileged to write from inside the whale; yet even those who have suffered similar outrages and tried to explain conditions or consequences to "outsiders" have been unable to create such a compendium of horrors.

The Gulag Archipelago should be viewed as a series of both national and personal experiences, a set of lessons in fear and courage, in being oppressed and in doing the bidding of the oppressor, in working the system and in being ground down by the system. Whatever polarities come to mind appear in *The Gulag Archipelago*, Solzhenitsyn has written the great antitotalitarian dialectic, the supreme work of literary and social analysis that finally placed the Soviet experience into a contemporary perspective that can at least be theoretically tested. Vague, didactic Leninist tracts on the withering away of the state; outrageous Stalinist equations of Communist life with the principle of happiness; the Brezhnev-Kosygin reduction of détente into a series of statements about mutual stagnation — these mythological politics give way, crack apart in the documentary history of Russian suffering before, during, and after the Russian Revolution.

Solzhenitsyn provided an experiential work that was the opening salvo in the collapse of the Soviet empire. It offered a framework of human resistance to degradation no less than an analysis of the longest-running totalitarian regime of the twentieth century. If the work saddens in the immensity of the horrors committed in the name of the state, it liberates in its appreciation that such a system has very poor staying power. As such, it remains, a decade after the collapse of the Soviet empire, a huge step forward in the development of a political understanding of genocide and its consequences.

The Gulag Archipelago brings to mind, with its documentary evidence of the slaying and imprisonment of tens of millions of Russians, comparison with the Japanese experience at Hiroshima and Nagasaki as recounted in Robert Jay Lifton's *Death in Life* and the Jewish experience of the Holocaust as recounted by Raul Hilberg in *The Destruction of the European Jews*. But the Soviet experience is unique, precisely because terror was self-inflicted, because Russians killed and maimed other Russians; albeit often of different national backgrounds.

In this sense, the banality of evil spoken of by Hannah Arendt is carried one step further; for the terror is not U.S. airplanes over defenseless Japanese cities or the destruction of European Jews at the hands of the Nazi Gestapo. However awful these other holocausts may be, the enemy, for the most part, was external. In the Soviet case, the enemy was also for the most part, internal.

The Gulag Archipelago offers a special sort of Dostoyevskian nightmare in which Russian spies upon Russian, Communist betrays Communist, Red Army officers destroy Red Army officers. All of this national self-immolation, in Solzhenitsyn's words "cauterized the wound so that scar tissue would form more quickly." But as Solzhenitsyn hints, there is more involved; the collectivist principle of criticism and self-criticism is raised to a pathological new high in which ideological purification is a consequence of purgation, in which intraparty struggle replaces in principle all party democracy, in which the notion of scientific evidence is overwhelmed by the notion of organization-inspired rumor.

For these reasons, *The Gulag Archipelago* has a fascination and a horror beyond even the literature of concentration camps. To die at the hands of a foreign tormentor or of a powerful adversary may be awful, but at least it is understandable. To suffer the same fate at the hands of one's own is a form of barbarism that permits Solzhenitsyn to consider Soviet Bolshevism as in a class with German Nazism. This point has thoroughly outraged Communist commentators on the book who have grown up with the belief that the fascist hordes were history's worst example of cruelty. Solzhenitsyn's comparison of the Soviet system to the fascist system — which in retrospect seems far more commonplace now than even a decade ago — must itself be ranked an act of extraordinary criticism and condemnation. He stepped over a psychological threshold of commentary few others dared to cross; at least prior to the collapse and exposure of the workings of the Communist system.

The Gulag Archipelago is the equation of political sociology with criminology and penology; that is, Soviet Communist praxis turned out to be the theory and practice of penology, of imprisonment. In Solzhenitsyn's paradigm of imprisonment, every aspect of the former Soviet system is converted into a science. There is a science of arrest, involving a structured system of questioning according to various criteria: nighttime and daytime, at home and at work, for initial arrests and recidivists, independent versus group arrests. Then there is the science of searches: how to conduct body searches, how to check out houses, even urinals; in short, how to flush out people.

Then there is the science of purge: how to isolate the victim from his own party apparatus, which Solzhenitsyn calls a grandiose game of solitaire whose rules were entirely incomprehensible to its players. The enormous impact on Communist cadres did not derive from their presumed vanguard position; rather, it was the other way around: it derived from their unique, studied ignorance of the real nature of Soviet society. The ordinary Russian peasant, spared the patina of Marxism-Leninism, was better prepared for the terror than the party cadre who bought the package labeled "dictatorship of the proletariat." All of these facts of the twentieth-century history of the science of the destruction of personality had very little to do with the lofty claims of egalitarianism and libertarianism made by the totalitarian leadership.

The Archipelago was a nation apart. Its victims were alone able to speak truth to power. It is as if the Archipelago alone had the right, ironically, to experience social science as social engineering, while the rest of society paraded forth under the mythical banner of Marxism.

We witness the amazing experience of social science emerging in the Soviet Union as a function of the rise of a prison system involving tens of millions of people. Distorted Pavlovian behaviorism, stripped of its humane ambitions, found its fulfillment in the Soviet state. This transition from Marxism to Pavlovianism was made possible because the Gulag Archipelago was more than a geographic sector. The prison system of the Soviet Union was far flung but it was connected psychologically, as Solzhenitsyn said, fused into a context and almost invisibly, imperceptibly, carried forward as a nation of the damned. It is not without irony that we still await a similar level of self-analysis from the German scholars studying Nazism.

Solzhenitsyn's *Gulag Archipelago*, while reminiscent of the writings of Raul Hilberg and Robert Lifton, also calls to mind the writings of Erving Goffman in *Asylums*. He combines these two types of macro- and microanalysis. It is a study of working within a system, surviving it and operating so as to make the system collapse under the weight of its self-imposed lunacy and limitless bureaucracy. A great deal of the book's social psychology has to do with the counterscience of prisoner life, the grim humor of survival in which a mistake means life, and hence a science that has to be equal or better than the various sciences of arrest, search and seizure, and imprisonment inflicted by the state.

One of Solzhenitsyn's major contributions is to note how terrorism functioned as a structural feature of Soviet society rather than as an episodic moment in Russian time. That is to say, Solzhenitsyn does not simply speak about the Stalin era or about special quixotic moments in that era when terror was high but of the entire period of 1918-1956. The Gulag Archipelago existed because the need for terror replaced the practice of liberty within Russian life. Indeed, there was not very much liberty to begin with, since the czarist era was hardly concerned with the distribution of justice. However, the revolution of mass democracy never took place, at least for Solzhenitsyn, and terrorism immediately became institutionalized. Within this structural framework there were special eras, for example 1929-1930, when 15 million peasants were either slaughtered, uprooted, or imprisoned; 1937-1938, when party personnel, intellectuals, and cadres of the military were entirely wiped out; and again in 1944-1946, when armed forces personnel, prisoners of war, and all persons having contact with the West were similarly destroyed or disposed of.

Only the purges of 1937-1938 were remembered because intellectuals and party personnel were able to articulate their mortification. Millions perished in this Yagoda epoch, but still more perished in the other two high-purge periods. Solzhenitsyn indicated that a fourth huge round of purges was being prepared in 1952-1953, this time against Jews and other national minorities. However, the costs were considered so high that even the other members of the Stalin-appointed Politburo withdrew in horror at the thought of another round. Solzhenitsyn does not clarify matters by confusing waves of terror with Soviet military acquisitions after World War II. The occupation of the Baltic countries was ruthless, but it cannot be placed in the same category as the civil war period of 1918-1922. By minimizing the gap between peaks and troughs in the exercise of terror, the need for analysis is highlighted. Fortunately, the work of scholars like Richard Pipes and Adam Ulam rounded out the narrative of Bolshevik history.

The most fundamental issue of social theory raised by *The Gulag Archipelago* is whether terror was intrinsic to the Soviet system or confined to the Stalinist epoch covered by the book. Solzhenitsyn's viewpoint is that terrorism is endemic to the totalitarian system as such, and hence the problems of Bolshevism continued to plague the Soviet system until its demise.

But there remained the more intriguing issue: whether terrorism was a special technique of Stalinism employed to stimulate development and industrialization in a uniquely backward set of social and cultural circumstances; and hence whether communism could present itself with a benign face — which indeed it tried to do during the Gorbachev *glasnost* period.

Of course, Solzhenitsyn did not have the benefit of hindsight in writing about the Gulag. His position is twofold: Terrorism was a technique employed by the czarist secret police with equally telling (but limited) effects. Hence it was not solely confined to the secret police (OGPU) under Bolshevism; rather, it is part of the history of modern Russia as such. Beyond that, the terror of wartime conditions is finite and determined by military considerations rather than party idiosyncrasies. This might better serve to distinguish the exercise of violence in the Leninist phase from the resort to terror characteristic of the post-1929 Stalinist consolidation. It might also help us understand the turn away from terrorism (and toward benign authoritarian rule) in the post-1956 Khrushchev era. But all of these nuances are linked to levels of state terror, not to alternatives to a totalitarian regime.

While Lenin in practice preferred norms of "socialist legality," nothing in the Leninist corpus would or could limit terrorism as a strategy and tactic of development. Stalinism is thus a direct theoretical consequence of Leninism, not at all its diabolical corruption. Thus on the very day in 1974 when the first volume of Solzhenitsyn's book appeared in English, a *New York Times* reviewer cautioned against reading *The Gulag Archipelago* as more than a Stalinist happening. But what was better understood by Solzhenitsyn than his critics was the surreptitious resurrection of the Stalin cult in Russia — a development that has since been repeated in the resurrection of the Communist Party as a leading force in Russian politics.

Even prior to the demise of the Soviet Union, Soviet society was transformed from totalitarian to authoritarian modalities. The rise of middle sectors, bureaucrats, teachers, party officials, technicians, skilled craftsmen, and so on created the seeds of a consumer society without a conflict society, a mass society without mass democracy. This authoritarianism permitted the continuation of Bolshevik legend and myths but does not permit the reinstitutionalization of the kind of terrorism that existed under Stalin. Soviet history moved in a peculiar way: not one step backward to generate two steps forward, as Lenin suggested; but, rather, nineteen steps backward to permit twenty steps forward, as Max Nomad has suggested.

To think in purely Communist terms, has meant, empirically at least, a betrayal of the ideals of mass democracy in favor of a code book of party elites. The connection between the freedom of individuals and the necessity of development is not an easy issue to resolve, especially in the light of foreign assaults upon the Soviet Union. Rather than speak the unspeakable about the limits of democracy, it is simpler for Solzhenitsyn to retreat into religious self-actualization. But the foreknowledge that history rarely moves in lockstep with justice may help us better appreciate why the Soviet empire ended in such an abrupt manner and with a relatively small amount of bloodshed. It is as if a social order had been emptied of all potential for terror by the excessive usage of force. At that point, essentially at the close of the 1980s, the Communist system came to a crashing halt, lacking the military might to stave off reform or the moral nerve to preserve its state power.

At the theoretical level, Solzhenitsyn is saying that Russia was not ready for socialism, indeed was unfit for it because of its backward economy and political and social conditions. But the leitmotiv in his thinking was that Russia was also not ready for democracy. The Leninists attempted to speed up, even defy history, flying in the face of Marxist assumptions that each social system must run its full course before there can be a normal transformation of capitalism into socialism. The very backwardness of Russian society overwhelmed the Bolshevik Revolution that consumed it in the long run. Instead of breaking the back of feudalism, the Bolsheviks wound up breaking the backs of their own followers and supporters. The very attempt to speed up the historical process of economic development in the face of lethargy and backwardness became the hallmark of Soviet development, of what might well be termed feudal socialism.

Coercion is a necessary component of development. In all likelihood, the sacrifice needed for high development would be impossible without a mythic sense of purpose. The Soviet state constantly spilled over, failing to distinguish coercion from terrorism, failing to distinguish the forms of state self-protection from the rights of citizens. Within such a system, the Soviet Union achieved a level of development that even today is lower than that of its capitalist adversaries. The outcome was

not simply political betrayal but economic stagnation and a
dangerous kind of frustration, not so much within the Gulag
Archipelago as among those who might point to the Archipelago as a major source of the central problem of Communist
life — the problem of legitimacy.

A central theme in the second volume of Solzhenitsyn's
work is the differential forms of punishment meted out to
common criminals vis-à-vis political prisoners.[4] The constant
denial of the existence of political prisoners by Soviets (and
one would have to add, Americans) becomes a charade to
mask the criminal nature of the state itself. Legislation is
created to distinguish forms of criminality: "For him [the thief]
to have a knife was mere misbehavior, tradition, he didn't
know any better. But for you [the political prisoner] to have
one was 'terrorism.'" Thus we have the master dialectic between crime and punishment, the individual and the state, the
rights of the person and the limits of authority, and perhaps
more painfully, the obligations of the citizen and rights of the
state. *The Gulag Archipelago* is compelling not simply as an
exposé of Soviet Party history or its penal system but as an
introduction to the entire gamut of normative issues that have
plagued Western civilization since its inception. Marx and
Engels recognized these issues and dealt with them by fiat,
declaring in principle that socialism would witness the withering away of the state. But in Stalinist practice such a diminution
of authority never occurred: Circumstances always blocked
the path of true historical necessity, and in the vise of this cruel
hoax, tens of millions of Russians were squeezed to death.

Solzhenitsyn's work suffers the defects of its virtues. Like
the U.S. prison literature of an autobiographical sort, it has a
searing intimacy that at times disguises a paucity of theory. No
large-scale explanation of the Soviet experience, no cost-benefit analysis is forthcoming. One is left feeling that no meaningful mass involvement in or defection from Soviet society was
registered throughout its entire seventy-five-year history. This
is clearly a point of view which is clearly unrealistic, first given

the Soviet Civil War experience, and above all, the large-scale popular support for the state generated during the war against fascism. It may very well be that the Russian people were fighting for the enduring features of Russian civilization rather than the Bolshevik system. Exactly such a pan-Slavic appeal was made by the Nazis (with mixed results, as the archives of Smolensk indicate), an appeal that seems to have left, at least in small measure, a mark on Solzhenitsyn and explains why little is said of repression and terror under czarism and why he offers so little in the study of continuities in Russian terrorism. It is as if terror that wore a nationalistic face was more acceptable to Solzhenitsyn than terror that came in a naked internationalist guise.

The theory offered to explain Soviet terrorism comes close to a conspiratorial view of history, as if a supreme being were masterminding the takeover of the Soviet world by the Devil and the expulsion of God: "It was essential to clean out, conscientiously, socialists of every other stripe from Moscow, Petrograd, the ports, the industrial centers, and later on, the outlying provinces as well. This was a grandiose silent game of solitaire, whose rules were totally incomprehensible to its contemporaries, and whose outlines we can appreciate only now. Someone's far-seeing mind, someone's neat hands, planned it all, without letting one wasted minute go by."

This is not to deny that real conspiracy existed. Wherever democracy is absent, the potential for conspiracy is present. But to explain such a gigantic event as the death and imprisonment of tens of millions of people as a conspiracy falls badly short of what is required at the macro level of explanation. The answer is right at hand: The fundamental impulse of both Stalinism and Leninism was rapid development. Industrial development can sacrifice consumer modernization along with the people it involves in the developmental process. One might argue that the amount of terror was not commensurate with the tasks at hand, that less terror and more benign forms of coercion might have achieved the same results; but the denial of the results is what weakens Solzhenitsyn's analysis. His myopia concerning Soviet achievements also denies him the possibility of a real theory explaining Soviet terrorism and returns him to a primitive Christian view of good and evil that even Christianity has abandoned.

Goethe once explained that the trouble with Christianity was its impulse to cast problems in terms of good and evil, when in fact the real ethical problems people face are choices between good and good. This choice of goods, or perhaps of evils, breathes real-life tension into social systems. And it is the absence of this awareness of the struggle between developmentalism and terrorism, between the creative life-giving forces no less than the death-making forces, that makes Solzhenitsyn's work a series of horrors relieved only by the author's personal genius as a writer.

But in summing up that first volume, it is evident that *The Gulag Archipelago* has given us what few believed would ever be possible: a series of case histories of the Communist Party of the Soviet empire — not a series of party visions and revisions, not a series of myths and illusions consecrated by the initial holders of power, but a study in state authority untrammelled and unfettered by popular will. The history of the Communist Party of the Soviet Union is ultimately the history of crime and punishment in the Soviet Union: the ultimate fusion of politics and deviance.

It really matters little that *The Gulag Archipelago* is not an entirely balanced or fair-minded work, that it fails to recount properly and fairly the heroic events of Soviet development and of the Soviet people in the face of all sorts of foreign military adversity. Were this a work balancing the worth of the Soviet system on a cost-benefit scale, we would simply have a volume in economic theory, or even worse, a bookkeeping, double-entry system that fails to measure in qualitative terms the monumental architectonics that made the Gulag Archipelago possible. What is so immense about this book is that one comes to realize that no one remained untouched by the Gulag

Archipelago, that the dirty little secret of the society as a whole was that the Soviet Union *is* the Gulag Archipelago, and that a description of prison life is a description of Soviet life. It serves little use to recite the joys of industrial achievement in the face of this awful truth. The Soviet Union became, at least between 1918 and 1956, a total institution.

What happened between the collapse of Stalinism as a system and a coda within communism to change the parameters of the game, to limit and curb the prison-house atmosphere of Russia is little explored by Solzhenitsyn. He never did tell us whether the Archipelago ended in 1956 or whether he simply stopped his story at a point beyond which he had no first-hand evidence. We are left not so much with a conclusion as with a giant ambiguity; one that is not removed by the publication of the remaining two volumes.

The *leitmotiv* of totalitarian systems is the painful and shameful absence of mass resistance. "Today those who have continued to live in comfort scold those who suffered." Solzhenitsyn adds rhetorically: "Yes, resistance should have begun right there, at the moment of the arrest itself." This sense of moral turpitude, not unknown to a generation of Israelis reflecting on the European Holocaust, is all-pervasive; not the least because Solzhenitsyn survived his own shame of silence. But he learned his lesson well. *The Gulag Archipelago* can be viewed as a lesson in courage, a statement of personal survival through conditions of imprisonment, intimidation, and indignities. In the fusion of biography with history, this masterpiece comes to fruition, and the dedication "to all those who did not live to tell it" is astonishingly redeemed.

We are reminded by Solzhenitsyn of the special circumstances in which his work was produced: "I am finishing it [*The Gulag Archipelago*] in the year of a double anniversary (and the two anniversaries are connected): it is more than fifty years since the revolution which created the Gulag, and a hundred since the invention of barbed wire (1867). This second anniversary will no doubt pass unnoticed." In this way a herculean project began as a testament in 1958 and completed in 1967 came into the world. But it took an additional decade to move this work into a larger Western democratic consciousness — long after the pageantry of the fiftieth anniversary of the Russian Revolution passed into oblivion.

The Gulag Archipelago is classic because it makes plain the essence of genocide in the twentieth century. The dialectic of the century emerges on countless pages and in endless details: in the guise of socialism we receive bureaucracy, in the place of popular control we are provided with elite management, instead of the liquidation of state power there emerges an augmentation of such power; in place of abundance through industrial development we get deprivation as the price of such development. And ultimately, in place of justice we get the law. If before Solzhenitsyn we were able to recite conventional platitudes about this century being the best of times and the worst of times, now we are forced to the grim realization that these have become simply the worst of times. In other troublesome ages, such as the fourteenth century, one must recognize as a redeeming virtue the perception that calamities were not deliberate, that they were the result of unconscious force of nature wreaking havoc with humanity. The conscious force of repression (called "racial destiny" by the Nazis and called "historical necessity" by the Communists) destroys so many people that the concept of humanity itself assumes a tenuous dimension.

It shall come to pass that the literate population of the future will be divided between those who have read and understood the lessons of the Gulag and those who have not read it — or even worse, read and not understood the broad implications of this "experiment in literary investigation." Already the cloudy voices of cynicism, fused with the fatuous voices of childlike optimism, have begun to assert the exaggerated political manners of Solzhenitsyn. Using as a pretext his Harvard commencement address on "The Exhausted West" (it is far simpler to make statements and render judgments on excerpts from a speech than to work through the experience of three volumes of *The Gulag Archipelago*), intellectual scribblers and political hacks assure one and all that Solzhenitsyn not only does not understand U.S. society but has already lost touch with Russian realities. Indeed, this same fate has befallen him upon his return home to Russia after the collapse of the Soviet empire. In the meanwhile, like a phoenix, *The Gulag Archipelago* remains beyond contest, beyond dispute, and — as is that rare characteristic of a masterwork — beyond good and evil doomed to repetition in Cambodia, Somalia, Bosnia, and only God knows where else.

The major accusation launched against Solzhenitsyn is of his emotivism and presumed mysticism. Underlying this charge is the more serious charge that he lacks adequate analytic categories; hence that his critique is one-sided, that it fails to take into consideration the positive achievements of Soviet industrialization. While it is doubtlessly correct that he uses emotional language, it is simply nonsense to claim that he preaches mysticism. Irony makes the sufferings described and the outrages committed bearable. The catalogue of evils presented never — *not on a single page in three volumes* — involves any mystical commitment to blind faith or self-destructive acts. To be sure, insofar as any act of heroism, courage, and self-sacrifice involves a transcendent belief in the human condition, Solzhenitsyn stands accused; but to the extent that mysticism is adaptation or surrender to antihuman behavior or acceptance of "man's fate," he is entirely innocent. This is, after all, a special variety of prison literature; and prisoners who write books seek freedom, not immolation. Indeed, the burden of the final volume is a testimony to rebellion, resistance, and retaliation. It is an effort to answer the question: "Can a man's urge to stop being a slave and an animal ever be reactionary?"

Solzhenitsyn's *Gulag Archipelago* has an implicit analytic scheme that deserves to be dealt with seriously, even profoundly. For in this towering statement of prison life in a totalitarian society there are "lessons" about twentieth-century social systems as a whole. The political sociology of Soviet society illumines the contours of a future that indeed can "work"— at least in short bursts. Herein lies its terrors for us all. And if that political sociology spills over into a political theology, it is nothing less than a consequence of universal ideologies confronting each other in mortal, perhaps eternal, combat. And if this creates an aura of Manichaeanism, of the substitution of good for right and evil for wrongs, reification in itself must be viewed as a consequence of political systems, of state power reaching out for an ultimate domination of individual life. The "evils" of capitalism that spawned its "goods" were an impersonal dialectical necessity for Marx in the nineteenth century; but the "goods" of communism that spawned its "evils" were a draconian choice made by Bolsheviks old and new and then advertised as a necessity.

Stalin enjoyed posing issues in a pseudo-Jesuitical manner. Every phenomenon became a rhetorical question. "Is such the case? Yes (or no) such is (or is not) the case." Hence he gave us the political question, the national question, the women question, and so on ad infinitum. Solzhenitsyn's *Gulag Archipelago* can be read as a parody of Stalinism. He takes these macroscopic "questions" and shows how they work in microscopic concentration camp circumstances. The marriage of Marxist theory and Russian realities was stress-laden from the outset. The bitter rivalries and factions within the revolutionary movement attest to this strain. Stalin's great achievement was to have consolidated the Leninist pivot and created a new orthodoxy. But to do so meant an end to rivalries, factions, and debate itself. The doctrine was saved while the intelligentsia was wasted. The depoliticization of totalitarian society is an underlying reality every dissident and deviant must contend with. The ordinary Soviet citizen went about his business, not unlike the ordinary Nazi citizen: self-consciously unaware of events and myopically closed to the human consequences of the Gulag.

Rebellion and resistance to human slaughter is such an unusual event that its recording by Solzhenitsyn becomes a major aspect of the third volume. While not quite reaching the epic proportions of the Warsaw Ghetto uprising, the record of resistance from Kengir to Novocherkassk — personal and political — forms the essential core of the third volume. But such uprisings remained sporadic and isolated. They are handled bureaucratically, involving scant potential for resistance. It is therefore not the character of rebellion that becomes startling, but the simple fact that resistance is even possible. Leviathan emerges as a total way of life, cut off from popular limits. But it was this isolation of leadership from membership in the civil society that finally emptied the system of its resolve, of its capacity for violence and murder.

The Stalinist decision to emphasize economic development and industrialization muted any efforts at personal liberty. Only when work norms were not met or when political confusions arose from a series of crises of succession were any displays of resistance tolerated. What Solzhenitsyn depicts is the first society in which economics is completely sundered from politics, or, better, in which bureaucratic systems management becomes the norm. Russia became a civilization without a polity, and without a people who determine the nature of justice, there can be no morality. Only political participants acting in complete freedom can determine the nature of goodness. The Soviet empire before its demise became the antithesis of the Aristotelian paradigm; it did not even measure up to the Platonic version of communism since the dialectic of the best and the brightest was reduced to the dynamics of the mediocre and mindless.

His Christian persuasion notwithstanding, Solzhenitsyn, quite like other exiles who preceded him, continues to be the conscience of a socialism gone awry. Like every Russian of the modern age, he grew up with a belief in the national question as resolved by the socialist system. Lenin and Stalin, in their wisdom, appreciated the fact that no revolution could be successful only in class terms. The ethnic and national variable was the crucial linchpin to the successful conclusion of the revolutionary phase.

> Only when the twentieth century — on which all civilized mankind had put its hopes — arrived, only when the National Question had reached the summit of its development thanks to the one and Only True Doctrine, could the supreme authority on the National Question patent the wholesale extirpation of peoples by banishment within forty eight hours, within twenty four hours, or even within an hour and a half.

The many nations of Russia that did not fit plans for totalitarian unification were extirpated singly and collectively: Chechens, Ingush, Karachai, Balkars, Kalmyks, Kurds, Tatars, Caucasian Greeks, Germans, Balts, Estonians, Karelo-Finns; and, as Solzhenitsyn reminds us, the Jews were being readied when Stalin came to his end in 1953. The numbers of peoples totally liquidated read like an anthropological Who's Who of European and Asian peoples. When one asks who inhabited the Gulag it becomes evident that these millions of minority people were declared the chosen ones; chosen for liquidation.

> Neatness and uniformity! That is the advantage of exiling whole nations at once! No special cases! No exceptions, no individual protests! They all go quietly, because they are all in it together. All ages and both sexes go, and that still leaves something to be said. Those still in the womb go, too, and are exiled unborn, by the same decree.

One might argue that this is the necessary price of national unification. But if that be the situation, it was a price extracted with a gigantic political myth, with the promissory note of the rights of all peoples and nations to self-determination. Ideology and reality were never further apart. What the West did with a melting pot the Soviets did with melting people; a system of hard labor, penal servitude, exile, and death. This became the style of Soviet totalitarian substance. Perhaps the end of ethnic groups is an anthropological and historical fact, but the end of people as individuals is a political and military policy. And the Bolshevik authorities saw fit to make no fine, hair-splitting distinctions.

Solzhenitsyn offers a traditional romantic vision of women. If they are not elevated in their nature, they are at least deserving of very special concern. But instead of this being an irritant, one realizes that this is not only a sincere sentiment frankly expressed, but a shrewd antithesis to the totalitarian equation of women's liberation with socialism. Indeed, the special pains Solzhenitsyn takes with their camp treatment, the abuse they endure as women, indicates that the Soviet revolution transformed society unilaterally, with the treatment of women no better or worse than the treatment of peasants, intellectuals, and ethnic minorities. But what does make matters worse is the special vulnerability of women: the unique torments of an unwanted pregnancy, gang rapes by violent criminals as a reward for their abuse of political prisoners, types of work that are brutal and serve as a special form of demoralization for women. The hypocrisy of the system was in calling attention to the special nature of the "Women Question" as an inheritance of Western democracy and capitalist servitude.

> The body becomes worn out at that kind of work, and everything that is feminine in a woman, whether it be constant or whether it be monthly, ceases to be. If she manages to last to the next "commissioning," the person who undresses before the physicians will be not at all like the one whom the trustees smacked their lips over in the bath corridor: she has become ageless; her shoulders stick out at sharp angles, her breasts hang down in little dried-out sacs; superfluous folds of skin form wrinkles on her flat buttocks; there is so little flesh above her knees that a big enough gap has opened up for a sheep's head to stick through or even a soccer ball; her voice has become hoarse and rough and her face is tanned by pellagra.

The women came to the Gulag sharing with the men the same illusions, and later, slow emergence of consciousness. Among the early women prisoners were those hauled off into the Gulag driven naked between formations of jailers and singing to their tormentors: "I know no other country / Where a person breathes so freely." But by the 1950s, these same women became the ferocious defenders of their fellow inmates; fused into solidarity by long sentences and desperate lives. "Events outstripped the casual contempt which the thieves feel for *females*. When shots rang out in the service yard, those who had broken into the women's camp ceased to be greedy predators and became comrades in misfortune. The women hid them. Armed soldiers came in to catch them, then others with guns. The women got in the way of the searchers, and resisted attempts to move them. The soldiers punched the women and struck them with their gun butts, dragged some of them off to jail (thanks to someone's foresight, there was a jailhouse in the women's camp area), and shot at some of the men."

> When the prisoners rebelled at one penal colony and won forty days of self-determination, this represented the first real breath of freedom these women had known. "The runaway escapes to enjoy just one day of freedom! In just the same way, these eight thousand men had not so much raised a rebellion as *escaped to freedom,* though not for long! Eight thousand men, from being slaves, had suddenly become free, and now was their chance to live! Faces usually grim softened into kind smiles. Women looked at men, and men took them by the hand. Some who had corresponded by ingenious secret ways, without even seeing each other, met at last! Lithuanian girls whose weddings had been solemnized by priests on the other side of the wall now saw their lawful wedded husbands for the first time-the Lord had sent down to earth the marriages made in heaven! For the first time in their lives, no one tried to prevent the sectarians and believers from meeting for prayer. Foreigners, scattered about the Camp Divisions, now found each other and talked about this strange Asiatic revolution in their own language. The camp's food supply was in the hands of the prisoners. No one drove them out to work line-up and an eleven-hour working day.

The Gulag does not offer a confrontation of traditionalism with modernity, but convention against barbarism. And in the

Gulag everyone knew barbarism would win out in the end. "Newlyweds observed each day as their last, and retribution delayed was a gift from heaven each morning." Irony of ironies: prisoners know a freedom denied to citizens of the Soviet society as a whole.

> The tension of the first two volumes of *The Gulag Archipelago* largely derived from the loggerheads at which "criminals" were juxtaposed over and against "politicals." Repeatedly, Solzhenitsyn shows how the regime re-creates a doctrine of brutal class warfare by utilizing criminals to intimidate and even assassinate political prisoners. The lumpen proletariat of Marx is deproletarianized under Stalin; but it performs the same tasks on behalf of the state: from strike-breaking to organized mayhem. The cynicism of this is displayed by the offering of women to the criminals, by moving them into camps where political trouble is brewing. Solzhenitsyn rises above the cheap claptrap of jailhouse lawyers who try to interpret every act of imprisonment as a political torment. He uses language exactly and precisely; in short, scientifically. Their commune, more precisely their world, was a separate world within our world, and the strict laws which for centuries had existed in it for strengthening that world did not in any degree depend on our "suckers" legislation or even on the Party Congresses. They had their own laws of seniority, by which their ringleaders were not elected at all, yet when they entered a cell or a camp compound already wore their crown of power and were immediately recognized as chiefs. These ringleaders might have strong intellectual capacities, and always had a clear comprehension of the thieves' philosophy, as well as a sufficient number of murders and robberies behind them. And what did their word "frayersky" — "of the suckers" — mean? It meant what was universally human, what pertained to all normal people. And it was precisely this universally human world, our world, with its morals, customs, and mutual relationships, which was most hateful to the thieves, most subject to their ridicule, counterposed most sharply to their own antisocial, anti public *kubla* or clan.

For two volumes these miserable, incarcerated creatures play out a living class struggle while the Soviet authorities offer metastases about the achievements of the Gulag: "a collective organism, living, working, eating, sleeping, and suffering together in pitiless and forced symbiosis." But in the third volume, the tension shifts.[5] Prisoners who are ordinary criminals learn, albeit slowly and painfully, the manipulative nature, essence of the regime, while the abused politicals learn to adopt the cutthroat ethic of the criminals in a kind of Darwinian trade-off. But it is one that worked for a short time at least.

> By 1954, so we are told, it was noticeably in transit prisons that *the thieves came to respect the politicals*. If this is so, what prevented us from gaining their respect earlier? All through the twenties, thirties, and forties, we blinkered philistines, preoccupied as we were with our own importance to the world, with the contents of our duffel bags, with the shoes or trousers we had been allowed to retain, had conducted ourselves in the eyes of the thieves like characters on the comic stage: when they plundered our neighbors, intellectuals of world importance like ourselves, we shyly looked the other way and huddled together in our corners; and when the submen crossed the room to give us the treatment, we expected, of course, no help from neighbors, but obligingly surrendered all we had to these ugly customers in case they bit our heads off.

It turns out that a third category of prisoner exists in Soviet labor camps, distinct and distinctive: the religious prisoner. This well-represented group was extremely important. They bore witness to tragedy, but they did so in a way that confronted the vacuum of Soviet ideology with the force of some higher and more noble belief. In their nonviolent commitments, they were the touchstone of conditions for all prisoners. When religious prisoners were tormented, maimed, or shot, that became a cue that all hope was lost. Only then was resistance viewed as the only recourse — futile and folly-laden though it might appear.

The Jews are represented in all three categories: common criminals, political opponents of the regime, and religious people dedicated to a higher set of principles. Solzhenitsyn does not make much of it; he does not have to. The surnames of Gulag residents reveal this fact. Hence Jews suffered a sort of triple risk: If they engaged in entrepreneurial acts they were reviled as bourgeois remnants; if they engaged in human rights activities they were condemned as Zionist plotters; and if they asserted their religious commitment to Judaism they were obscurantists and fossils substituting ancient dogma for the "science" of Marxism-Leninism. This threefold persecution makes the Jewish condition especially poignant and dangerous. The liquidation of the Jewish population of the Soviet Union is just as much an agenda item as their liquidation by Nazi Germany. The Nazis were cruel: They wanted dead bodies as dead souls. The Soviet authorities were willingly ready to settle for dead souls only; hoping, like the Inquisition, that the living bodies would convert to communism, becoming in the process productive workers of the state. That many died in the process distinguished Communist from Nazi forms of anti-Semitism. In the Soviet scenario, such death was an accident, in the Nazi program, such death was a planned, central feature of state power as such.

But the gap between Nazi plans and Communist accidents cannot be exaggerated. As the newer post-Soviet literature makes clear, there had been collaboration on a broad scale between the Ukrainian police and the German military. As John and Carol Garrard make clear in *The Bones of Berdichev,* the idea that two dozen Germans had killed 30,000 Jews was preposterous. The Ukrainian police had participated not only in the round up of the Jews, but also in the actual killing; and the property of the Jews had been looted by their neighbors. As Walter Laqueur notes in reviewing this sad episode, "Berdichev had been the rule rather than the exception."[6]

The participation of some Russian citizens and Communist cadres in their own degradation helps to explain why Solzhenitsyn's *Gulag Archipelago* has the capacity to shock and disturb. Surely it is not for lack of a literature on the subject of Soviet state terror. The archives are filled with scholarly treatises and personal testaments alike. And such early efforts as Vladimir Tchernavis's *I Speak for the Silent*; Pitirim Sorokin's *Leaves from a Russian Diary*; and Ivan Solonevich's *Russia in Chains* have the capacity to evoke similar powerful moods and sentiments. To be sure, Solzhenitsyn exhibits an exactitude as well as a collective judgment rarely before assembled in such force. And there can be no question that his fame as a great writer, not to mention the circumstances of his exile from the Soviet Union, also played a part in making *The Gulag Archipelago* special.

Another element is present, one with ominous consequences. Our analysis of totalitarian society is, like our analysis of nuclear conflict, too easily based on a spurious exchange theory, on a trade-off between industrial growth to postwar survival and the number of deaths involved. We are inclined to accept certain levels of death or even mass annihilation if the ends in view can be achieved. Thus, we are inclined to say, if it takes 30 million lives to create a Soviet beatitude, then so be it. But which 30 million? And why one number and not another? Could the same results have been achieved with fewer deaths or less suffering? What in past centuries was a sense of historical cost, even necessary cost, for social change and economic expansion in our century has become a willing, and even an enthusiastic, endorsement of the idea of costs to achieve not infrequently spurious benefits.

I submit that the special nature of Solzhenitsyn's impact derives from his keen awareness of the substitution of engineering for ethical criteria in evaluating the human soul. He does not speak *against* development but, rather, *for* those countless millions who paid the price for development. And in compelling a fresh review of the actual costs paid and the dubious benefits received, he has restored the balance between political realities and moral possibilities. This is by the close of the final volume in the trilogy not just the story of a people or even of a system, but of decision making by political rulers intent on preserving their system and their privileges within the system.

Even a masterpiece may have flaws. Solzhenitsyn's single-mindedness would make that inevitable. The major problem in the final volume of *The Gulag Archipelago* is the rather weak empirics of concentration camp life between 1957 and their closings. The transition from totalitarianism to authoritarianism in the final phases of Soviet life is left unexamined in favor of a vaguely stated premise that only a total overhaul in the Soviet system, indeed a counterrevolution, would change the internal dynamics of Russian life. But in point of fact the killing fields were closed before the collapse of Soviet power. And at the other extreme, Solzhenitsyn despairs about a post-Soviet generation of Russian youth who walk about with their portable radios and with their arms around their shaggy girls, and who could not care less about the Gulag system that was. But is that system the same? Is it merely a shell of its former self? Is this a work of history or social life?

In terms of values and norms, Solzhenitsyn answers in the affirmative; that the Gulag lives. And we have every reason to believe this to be the case. Predetermined prison sentences of dissidents continued until the collapse of communism. Persecution of the politicals has few rivals in the world. The same dried-out Leninist rhetoric continued unrivaled again until the end of the Gorbachev epoch.

Still, there did seem to be growth in the middle sector, and concomitant demands for observing legal norms that did not formerly obtain. The sheer reduction in numbers within the Gulag requires some sort of explanation that Solzhenitsyn is seemingly unable to provide. Indeed, in his later musings, after returning to Russia in the early 1990s, he confused his assault on the genocidal character of the Stalnist regime, with the opulence and uneven distribution of wealth found in the Yeltsin regime. In this sense, it might well have been that the depoliticization of Soviet society was so thoroughgoing that the need for an immense Gulag was reduced to manageable proportions in the post-totalitarian phase of the Soviet regime. Perhaps this is more frightening than the Gulag itself, implying as it does a society that has itself become a willing penal colony, where good people are given time off for good behavior as long as they strictly observe one rule: Thou shalt not question the political regime and its bureaucratic processes. But the current evolution of a multi-party system has infused Russian society with precisely the pluralism that those who suffered under previous regimes find most difficult to explain.

By the time *The Gulag Archipelago* was completed, a work the author never saw in its entirety as a unity prior to publication, Solzhenitsyn realized its literary imperfections: repetition and jerkiness — what he calls the mark of a persecuted literature. But such repetitions, far from being superfluous, are essential. The apostles each repeated the story of Christ's crucifixion and redemption. The magnitude of human suffering is no easy lesson absorbed at one sitting. The Afterword offered by Solzhenitsyn is one of those rare moments when the "hyphen" in the Judeo-Christian heritage is breached, and the Father of historical redemption fuses with the Son who bears special witness to human suffering:

> I want to cry aloud: When the time and opportunity come, gather together, all you friends who have survived and know the story well, write your own commentaries to go with my book, correct and add to it where necessary. Only then will the book be definitive.

When the history of the Soviet genocide is published in full, and in one of those huge multivolume editions Russian publishing was famous for trumpeting, then we shall have an operational test of the potentials as well as limits for freedom within totalitarian states.[7] And while this process of recovering the past is now painfully underway in Russia, Solzhenitsyn's towering trilogy still stands as the century's landmark effort in preventing us from going gently into the totalitarian night.

Part III

FUTURE AS MEMORY

11

Memory as History

We need to force ourselves to think beyond the platitude that genocide is an abomination, and to understand the more difficult thought that it represents an unending moral temptation for mankind. The danger of genocide lies in its promise to create a world without enemies. Think of genocide as a crime in service of a utopia, a world without discord, enmity, and suspicion, free of the enemy without or the enemy within. Once we understand that this utopia is the core of the genocidal intention, we have to realize that this utopia menaces us forever. Once we understand genocide as utopian, we understand also the vulnerability of universalism.

— Michael Ignatieff[1]

IN HIS THOUGHTFUL VOLUME ON *A HISTORY OF THE JEWS*, PAUL JOHNSON NOTED A SPECIAL property of the Nazi regime in power: its frightening dualism. "Right to the end, Jews were the victims both of sudden, individual acts of thoughtless violence, and of systematic state cruelty on a mass industrial basis."[2] The diary of Victor Klemperer and the memoir of Peter Gay, each in their own distinctive ways, illustrate this dual character of Nazi terror. The intensely psychological nature of these works, which internalizes the disintegration of civil society in Germany after the rise of National Socialism, especially in the 1933-1939 period, are important as records of the period. They also constantly remind us that this murderous regime took root in the most advanced, cultivated and highly educated nation of Europe. Those who believe in and write of the Enlightenment, like Peter Gay[3] and Victor Klemperer[4] themselves, are thereby compelled to struggle with a paradox that seemingly does violence to our collective sensibilities. We want to believe that owning a dog, eating healthy food, listening to a Mozart quartet, reading a novel by Thomas Mann, enjoying the poetry of a Heinrich Heine, are the mark of civility itself. Otherwise, of what use is higher education, of what value is learning in itself? Let it be said at the outset that the dichotomy between personal cultivation and moral standing is not resolved by these two efforts. Klemperer and Gay, as is characteristic of a particularly enlightened Jewry, live in a world where religious identification matters a great deal, but God hardly at all. Still, the enormity of this "frightening dualism" of random violence and organized terror haunts these works.

Those two distinguished intellectual and literary historians share with us their personal and intellectual experience with thoughtless violence and systematic terror. The duality of Nazism is an evident leitmotif throughout both works. But the larger contradiction is compounded by personal contradictions. Here are two brilliant scholars, Gay writing an essentially autobiographical work of remembrance, and Klemperer maintaining a diary so that the rest of us will remember, whose essential intellectual commitment has been less to German order than to French freedom. Peter Gay is the author of a magisterial two-volume work on the Enlightenment as well as a work on Voltaire, while Klemperer much earlier had completed a major work on eighteenth-century French literature with a special interest in the *philosophes* before he concluded his diary. This attraction to a presumably democratic and secular culture in France strikes me as a typically Jewish characteristic. I suspect that even Gay's long-standing interest in Freud and the European bourgeois condition has more to do with the emergence of a European consciousness, of which Jews felt more at ease, than with any nationalist claims. Both Gay's and Klemperer's works set in motion a clash of high cultures: European culture with its center in the German language, and Jewish culture with far weaker claims on their loyalties. As painful as it may be to acknowledge, for both men Nazi terror rather than Jewish or Hebrew training imposed a sense of Jewish consciousness. To the credit of both, such basic shifts in value structure from generation to generation are not disguised. Indeed, both love the German liberal tradition, and this provides a certain tension to each of these radically different literary enterprises.

Victor Klemperer was one of only 198 registered Jews from the city of Dresden who survived the war. The remaining 1265 had been deported to Riga, then to Auschwitz and Theresienstadt to meet their terrible fate. Most were shot or gassed upon arrival. Klemperer was spared deportation; the Allies saved him one day before his number was up with the enormous February 13, 1945 bombing of Dresden. In the confusion that followed Klemperer and other Jews removed the yellow Star of David identifying them as Jews, and spent the next three months on the run until they made it to southern Bavaria in a section occupied by American forces. In this way, a narrator fearful of death throughout the war manages the miracle of survival. And we have the benefit of an extraordinary memoir, one that offers a mixed message in describing personal fortitude and moral acquiescence.

It is almost as if the evils of Nazism are a given, and what needs to be reported is the quotidian horror inflicted by a totalitarian regime on an essentially non-political figure, raised in a liberal Jewish atmosphere, who later converts to Protestantism more as a matter of convenience and respect for the woman of his life who was to become his wife. The bare bones of the story are well told by the diarist and his translator in a Preface. But it is clear that this is a work of more than casual significance—its sales history in the original German language edition itself bestows upon *I Will Bear Witness* a special position.

In his diary entry for February 23, 1938, Klemperer imagining a post-Hitlerian world, asks himself: "What would be different for me in the Fourth Reich, whatever form it took? Probably I would only then face the very greatest loneliness. Because I could never again trust anyone in Germany, never again feel myself to be uninhibitedly to be German" (p. 251). Gay, for his part, relates a moving experience with the outstanding Franz Neumann, his older Columbia University colleague: "Here were two intelligent academics dangerously near a quarrel, both men of goodwill, both German born, both émigrés who had had a close call. We let it drop; though I did not stop thinking about the incident. I did not realize it then, but the episode was evidence that there was no 'correct' attitude to take toward the Germans. Individual experiences and private emotions, not all of them directly related to life under the Nazis, justified whatever attitude we took" (p. 4).

The reflections of an already mature scholar like Klemperer are obviously not as benign or as sanguine as those of a mature scholar looking back on his childhood—for Gay's book is essentially a memoir of a childhood long past: He was an outstanding student, stamp collector, sports enthusiast—one better watching than playing. This is a story of a child within the "German inferno." but still remote. Germany was a land filled with hatred, but it had yet to bubble over into the Holocaust. By self-definition, Gay was a good boy, attentive and serious. One is repeatedly struck by the sense of comfort and class, a good boy from a good family. He endured only occasional anti-Semitic taunts from teachers and student at the Goethe Realschule where he was a pupil from 1933 to 1938, and spent his first thirteen years in a quiet street in Wilmersdorf in the western part of Berlin. Gay lived in a world of supportive people—Jews and Christians, good Germans all. There were family friends and business associates like Emil Busse, and neighbors like Walter Schrieiber who owned and shared the collected works of Charles Dickens. But a dark undercurrent was omnipresent. As Gay observes: "in Nazi Germany, jokes were no joking matter." Even his departure from Germany was shrouded in ambiguity—he recalls the terrible episode of the St. Louis failing to secure landing rights in any U.S. port after the Cuban ruler invalidated the landing cards of its near 1000 Jewish passengers. The episode left Gay wondering about the United States as well.

Gay writes feelingly of his years in the United States. His studies, his dissertation on Eduard Bernstein, the leader of German social democracy. The work ends on a note of reconciliation. For Gay this means giving as much attention to German as to French and British sources for the Victorian bourgeoisie and the European Enlightenment.

In the final analysis, Gay distances himself from those who have a "preoccupation" with Nazi Germany and its consequences. He frankly admits that "I understand this preoccupation but I do not share it." In a bitter finale, he declares that "I have deliberately refused to dwell on the mass murder of Europe's Jews. I have avoided movies that deal with it, even important ones, like *Shoah*. It results in a continuing feeling of ambiguity, "no closure to offer."

His memoir ends on a curious note. He adds his voice of protest to a tenure decision on Elizabeth Noelle-Neumann, the German political pollster who worked in Goebbel's propaganda ministry. He concludes the book by saying "Noelle-Neumann is guilty until she is proved innocent. Is this fair? Is that objective? Certainly not. It only shows that Peter Fröhlich of 1938 and 1939 is still alive in Peter Gay in 1997." One is left with the ambiguity felt by a scholar, an ambiguity stemming not from ignorance, but perhaps from knowing too much. Gay's life and memoir are not likely to satisfy fanatics, zealots, or nationalists. He is not a religious man, not a devout Jew, not a Zionist. He permits you to read his memories and make your own judgment. The sad part is that we cannot help him, and he cannot much help us. So much death, carnage and disruption—and its legacy is "to be continued" But most likely, memoirists other than Professor Gay will continue it.

Peter Gay has called Klemperer "one of the greatest diarists—perhaps the greatest—in his review of *A Diary of the Nazi Years* (in the German language). Regardless of whether such a judgment will stand the test of time, (frankly, I think that it will) the fact remains that the two books, *My German Question* and *I Will Bear Witness* are yoked by ambiguity as much as analysis. For Klemperer the ambiguity is even deeper than for Gay, since he was a convert to Protestantism, and hence views cases of other converts being denied burial rights in Church grounds as "moral suicide." Klemperer writes as Simmel's outsider to everything: outside the Nazi State, outside the Jewish community, outside the intellectual world. Indeed, it is precisely this sense of externality, of peering through a looking glass darkly, that gives his extraordinary diary (of which this is but the first volume, the second to be issued next year) its poignancy. There is a certain non-judgmental approach in entry after entry. The special tax on Jewish assets (from 20 to 25 percent in 1939), and the requirement that supplementary name "Israel" be added to all Jewish entries in the telephone directory on pain of punishment, are greeted, as nearly everything before and after, from a narrow viewpoint. These outrages "affects me as little as the telephone. Poverty also has its advantages" (p. 319). Repeatedly, Klemperer admits to "feeling emotionally cold." The only exception is Klemperer's feelings for his seriously ailing wife Eva, for whom he has a "real love." In his own words, Klemperer notes his highly personal aim. "The main events aren't as important for my record as is the everyday of the tyranny, which might be forgotten. A thousand gnat bites are worse than a single blow on the head. I observe, I note the gnat bites."

What gives Klemperer's diaries their special brilliance is the consistency of his clinical style, The Jew-baiting characteristics of *Der Sturmer*, in which Goebbels speaks of the need to "exterminate [Jews] like fleas and bedbugs" is followed not by analysis but oblique references to Hegel, Condillac and Helvetius (p. 128).

It is almost as if intellectual life cauterizes emotion so as to limit the damage of reality. When Klemperer encounters a traffic jam caused by a young man shouting, "Whoever buys from the Jew is a traitor to the nation!" he says only "After a while, I walked on" (p. 133). The migration of friends and colleagues to far away place becomes a backdrop to having a pension, owning a car, and learning to type (pp. 142-43). In the midst of sad discussions on emigration, random comments on decision and District Court rulings, there are careless sentences like "And in what way are the Zionists different from the Nazis?" (p. 199). Visits by Hitler to Mussolini are noted with random remarks about the diarist's "heart condition."

Indeed, a constant preoccupation with personal health is evident in frequent visits to doctors and optometrists. Self-referential remarks about his book in the making makes one wonder if Klemperer actually ever understood the relationship between the larger political world and his private world. Indeed, not until the end of volume one, does a sense of linkage, of connectedness emerge—all too late for him and his fellow victims of the Nazi Era. The year 1941 was his most dreadful: "Dreadful because of our own real experience, more dreadful because of the constant state of the war, most dreadful of all because of what we saw others suffering (deportations, murder)." It took much travail for Klemperer to rise above his own dislikes and aversions — and they were many — into some sense of the collective suffering.

Ultimately, the problem with Daniel Goldhagen's thesis of the Germans as a whole being infected with eliminationist anti-Semitism,[5] and no less with Peter Gay and Victor Klemperer's emphasis on individual guilt or innocence, is the absence of anything other than a psychoanalytical vision of the Holocaust. In fact, the issue turns not on guilt or innocence, collective or individual, but on decisions and policies of a totalitarian State determined to eliminate the Jewish people from the face of the earth. What started as a secondary element in the conduct of a supposed thousand-year Reich was transformed into the goal as the survival of the Third Reich beyond a few years became patently dubious. Memoirs and diaries, however brilliant and illuminating, have severe limits. Above all, they cannot make plain the character of a political system and a social structure that can destroy all private lives and all good wishes and all selfish intentions. We are mesmerized by the work of Klemperer or Gay, not because of the brilliance of the writing or the fair-mindedness of their judgment, but by our retrospective awareness that what took place is so far beyond the real intellectual reach of the psychoanalytical or personal.

I suspect that Peter Gay, and perhaps being called utopians, although in the case of the latter we shall never know would disturb Klemperer. But both of these works suffer from utopianism: a continued belief in the eighteenth-century idea of progress, the nineteen-century idea of socialism and the late twentieth-century idea of being a European. These are civilized authors for whom rationality in thought and centrism in politics is a way of life. This nationality led to a certain disarming sensibility as to the meaning and the content of being Jewish. Gay hardly disguises his marginality to all things Jewish, while Klemperer was a convert to Protestantism and married to an "Aryan woman" whose special status spared Klemperer a train ride to a Nazi death in 1945. But just as World War One witnessed the dissolution of the idea of a working class International led by the Communists, and the emergence of intense nationalisms that enlisted Germans. Frenchmen, Englishmen, Italians, and finally Americans, to engage in another war to end all wars, so too, did the emergence of Nazi Germany make clear that the idea of Europe was a myth, crushed under the weight of national destiny and racist extremism. These two fine works by scholars, who did not blink in the face of what they saw and lived through, must be taken as a half-measure to an understanding of Nazi Germany. Ethnography is not yet sociology; memoirs and diaries from the trenches are not yet histories and policies orchestrated from the top.

Yet this, too, must be said. If we require evidence that such testimonials and diaries as provided by Gay and Klemperer are very much needed, not only in the name of personal therapy but no less as a requirement of history, we have other examples to consider, such as the work of Professor Hagen Schulze. For the only sense in which his *Germany: A New History* is new is its date of publication.[6] One can hardly imagine a more old fashioned type of history. It is essentially a pictorial record emphasizing the positive accomplishments of a Germany before and after the Nazi hordes seized power. The degree to which such an effort can be described as history or apologetics is something better left to those students of Germany who have made the study of that nation a lifetime chore. I confess to have enjoyed the pictures, even though their connection to the text is sometime obscure, and even contradictory—as was the use of Heartfeld's illustrations of Hitler receiving financial support from the bourgeoisie, when the text claims, I believe correctly, that Nazism was a mass movement rather than an elite movement. What does concern me is the astonishing periodization of German history in Schulze's text.

One of the most acute and compelling tasks of historians is carving up or segmenting the universe. How the historian frames the "picture" tells us much about his biases and preferences. In this case, the Hitler Epoch is divided between the seizure of power in 1933 through the invasion of Russia in June, 1941 and the entry into the war of the United States on the Allied side in December, 1941. My own view, and I believe that of most historians, sees the pivotal point of the Hitler Epoch as the invasion of Poland, and the consequent declaration of war by England and France as constituting the actual start of the Second World War—this was in September, 1939. One might also view December, 1941 as the period in which the fateful decision was made at the infamous Wansee Conference, that 1942 would begin the monumental shift in Nazi war aims from the liquidation of the democracies, to the extermination of the carriers of democratic values—the Jews. But Professor Schulze has his own agenda, his own sense of German history which disguises apologetics in the long view—one in which Nazism is an unfortunate twelve-year blip in an otherwise distinguished record of national achievement.

Schulze attempts to camouflage the final years of the Third Reich of Adolf Hitler by linking them with the post-war Germany of Konrad Adenauer, thus artificially creating a single period from 1942 to 1949. In this way, the period of mass extermination, of the Holocaust, is neatly incorporated into the period of gradual reconstruction and denazification. That this piece of historical legerdemain is actually carried off without a bow to the overwhelming facts of the 1942-1945 period is an assault at the work of countless historians, Jewish and German, who have recognized the special nature of this period of the Nazi regime, moving from random, sporadic assaults on the Jewish communities, to terrible harassment and humiliation, to a systematic utilization of State power to murder millions of people. Schulze can scarcely bring himself to even mention the Holocaust. And in burying this defining moment of the century, indeed, the millennium, in his description of a gradual movement from totalitarian to democratic regime, he commits a terrible moral sin, something more serious than an error of historical judgment.

By such a strange distortion of history, Schulze attempts to disguise through obfuscation the most obvious fact of post-war reconstruction: that it came about through military defeat of the Nazi behemoth by the combined armed forces of the United States, Great Britain and the Soviet Union. Indeed, the change of regimes in Germany was not an internal or evolutionary element, but the result of external forces on the ground. At a time in history when life was measured in days and hours, when the Nazis tried in sheer desperation to snatch victory from defeat, in a victory measured by the body count of innocent people, the need to emphasize 1945 as the end date of Nazism is evident. The glossy paper, the high resolution photographs, not to mention the apologetics masquerading as history, makes one suspect that this work had the support, spiritual if not material, of something more than Harvard University Press, its publisher. Slick paper and slick thinking notwithstanding, this volume does not represent the high point in that esteemed press's history. But Schulze's work does remind us that the struggle for the memory of the century is not over. The testimonials of survivors in exile or at home in an alien world transform the Jewish conscience into a living presence. Such works as those provided by Gay and Klemperer will help prevent callous indifference to Nazi totalitarianism. The loss of memory by the young is a far more serious concern than denial of the Holocaust at the fringes of academic respectability by the old and the foolish.

George Steiner wrote an essay in 1959, recently reprinted, on contemporary Germany called "The Hollow Miracle," where he notes that "everything forgets; but not a language. When it has been injected with falsehood only the most drastic truth can cleanse it. Instead, the post-war history of the German language has been one of dissimulation and deliberate forgetting. The remembrance of horrors past has been largely uprooted."[7] Steiner probably would have been wiser to say suppressed rather than uprooted, since no phenomenon as devastating and thorough as the holocaust can be uprooted.

That it took until 1986 to open up such a discussion, and in the process, to revitalize what Steiner thought to be dead—the German language—is hardly a wonder. But in this act of consciousness, however clumsy and filled with apologetics, the restoration of not just the German language but the potential of the German nation can be detected. *Forever in the Shadow of Hitler* is a collection without an introduction. It lacks even the semblance of order, and is drawn from a variety of authors with diverse (to put it mildly) views. The volume has been published in a physically pedestrian way, and if it can be believed, was prepared without an editor. Nonetheless, it is must reading; an awful phrase usually reserved for popular novels that hardly last out a publishing season.

The *Historikerstreit*, as the battle over the nature of the Nazi legacy has come to be called, contains the raw texts, and perhaps reveals the raw nerves of current debates by German sociologists and historians of the Nazi Epoch. This is not simply a debate between Ernst Nolte and Jürgen Habermas over whether the Holocaust was real, rather, it is a discussion of whether the Holocaust is unique, or a continuation with genocides the world over, and totalitarian regimes that raged throughout Europe under the flag of international communism in Russia no less than National Socialism in Germany.[8]

German historians and sociologists, in seeming obliviousness to Jewish literature examining the same issues, argue whether the Holocaust committed by the Germans against the Jews is a unique event in history, or one of many inflictions visited upon oppressed peoples. Both Nolte and Habermas treat these issues from the viewpoint of a perpetrating culture; the effort is viewed by both as an attempt to settle accounts with the meaning of German national identity. Habermas's charge of apologetics is complex; stating that the guilt of Germany is being wished way by Nolte in the general upsurge of totalitarianism of all sorts. Nolte in turn charges Habermas and his followers with emphasizing the Holocaust not so much to remind the German people of the atrocities committed by the Hitler regime, but as a mechanism to minimize similar atrocities perpetuated by Stalinists in the name of the Russian people.

The passions which German historians of culture bring to the subject are sufficiently complex to rescue the discussion from banality. Still, in contrast to Jewish historians like Raul Hilberg and Lucy Davidowicz, both sides lack a scalpel-like exactitude in describing the Holocaust: there are no discussions of numbers, techniques, or the timing of destruction. The German penchant for "abstract thought" permits the people of Germany to choose sides between the uniqueness of the Holocaust and the universality of totalitarianism without quite coming to terms with concrete history as such.

The bitterness of the debates notwithstanding, and without choosing sides, these are not evil historians or social critics. They are rather people whose craft comes upon issues that cannot be solved simply by appeals to evidence, tradition, or convention. Both Nolte and Habermas face this essential problem, albeit in different ways. Nolte must place the Holocaust in the context of a generalized expression of totalitarianism during the period of 1918 to 1991, with special emphasis on commonalties between Hitler's National Socialism and Stalin's international communism. He does not excuse the crimes of fascism any more than Bullock did in comparing the careers of Hitler and Stalin, but he sees them as part of the crimes of totalitarianism. Habermas for his part seems unable to acknowledge the destruction of many ethnic peoples under Stalin, and the continuities of a centrifugal ideology that the Soviet system shared with the Nazi system.

On this point Habermas scores heavily against Nolte and his formidable associates. He examines the uniqueness of the Nazi assault against the Jews, over and against the more "rational" objectives of the Nazi war machine. For Habermas, the question of moral responsibility inheres precisely in this assault on a people rather than the conduct of a war. For if the destruction of the Jews was simply an extension of a general assault by totalitarians against ordinary people, then we are dealing with a quantitative continuum, not a qualitative break, from the past. And for Habermas, this becomes Nolte's apologetic escape hatch, an opportunity to link Nazism with Communism, even in its treatment of Jews and other national minorities.

The essays in this volume provide testimonial for one or another variety of the contrite conscience. In the process, a great deal of light in shed on the German mentality, especially its capacity for extracting a problem of scholarship from the

ashes of its own inspired tragedies. It is less the moral thundering of Habermas and Nolte than the effort to define a national
identity (a phrase heard often in these essays) and biological
liquidation that is the leitmotif of the minor figures in particular. Andreas Hillgruber's linkage of the "twofold fall": the
military collapse of the Third Reich and the murder of the
European Jews need to be examined more closely. He lacks a
sense that the murder of the European Jews became an end
unto itself for fascism, whether or not the Nazi Empire or its
advanced posts survived or crumbled.

The best of German scholarship assaulted this cleansing
effort, this attempt to relativize national socialism. The work
of Hans Mommsen, Wolfgang J. Mommsen, and Jürgen Kocka,
Robert Leicht, Kurt Sontheimer, and Martin Broszat take on
the challenge. One gets the impression that the democratic
historians won the battle, while the revisionists like Nolte won
the popular war. The parallels between German defeats and
Jewish destruction and between the unfairness of Nazi guilt as
similar to the guilt charged to Jews are effective. Finally, the
wild assumption that the 1939 statement by Chaim Weizmann
and the other leaders of the Zionist Movement declaring
Nazism as the enemy of the Jewish people, somehow entitled
a Nazi response, in effect reverses cause and effect. Nolte's
blame's Jews for stimulating the Nazi policies that were crys-
tallized in the Wansee Declaration and ended in the slaughter
of European Jewry.

Neither side to the debate tries to explain the specific timing
of the Holocaust. Why was the actual slaughter of the Jewish
masses actually undertaken between 1942 and 1945, when all
but the most desperate within the German high command
knew that the war against the Allies had essentially been lost?
The Nazi epoch reigned for thirteen years. But the actual
slaughter of the Jews was confined to the last three. The first
ten could be considered prologue. One might argue that the
goals of war shifted for the Nazis—from the defeat of the
Allies to the slaughter of the Jews. The decade of softening up

public opinion had been sufficiently successful to make possible this shift of gears in Nazi goals. To the German Right the shift in goals makes sense only as a response to the Jewish Menace, while to the German Left it was part of the reactionary nature of the regime. Neither side wishes to deal with the consensus that the Nazis had established to find a victim to blame for the loss of the war if it could not find a cure to the cause of the war. If Jewish historians are missing from the analysis, then the German people are missing from the text altogether.

Both sides are essentially correct in their critique of the other, but less than convincing in defense of their own views. Habermas and his colleagues do indeed emphasize the unique nature of the Holocaust. They do so not just to give the Jewish people their due, but to weaken the sense of their own culpability in past left-wing totalitarianism. Nolte and his supporters correctly suggest the unity of totalitarian systems. But they sometimes do so not in order to excoriate the foundations of such a global phenomenon, but to restructure and weaken the sense of unique responsibility of the Nazi regime and the German people for the unscalable Holocaust. Karl Dietrich Bracher put the matter most succinctly: "The shame about the failure of a cultured civilization, one that believes itself formed by the values of Christianity, humanism, and the Enlightenment, can help us to recognize the dangers of totalitarian manipulation. References to similar phenomena in other civilizations should not relativize that experience; rather it should broaden it and make it general. That means not only a remembrance of the past but also a warning for the present and the future."

Unique events in the history of societies can always be linked to historical processes that have taken place elsewhere, while continuities in the tragedy of human destruction clearly reveal unique elements depending on the culture and climate of a people and a place. One suspects that Nolte and Habermas know this. But the question of the uniqueness or universality of German culpability, if it has no empirical content, must have a moral answer, since a people as powerful and central to fin de siècle economy and polity can hardly claim the mantle of victim. The issue rephrased becomes: do Germans get on with the task of being dominant admitting the ultimate sin of massive life-taking, or do they get on with the task of remaining dominant by relativizing their sins, linking them to a tradition of twentieth century tragedies.

In short, for this book, the Holocaust is a German Question, not a Jewish Question. These are essays and articles written for the most part in *Frankfurter Allgemeine Zeitung* and *Die Zeit*. They are not aimed at foreign consumption, nor intended to assuage foreign opinion that Nazism haunts the German soul. I suspect this is not only or even primarily because of what happened to the Jewish people, but instead what happened to the German people. The discussion will not hardly please the Jewish people with the level of understanding shown, nor will it give the remainder of Europe a sense of confidence that Germany is capable of anything other than a highly formalist notion of democratic order. And it is Nolte that senses this better than Habermas since it is he who appreciates the totalitarian temptation that lurks beneath the views of Habermas.[9] In the very act of condemning the uniqueness of German guilt, there is an implicit denial by Habermas of the Soviet system, a system to which he gave more than lip service during most of the post war/cold war epoch.[10]

Despite the sharper overall intellectual understanding of totalitarian politics by Nolte, neither and even less so, Habermas carry the ideological day. Those who took a middle position as Immanuel Geiss, sense as much. Only those capable of "walking the tightrope" emerge as rational, if inconsequential actors. The crimes of Nazism and the crimes of communism have become melded and blended over time. The moral fervor with which Habermas and Rudolf Augstein assault Nolte is contrasted to the moral obtuseness of the latter. But neither side to this debate comes to terms with the Holocaust as an event unto itself, apart from Nazism and Communism as systems of competing totalitarianism. Astonishingly enough, we are left with a sense of Christian revival, a "worldwide renaissance with fundamentalist trends in the various religious communities."

What begins with a discussion by professionals of the place of Nazism in German history, ends with the place of German history in the revival of, and redemption offered, by Christianity. Little wonder then that the great debates in Germany on the Holocaust fizzled out into self-examinations of a rather puerile sort. The German self-evaluations end by leaving victims and vanquished in essentially the same relationship they were prior to the entrance into this *kulturkampf* by German men of learning. With German identity rooted in the realm of economic growth, Jewish identities have seemingly faded into the background, left to argue the realm of symbolic politics among themselves and their survivors. But at least, in this very bitter debate, some possibilities for the restoration of the German language in its classic form have reemerged. These debates within German academic life provide the English speaking reader with a window of opportunity to understand and penetrate the new German ideology. We learn not so much why the Holocaust happened, but appreciate how it could happen again. This is the consequence of a people and a regime that continues to retain the idea of utopia as rooted in the world of totalitarian social order.

12

Banality of State Power

The results clearly and decisively show that democracies commit less democide than other regimes. This is the underlying [principle] of all my findings on war, collective violence, and democide. The less freedom people have, the greater the violence, the more freedom, the less the violence. I offer this proposition here as the Power Principle: power kills, and absolute power kills absolutely.

— R.J. Rummel[1]

THE ISRAELI WRITER, AMOS ELON, CUT THROUGH THE DE-BRIS of celebration and condemnation by noting that "Hannah Arendt made many small errors for which her critics will never forgive her. But she also got many of the big things right, and for that she deserves to be remembered."[2] It is my contention that Arendt along with Solzhenitsyn were the two most important figures in the postwar effort to explain the relationship between totalitarianism and life taking. Together they have redeemed the conscience of German and Russian humanity.

Hannah Arendt was born in Hanover, Germany, of German-Jewish parentage in 1906. She was educated in Koenigsberg and later Heidelberg. After fleeing to France from Germany in the late 1930s, she immigrated to the United States in 1941. She was naturalized as an American citizen in 1950. Most of her life was spent in the academy. She was a Guggenheim fellow in 1952–1953; visiting professor at the

University of California at Berkeley in 1955; the first woman appointed to a full professorship at Princeton University in 1959; and visiting professor of government at Columbia University in 1960. From 1963 to 1967 she was university professor at the University of Chicago. And in 1967 until her death in 1975 she served as university professor at the New School of Social Research. It is fair to say that Arendt was an intensely urban person, and that being proximate to San Francisco, Chicago, and New York meant at least as much to her as the university affiliations as such.

The publication of *The Origins of Totalitarianism* in 1951 established her as a major figure in post-war political theory. In that work she attempted to provide a unitary approach to totalitarianism as such, seeing differences between National Socialism and Communism as of lesser significance than the organizational and cultural linkages that such systems have with each other. Such systems have a common base in the leadership principle, in single party politics based on mass mobilization rather than individual voluntary participation, and not the least, in a near insatiable desire to expand from nation to empire—whether directly through military adventure or indirectly through political infiltration.[3]

Anti-Semitism functioned differently in Germany under Hitler and in Russia under Stalin, but they had the same common roots: the existence of disparities between social classes and the need for objectivifying an enemy responsible for all shortcomings and defeats suffered by nations and systems. Arendt's powerful critique of anti-Semitism was directly linked to her participation in Jewish affairs once she came to the United States. She served as Research Director of the Conference on Jewish Relations between 1944 and 1946; and then as executive director of Jewish Cultural Reconstruction in New York between 1949 and 1952; or just prior to her fame and assumption of the round of university posts mentioned earlier.

Arendt's views on genocide extended far beyond her *Eichmann in Jerusalem* volume. Indeed, unconstrained by journalistic narrative, she developed a general theory of totalitarianism, in which the subject of genocide was thoroughly explored. In defining Nazism, she argued against the idea that it is simply a distorted extension of Western culture as such. "Nazism owes nothing to any part of the Western tradition, be it German or not, Catholic or Protestant, Christian, Greek or Roman... On the contrary, Nazism is actually the breakdown of all German and European traditions, the good as well as the bad."[4]

Arendt, rather than view genocide as a special property of Germans or Austrians (or any other people) considered it as nihilism in action, "basing itself on the intoxication of destruction as an actual experience, dreaming the stupid dream of producing the void." Not a few of Arendt's critics consider this formulation as apologetics, a way in which she was able to reconcile personal relationships with politically conservative mentors and lovers like Martin Heidegger with a larger series of politically liberal, and sometimes radical, claims. But whatever the truth of such strongly biographical claims, her views on national types are well within the mainstream of twentieth-century social theory.

The single most important element in *The Origins of Totalitarianism* as it pertains to genocide is that prospects for mass murder and selective mayhem are embodied in the structure of totalitarianism as a system rather than the special national characteristics of any particular people. The forms of totalitarianism may vary—Nazi, Fascist, Communist—but the content allows for genocidal acts regardless of the ideological proclivities of the extremist regimes.

The ground for such genocidal actions is prepared by the denial of citizenship, of political and legal rights of the victim class. Arendt offered a brilliant examination and support of Edmund Burke's critique of abstract arguments of human rights that are divested of concrete sentiments of those natural rights that spring from being part of a nation. Arendt notes that "The survivors of the extermination camps, the inmates of concentration and internment camps, and even the comparatively contented people could see without Burke's arguments that the abstract nakedness of being nothing but human was their greatest danger. Because of it they were regarded as savages and, afraid that they might end by being considered beasts, they insisted on their nationality, the last sign of their former citizenship, as their only remaining and recognized tie with humanity." And in a stunning conclusion to the segment on imperialism, Arendt points out "that a man who is nothing but a man has lost the very qualities which make it possible for other people to treat him as a fellow man." And this stripping the Jews of legal rights through deprivation of the rights of citizens *per se* is the essential necessary (if not sufficient) condition for genocide to take place.

There is an ambiguity in her formulation, in that at times, it is the size and power of government as such that provides the seeds for totalitarian rule, while at other times, it is the cultural and psychological conditions that define prospects for totalitarian domination. So it turns out that totalitarianism depends on the assumption of power by the extremists at a point in time when state machinery is "frozen," that it is calcified and unable to remain a process. But it also turns out totalitarianism is made possible by the widespread installation of fear and what she calls "total terror." And the totalitarians' system is one in which victims and executioners alike are selected without regard to personal conviction or sympathies, but only in terms of rigid "objective standards" — i.e., who is a Jew and who is an Aryan.

The Origins of Totalitarianism ends on a creative ambiguity, one hardly restricted to Arendt. A great deal of argument within political theory after World War Two focused on just such examination of the causes of extremism and the breakdown of law and democratic order. We need to know whether it is politics or culture that defines the limits of power. For

otherwise, not only are we limited in understanding or responding to such ultimate horrors as the Holocaust, but the
nature of democratic options as such remain in precarious
limbo. For we need to determine whether totalitarianism is but
an extension of political processes mobilization and massification as such, or something quite different and antithetical to
those processes.

Arendt attends to this ambiguity in a work that appeared a
decade later. After *The Human Condition,* which might well
be seen as an interlude rather than continuation of the earlier
arguments about her fine German mentor, Karl Jaspers, she
returns squarely to the problem of totalitarian systems and
political change in what may well be her most underrated
effort:[5] *On Revolution.* Indeed, this work too is dedicated to
Jaspers, when she noted that he uniquely in *The Future of
Mankind* "dared to face both the horrors of nuclear weapons
and the threat of totalitarianism." *On Revolution* addressed
the world one step further. With the nuclear powers at a
stalemate, revolutions have become the principal political
factor of our time. To understand revolution for her became
the key to unlock the future.[6]

While *On Revolution* does not directly address issues of
genocide, Arendt does illumine new directions. In coming to a
psychological profile of political absolutism, a sense of how the
"passions" and the "taste" for power lead to the genocidal
state emerges. She takes Robespierre's theory of revolutionary dictatorship as the quintessential model of the European
encounter with politics, an encounter that ends in anti-poli-
tique. "The thirst and will to power as such, regardless of any
passion for distinction, although characteristics of the tyrannical man, is no longer a typically political vice, but rather that
quality which tends to destroy all political life, its vices no less
than virtues."

With the appeal to the political as a framework for rational
discourse, the sort of unique qualities that endeared American
and British civilization to Arendt, there can be no democratic

society. So that even in Revolutionary France from 1789 to 1794, the shouts of the day were "Long Live the Republic," and not "Up with Democracy."

Arendt remained in all her works the jurist, the legal analyst. Her concerns were to plumb the depths of legitimacy, not as an abstract discourse on nationalism, but as an effort to review the grounds that permit a people to survive even harsh and tyrannical conditions. In this, she was neither a conservative nor liberal, at least not in any conventional modes of those concepts. To be sure, this difficulty in easy characterization may be that property in Arendt that has proven most irritating as well as elusive to critics.

For example, Arendt saw in modern conservatism (in contrast to the writings of ancient Greek philosophers) a profound two-hundred-year response to the French Revolution, seeing it as a polemic in the hands of Edmund Burke, Alexis de Tocqueville, Eric Voegelin, and their modern followers. While liberals, for their part, were doomed to provide an uneasy rationalization for a totalitarian Revolution they could neither quite understand, accept in full, nor reject. But the ambiguity of such formulations notwithstanding, in this way, she compelled a fresh reading of historical events of enormous magnitude.[7]

It is questionable, and not at all certain, that Arendt had her causal ducks in a row on this theme. It would seem that Jacob Talmon, who also wrote on *The Origins of Totalitarianism* at the same time and with remarkably similar conclusions, was closer to the mark in suggesting that the radical segment of the French Revolution, and the French Enlightenment before that, were the human carriers of polemics as a way of political life. They cultivated conflict both as a style suited to ideological thinking and as a substantive way to treat political power. But that said, it may well be that conservatism for so many years did reveal re-active rather than pro-active tendencies. It did so until that point in time when it was once more linked to mass politics and political party life in America. But of course,

Arendt died just at that point in time when the transformation of conservatism from a class based theory to a mass-based practice was commencing. But these are considerations within democratic cultures that were far removed from the monolithic world of totalitarianism that allows for genocides.

As someone steeped in classical Catholic thought and the German legal tradition, the juridical order of things was critical to Arendt through her career.[8] The legal system is that logical artifact that both makes possible and calls forth the loftiest aims of human beings. At the other extreme, the appeal to law prevents or at least curbs the implementation of their most venal desires. These strongly ancient Jewish and classical Greek appeals to the legal as the logical were invoked by Arendt both to illustrate the survival of the human race, and its function to limit and ultimately thwart the totalitarian temptation behind the genocidal invocation.

On Revolution is a continuation of discussions first broached in *The Human Condition* and in *The Origins of Totalitarianism*. Since this work is something less than social science and something more than mere speculation, perhaps a prosaic ordering of Arendt's materials is not only forgivable but necessary. Overlooking her contempt for the "modern debunking 'sciences' psychology and sociology," I shall state her position in proposition form and offer possible lines of disagreement and further inquiry.

War and revolution have violence as their common denominator. Conflict derives from fratricidal instincts, and political organization has its roots in crime. Crucial to revolution in the modern age is the concurrence of the idea of freedom and the experience of new social beginnings, of apocalypse.

Revolution gains a new significance as war, its partner in violence, becomes an implausible way to effect social change. Total annihilation has transformed the character of the military from protector of *civitas,* into a futile avenger. Even prior to the nuclear age, wars had become politically, though not yet physically, a matter of national survival because of the wide-

spread fear that the vanquished power will suffer the subjugation of its political organization. Non-technological factors in
warfare have been eliminated so that the results of war may
be calculated in advance with perfect precision. Foreknowledge of victory and defeat may well end a war that need never
explode into reality. If we are to survive, this cannot become a
century of warfare, but it most certainly will become a century
of total revolutions. The universal goal of war is revolution. But
even without the possibility of limited agreements, revolution
will come to define the character of the modern uses of violence and the present impulse toward freedom and liberty.

Revolution in the modern age has been concerned with two
distinct drives: liberation (absence of restraint and increase in
social mobility) and freedom (political level of life). While
liberation is consonant with various forms of government,
freedom is possible only through a republican form of government, which explains why the American, French, and Russian
revolutions all adopted this form of rule.

The two fundamental models of revolution are the American and French revolutions-though only the French Revolution became the basic model for Marxism. The American
Revolution adhered to the original purpose of revolution—realizing freedom—while the French Revolution abdicated freedom in the name of historical necessity. The American
Revolution was at one and the same time profoundly political
and anti-historical and no less, anti-political and quite historical.

The French revolutionary model, the model adopted by
Marxism and which penetrated the ideological and organizational aspects of the Russian Revolution, was concerned with
the social question—with problems of exploitation, mass al-
ienation, and poverty. It was inspired by the idea of compassion
but ended in a mindless passion. The American revolutionary
model was concerned with the political question, with problems of politics and the predicaments that flowed from an
elitist theory of mass human nature. Its revolutionary passion

was mediated by norms and hence ended in compassion, or at least a sense of the worth of the process whatever the success of the policy.

The weaknesses of the classic French model are revealed in the abortive aspects of the major revolutions of the modern era—the Paris Commune, the Russian Revolution, and the Hungarian uprising. In each case there was the rise of two distinctive forces: the party, acting in the name of the people, and the voluntary associations (workers' councils, soviets, communes,) or the people as a collective. In the betrayal of the revolution, the force of power over the people came through the consecration of political parties, whereas the council system because it failed to realize itself as a new form of government (as in the American Revolution) tended to be short-lived. It is this fact that accounts for the perfidy of modern revolutionary movements—the breakdown of voluntary association and its replacement by a swollen bureaucracy.

These propositions indicate Arendt's morphology of revolution. Although it is not possible to argue this book's thesis in terms of right and wrong, a number of questions arise. The key problem is the relative absence of evidence. How does one evaluate such speculations? The abundant confidence with which *On Revolution* is written is far from persuasive. The unsystematic prose style, which keeps the reader hopping about looking for the continuing threads, does not enhance a ready acceptance of her perspectives, even as one is drawn to her sentiments.

Arendt reveals little knowledge of modern warfare, that is, little about the ambiguities of modern conflict—counterinsurgency, paramilitary struggle, police action, guerrilla action—that would show that war is becoming obsolete. It might be correct to note that thermonuclear warfare would make total international conflict obsolete—since it is like a gun with two barrels pointing in opposite directions. But the absence of any distinction between war and annihilation throws all of the weight of her discussion on revolution into the questionable assumption that war is obsolete by reason of self-interest.

The absence of knowledge about problems of contemporary warfare is excusable—war and peace studies are dismal—but conceit is no reply. And when the author states that "the only discussion of the war question I know which dares to face the horrors of nuclear weapons and the threat of totalitarianism, and is therefore entirely free of mental reservation, is Karl Jaspers' *The Future of Mankind,*" she is only revealing her ignorance of a widespread and valuable empirical literature that has just this relationship as its central concern. Nor is the definition of revolution particularly enlightening. To see revolution as having everywhere a violent quality is to fail to distinguish between change in social structure and strategies sometimes used in such changes. Even if we generously assume that Arendt is speaking exclusively in terms of political revolution, violence is not a necessary or sufficient component.

Contradictory statements blemish her presentation: "The part of the professional revolutionists usually consists not in making a revolution but is rising to power after it has broken out, and their great advantage in this power struggle lies less in their theories and mental or organizational preparation than in the simple fact that their names are the only ones which are publicly known." But elsewhere she says that "without Lenin's slogan 'All power to the Soviets' there would never have been an October Revolution in Russia." Which cliché should be believed? Arendt's repeated assertion that the consequence of revolution is always less freedom and liberty than previously existed is belied by an appreciation of the positive outcome of the American Revolution. Indeed, it is precisely her dislike for revolutionary process that causes her to search out special features in the American Revolution not found in Europe.

Arendt belongs in the unusual category of a revolutionary conservative. For although she is bent on demonstrating the negative aspects of Thermidor and Robespierre and the positive aspects of the *Federalist Papers* and the founders of the American Republic, she nevertheless is seeking at the deepest level for a way to make revolutionary movements responsible to revolutionary men. Thus it is that councils of workers, soviets, and so forth are held to be useful models of voluntary control. The revolutionists constitute a "new aristocracy" that would properly spell the end of general suffrage. As Arendt puts it: "only those who as voluntary members of an `elementary republic' have demonstrated that they care for more than their private happiness and are concerned about the state of the world would have the right to be heard in the conduct of the business of the republic." The revolutionary elite would be guardian of the nation. How this differs from the betrayal of revolutions by political parties and how this guardianship could avoid becoming a political party, is not discussed.

Arendt respects the "spirit of revolution" but scores its failures to find an "appropriate institution." She has located such an institution in the voluntary councils that accompany revolutions, but what is amazing is her unwillingness to support her theory with evidence: for example, there is no discussion of the actual strengths or shortcomings of the late, lamented Yugoslav worker councils or of the Israeli *Kibbutzim*. This is a result of her reticence to address the political revolution of freedom in relation to the social revolution of abundance. Her comments in this direction reveal an awareness of the potential antagonism between economic development and political freedom, but not a consistent understanding of how and where State and society intersect; or toward what ends.

The big unanswered question of revolution is precisely the mix between economic rationalization and political reason. Polarization of these may make a stimulating treatise, but it cannot define the experimental character of most contemporary revolutions. For Arendt, the French and American revolutions were creative opposites. For peoples of revolutionary lands, both stand as selective options in searching for the new. If massive revolution defines the century, it might be wiser to reach for new combinations of policy and publics rather than to look with nostalgia upon the Greek city-states and their prudent elitism, for solutions to modern problems of caste and class.

The various strands in her thinking on law, revolution and the social order come together in concrete form in her "report" on the Nazi destruction of the Jewish people, *Eichmann in Jerusalem*, to which we now turn. It is undoubtedly the most explosive statement on the trial of Adolf Eichmann that was held in Jerusalem in 1961 after his capture by Israeli security forces in Argentina. The work originated in a commission by *The New Yorker* magazine to cover the trial, and was finally written up in the summer and fall of 1962 while Arendt served as a fellow of the Center for Advanced Studies at Wesleyan University. The book itself was published in 1963, with a 1964 version that carried a postscript and reply to critics.

The work has been subject to such repeated and withering assaults and no less fatuous praise from sources remote to Hannah Arendt's way of viewing and thinking that it is not amiss to hearken back to the text itself. For the biggest surprise in store for the viewer is that the overwhelming burden of the book is a straight, legal narrative of the trial of one man in one courtroom for specific crimes against one people—the Jewish people. The Arendt volume shares the position of the Israeli judicial system: that Eichmann was guilty of heinous war crimes, and that Israel, as the representative of the Jewish state and its people, had every right to execute the culprit.

The largest portion of *Eichmann in Jerusalem* is taken up with exposition and narrative: moving from the character of the German judicial system and its corruption under Nazism, to a biographical profile of Eichmann, onto the stages in the development of the Nazi plan for the genocide of the Jewish people leading up to the Wansee Conference. The next large portion of the work is taken up with a series of brilliant historical sketches of deportations. The first wave came from Germany, Austria and the Protectorates. The second wave from Western Europe, France, Belgium, Holland, Denmark and Italy. This was followed by a third wave of deportations, from Central Europe, especially Hungary and Slovakia. At the level of historical sweep, the Arendt volume stands side by side with the works of Lucy Dawidowicz[9] and Raul Hilberg.[10]

The controversial elements are actually restricted to the Epilogue and Postscript. Indeed, even Arendt's description of the Nazi killing centers at Auschwitz, Bergen-Belsen, Theresienstadt, and recitation of the evidence and eyewitness accounts of the Holocaust follow a familiar path. There is no effort to dismiss, denigrate or become disingenuous about the existence of the Holocaust, or even that it was warfare aimed at the specific liquidation of the Jewish people. To be sure, it was the very specificity of the Nazi crimes against a specific sub-set of humanity that permits Arendt to reason that Israeli courts had full jurisdiction in the matter of the disposition of Eichmann, no less than the precedent set by the Allied courts after World War Two in the Nuremberg Trials.[11] So we must look at the ethical and psychological aspects of the Arendt volume for an answer as to why her work aroused such passions among scholars, politicians and Jewish communities the world over.

The problem inheres in the sub-title rather than the title: *A Report on the Banality of Evil.* The choice of words was not casual or accidental. Arendt was in search of the why of the Holocaust even more than operational details. She aimed to understand how this SS colonel could perform such a hideous role in modern history, show little remorse, yet also display keen analytical insight into the trial processes no less than the killing fields he helped organize and supervise. Arendt located the problem and her answer in terms of the nature of the bureaucratic mind—a world of operations without consequences, information without knowledge. In this strict sense, she felt that banality was the most appropriate single-word description of Adolf Eichmann.

And while not even Arendt's most bitter opponents would accuse her of being a Holocaust denier, there is a problem with the word banality. It strongly implies the mundane, the ordinary, the everyday inconveniences experienced by all creatures—great and small. To use such a term to describe Eichmann thus appeared as a form of clever apologetics, making him into an everyday functionary—interchangeable with other unimportant people and their passive followers. At the same time, one might point out that for Arendt there is also a banality of goodness. In this category one might easily place Oskar Schindler—womanizer, profiteer, Nazi Party member, and savior of one thousand Jews from the ovens of Auschwitz. It was Arendt's special ability to appreciate the mixed motives from which human beings operate that accounts for good and evil alike. In this sense, her Kantian philosophical roots served her well as a student of the Holocaust.

The question thus arises, and Arendt admits to it, whether the trial was actually intended to punish a single person for his specific crimes, or a symbolic assault on the totalitarian regime that existed in Germany between 1933-1945. In response, Arendt argued that the use of the word banal meant nothing more or less than a factual description of an evil man, but not a deranged one, an ambitious bureaucrat rather than a dedicated ideologue. Arendt observed of the judges in the Eichmann trial, "a conspicuous helplessness they experienced when they were confronted with the task they could least escape, the task of understanding the criminal whom they had come to judge" (p. 276). As might be imagined, this only rubbed salt into a wound—one that still has not healed or even abated.

Arendt placed her finger on the soft underbelly of the trial, not only of Eichmann but of his likeness: to single out on the one hand the most monstrous of perverted sadists, and yet claim that he was intrinsically little else than a cog in the Nazi war machine, a figure representing the entire Nazi movement and anti-Semitism at large. While this might have passed with a disturbing nod, Arendt's further claim was that the physical extermination of the Jewish people was a crime against humanity, perpetrated upon the body of the Jewish people, and not the nature of the crime against that people was subject to punishment. But again, the issue was joined between Arendt and her critics, since there was a subtle denial of the uniqueness of the Holocaust in the long history of human savagery.

Arendt's careful outline of how the Wansee Conference decisions to exterminate the Jews, to make Europe *Judenrein* or Jew-Free, is chilling and numbing. It is among the best writing she was able to muster.[12] And if there were strange elements, such as linking Eichmann to the Kantian precept of obedience to the law and a moral obligation, the actual savagery and fury of the Nazis and their more than willing helpers among the occupied nations, can hardly fail to elicit a powerful response in readers even now.

The one element that did arouse additional anger was a subtle equation of the victims with the victimizer. The participation of Jews in all sorts of Jewish Councils and Zionist emissaries (exempt from the normal victimization) in bad bargaining and at times even in bad faith, efforts to save Jewish souls by trafficking into monetary and commodity bribes to the Nazis—which while not condemned by Arendt, are dealt with in less than sympathetic terms. That transport lists to concentration camps were often put together by Jews that sent many to their deaths and preserved the lives of some, has been well documented. But in Arendt's hands, such acts of complicity only deepened the notion of "banality" as a common feature of the tormentors and the tormented.

One can say that Arendt's book is a landmark in the psychology of the Holocaust. *Eichmann in Jerusalem* provides a foundation that makes possible a political psychology of Nazism far beyond earlier works—even of her own efforts to study the nature of totalitarian power and mass movements. If *Eichmann in Jerusalem* was found even by its admirers such as

Stephen Spender as "brilliant and disturbing," and Hans Morgenthau as "troubling our consciences" it is because the psychological profile makes the Holocaust not a special event but a common human failing of civility and decency; induced by either an absence of or a breakdown in governance as a response to the human need for tranquillity. Arendt wrote a work on Jews worthy of a German scholar and a classical Greek humanist. Whether the work captured the ultimate tragedy of the Jewish people in the twentieth century, or even the imagination of the Israeli citizens at the time, remain open issues. But whatever turns out to be the ultimate judgment, this is clearly one of those rare works in which the object of the discourse is of great significance along with the subject of investigation.

The Life of the Mind represents a culminating philosophic effort to understand the life of the State. To be sure, it is not quite complete, but something less than one-third to be guessed at. Even stating the obvious is bound to create some misunderstanding, since Arendt disclaims being a philosopher or "professional thinker." Indeed, publication of a large part of the first volume on *Thinking* in *The New Yorker* magazine, not to mention that a widely respected but thoroughly commercial publisher issued the two volumes, might lend some weight to such a disclaimer. But in fact, the work is thoroughly philosophical in the German classical tradition of Kant, Hegel, Nietzsche, and Heidegger. It is a measure of Hannah Arendt's justifiable fame as the author of such works as *The Origins of Totalitarianism, The Human Condition, On Revolution, Eichmann in Jerusalem,* among others, that a work so demanding, so requiring intimacy with major figures of philosophical history, would receive wide hearing. Under the circumstances, one might well have anticipated commercial drivel from editor or publisher. It is to their lasting credit that no such posthumous exploitation is attempted. McCarthy's postscript is entirely professional and pellucid. Everyone connected with this project exhibited at least one central element of good judgment ("judging" was to have constituted the final volume of this trilogy). That element is good taste.

The Life of the Mind picks up on themes first expressed two decades earlier in *The Human Condition.* The first two parts of the new work, offered as the Gifford Lectures for 1973 and 1974 respectively, seem to express polar opposites. The earlier work emphasized the active life—comprised of what we are doing: labor, work, and action. The new work involves the contemplative life: thinking, willing and judging. But this triad is only superficially antithetical to the earlier one. Labor, work, and action are interconnected as biosocial activities, whereas thinking, willing, and judging occupy far more autonomous realms in the contemplative life. The triads remain and the polarities remain. But the special nature of philosophical activities is in asking unanswerable questions and hence establishing human beings as question-asking beings. In this way Arendt sought to get beyond the atomism that afflicts the social sciences in particular—the search for the magical key word: *society* for sociology, *culture* for anthropology, *polity* for political science, *money* for economics, and *personality* for psychology. The magic key is less in the artifact, as stated in *The Human Condition,* than in the demystification of all artifacts, as in *The Life of the Mind.*

The temptation to review this work as if it is flawed by virtue of being incomplete is not simple to resist. But there are so many broad hints, fragments from lectures, and outright statements on judgment, that the work can be examined as a complete effort. The relationships between thinking, willing, and judging are set forth early in the first volume. And like a profoundly risky move in chess, the disallowance of any intertranslatability between the three categories drastically weakens the work. For instead of searching out areas of analytic linkages (i.e., ways in which the act of thinking involves willing and judging), instead of considering each of these as aspects of a naturalistic theory of mind—perhaps along the lines H.G. Mead or Y.H. Krikorian—we are required to see each aspect a windowless monad. It is curious that this should be so, since Arendt was so familiar with Aristotle and the remarkable way a sense of emergence created linkages—biological issues into social, social into political, and political into ethical. Indeed, these basic categories have survived 2000 years, and if the contents of modern science are no longer Aristotelian, the twentieth-century impulse toward the unity of science remains inspired by the Greeks. This major dilemma notwithstanding, Arendt's work is such a thorough examination into basic concepts that it transcends its own checkmate. She can at least claim a draw between the idealistic and naturalistic traditions that propel her work.

These volumes consecrate Hannah Arendt's life's work, even if they do not effect a synthesis of epistemology and ontology. For the essential statement in *Thinking,* made many times over as variation on the theme of mind, is the quintessential point about twentieth-century existence: that it is not the struggle between theory and action that is central but the struggle between theory and theory. Thinking is the hallmark of a free person living in a free society. To reduce action to behavior and then interpret behavior as if it were thought is for Arendt the shared fallacy of dialectical materialism and behavioral psychology. Whether in the language of revolutionary act or operand conditioning, the pure activist fails to understand that reducing thinking to doing is the end of the process of thought and the beginning of thought control or behavior modification.

In place of the casual slogan about theory and its issuance into practice, Arendt early on poses the question: "What are we 'doing' when we do nothing but think?" For the totalitarian temptation is to assume that those not engaged in the collective will, in the process of bringing about progress, is doing nothing. This is the metaphysical equivalent of the theological fear that idle hands make for idle minds. The reduction of metaphysics to a form of poetry by the positivist tradition is in fact a call for the repudiation of speculation as a human

activity in itself. Arendt shrewdly notes that the crisis in philosophy, ontology, theology, social theory, etc., comes into being
as a result of pronouncements by the intelligentsia itself. But
what makes such premature deaths of disciplines so risky is
that what begins as a disputation among intellectual elites,
concludes with popular disbelief in the worthiness of thinking
as such: "These modern "deaths"—of God, metaphysics, philosophy, and, by implication, positivism-have become events
of considerable historical consequence, since, with the beginning of our century, they have ceased to be the exclusive
concern of an intellectual elite and instead are not so much the
concern as the common unexamined assumption of nearly
everybody. With this political aspect of the matter we are not
concerned here. In our context, it may even be better to leave
the issue, which actually is one of political authority, outside
our considerations, and to insist, rather, on the simple fact that,
however seriously our ways of thinking may be involved in this
crisis, our *ability* to think is not at stake; we are what man has
always been—thinking beings ... men have an inclination,
perhaps a need, to think beyond the limitations of knowledge,
to do more with this ability than use it as an instrument for
knowing and doing."[13]

Bridling the will is no small matter. Its subjugation to reason
is more than an indication that in the hierarchy of thinking,
willing, and judging, willing comes in a distant third. That this
portion of *The Life of the Mind* was completed before only
fragments of the portion on judging were done should not
suggest that the will somehow mediate the claims of thought
and taste. Arendt is the political philosopher par excellence;
and unlike Kant, her sense of philosophic categories was
filtered through twentieth-century awareness of totalitarianism. She sees will as a constant clash with thinking. In her
words, "the will always wills to *do* something and thus implicitly holds in contempt sheer thinking."[14] Moreover, this impulse to will translates itself into the constant search for the
novus ordo seclorum. The will remains the final resting-place

of "men of action." Such activists demand forever new foundations, constantly destroying what was and is, in the name of the new and the yet to be. Perhaps in this Arendt's strong conservatism emerges, certainly her critique of the men of action would so vouchsafe: "There is something puzzling in the fact that men of action, whose sole intent and purpose was to change the whole structure of the future world and create a *novus ordo seclorum,* should have to go to that distant past of antiquity, for they did not deliberately [reverse] the time-axis and [bid] the young 'walk back into the pure radiance of the past.' They looked for a paradigm for a new form of government in their own 'enlightened' age and were hardly aware of the fact that they were looking backward. More puzzling, I think, than their actual ransacking of the archives of antiquity is that they did not rebel against antiquity when they discovered that the final and certainly profoundly Roman answer of 'ancient prudence' was that salvation always comes from the past, that the ancestors were *majors,* the 'greater ones' by definition."

I suspect that more than conservatism is at stake. For theorists of the act, of freedom, always had a way of terminating their freedom with their own visions of society. Since for Arendt the capacity of beginning is rooted in the human capacity for renewal, it requires no end point. Terminus is not freedom but death. In this sense, freedom as system is a doomsday called utopia. That is why judgment becomes so important for her. For judgment makes transcendence of will possible without a denial of reason. The aesthetic sense is not an accouterment but a necessary faculty that tells people that what is perfect to one person or one ruler may be imperfect to another person or ruler and downright ugly to yet a third person and a third ruler. She locates the source of democratic survival in the pluralism of judgment.

What has consistently infuriated neo-Platonists and Marxists alike about the Kantian view of aesthetic judgment is its distinction between beauty and taste on one hand and applicability and moral purpose on the other. Arendt states the Kantian argument quite bluntly: "If you say, 'What a beautiful rose!' you don't arrive at this judgment by first saying, all roses are beautiful, this flower is a rose, hence it is beautiful. The other kind, dealt with in *the second part*, is the impossibility to derive any particular product of nature from general causes. Mechanical in Kant's terminology means natural causes; its opposite is 'technical' by which he means artificial."[15]

Judgment thus is concerned with that "enlargement of mind" that derives from evaluating "something fabricated with a purpose." But far from supporting an elitist vision of aesthetics or culture, Arendt draws precisely the opposite, namely a populist, conclusion. Taste is a community sense (*gemeinschaftlicher Sinn*), and hence while not all people are geniuses, all people are capable of rendering judgment. What is so terribly important about this populist vision of judgment as both autonomous from thinking and willing, is that it provides the solution to the problem of democracy and also that basis of unity amongst the *polis*.

Arendt still leaves us with a problem: the contradiction between the idea of progress as the law of the human species and the idea of human dignity as an inalienable aspect of individual human beings. This presumably would have formed the nexus of the third volume on Judgment, *The Life of the Mind*. For those to whom limitations on knowledge are a fact to be overcome rather than celebrated, the problem bequeathed by Kant and now by Arendt is a challenge of no small magnitude or light consequence.

Arendt suffered a dialectical passion, or at least a commitment to the reality of reification: the warfare between thought and common sense, the Greek question and the Roman answer, the gap between the past and the future, thinking and doing, the active life and the contemplative life, the impotence of the will versus the omnipotence of the will. This gives her writings a tremendous tension, a dramaturgical sensibility that has virtually disappeared in the empirical tradition. Perhaps that is why she can so readily and categorically dismiss Hume's dictum on reason being the slave of the passions as "simple minded," while Locke does only a trifle better as a believer in "the old tacit assumption of an identity of soul and mind." Indeed, the British empiricists fare less well at Arendt's hands than those of her master, Kant.

It is to Kant that the work is really consecrated. For her divisions of thinking, willing, and judging derive in great measure from Kant's great works: *Critique of Practical Reason, Foundations of the Metaphysics of Morals,* and *Critique of Judgment.* From the transcendental dialectic of the *Critique of Pure Reason* she drew the cardinal lesson: the insolubility of the nature of providence, freedom, and immortality by speculative thought. But what Arendt does, what is so unusual about her work, is to infuse Kant's deadly logical prose with the excitement of Hegel's dialectical scaffold. Whether by intent or accident—and to know Hannah Arendt and her work, is to know that scarcely a word, much less a concept, happens randomly—Kant is given the ultimate victory in the classical philosophic struggle. This is no cheap victory, but a victory over titans like Plato and Hegel. For Arendt, it is Kant who gives us conscience as a realm of freedom unto itself; it is Kant who understands that judgment is something that can be practiced but not taught, and it is Kant who sat astride the will, uniquely understanding it as neither freedom of choice nor sheer spontaneity of activity. Kant's will becomes Arendt's will, "delegated by reason to be its executive organ in all matters of conduct." Karl Popper's proponents of the closed society (Plato and Hegel) now meet their match in Arendt's proponent of the open society (Kant).

Arendt points to a great divide in modern scientific quests: on the one hand is the positivist quest for truth, and on the other is the rationalist quest for meaning. For her, it is a basic fallacy to confound the two, a fallacy to which even such figures like Heidegger fall prey. The distinction between the urgent need to think and the desire to know, is an operational way of distinguishing thinking from doing. And here, although the Greeks are called upon to bear witness to this distinction, I dare say it is Arendt's Jewishness that provides the missing link. For it is the historical role of the Jews to search and not find redemption and the redeemer, in contrast to the truth announced by Christianity of redemption through the Son of God, that really distinguishes Arendt's claims for thinking as the ultimate act.

There is a strange myopia in Arendt, an all-too-conventional vision of the history of philosophy as a movement from the Greeks to the Romans to the Christians to the Medieval Schoolmen, and finally to the Germans. But such a mechanical rendition of the history of philosophy fails to explain why Heidegger the existentialist falls prey to the same error as Carnap the positivist. Why does the metaphysical impulse to certainty take precedence over epistemological distinctions? Is not the answer at least in part located in a shared scientific vision of the age in which the quest for meaning is seen as less urgent than the delivery of truth, even the imposition of truth on non-believers, infidels, and heathens? Perhaps in the third volume on judgment such matters would have been addressed. I suspect otherwise. Having rejected the philosophic dialogue written by opponents of the open society, she was powerless to cope with the betrayal of that life in its post-Kantian phase. The elementary forms of democratic expression are described as in mortal combat with the evolutionary Nazi and historical Bolshevik forms of anti-democracy. The allies of the demos are left disarmed so to speak, wrecked by intellectuals announcing the death of intellect.

There was a point in time when one would have had to shuffle in embarrassment for reviewing a metaphysical work. But these are not such times. With figures such as Marx, Durkheim and Weber anchoring major tendencies in current sociology, no apologetics for reading such a masterful treatise is required, nor need it be hidden under sociological pillows. To be sure, those who represent phenomenological, symbolic

interactionist, and humanistic varieties of sociology will probably be far more attracted to these pair of volumes than
advocates of behavioral, functional, or physicalist sociologies.
But to disentangle a potential audience for such an undertak-
ing is aptly evocative of what Arendt understands as the
topsy-turvy world of action and theory: "The Marxian and
existentialist notions, which play such a great role in twentieth-century thought and pretend that man is his own producer
and maker, rest on these experiences, even though it is clear
that nobody has 'made' himself or 'produced' his existence;
this, I think, is the last of the metaphysical fallacies, corresponding to the modern age's emphasis on willing as a substitute for thinking. And this is of some relevance to a whole set
of problems by which modern thought is haunted, especially
to the problem of theory and practice and to all attempts to
arrive at a halfway plausible theory of ethics. Since Hegel and
Marx, these questions have been treated in the perspective of
History and on the assumption that there is such a thing as
Progress of the human race. Finally we shall be left with the
only alternative there is in these matters—we either can say
with Hegel: *Die Weltgeschichte ist das Weltgericht,* leaving the
ultimate judgment to Success, or we can maintain with Kant
the autonomy of the minds of men and their possible inde-
pendence of things as they are or as they have come into
being."

As long as thinking, willing, and judging are viewed as three
basic mental activities that "cannot be derived from each
other" and that "cannot be reduced to a common denominator," the very edifice Arendt attempts is subject to the same
criticism as any other absolutism. In twentieth-century terms,
her work consecrates the collapse of acceptable paradigms in
social science and philosophy. Hence the trinitarianism of
thinking, willing, and judging can do no more than confront
each other in field after field, discipline after discipline. But if
Arendt did not effect the grand synthesis (nor does she claim
at any point to be after such a Holy Grail), she sheds a great

light on what is ailing our social and behavior disciplines. We at least know what the sources of division are with a precision and a clarity that makes possible new creativity. And that is ultimately what the life of the free mind is all about.

It is ironic that the author of *Eichmann in Jerusalem* should also be a supreme devotee of German high culture. Despite her cosmopolitan style, there can be no mistaking that in philosophy, law, and politics, Hannah Arendt was a complete product of the German *Aufklärung*. The century has been rolled back with these volumes: as if Hitler and Nazism had not happened, as if German liberal thought were an unbroken chain of continuities.[16] But this is not the case. And Arendt in her towering works has been a prime mover in enabling us to understand the essence of the totalitarian persuasion. But at the last, she remained true to the tradition of German liberalism. The French language, which she loved, counted for little more than a Cartesian footnote; the English constitutional tradition, which surely nourished her faith in compassionate justice over and against impassioned (non-rational) vengeance, counted for little. Russian democratic thought from Herzen to Solzhenitsyn scarcely existed for her. And perhaps most shattering to those who saw her primarily as a Jewish writer, the Hebrew tradition was reduced to several hyphenated footnotes to Christian theology.[17] In the end, in the long pull, this remarkable woman, scholar, critic, exile, teacher turned out to be not an avenging angel remorselessly pursuing her totalitarian quarry but the last loving product of German Enlightenment: the keeper of a flame she herself had helped resurrect from the charnel house of postwar Europe. The dialectical process is indeed mysterious and insoluble as Kant insisted. It brought forth, fifty years late in a foreign language by an exile from Nazi repression, the last hurrah of the Weimar Republic.

13

A Natural History
of the Holocaust

*The planned total murder of a people was an unprecedented
catastrophe in human civilization. It happened because it could
happen; if it could not have happened, it would not have done so.
And because it happened once, it can happen again. Any historical event is a possibility before it becomes a fact, but when it
becomes a fact, it also serves as a possible precedent. And although no event will ever be repeated exactly, it will, if it is
followed by similar events, become the first in a line of analogous
happenings. We ought to do everything in our power to make sure
it is a warning, not a precedent.*

— *Yehuda Bauer*[1]

IT IS NOW 55 YEARS SINCE THE CLOSE OF WORLD WAR TWO.
EVEN IF A CERTAIN CONSENSUS has been reached on the
broad scope of the Nazi war against the Jews, causal questions
remains as vexing now as ever. The policy decisions that led to
the cross-over by the fascist powers from a stated ideological
hatred of Jews to a systematic implementation of the "final
solution" is still being debated. There also remain considerable
differences of opinion in the extent to which the fascist forces

substituted the war against the Jewish people for processing the war against the allied forces. It is almost as if the more details are uncovered about the Holocaust, the less certain have we become as to the causal chain of events involved. My belief is that in bringing a human rights perspective to the study of the Holocaust allows us to appreciate both its uniqueness, and also how it is part of an expanding pattern of genocide. My aim here is to develop what might be termed a natural history of studying this unnatural assault on a singular people in a certain time and place.

There are four identifiable, if overlapping stages in Holocaust studies. None of them entirely resolves ambiguities and confusions about actual events, but they do lead to a more precise accounting of the motives and goals of the perpetrators of genocide and pinpoint its victims. These four stages laid the groundwork for developing an early warning signal for detecting emerging patterns of genocide. In this sense, the terrible tragedies of the twentieth century may serve as an anchor for social and behavioral scientific efforts of the twenty-first century to study human aggression at its extremes. I believe we are reaching an emerging synthesis in Holocaust studies, or specifically, how and why the largely successful Nazi extermination of the Jewish population of Europe was carried out. Hopefully, such exercises will not be required in the future in order to provide the human race with yet a lower bench mark with which to demarcate human civilization. However for now, such hopes cannot be viewed as facts.

The first stage in Holocaust Studies is what might best be called the literature of the witnesses. Libraries have logged some 2500 published books, diaries, memoirs, and monographs (in English alone) of a first person, narrative variety. Each of these accounts is unique, and many provide moving insights in their own right, as a whole and as a collectivity. They provide the raw material for the systematic review of the Holocaust. These works, often written by the victims, survivors of the death camps, provided emotional fuel for recognition of the great harm done to the idea of human solidarity by the Nazi system. In the act of expiation, all types of psychological issues of guilt and innocence, instinct and reason, punishment and rehabilitation, orthodoxy and apostasy were translated into raw numbers and personal narratives. That this first stage remains a viable part of current efforts to study the Holocaust is indicated by the Elie Wiesel Foundation urging the establishment of a resource center for the collection and eventual publication of an estimated four to five thousand additional memoirs now in private circulation.

THE SECOND STAGE MIGHT BEST BE DESCRIBED AS THE HISTORICAL AND JOURNALISTIC STAGE. Memoirs and recollections became a source for historians and journalists to understand the where, when, and how of the Holocaust. Joined by a variety of researchers, historians developed an accounting of the origins and outcomes of the Holocaust in a difficult climate, but dispassionate way. This second level provided some insights into the scope and depth of the Holocaust. However, this style of work came to an impasse when confronted with multiple questions of a comparative nature. Why was the Holocaust more severe in one nation and less in another? Why did the behavior of the perpetrators vary from one concentration camp to another, one village to another, one person to another? Why did the actions of victims run the gamut of possibilities from outright acquiescence to active resistance?

In short, historical and journalistic research opened up prospects for a next stage; one in which social research took on a strong analytical mode. Perhaps the greatest contribution was in the appreciation by historians like Lucy Davidovich,[2] Raul Hilberg,[3] and Nora Levin[4] that the Holocaust was at its center a war against the Jews. Indeed, as the defeat of the Axis powers war by the Allied powers became manifest, the *raison d'être* of World War Two increasingly shifted from an external struggle against capitalism in the West and communism in the

East, toward a war against Judaism. The mythic Jew was labeled as the conspiratorial source of both world systems. This provided an enormous breakthrough, not just in the study of genocide, but in the unitary character of totalitarian regimes.

THE THIRD, SO-CALLED PSYCHOLOGICAL AND SOCIAL SCIENTIFIC STAGE TOOK UP THE DIFFICULT TASK of integrating personal psychological issues with long-term historical considerations. Those ranged from geo-political considerations in which the major powers dealt with the Jews as part of global considerations, to examinations of ethnic and religious differences in terms of national policy-making. The social science literature began to inform us of different forms of genocide: systematic vs. random, those performed by backward dynasties in distinction to those performed by modern totalitarianism.

We were compelled to disaggregate systems like Nazism and Fascism and introduce the cultural variable to explain differential responses of Germans and Italians. It became apparent that the formal mode of government and party apparatus did not in itself explain responses to the Jewish masses. The social sciences took up big issues of national difference such as the low rate of cooperation with the assassins in small countries like Denmark in contrast to the high rate of cooperation with these same assassins in other small countries like The Netherlands. Perhaps the most advanced work done in this third stage was to appreciate the structural, organic nature of the Holocaust—as it charted the cancerous growth of totalitarianism as part of a society now relieved of its humanity by its sense of destiny.

WE ARE NOW ENTERING A FOURTH STAGE OF ANALYSIS, ONE IN WHICH ELEMENTS OF EACH of the previous three stages are absorbed and perhaps synthesized. This stage is coincidental with the recognition that life and death are the lodestones of the human sciences as such. The measure of a civilization is its promulgation of life or its promotion of death. This becomes a continuum for the study of human beings. In this stage, people working in this area of Genocide Studies arrive at a unity of purpose. Its specialists are linked to one another—across inherited professional boundaries—and hence begin to speak of Holocaust and Genocide Studies as a field unto itself, with personalities, chairs, departments and journals. The paraphernalia of research and scholarship can sometimes dangerous. The professional rigors of intellectual life can cause one to become unfeeling and unresponsive. But the existence of this new stage, this new level, is now clear.

The movement from macroscopic to microscopic analysis characterizes this stage. It represents a movement away from the metaphysical to the material conditions under which the Holocaust actually took place. This is not a breakdown in feelings, but a realization that prevention of future genocides requires an appreciation of the highly specific elements that made such a catastrophic event possible in the first place. It attempts to steer a course somewhere between the sentimental elements that are inevitable in autobiographical profiles and at times insensitive, overly mechanical aspects of the examination of totalitarian rule. This is also a movement from large-scale to small-scale study of phenomenon, not because of an innate preference for the latter, but because incongruities, dilemmas and contradictions posed by large-scale analysis compel a search for answers in more specific contexts.

In addition, as a surviving generation passes away, Holocaust deniers—some crude and others sophisticated—emerge to challenge the historical record. And refutation involves a study of intimate details that in the past were taken for granted. For example, the 1300 pages of notes written by Adolf Eichmann while imprisoned in Israel, provided the basis for verifying the precise use of gas chambers and incinerators in the scientific liquidation of the Jewish people. This is apparent in the study of the Holocaust as we enter not just a new millennium but a new condition, one in which the issues must be resolved by a post-survivor generation in appeals to hard data rather than personal memoir. In such a new epoch, research must search state archives, corporate decisions, and military minutes. A large plus in this effort is the opening of archive materials of former totalitarian closed states. In this fourth stage, not only is there a need for sophisticated analyses, but even more, complex methods of data retrieval.

There is the inevitable movement from witnessing, commenting, and reflecting to analysis and explanation. We have not been lacking in the latter. Indeed, many of the best and the most talented minds of the social, cultural, and historical disciplines have blessed the study of the Holocaust. Many have envisioned what each professional would like to forget would be remembered, even if it took a near endless stream of memorials and commissions to do so.

The movement to microscopic analysis is not simply a function of generational change, but of the aforementioned problems encountered in explaining the Holocaust in large-scale measures alone. Why did European countries with similar characteristics, such as Denmark and the Netherlands, have such different records of support for their respective Jewish communities? Why did Jewish community life retain its vitality in one dictatorial country such as Romania, but not in another adjacent neighbor such as Hungary? How do we account for the mass popular support in Nazi Germany for the war against the Jews, but the relatively limited support for such a war in its wartime ally, Fascist Italy? How can it be that the Nazi regime is described as pagan and opposed to Christian beliefs, yet its architects of the Holocaust employed as a standard measurement of who lived and who died precisely the religious background and affiliation of its citizens?

These are large concerns, and we cannot hope to resolve them in a brief survey paper.[5] But we can and should address with candor the need for microanalysis. This should be done not as a function of trivialization or even specialization, but as a mechanism to get beyond present dilemmas into a larger, more meaningful explanation of the greatest catastrophe of the twentieth century. The use of genocide as a function of state policy characterized the Holocaust as well as varieties of genocide that both predated and postdated what the Nazi War against the Jews.

This war, while taking six million innocent lives, was not the worst of the century in life-taking terms. The Stalinist period in Russia killed anywhere from 35 to 50 million people, while the Maoist period in China caused the deaths of about 23 to 35 million people. In genocidal matters we are not dealing with totalitarian excesses or human loss as such as such. Rather, we are dealing with a special phenomenon: the effort to exterminate an historical people, a major world religion, and a culture that parallels in its offerings what we owe to the Greek and Roman worlds. A proper understanding requires close detailing of specifics and the capacity to move beyond horror to examine situations aimed at total or partial destruction. We must make a Herculean clinical effort to put moral issues to one side and hold pathologies that are clearly present in momentary abeyance, in order for the analytical distinctions necessary to be sharpened. One of these is Steven Katz's distinction between a genocidal regime as such and one with mediating approaches to victim groups.[6] In this way, these moral issues can be taken up as a series of gradations in measuring the nature of political regimes in a more meaningful and operationally more durable fashion.

Let us start by tackling head-on the issue of six million Jews. As we hardly need reminding, Holocaust deniers are prepared to write all sort of absurdities about the "myth of Auschwitz" and enter disputes about numbers and the location of gas chambers. Well yes, they say, many innocent lives were taken but these were random, not religion specific, and do not add up to the six million mark claimed. Perfectly decent researchers have even become embroiled in such discourse. The number six million is important because the Nazi regime conducted two wars on two fronts. The first war was to defeat the Allied powers and clearly was lost in 1943 if not earlier. The second war was for the destruction of the Jewish people and was largely successful. The effort devoted to the second war was redoubled precisely as the external war was going badly. The struggle over numbers is therefore not simply quantitative in character. It serves to answer issues of the ferocity, totality, and wickedness of the Holocaust. It also helps us to understand the clash within the hierarchy of the Nazi regime between those, like Heinrich Himmler, who wanted to shut down the gas chambers in 1943, and others like Adolf Eichmann, who in disregard of such orders, fearfully accelerated the pace of mass executions. Once the mass extermination of Jews became Nazi policy, it became impossible to shut down the spigots, despite ambivalence and confusion in the highest reaches of Nazi power.

The force of Nazi extremism "on the ground" is demonstrated by the death march in Koenigsberg of 7,000 young women and children in 1945—four days after the fall of Auschwitz to the Red Army. What is now the Russian town of Yantarny witnessed a massacre conducted by the SS. It became killing seashore, but there were no memorials, no acknowledgments by the Stalinist regime. Something like sixteen people survived. Several of the witnesses were Christians who documented a slaughter of horrifically brutal proportions. This is important in the overall scheme of things because this event took place after Auschwitz, in full recognition that the war against the Allies was over. Hence, it serves to make it clear that in the eyes of the perpetrators, the dirty war, the war against the Jews, had to be won quickly and at all costs in the remaining days of the European conflict.

This event also documents the communist style of denial through assertion. The Stalinists converted the murder of seven thousand Jews into the fictitious murder of seven thousand Red Army troops and assorted civilians. Soviet ideology could not admit the reality of the Nazi war against the Jews because the Communists themselves were involved in a corresponding war against the Jews that would continue through Stalin's death. The events at Yantarny/Koenigsberg also give powerful fuel and ammunition to the Goldhagen thesis: that the German civilian population largely colluded in, and derived material benefits from, the murder of Jewish innocents.

The universal silence about such a large-scale death march at Palmnicken (Koenigsberg) seriously weakens the pleasant idea of German innocence versus Wehrmacht guilt. My point is not to recite the horrors of one among many death marches. It is to indicate how exact analysis of a singular event can illumine the whole specter of totalitarian evil in a special way. The work of Evgeny Grossman and Ilya Ehrenburg on the *Black Book of Russian Jewry*[7] was denied publication because in making plain the death of the Jews as a unique series of events, it undermined the Marxist-Leninist notion of the class character of World War Two. This constant impingement of ideology on the consciousness of the investigator is itself a factor, a problem, in the contemporary study of the Holocaust.

This fourth stage of work also refines the analytical tools needed for the study of the Holocaust and the possible future genocides that one might wish to avoid. The work of Christopher Browning, a historian by training, illustrates these new research trends. His work, *Nazi Policy, Jewish Workers, German Killers* focuses on how Nazi Jewish policy evolved during the first years of the war. At what point did the Nazi regime cross the historic watershed from population expulsion and decimation to total and systematic extermination? What contradictions emerged in a policy that aimed to exterminate at one level and to exploit Jewish labor at another? What role did local authorities play in shaping and carrying out Nazi policies? What sort of divisions could one detect among the Germans—the place of opposition (very low) passive non-compliance (10-20 per cent range) and active support of exterminationist policy?

In short, Browning absorbs the earlier three stages at the
vertical level, and clearly moves from the macroscopic to
microscopic level of analysis at the horizontal level.[8]

Another analytic development is the effort to determine
who did the actual killing of the six million Jews. It is not at all
evident that the Nazi regime was directly responsible for all of
the killing fields. For example, a young Canadian historian,
Mark Biondich, has determined while microfilming all available data in Croatia, that the Ushtasa did not simply create
anti-Semitic legislation and deports Jews to death camps. Indeed, although Croatia was a satellite state under the direct
rule of the German and Italian fascists, the Croatian government itself killed more of its own Jews than it deported to the
Nazi-operated death camps. Biondich indicates that the evidence shows the Croatian authorities quickly realized that
they, rather than their masters, could reap significant economic
benefits by confiscating monies and property—and they did
so in the name of solving the so-called Jewish Question. Recent studies of Vichy France have brought to light the active
participation of French collaborators in rounding up and exporting the Jewish communities for shipment to their death in
concentration camps. In short, there was intense competition
among the thieves and murderers. The line between good and
evil is not exactly parallel to the line between invaders and
invaded.

While there have been attempts to identify and locate
righteous Gentiles and those who stood in opposition to the
death camps, a certain revisionism is taking place. Those who
were earlier identified as resisting the Nazi Holocaust are now
being examined in the other direction. Everyone from Pastor
Martin Niemoller to philosopher Martin Heidegger has been
shorn of his or her rationalizations.

It seems clear that Niemoller defended Jews who were
converts to Christianity, not the autonomous rights of the
Jewish religious community as such. Breaking myths also extends to larger demographic issues. For example, the idea that

German Jews were satisfied and reticent to leave Nazi Germany is undermined by the work of Herbert Strauss. He statistically documented a continuing pattern of emigration from 1933 through 1939, and found that nearly all-remaining German Jews had made plans to leave that were thwarted by the regime.

As the two volumes of *Notebooks* and *Diaries* left behind by the philologist Victor Klemperer make abundantly clear, there was absolutely no pattern of zealous support among the Jews for the Nazi regime, and even fewer illusions. Nearly two-thirds of German Jews left, and the third that remained were often constrained by the need to protect elderly family members. So the new demography also has been enlisted to create a microscopic analysis of great worth.

The fourth stage literature on church-state relationships as they impacted totalitarian regimes likewise is more nuanced and complicated than earlier imagined. It is a story not just of obstinacy at the top, i.e., of two strikingly different popes — Pius XI and Pius XII — but of a variety of papal emissaries who had a wide number of views on how to handle the Nazi system and its war against the Jews. The long record of Catholic anti-Semitism was not exactly fertile ground for shared resistance to Nazism. That said, it is evident that the Church was itself torn between public declaration of opposition to the Nazi pogroms, public support for such behavior, and the more easy path of the epoch: silence in the face of disaster.

The Nazis were for their part also conflicted with respect to the Church. They had to balance Protestant fears of Catholic power—a strong leitmotif since Luther, and no less with what George Mosse often noted was their own ideological emphasis on paganism as a response to what Nazism deemed the religion of cowardice, Christianity. Operationally, the Nazis were confronted by the need to define the Jewish community in terms of who was a Christian no less than who was a "mixed breed." The theological claims that Nazism is illustrative of paganism, Christology, or as is more popular in recent years, modernism as a technology, all come upon a complex set of factors. Whatever the rubric or tactic, the Nazi goal was the total annihilation of the Jewish people; starting with the European Jews. This compelled them to carry out their hideous mission under a variety of legal and cultural guises.

While the literary works on Holocaust denial continue to capture headlines, including the failed lawsuit brought by David Irving in British courts against the American historian, Deborah Lipstadt, here too there has been a subtle shift. No longer is the agenda filled with arguments about whether or not the Holocaust took place. The deniers have moved toward a second stage, one based on Holocaust evasion and reduction. If the struggle about the Holocaust is purely about numbers, or if one can demonstrate that five million rather than six million people perished in the Shoah, the assumption is that there is a general misunderstanding of the Nazi epoch as such. David E. Stannard provides another variation on this statistical parceling. Specifically at stake is his assertion that "the Nazis killed 60-65 per cent of European Jews, compared with the destruction by the Spanish, British and Americans of 95 per cent or more of numerous ethnically and culturally distinct peoples in North and South America from the 16th through the 19th centuries."

Though the ultimate aim of the Nazis was to destroy 11 million Jews or all of them in Europe at the time of the war, the Nazis were never able to destroy the Russian Jews, since they were unable to conquer the Soviet Union. But of the six million Jews within the domain of the Nazis, more than 95 percent were in fact brutally eliminated. It is clear that this new stage in Holocaust studies is not simply a function of expanding knowledge, but of a rising tide at the political and academic fringes of those who would preserve Nazism as an ideology and an organization purged of its presumed excesses.

It is assuredly of small comfort to the victims of the Holocaust to know that other genocides have taken place. Few scholars deny the extent of genocidal patterns in the twentieth century. The issue of uniqueness should no longer become a smokescreen for trivializing or minimizing the specific horror of the systematic engineering of death of European Jewry within the National Socialist sphere of influence. The movement to Holocaust evasion and away from Holocaust denial is the other side, the dark side, of the microanalytic situation that now obtains in genocide research. At stake is the diminution of the meaning of the Holocaust by relativizing its nature, by making it one of many horror stories of the twentieth century. There is a fine line between asserting the unique nature of the Holocaust and its place in a long list of genocidal outrages. The new generation of scholarship must walk that fine line without becoming ensnared or enraged in parochial disputations—a task admittedly easier to assert than to live by.

It would be both dangerous and foolish to give undue weight to either those who would deny the reality of the Holocaust or evade responsibility for its occurrence. There are both ethical and practical risks in taking refuge in extreme relativism, in which the systematic extermination of an innocent people is reduced to everything from cultural repression to random deaths in civil conflicts. On this, one must speak plainly or find the study of the Holocaust washed away in the bathos of sentimentality and the pathos of victimology. Here too there is an organizational component to the fourth stage: the Holocaust has emerged as the focus of more than 175 separate voluntary associations worldwide. These associations, ranging in size from small groups with a handful of volunteers to the United States Holocaust Memorial Museum with over 400 salaried personnel and 300 volunteers have changed the organization map of Jewish life in the Western World. They have also become vanguard agencies for the promotion of broader human rights activities.

There are, to be sure, risks in the professionalization of Holocaust studies—perhaps none greater than to convert an enormous human tragedy into a series of academic groupings debating minutiae as if they were picking through the final hours of a rummage sale. But such problems are a concern for select academics that spend careers on the subject. Ordinary people who show solidarity with the worst moment in Jewish history, from young children to old survivors are spared such self-imposed agonies. Expressing the continuities of Jewish life is the ultimate rebuke to Holocaust deniers and evaders.

Thorny issues have arisen in the current fourth stage that is beyond the scope of analysis in this essay. For example, there are legitimate and unresolved issues connected to reparations and repayment. There is a fine literature on the monetary measurement of values—extending from Georg Simmel[9] to Viviana Zelizer[10]—that help us arrive at an understanding of this difficult issue. But the fact remains that placing a dollar amount on human death can be viewed as sacrilegious and destructive of Jewish or any religious tradition.

It is little wonder that the Jewish community has been roiled between those in support and those in opposition to monetary compensation schemes for Holocaust survivors. This has come to the fore in recent debates that took place in the pages of *Commentary* between those who believe that Holocaust is seriously cheapened by monetary reparations and those who view such fiscal settlements as appropriate, symbolic rather than reductive in character.[11]

But it does appear that in the secular world, money remains a measure of how a guilty party acknowledges and atones for past errors. In short, the emergence of a fourth stage in the study of the Holocaust hardly moves us closer to moral closure, or for that matter, to a new synthesis. Quite the contrary, what has taken place in the last sixty years is evidence that life taking by State systems very rarely resolves ethical concerns or philosophical paradox.

There are non-monetary considerations in this new stage that are no less nettlesome. Jan T. Gross has uncovered a situation that took place in July 1941 in which 1600 Jews were burned alive in a town of Poland called Jedwabne. A monument was erected to memorialize the event by Polish authorities, the Nazis actually disputed the allegation, and it turns out that the actual perpetrators were many of the other 1600 non-Jews who lived in the same town. So we have the anomaly of victims serving as victimizers. Adam Michnik pointed out that Poland was a nation in which "not a single Polish family was spared by Hitler and Stalin. The two totalitarian dictatorships obliterated three million Poles and three million Polish citizens classified as Jews by the Nazis." And while Michnik fails to note that the murder of Poles represented ten percent of the population, while the murder of Polish Jews nearly one hundred percent of the population, he does speak with deep contrition about "the lives of those Poles who felt guilt." They were "the ones who moved into the houses vacated by Jews herded into the ghetto ... There were some Poles who turned Jews in and others who hid Jews for money."

In short, the most advanced analysis of the Holocaust permit us to appreciate the role in one and the same person and in one and the same community of victim and villain.[12] If this fourth stage of analysis does not resolve the issues of responsibility and execution, it does at least provide a sense of good and evil, right and wrong, far more complicated and even convoluted than previously imagined.

So then where are we now, what have we learned from this evaluative process? Better stated, how have we been advantaged by this new fourth stage of information and knowledge about the Holocaust—and by extension to other genocides of the twentieth century?

- ▸ *First,* the research community has moved from blanket indictments of perpetrators and blanket absolution for victims to study the struggles inside the social structures of each end of the human scale. The stresses and strains within the Nazi leadership were few, but their need to mobilize the German people created conditions for subterfuge and deception, which led to differences in strategies and policies.

- ▸ *Second,* economic development or cultural sophistication did not uniquely define the extent of public support or opposition to the

Holocaust. Danes and Dutch alike share many characteristics in common—but the treatment of the Jews and minorities differed substantially. So we require a further study of the moral foundations of economy and culture alike as a measure of response as such.

▸ *Third,* the very occurrence of the Holocaust brought into play a congruence of objective events and subjective ambitions. The older tradition of choosing either impersonal history or personal narrative to explain the pattern of genocide has given way to a common sense set of realizations. It is the interaction, more, the incubation, of objective structures and personal decisions that changed the situation under Nazism from the random denunciation of the Jews, to the deprivation of their civil liberties and livelihood, and finally to their systematic annihilation. In the real world, the divisions between academic fields such as political psychology and political sociology are merged and ultimately dissolved in the decisions taken and then executed.

▸ *Fourth,* in the long process of discovery a new and essential field of social and political organization has been hammered out. The struggle for human rights is now anchored in the definition of civilization. Survival has itself become a problematic rather than a given. The highs of a civilization are the life-giving propensities of peoples; the lows are the life taking propensities of states. In human life there is volition as well as determinism in behavior. It has taken a while to find a common ground, but having done so, we now are able to find a common voice.

Every field of endeavor requires standards for measurement of advancement. Engineers will use the degree of electrification as guidelines. Communications people rely upon the extent of computerization. Economists employ the stability of currencies and purchasing power to measure national wealth. Political scientists emphasize the number of people involved in the electoral process to determine democratic propensities. Entertainment industry moguls record the number of film theatres and recording sales. This list is long, but scarcely infinite or irrelevant.

Through this long process of discovery we have all shared recognition of the extraordinary place of genocide and state killings in the twentieth century. This has taught us, or at least should have that as dedicated experts in the study of such destructive phenomena, we have our own measure of advancement — the implementation of a human rights perspective based on social equity and personal respect. This is the degree of regimes that practice life giving over and against those that practice life taking. That is the human rights standard of measurement. It is a perspective that uniquely permits us to sit in moral judgment of our age — and also of past ages.

14

Jewish Survival in a
Post-Holocaust World

Our tale was not about Jews alone. It was about what had been done to Jews by others. Because of its magnitude and its ontological nature, the Holocaust will forever remain a challenge to this generation and perhaps to all generations. Some of us have chosen to stay within its fiery walls so as to explore and perhaps redeem its hidden truth. Whatever we do, whatever we say, must be measured against its background. If at times we sound oversensitive to certain words, if at times we overreact to certain events. It is that we have chosen to remember the time when Jews seem to have been forgotten by all men.

— *Elie Wiesel*[1]

BY COMMON CONSENSUS, THE TWO MOST EXTRAORDINARY EVENTS OF TWENTIETH CENTURY Jewish history were the destruction of European Jewry in the Holocaust, and the construction of the modern State of Israel. They bracket the 1940s, and they define Jewish parameters in the new millennium. Whatever the interpretations of these events, they clearly conjure up powerful and contradictory emotions: defeat and victory, peripheries and centers, helplessness and heroism, and of spirit and matter itself. The purpose of this chapter is to identify Jewish survival prospects in a post-Holocaust world, and in a world in which Israel has already marked one half century of its existence as a modern nation-State. Even if there is a consensus that the arbitrary taking of life by a State is an unmitigated disaster, the converse is by no means quite as obvious, that the State is as an unmitigated good.[2]

How Jewish religions, national integration, and cultural identity are forged in light of these two immense events is the burden of this analysis. It is evident from any close examination of the stated subject of this analysis that contradiction is far more characteristic of Jewish life than consensus. This was the case in the Jewish past and remains so in the present. Struggles between orthodoxy and reformism, nationalism and cosmopolitanism (for want of a better word), Israeli national interests and Jewish universalistic claims, and capitalist individualism and socialist collectivism, have all hardened into postures rather than been resolved over the course of the century. Add to this mix such volatile private concerns as intermarriage, conversion, ethnic heritage, secularization, and the task of analysis appears daunting, while that of synthesis seems well nigh impossible.[3]

Policy-makers repeatedly claim that even were Israel not to exist, conflict among Arab and Moslem interests would continue to fester. Dare one add in reverse that even were Arab hostilities to Israel and Moslem animosities toward Jews were to magically dissolve all at once, conflict among Jewish interests—political and religious—would continue in force. Urgent questions have been raised about generation concerns: the evolution of Israel as a national entity with "normal" state proclivities to monopolize force, and the prospect that Judaism may become a minority religion even within Israel, much less within the context of most open societies. It behooves the social science community to answer whether Judaism is any different than other world class religions, and what constitutes Judaism as a frame of reference in national and cultural terms with nominal regard to issues of religious observance or theological discourse.

There is also the thorny, if largely unspoken, issue of how strategies of becoming Jewish enhance or impede principles of scientific research. Concerns for Jewish survival strongly imply that such survival is a positive value. But whether a moral center of gravity much less teleological purpose can be deduced from the history of religions as a sociological concern merits examination. Within these heavy domains of relevance I should like to consider minimal and maximal approaches to Jewish survival. To be sure, the topic of Jewish survival in the period ahead is so broad and pervasive that the potential for saying something new, much less presenting a startling set of findings of conclusions is more presumptuous than ambitious. Yet, it is in the nature of human nature to persist in lurching forward, no matter how slightly, and to seek closure no matter how tentative.

I take as my text a highly personal point-counterpoint as it were: the collection of my essays published nearly thirty years ago under the rubric: *Israeli Ecstasies and Jewish Agonies*, and the work I have pursued in the intervening years called *Taking Lives*. Risking a digression before addressing the wider issue of Jewish survival directly, I should like your indulgence on how I view my own work in tandem, as bookends separated by a considerable amount of time.

The purpose of *Israeli Ecstasies and Jewish Agonies* was to explain how a dialectical set of relationships emerged as a result of a new centrality for Jewish life, Israel; and the evolution of a new periphery as well, in North America.[4] For what seemed to be at stake in the late 1960s and early 1970s was the serious weakening of Jewish life. In the West it appeared as an entity of value apart from the existence of Israeli society. Now, the situation is curiously reversed. There is a widespread recognition of life in the Jewish periphery, from wide ranging histories of the Diaspora to the revitalization of Jewish literature and music. But there is also a growing skepticism, even fear, of the centrality of the Israeli center.

My intentions in *Taking Lives* were somewhat less global: to develop a social scientific framework for understanding the Holocaust in terms of state legitimacy, or more specifically, variables of class, status and power familiar to those who work in the Weberian tradition.[5] Curiously, we have a huge literature based on personal testimonials and biographies, and only a slightly smaller amount of writings exploring theological and religious considerations that emerged from the Holocaust. The social analysis of this monumental tragedy is only now receiving its proper due. Moreover, it is becoming plain that the thin line between the personal and the political, the subjective and the objective, dissolved on the ground, in the quotidian world all human being inhabit. What makes the study of Jewish identity complex is that we are not dealing with a unilinear phenomenon, but one more akin to a multiplexed phenomenon moving in a variety of historical as well as structural directions. To discuss the Jewish condition is to examine religiosity, nationality, and culture all at once as well as one at a time. Indeed, to disaggregate these elements of Judaism results in distortions and reductions that can, and sadly enough often does, lead to little light and much heat.

To be sure, the arguments between those who emphasize issues of class stratification on one side and cultural identity on the other indicate that exaggerated claims for any one sort of social scientific approach to life taking issues are likely to result in frustration and futile argumentation. I turned from a study of Israeli-Jewish relations to an examination of the deeper roots of the Jewish condition as such, because the explosion of literature on the Holocaust led to serious distortions in the intellectual landscape; and no less important, the social scientific accounts, while attempting to repair such distortions resulting from a variety of reductionists in the popular literature, introduced a few new sins of their own.

We have an astonishing amount of personal narratives (some serious, others self-serving) providing eyewitness reports of horrors and human degradation, but failing to place the final solution in any larger context. So what we are left with is a series of uplifting or depressing stories of living with the past, or getting beyond horror and degradation. The other end of this is what might be called the theological exegesis, in which issues of an ultimate sort are examined: from can we believe in God's goodness after the Holocaust, to a variety of messages, intentional or otherwise, that serve as Providential warning signals for those who fall from grace. Again, the quality of such human examinations of providential intentions shifts from profound to the trivial and worse.

Because a collectivity, the Jewish people, were uniquely singled out for total and complete annihilation, Christian and Hebrew scholars alike have tried to interpret the Nazi war on the Jewish people in Biblical, revelatory terms; frequently laced with reflections on the historical status of Jews living in a Christian world, and extending into the particular economic drives, political motives, and cultural longings of each world religion in relation to the other.

In the midst of these larger trends, what we may call the biographical and the theological respectively, a third trend has emerged: the empirical study of how the Holocaust took place, what it happened when and where it did, and why it surfaced in relation to the Jews of Europe. The major and admittedly bowdlerized answers given are: first, Germans have a unique propensity for racial purity and animus toward strangers in their midst who do not share in the national value system; and second, it is not the nation but the system, the National Socialist system that created the foundation for implementing the final solution.

I do not want to enter a polemic with other viewpoints, or argue issues examined at length in other parts of *Taking Lives.* Rather, I want to note emphatically, that my own view is that however multiple the sources of anti-Semitism, and however broad the base of emotive support for the Final Solution, the actual implementation and execution of the Holocaust was a function of State power, of the legal and military monopoly of power that resided in the hands of the National Socialist state which allowed for the Holocaust to move ahead in its grinding, vicious wholeness. The emergence of Israel as a state after World War Two implicitly recognized as much. It made Jew and non-Jew alike aware of the modern as well as ancient sources of power and authority. The monopoly of power rather and the protective cover of borders rather than the beneficence of rulers became the touchstone of Jewish life after the Holocaust. The special fusion of secular politics and a religious-cultural tradition provided the grounds of legitimacy for the Jewish State of Israel.[6]

However "banal" the perpetrators of the Holocaust may have been as private persons, they acted in concert as part of a killing machine, comprised of a hugely expanded and swollen bureaucracy dedicated to surveillance, a military establishment that dwarfed anything hitherto known in the annals of European armed force, and a disciplined political party apparatus that had as its exclusionary membership mission the extirpation and destruction of Jewish life wherever Nazism held sway, including occupied zones and lands not known in earlier eras for anti-Semitism as national preoccupation. In this sense, *Taking Lives* is an effort to concretize the work of political sociology, of the interaction between state and society. It is also a way to lay claim to the fact that the very act of taking lives and counting bodies is the sociological equivalent to locating the essential variable by which a society and a state are to be judged.

The analysis of Jewish survival in post-Holocaust terms is immediately made complex by its triadic nature: We must simultaneously deal at once with the state of Israel, having a model of democratic rule rooted in Westminster; a divinely inspired Torah passed on to Jews over centuries and millennia as a guide to ethical and legal behavior; and a Jewish culture filtered through many nations and conventions and languages that are summarized in an adherence to some form of community living and personality characteristics. Add to this mix relationships between persons who claim a common adherence to Judaism in philosophic terms, and any ensuing analysis of the Jewish condition becomes numbingly complex. That as it may be, our common task is to clarify these relationships, so that we have an analytical model rather than a clerical muddle. Essentially, I do so by taking a minimalist, rather than maximalist view of the Jewish-Israel relationship. Along with Abba Eban,[7] I assume that being a Jew implies commitment to the fate and fortune of Israel and to a community of like-minded souls. Whether being an Israeli implies, in reverse, a commitment to the fate and fortune of world Jewry, is a question perhaps best left in abeyance for the present. Let me immediately note that this minimalist approach carries risks. Marginalization within Jewish religious life can, and often does, readily translate into complete secularization, or as is sometimes the case, into varieties of alternative civil religious persuasions.

Before we examine current struggles, it might be useful to remind ourselves how military matters stood only a quarter century ago. It might help explain why I referred titled my work *Israeli Ecstasies and Jewish Agonies.* In the period that followed the euphoria of the Six-Day War in 1967, it is understandable that a dominant wing of Israeli leaders could argue as David Ben-Gurion had earlier, that commitment to Zionism could have no validity without Jewish immigration to Israel. Without such a pioneer vision, Jewish life in the Diaspora was bankrupt.

I don't know how long it will take, whether ten years or fifty years, but in time, America will be a unitary nation, just like any other nation. It is entirely different with Jews in Israel. The roads in this country are Jewish roads; they were built by Jews. The houses that you see here were built by Jews. The trees are Jewish trees; they were planted by Jews. The railway is a Jewish railway; it is conducted by Jewish workers, by Jewish engineers. The papers are Jewish. We do not live a group life. Here we are living a national life. There is another difference between Israeli Jewry and Diaspora Jewry. We are also an independent factor in international life. We appear like any other free people at the United Nations. We meet with representatives of large and small states on an equal footing. We do not need *shtadlanim* (intercessors) any more.[8]

Those amazingly proud words uttered in the glowing aftermath of military victory now appear quaint, inspiring more response than regard. As a consequence of military struggle, one, which resulted in a political stalemate, redefinition of Israeli realities topped the agenda. Claims of sovereignty and autonomy have been tempered by a renewed realization of the special relationship between Israelis and Jews, without much outward concern for who is preeminent in this interaction network. Thus, in a new book by Geoffrey Wheatcroft on *The Controversy of Zion* we have a summary of arguments against Zionism that have become as strident as they are commonplace.

It is the very absence of the kind of ethnic nationalism and cultural homogeneity exemplified by Israel that has made possible their own triumphant story. What Jews outside of Israel have come to recognize very clearly is not only that Israel is not their home, but that the Israelis, however much they admire them, are no longer their people.... The final paradox might be that Zionism has succeeded in everything but its ostensible purpose; to resolve the Jewish Question by normalizing the Jewish people and to end their chosenness.... And yet the Jews remain in some manner chosen.... Today there is a Jewish state, which is a source of healing pride for millions of Jews, but also a source of anxiety. Should they defend the religious zealots and right wing settlers who play an ever-larger part in Israeli life? Or is Israel increasingly irrelevant to the fabulous success story of the Jews of America?[9]

More contradictory general propositions on Israeli-Diaspora relations are hard to envision. But we need to determine whether such varied sentiments represent something deeper than the changing fortunes of warfare and statecraft. Do these two ideological frameworks define not only the limits of Israeli existence, but also the survival capacities of the Jewish people as a whole? In exploring this question, we must confront a reality in which a center (Israel) remains relatively weak while a periphery (American Jewry) is relatively powerful.

Israel's geographical rationalization, in the current period, and the Arab countries' own continuing struggles between tradition and modernity, have led to a renewed search for religious, ethnic and cultural elements within Judaism. Do the political and social structures that divide Jews along national lines permit unity or fusion in religious and cultural terms? I suspect that even posing the issue in this way makes a positive answer possible. Definitive political and theological responses cannot be concluded with respect to Israeli-Jewish relationships. Dialectical people have a habit of maintaining long-standing differences, broken in moments of crisis by tactical synthesis. This certainly characterizes the present condition of Jews and Israelis. The state of Israel is an irreducible fact, one that Jews must live with—even those who might not celebrate such a fact. In this sense, Zionism and anti-Zionism are fewer policies than postures in present-day Israel. National realities now seem indifferent to internationalist ambitions.

In a broad series of stages, the Arabist effort to convert Jews into a pariah people and Israel into a pariah state have failed. This is no small accomplishment in its own right. Beyond these, a series of issues within Judaism were also resolved in the past quarter century. Arabic adversaries, by ceaselessly questioning the legitimacy of Israel as a "settler state", provided the foundations for wide-ranging reexamination of the contemporary state of Jewish affairs, culminating in relatively successful efforts by Israel to come to terms with its position in the Middle East. Again, no small achievement for a land that felt far more tied to Europe than the Middle East only a quarter century ago. Such self-exploration might be a constant in Jewish affairs without external pressures, but with them. the sense of immediacy takes on dramatic proportions.

The repudiation of the Zionist as racism canard, with the firm support of Western democracies, was also coupled with a series of negotiated arrangements starting with Egypt and Jordan, and now expanded to include Palestinian Moslems and Syrians. A variety of diplomatic as well as military arrangements have modified the sense of Israeli estrangement. The question however remains whether weakening the threat to Israel as a pariah State translates into a weakening sense of identification of Jews with the fate and fortune of Israel. More bluntly, do Jews now view Israel as a place to visit archaeological sites and go scuba diving rather than a place to restore political commitments or make an issue out of vigilant support?

Debate about whether Israel is central or peripheral to the Jewish experience in the United States or elsewhere in the Diaspora is only one half the essential paradigm. The other half is whether Judaism is central to Israeli political integration. It might well be that underlying these questions is whether Judaism is central to Jews wherever they are. Posing the issue in these admittedly harsh terms is not an exercise in dialectics, but an effort to examine the empirical state of affairs that makes the issue of Israeli sovereignty profoundly meaningful. For example, if migration from Israel to America far exceeds Jewish-American immigration to Israel, does this automatically weaken or strengthen world Jewry?

If one believes in the organic incompleteness of Jewish life outside Israel, the answer is self-evident. But for those who believe that the Jewish nation resides wherever a Jewish congregation exists, temporal problems of the state of Israel are of only limited significance to what Herzl called "the Jewish Company." The extent to which orthodox positions on Israeli centrality have broken down is best illustrated by the current demographic situation. At least 10 percent of Israelis, or approximately 450,000 of Israel's citizens, are currently living in the United States on a relatively permanent basis. Beyond that, new migrants to Israel from Russia are often interested in moving to the United States, Canada, New Zealand, or Australia, what might be referred to as the Anglo democracies, rather than staying in Israel. Whatever the explanations offered—hardships of settlement in Israel, limited knowledge about or interest in Jewish religious life, fears of new military hostilities, oppression of tax burdens, or limits to upward mobility and career opportunities—Jewish dedication to Israel remains highly questionable under present-day circumstances.

Whenever the existence of Israel has been threatened by hostile, military dominated states, and the survival of the Jews of Israel is clearly imperiled, Jewish solidarity has been evident and made near total by the "facts on the ground" total. Witness the outpouring of international Jewish support for Israel in the 1967 and 1973 Arab-Israeli conflicts or, most recently, the solidarity of Jews against Iraq, Libya and Iran, i.e., the so-called terrorist states. Ultimate questions about survival always obviate niceties of discussion and disputation. The choice between social life and death, like individual life and death, makes intellectual hairsplitting seem fatuous. To the extent that the Jewish State has, from its inception, been engaged in a survival-crisis-response syndrome, one can speak with confidence of the centrality of Israel to the Jewish experience.

However, when minimum conditions of Israeli security are met and, in consequence, the needs of a large portion of Jewish peoplehood are met, the question of the centrality of Israel to Jewish life becomes thorny. When Israeli survival is not in jeopardy, but to the contrary, relatively normalized, conventional distinctions between socialism, nationalism, and religiosity, slip back into the rhetoric ordinarily employed by Jews inside and outside of Israel. The state of normality thus unleashes national rather than overseas concerns. The relative lack of such normal, peaceful, conditions in the Middle East since the founding of Israel has obscured real differences between Jews in the Diaspora and in Israel with respect to a variety of issues affecting the international Jewish community. The data indicate some clear guidelines in this respect.[10]

▸ *First,* reform Jews, adults and youth, who are presumably representative of American Jewry as a whole, rate the relationship of American Jews to Israel as very important; but only a quartile agree with the statement that Israel is the center of contemporary American Jewish life. As orthodoxy continues to hold sway in Israel, and reform and conservative religious movements inside Israel are confronted with problems of legitimacy, even that figure may be inflated.

▸ *Second*, regional studies of American Jews reveal noticeable differences in the strength of Zionism between fathers and sons. Fathers scored significantly higher on indicators of Zionist persuasion. For the most part, all available data support the argument that the Zionism of American Jews is less intent to migrate than a general belief in Israeli claims. Pro-Israel sentiment is directly linked to perceived threats to the survival of the Israeli State.

▸ *Third,* American Jewish attitudes vary significantly depending on whether Middle East wars are perceived to have negative consequences for the United States. Thus, the reaction of American Jews to the Six-Day War of 1967 was more favorable than their attitudes toward the Yom Kippur War of 1973 or the Lebanese adventure of 1982 precisely because the synergy and consistency of American and Israeli interests in the earlier war did not obtain for the later conflicts.[11]

Israel has registered genuine achievements in various spheres of life science and medical research, cyberspace technology, humanistic education in kibbutzim, folk music and dance, basic agricultural self-sufficiency, army efficiency and *esprit*, etc. Beyond these areas, the caliber of Israeli society is not notably higher that say, Western Europe. In politics, academic life, industry, labor leadership, religion, *belles lettres*, the media, the dramatic and fine arts, Israel, while surely not lagging too far behind other developing countries, Israel is far from producing standards of excellence sufficient to inspire its own citizens or the Jewish Diaspora. As long as the relationship of the Diaspora to Israel is strictly financial, with no genuine joint responsibility in planning for Israel's development, or real accountability to contributors abroad for the funds collected, one cannot (outside the religious clusters) expect thoughtful Jews the world over to express a sustained sense of personal involvement in Israel at the intimate, or subjective levels.

It may be argued that an adequate reexamination of Israeli-Diaspora relations should begin by understanding Israel as both a Third World entity and a European democracy operating in a unique context. Perceived in this way, tendencies toward growing separation of Jewish life in the Diaspora from identification with Israeli society might be seen as part of a long-run secular trend distinguishing nationhood from religiosity and ethnicity. Diminishing Jewish involvement with Israel may have long-run benefits as well as costs for center and periphery alike. For Israel, such secularization could lessen overseas pressure in the formation of national and international policies, and hence permit Israel greater flexibility in its decision-making processes. For Diaspora Jews, such a distinction might compel greater attention to Judaism as such, to the role of religion, culture, and ethnicity in the contemporary West, apart from concerns about military annihilation currently shrouding Middle Eastern affairs. Evolution of the debate over Israeli centrality and Diaspora marginality has moved a considerable distance beyond inherited Zionist and anti-Zionist shibboleths.

Magic wands cannot resolve the question of Israel's centrality to Jewish life. The inner reality of Jewish life is triploid; it is not simply manifested in choices dictated by Statist considerations. Judaism has had its own special religious Trinitarianism: Israel, the Torah, and God. Corresponding to that, in secular terms is first, Israel as a state (in the Hobbesian sense of

retaining a monopoly of power). Second, peoplehood, in which
the sacred documents are invested in the Jewish people as a
whole, a legal entity without a physical nation, but a national
people. Finally, there is the Hebrew God, in which a collection
of moral sentiments, legal precepts, and cosmological concepts
are joined and fused to make Judaism a religion.

The centrality or marginality of American Jews to the Israeli
experience can similarly be broken down into a kind of tripartite arrangement. Survey data have repeatedly shown that
American Jewry's response to Israel depends on whether
Israel is being talked about as a nation-state, as part of a
worldwide communion of Jewish people, or as a theological-
religious phenomenon having transcendental as well as imma-
nent goals. When Israel is physically threatened by military
activity, there is a high degree of international Jewish mobilization. But it is hard to imagine any responsible American
Jewish leader calling on the Jewish people of the world to
respond exclusively to Israeli needs as a state power in the
Middle East, or for that matter even to urge support of the
specifics of everyday life in Israel.

The historian Melvin Urofsky who has done significant
research in American Zionism, put the matter of Jewish response to Israeli appeals forcefully: Being Jewish is not the
central concern of most American Jews: being American is.
With the exception of one or two "gut" issues, such as anti-
Semitism or Israel, American Jews are divided, indeed fragmented on every other question.[12] They want to consider
matters relating to religion as private, secular issues, even
those that might affect Judaism, are to be treated in a secular,
an American manner. Another way to express this same opinion is to observe that Jewish communities are themselves
seriously affected by the centrality of American society and
economy as a whole to the continued existence of Israel. In
this sense, to the extent Israel as a society remains peripheral
to American centrality, Israel compromises its claims for cul-

tural or religious centrality with respect to Jews, especially those who live in the United States.

The notion of centrality, or the direct impact of Israel on a peripheral Jewish population, has three distinct frames of reference: the state of Israel, the Jewish people, and the Hebrew religion. This is a critical differentiation inherent in the history of Judaism. Its tripartite character underscores a great deal of ambiguity in Jewish life. But it also gives Jewish life considerable strategic resilience. What falsifies a great deal of data and statistics on whom is or is not a Jew, or *when* a Jew becomes a non-Jew, and so on, arises precisely within the American context, where this kind of tripartite structure becomes intolerably manifest. National Jews, ethnic Jews, and theological Jews all confront each other as total ideological solutions (i.e., assimilationist or survivalist) to fragmented political frameworks. As a result, contemporary Judaism exemplifies a feeling of pluralistic peoplehood that involves many diverse elements. Judaism cannot easily be destroyed or eliminated: but neither can it be easily synthesized into a single supreme frame of reference.

The universalism, or if one prefers, the very porosity of Judaism, even if it causes moments of grief to Israel's particular concerns, provides residual strength to Jewish survivalist impulses. One indicator of this strength is the multiple problems encountered in conversion efforts. The source of so many failures in evangelical efforts to "convert" Jews is the narrow fundamentalist definition of what constitutes Jewishness. Christian fundamentalism tends to limit its interests in Judaism to one of theology. To the extent that Islamic theology also sees Judaism as exclusively a religious faith, it has the same interpretive problems as the Christian West. Consequently, their efforts to eliminate Judaism via theological conversion have had limited success. Jewish strength resides in its plurality, clerical and secular alike. The gigantic historical ambiguity involving God, ethnicity, and nation is a positive and healthy factor in Judaism's survival. But it also makes it exceedingly difficult to reach a definitive answer to the question of how central Israel is to Jewish life.[13]

In the past, Israeli centrality implies Jewish marginality. The ideological bridge between Israel and Jews is much more heavily traversed in one direction: from the Diaspora to Zion. Yet in demographic terms, the bridge carries more traffic from Zion to Diaspora. Increasingly, an older pattern, in which Jewish leaders are frequently asked to define the role of Israel in the life of the individual American Jew, is being replaced by a newer pattern, in which Israeli figures must begin to explain the role of Diaspora Jews in the life of individual Israelis.

As this pattern of intellectual cross-fertilization ripens, the foundations of Zionism themselves undergo scrutiny. The totality of the destruction of the European Jewish communities that thrived between 1789 and 1939 served to vindicate classical Zionist persuasions. But the continued vitality of Jewish life in Anglo-American democracies has, with equal force, compelled reconsideration of Zionist ideological tenets. Earlier maximalist demands that Diaspora Jews resettle in Israel have reduced themselves to a minimalist approach. Now the durability, permanence, indeed, the absolute necessity of a viable Diaspora has replaced older, more religious-oriented visions of a return to Zion. What this does to Israel's centrality in the lives of world Jewish communities becomes a question of some urgency.

Do Conservative and Reform varieties of the Jewish religion have anything to contribute to Israeli society or theological attitudes in Israel? To ask this question is to ignore the most pronounced tendency in present-day Israeli society itself, the manifestly weak levels of religiosity and religious participation in Israeli society. Israel's secularization approximates those characteristics of other modernizing societies. Regular synagogue attendance is probably lower than Sunday morning churchgoing in American society. Indicators such as worship in a synagogue may prove little, by themselves, but at least they help make quite plain the differences between support for

Israel and active participation in Jewish community or religious experience.

We need to confront uncomfortable questions within both Jewish life and Israeli society. To what degree can one have an American Jewish identification that corresponds to a highly secularist Israeli society? This is a more difficult question than whether one identifies with Israel in a strictly crisis scenario. Here the touchy issue becomes under what global conditions might support for Israel not be forthcoming by American Jewry? For example, what kinds of military action or capabilities would make it permissible or even theologically mandated to withhold support of Israel by Jewish communities? We witnessed the beginnings of this sort of distinction in the Israeli-Lebanese struggles in the early 1980s. Israeli military victories in the field were greeted with far more unease than threats to Israeli society in earlier periods.

Such extremely sensitive questions are being raised with increasing frequency. If Israel enters a period of protracted political stalemate, in which it is part of pluralistic goals, and dynamic development in the Middle East as a whole; the capacity for quick mobilization of world Jewish support will diminish. As the war-peace syndrome recedes, stagnation-growth issues emerge. In such a scenario, matters taken for granted between Jews in the Diaspora and Israelis in Zion, are far fewer and less compelling than in the grand dialogue of the formative period of Israeli existence.

Whether the Jewish question rather than the Israeli question has once more become central is the thorny problem of the present decade. Throughout the twentieth century, every decade has thrown up a master problem that has occasioned realignment, reshuffling, and rethinking. Old alliances tend to dwindle with a decade's end. Those who found themselves united around opposition or support of the Vietnamese conflict in the 1960s, found old alliances sharply curtailed alliances in the 1970s under the impact of the Middle East crisis. This is not to say that new forms of association between Jews as an "interest group" and other social movements cannot be forced, only that the foundation of such associations tend to be more domestic than global concerns.

The American experience has become more intertwined with Jewish experience than at any time in the past. Quite apart from military support to Israel, whether posed in terms of integration of Russian Jews, Jewish settlements in the West Bank, or impact of Latin American and South African Jewish communities on new immigration patterns, all become central considerations for those charged with rethinking democratic premises in American Jewish organizational affairs. The special concerns of Israel must somehow be placed within a Jewish context so that policy choices are not reduced to Israel's impact on America, but rather the more complex issue of Israel's reflection of, no less than impact upon the so-called Jewish question.

The existence of Israel has led to a realignment of forces. Because of the compelling fusion of objective circumstances and subjective sentiments, the Jewish people are no longer the people they were between the *Anschluss* and Auschwitz. Jews no longer exhibit the same circumscribed commercial concerns or the same focus on survival. Whether or not this shift from economic survivalism to political participation is celebrated, the fact that the Jewish question has become central to international debates in the 1990s is incontrovertible. It is profoundly intertwined with problems ranging from energy supplies to military preparedness, to profound reconsideration of the Holocaust and the behavior of nations under stress. Within this global context, the Israeli issue is profoundly meaningful to all peoples and parties. Outside of that context, Israel is of special meaning primarily to the Jewish peoples.[14]

Given the plural status of Jewish identification, what then should be the posture of the individual Jew toward the question of national allegiance to Israel and political participation in matters of importance to Israel? This question is specifically anguishing for the American, Canadian, and West European

Jews (in that order) since there is only limited potential for full citizen participation in Latin America, South Africa, Russia, Eastern Europe, and portions of the Third World where Jews exist in large numbers. Past Jewish participation in these home countries of the Diaspora has been at the economic and social levels. As a result, the problem of dual or multiple political allegiance remains, for such people, largely an abstraction.

Diaspora participation in the affairs of state in Israel is limited to rhetorical flourishes and editorial anguishes. It is true that certain key leaders in the American Jewish community have some marginal voice in Israeli life. But this is primarily a consequence of philanthropic and monetary power; not any special policy making acumen that is essential to Israeli political affairs. Prominent wealthy American Jews have the same input into Israel as the International Monetary Fund does in any Third World country. A central problem in consequence is the extent to which Jewish solidarity, in times of Israeli military crisis, can or should be brought to bear on one's own country or countries. Jewish mobilization in support of Israel by no means violates their citizen obligations to the United States or anywhere else in which they have a vote as well as a voice; but the United States is particularly sensitive to large interest-group pressures.

The arguments, which have raged concerning divided loyalties of American Jews, are largely chimerical if not entirely fictitious. Certainly, throughout the relatively brief history of the state of Israel, Jews have never surrendered political loyalty to another state. If anything, Jewish communities have drawn closer to the American political mainstream as Israeli interests have become intertwined with those of the United States. In the absence of any impulses in the opposite direction, the issue of dual loyalties remains of marginal importance. Only in special circumstances, such as the Pollard spy case, are uncomfortable issues of any relevant sort introduced.

While conceptually possible, it is empirically unlikely to envision a condition under which American and Israeli inter-

ests diverge so sharply as to compel Jews to confront the
pluralistic premises of this viewpoint with the monistic requirements to chose between either the United States or
Israel. At such a time, the very essence of the American
commitment to pluralism or, perhaps, the Israeli commitment
to democracy would be sorely strained. And in such moments,
abstract guidelines must yield to historical specifics; such is the
character of decision making in times of national strife. The
great advantage of Israel, its basic bargain with Western civilization, is its explicit commitment to democratic government
and pluralistic outlooks, presumably a milder form of commitment that Americans have to the United States. If this delicate
equilibrium breaks down on either side a decision might be
forced. But to presume so on a priori grounds would represent
an extreme form of unwarranted historical pessimism.

Jews have traditionally lived in a partial, fragmented world.
Tensions and polarities are built into the substance of Jewish
lifestyle. Marginality is a consequence of a people dispos-
sessed, displaced, and well traveled. More pointedly, marginality is also a condition that makes possible facing problems
of the world with a maximum amount of objectivity and a
minimum amount of undiluted fanaticism or ideological investment. Perfect integration into any national system, even
that of Israel, could well represent negation of positive Jewish
values. It would also signal a collapse of the pluralistic sources
of American politics and traditions. Presently, neither of these
outcomes seems imminent. Jewish concerns can remain
largely focused on positive solutions to practical issues; including the status of Israel. But as Charles Liebman has rightly
pointed out, that given Israel as a state with a moral purpose,
neither Israelis nor Jews can quite accept in theory much less
the practice of unlimited democracy. As a result conservative
values coexist in uneasy alliance with liberal politics.[15]

What seems to have taken place is a huge shift in cultural
fault lines, a transformation of values that has seen the emergence of problems of secularization and national identity that

are characteristic of emerging free societies the world over. While concerns about individualism and identity clearly enlist the sympathies of Jews the world over, they do not exhaust the *Geist* or *Weltanschauung* of the Jewish people at century's end. Varieties of specifically Jewish clerical belief, from pragmatic reconstruction to cabalistic mysticism abound.

If the current situation hardly permits euphoria or ecstasy, the processes underway in Israel do serve to refocus Jewish energies and enlarge its visions. The Holocaust remains the tie that binds the Jewish people to the State of Israel. But by the same token, the State of Israel is inextricably tied to the Jewish people and its history. It is scarcely an accident that in the Arab assaults, from abusive rhetoric to physical assaults, on the Israeli State, the easy slippage in language from Israelis to Jews is a sad reminder that the State does not define the Jewish people. But by the same token, the State remains the protectorate of the Jewish people.

If this is an uneasy and disquieting dialectic, it remains the price paid for a century of genocide. That so much change has occurred in the past half century is a tribute to the maturation of Israel. However, it also speaks to the survival capacities of Judaism as such. Israel is the pre-eminent example in our times on how political and emotional flexibility are special characteristics of small new nations and big historic peoples. This uneasy alliance of modernity and tradition is the solution on the ground to an earlier universe of Jews without a State, and a State without Jews.

Part IV

TOWARD A GENERAL
THEORY OF
STATE-SPONSORED
CRIME

Functional and Existential Visions of Genocide

In the ashes of the past we can taste the ashes of the future, and from both we try to create the present and to awaken life. We pass by and, precisely because now and again we do awaken life, that which is called real life is so precious to us — precious because we know what society, if it wishes to remain itself for even a week or two, must not allow itself to become aware of: that transience and death are always at the door, that all will turn to ashes.

— Heinrich Böll[1]

EVEN THE MOST RUDIMENTARY EXAMINATION OF VARIOUS TOTALITARIAN SYSTEMS REVEALS serious shortcomings in conventional social science modes of dealing with the interrelations between repressive regimes and mass murder. The attempt to locate "bad" practices in bad states is as flawed an approach as is the attempt to locate "good" practices in good states. Such neat Platonic tautologies just fall apart in practice. There are "bad" fascist states, like Germany, that took lives with impunity; there are other fascist states, like Italy, that rarely took lives. There are "good" democratic regimes, like England, the Netherlands, and Belgium, that would never dream of violating the civil liberties of their native citizenry. But these same regimes, when operating in imperial contexts, whether in Africa or Asia, had few compunctions about engaging in near-genocidal practices against native populations.

This chapter takes up functional and existential perspectives on genocide. It is an effort not so much to discredit earlier efforts as to make evident the need to further explore cultural forms, ignored by such inherited frameworks, for the purpose of arriving at a new synthesis. If the theory and practice of social science is to measure up to the needs of understanding, much less correcting, some of the most extreme yet typical behavioral characteristics of our times, we must engage in a sober look at the politics of social systems and their responses to the protection of, or prohibitions against, human life.

Defined in strictly organizational terms, fascism is a system in which the state regulates labor and management functions while the bureaucracy grows exponentially with respect to the rest of society, and in which the state apparatus, from the educational establishment to the military, is harnessed toward ensuring the state's own survival and expansion. State preeminence creates conditions for authoritarian domination over vast populations, national and even international. There are other characteristics of fascist systems. An organizational chart would show that countries such as Italy during 1920-1943 and Germany in 1933-1945 had considerable similarities: the one-party system, the permanent charismatic ruler, and the orchestrated mobilization of masses by state-controlled agencies. These are important categories in any discussion of fascism. Yet for those who had to (or rather could) make rational decisions about where to live in the 1930s, Rome in the fascist period was a far less austere and grim choice than Berlin in the Nazi period. In other words, a rational choice does not necessarily flow from a structural design.

The difficulty with functional description is best appreciated by considering Talcott Parsons's macroanalysis of fascism as linked to "the generalized aspects of Western society."

Abstraction as a sociological style is stretched to the limit. Included in the Parsonsian shopping list of fascist characteristics are the emergence of an emotional, fanatical mass movement closer to religion than to political movements; huge and sudden shifts in population and demographic patterns; the emergence of nationalization and nationalism; and the unwillingness of privileged classes to yield their prestige and power to newer, emerging classes.[2]

While these are certainly pivotal elements in fascism, they do not provide a sufficiently sensitive characterization of fascism as a social system. They offer meager guideposts in distinguishing between fascisms — for example, the cultural emphasis of Italian fascism in contrast to the biological determinism of German Nazism. Functional indicators of fascism are so general that they often serve to describe characteristics displayed by every advanced industrial system. They lack sufficient refinement to permit meaningful distinctions between fascism in Italy, National Socialism in Germany, and Falangism in Spain and other varieties of fascism elsewhere, or differences between fascist and other "totalistic" social systems.[3]

Whatever be the results of current debates concerning the uniqueness of the Holocaust, few events in the annals of twentieth-century genocide equal in horror the treatment of European Jewry by Nazi Germany. The dropping of the atomic bomb on Hiroshima might well equal it in terror but not in sustained magnitude. Likewise, the treatment of the Gypsies by the Nazis may have equaled the Holocaust in approach, but it did not approach it in size. On 20 January 1942 Hitler's government held a conference in the Berlin suburb of Wannsee, at which time the central administrative authorities of the Third Reich prepared to carry out Field Marshal Hermann Göring's order to "make preparation for the general solution of the Jewish problem within the German sphere of influence in Europe." The total number of Jews slated for extermination was 11 million.[4] The Nazi war machine fell short of realizing this number by approximately one-half, since the bulk of Soviet Jewry survived the war and nations like England and Switzerland were never occupied and hence their Jewish populations fell outside the Nazi sphere of influence. Even so, available data indicate that nearly 6 million Jews were arbitrarily and collectively executed between 1939 and 1945 at the hands of the Nazis for the "crime" of being Jewish.[5] This figure does not include other groups who also died in concentration camps, such as Poles, Gypsies, and other "undesirables." But the treatment of other peoples remained relatively random in contrast to the highly rationalized and total destruction of Jews under Nazi occupation. One-third of world Jewry was exterminated during Hitler's rule. The 16 million Jews of 1939 were reduced to less than 11 million by 1945.[6]

Rationalization of the Nazi program of assassination moved by stages: First came the 1933 declarations that the Jewish problem was uniquely a German curse, the slogan being "The Jews are our misfortune." Next came the 1935-1937 period in which the Nuremberg Laws were enacted, decreeing that only persons of German blood, or Aryans, could be citizens of the German Reich. The third stage, covering the 1938-1939 period, was one in which the first concentration camp was opened at Buchenwald and mass anti-Jewish riots occurred in both Berlin and Vienna. The fourth stage, of 1939-1940, was one in which World War II began and ghettos were sealed and converted into concentration camps. In the fifth stage, 1942-1944, the bulk of the Jews were exterminated in the many concentration camps that had been developed after the Wannsee (Berlin) Conference. It was also during this period that the liquidation of all ghettos throughout Europe was carried out with demographic precision. The sixth and final stage took place in the last year of the war, 1945. Once it became apparent that the Nazi war machine had been beaten, every attempt was made to obliterate all traces of the various and sundry activities committed in the name of cleansing the Third Reich by destroying its captive Jewish remnants.

The natural history of the Nazi genocide, its progression by stages, had a powerful psychological deterrent to mounting any resistance. There was the difficulty that the general population found it hard to believe that genocide was actually taking place. The literature on this is legendary as well as legion. Even those taken to the final death marches were willing to believe that they were simply to be taking showers, or in the process of being reunited with families. The very momentousness of genocide as a state practice makes it difficult for participants to recognize the phenomenon — those performing the executions no less than those being executed. Interesting in this regard is the case of the U.S. Jewish community during World War II. Despite its large size, it placed scarcely any pressure on the U.S. administration because of its relative disbelief in the magnitude of the Nazi Holocaust. As Henry Feingold reports in *The Politics of Rescue*, a volume on the Roosevelt administration and the Holocaust:

> In the case of the Jews the Roosevelt Administration had no popular mandate for a more active rescue role. Public opinion was, in fact, opposed to the admission of refugees, because most Americans were not aware of what was happening. A Roper poll taken in December of 1944 showed that the great majority of Americans, while willing to believe that Hitler had killed some Jews, could not believe that the Nazis, utilizing modern production techniques, had put millions to death. The very idea beggared the imagination. Perhaps there is such a thing as a saturation point as far as atrocity stories are concerned. In the American mind the Final Solution took its place beside the Bataan Death March and the Malmédy massacre as just another atrocity in a particularly cruel war. Not only were the victims unable to believe the unbelievable, but those who would save them found it extremely difficult to break through the "curtain of silence." The State Department's suppression of the details compounded the problem of credibility.[7]

Thus the question of genocide is made hard for those living in other social systems to comprehend, in part because it continues to be viewed as an aberration rather than a system.

The purpose of reciting these well-known details of Hitler's Germany is to illustrate that the precondition for mass extermination was engineered dehumanization: the division of the citizenry into organic members and alien intruders. This took places in stages: first by executive decree, then by legislative enactment, and finally by judicial consent. These legal and social events represented the precondition for the technical performance of genocidal policies by totalitarian states. This progressive delegitimization of minorities had its parallels throughout the Stalinist era. There is no question that large numbers of Ukrainian people were exterminated by the Soviet system and its secret police for failure to conform to the canons of the national question.

Still, a strong difference between communism and fascism was the hard-core ideology derived from Leninism, which argued that anti-Semitism and other forms of national discrimination were capitalist aberrations. The Soviet regime was always torn between attacking Jews and other "nationalities" for their "petty bourgeois" manifestations, and attacking anti-Semites and other chauvinists often on the same ideological grounds.[8] But confusion in theory did not prevent massacre in practice. In the *Gulag Archipelago*, Solzhenitsyn outlines the high points of the Soviet system of terror, its origins, duration, and structure. Literary devices notwithstanding, one is reminded that we are dealing with the liquidation of roughly 20 million Soviet citizens by the Soviet state; or a number that roughly parallels the number of those destroyed by the Nazi state:

> When people today decry the abuses of the cult they keep getting hung up on those years which are stuck in our throats, '37 and '38. And memory begins to make it seem as though arrests were never made before or after, but only in those two years. The wave of 1937-38 was neither the only one nor even the main one, but only one, perhaps the biggest of the three waves which strained the murky, stinking pipes of our prison sewers to bursting. *Before* it came the wave of 1929-30, the size of a good River Ob, which

drove a mere fifteen million peasants, maybe even more, out into the taiga and the tundra. But peasants are silent people, without a literary voice, nor do they write complaints or memoirs. No interrogators sweated out the night with them, nor did they bother to draw up formal indictments — it was enough to have a decree from the village soviet. And after it there was a wave of 1944-46, the size of a good Yenisei, when they dumped whole nations down the sewer pipes, not to mention millions and millions of others who (because of us!) had been prisoners of war, or carried off to Germany and subsequently repatriated. (This was Stalin's method of cauterizing the wounds so that scar tissue would form more quickly, and thus the body politic as a whole would not have to rest up, catch its breath, regain its strength.) But in this wave, too, the people were of the simpler kind, and they wrote no memoirs.

But the wave of 1937 swept up and carried off the Archipelago people of position, people with a party past, educated people, among whom many had been wounded and remained in the cities and what a lot of them had pen in hand! And today they are all writing, speaking, remembering: "Nineteen thirty-seven!" A whole Volga of the people's grief![9]

The efforts of Wilhelm Reich to place the Soviet and German experience in a similar cultural perspective, despite their differences in social systems, are particularly noteworthy. One may argue with his arcane linguistic formulation, but there can be no question as to the empirical accuracy of his evaluation:

The German and Russian State apparatuses grew out of despotism. For this reason the subservient nature of the human character of masses of people in Germany and in Russia was exceptionally pronounced. Thus in both cases, the revolution led to a new despotism with the certainty of irrational logic. In contrast to the German and Russian State apparatuses, the American State apparatus was formed by groups of people who have evaded European and Asian despotism by fleeing to a virgin territory free of immediate and effective traditions. Only in this way can it be understood that, until the time of this writing, a totalitarian State apparatus was not able to develop in America, whereas in Europe every overthrow of the government carried out under the slogans of freedom inevitably led to despotism.[10]

Reich also understood the common roots of Nazi biologism and Communist historicism: the search for "a new man." And if one could not be found, then the ideology was set in place to bring about such a new person, a clean person purged of sin and error. In short, a human god — vengeful to enemies of the state but compassionate to those who dedicated their lives to such a secular providence.

To see how ubiquitous the use of labels such as "fascism" can be, one need only contrast the situation in Germany with that in Italy, both in respect to the general nature of Italian fascism and its particular attitudes toward the Jewish question. In Italy, the Special Tribunal for the Defense of the State was a judicial body created ad hoc by fascism in the Exceptional Laws of 1926, with a view to prosecuting political opponents of the regime and removing them from the jurisdiction of the ordinary magistracy, which had more respect for legality.

The Special Tribunal was therefore by its very nature a contradiction in terms: an extralegal judicial body, which often made no effort to give a coherent juridical basis for its sentences or to conceal the political persecution that was its function. Between 1927 and 1943, the Special Tribunal passed 4,596 sentences for a total of 27,735 years of imprisonment. Death sentences numbered forty-two, of which thirty-one were carried out. Those sentenced were members of every social class and of various parties.[11] The source of this information on the relatively benign condition of Italian fascism is no less an authority than Antonio Gramsci. The great distinction between genocidal societies and incarceration societies is precisely what permitted Italian communism to survive and what made German communism die — only to be reborn in postwar East Germany as an appendage of Soviet occupation.

In retrospect, the differential attitude toward Jews seems a touchstone of Italian fascism and German Nazism. While both had similar forms of political organization, Italy represented, at its worst, an incarceration society; whereas Germany from the outset used the legal machinery to institutionalize a genocidal society. The passage of the Racial Laws marked the fundamental rupture between the fascist state and the Italian bourgeoisie. From 1938 to its collapse in 1943, the bulk of the Italians, and not simply those in one class, began to view the regime as something alien to them. The emergence of official anti-Semitism, restricted though it was to a juridical model, marked the beginning of the rejection of fascism by large numbers of Italians and began the period that produced the eventual downfall of the regime.[12] It was argued that fascist anti-Semitism was both unnecessary and extrinsic to the Italian class system and its cultural components. Various observers have seen Italian anti-Semitism as a fundamental component and fatal cause of the demise of the fascist role in Italy.[13]

With respect to distinguishing fascism from Nazism, it is exactly the different genocidal potentials of each that become crucial. Whatever formal or structural similarities, for example, between Italian fascism and German Nazism, it would be dangerous to see Nazism as a mere variant or extension of fascism. Whatever their organizational similarities, there is a need to distinguish between the two, precisely because significant, substantive differences exist in matters of life and death.

The emphasis on biological determinism within Nazism is in marked contrast to the cultural permissiveness of fascism. This is a crucial distinction, involving the definition of the national idea of fascism as against the racist idea of Nazism. While the two systems may have in common a high degree of antiliberalism and anticommunism and may be defined by an excessive amount of government authority in all areas of life, the biological when seen in political terms, that is, in its modus operandi, has to do with nothing less than the purification of race and hence the domination by a certain people and the liquidation of others. Italian fascism was born of a political tradition; German Nazism incorporated a biological purification of race. Even if totalitarianism represents a common denominator of fascism and Nazism alike, this does not necessarily mean that they performed in similar terms with respect to its own citizenry; or for that matter, foreigners under its temporary dominion.

A sophisticated appreciation of the political character of fascism is contained in an essay by Zeev Sternhell. He understands that the coming to power of the fascists in Western Europe was a function of the weakness of the Right and represented a political standpoint throughout:

> It was where the right was too weak to hold its own ground that fascism achieved its most marked successes. In times of acute crisis the right turned to the new revolutionary movement — the only one capable of confronting communism — for assistance, but never treated it with anything less than the deepest suspicion. By contrast where the right was sufficiently confident to face the Marxist left itself, where its positions were not unduly threatened and it had a solid social base, it did everything in its power to prevent the fascist phenomenon from getting out of hand. It concentrated above all on manipulating fascist troops and spending money to safeguard its own interests. Western Europe, Spain included, is a good case in point. It was not the strength of the right but its relative weakness, its fears, and its fits of panic, which created one of the essential conditions of fascist success.[14]

This stands in considerable contrast to the successes of German Nazism, where the "fascist phenomenon" did get "out of hand" and where the traditional Right proved inept and incapable of holding the line.

This brief description of the relative absence of mass murder in an incarceration society such as fascist Italy is offered not only to demonstrate that cultural variables are unique determinants of behavior in a social system but to demonstrate that defining a social and political system solely in terms of formal characteristics falsifies a comparative analytic framework. To argue the case for a great world historic struggle between fascism and communism on the basis of fine ideological distinctions seems less persuasive when we make central the question of officially inspired deaths. On the basis of raw data concerning their official assassination of citizens, Nazi Germany and Stalinist Russia are more proximate to each other than either is to Italian fascism or, for that matter, if official murders are a yardstick, to Chinese communism. When we compare the Italian and German experiences with fascism or the Russian and Chinese experiences with communism, we have the beginnings of a fundamental existential perspective toward social and political life.[15]

Some fascist or socialist countries announce virtually no death by state decrees, while in others carrying similar political labels, death may be a commonplace event. This existential dimension of the sociological enterprise must therefore be taken seriously. Whether people live or die is a fundamental distinction that may enable us to make a science of society a fundamental discipline; one based on the fusion rather than the further disaggregation of social, cultural, and personality dimensions.

It is not my purpose to discuss the entire range of issues related to life and death: deviance, suicide, random assassination, crimes of passion. These are being placed to one side, although they are certainly important; indeed, they are central to any social scientific definition of the social system. Rather, I want to emphasize a specific problem: the possibility of defining the state not in structural-functional terms of communism, liberalism, or conservatism, but in terms of whether, and to what degree, any state system permits the official and arbitrary termination of the lives of its citizenry.

Conventional war, to the extent that such conflicts adhere to distinctions between military and civilian activities, have largely been excluded from the purview of this discussion. Deaths occasioned by conflict between states are subject to so many interpretations, such as the right of survival of the state over and above the obligation of individuals to that state, that it is operationally imperative to distinguish warfare from genocide. This decision is further warranted by the weight of current empirical research that indicates that domestic destruction and international warring are separate dimensions of armed struggle. "There are no common conditions or causes of domestic and foreign conflict behavior."[16] And while this disjunction between domestic repression and foreign forms of decimation may seem incongruous, even a brief reflection will reveal how often foreign détente permits internal mayhem.

Life-and-death issues have a bearing beyond particular concerns of class or stratification. The subject of the arbitrary termination of life involves a general understanding of the merits and demerits of the social system as a whole, and the place of social order within the system. Emile Durkheim well understood this relationship:

> The questions it raises are closely connected with the most serious practical problems of the present time. The abnormal development of suicide and the general unrest of contemporary societies spring from the same causes. The exceptionally high number of voluntary deaths manifests the state of deep disturbance from which civilized societies are suffering, and bears witness to its gravity. It may even be said that this measures it. When these sufferings are expressed by a theorist they may be considered exaggerated and unfaithfully interpreted. But in these statistics of suicide they speak for themselves, allowing no room for personal interpretation. The only possible way, then, to check this current of collective sadness is by at least lessening the collective malady of which it is a sign and result.[17]

I would like to extend this line of analysis to the area of deaths due to reasons of state. Genocide differs markedly from suicide. Taking one's life, dying for oneself, out of anomie, altruism, fatalism; or dying voluntarily for one's state in order to uphold the boundaries of a nation; or to uphold the laws of a nation, such as the Socratic death — these represent a phenomenon apart. We are concerned with the arbitrary termination of life against the will of the individual and on behalf of the collective will of the state. The burden of these remarks is restricted to legal murder in which no one is punished other than the victim; that area of state power that terminates one life or many on behalf of an abstract political principle, whether it be national or international in character.

Hannah Arendt put the matter in proper perspective when she pointed out that there is a fundamental difference between totalitarian and libertarian concepts of law:

> At this point the fundamental difference between the totalitarian and all other concepts of law comes to light. Totalitarian policy does not replace one set of laws with another, does not establish its own *concensus juris*, does not create, by one revolution, a new form of legality. Its defiance of all, even its own positive laws implies that it believes it can do without any *concensus juris* whatever, and still not resign itself to the tyrannical state of lawlessness, arbitrariness, and fear. It can do without the *concensus juris* because it promises to release the fulfillment of law from all action and will of man; and it promises justice on earth because it claims to make mankind itself the embodiment of the law.[18]

It is now well understood that within totalitarian regimes the legal breakdown of normative behavior universally applied is a prelude to carrying out the most extreme forms of mass murder. Underlining the absence or the corruption of legality is the idea that the state demands a higher legality than may be called forth in the name of nature, divinity, or history. The source of authority is no longer human or even transcendental. Instead, there is a fanatic commitment to notions of state absolutism that make death not only possible but thoroughly justifiable. What can one do with those of inferior genetic worth and in opposition to the best of racial man? Posing the issues in this way makes possible not simply a collapse of impersonal law but its displacement by personal law, which in permitting certain societies to mandate the arbitrary taking of lives equates to no law at all.

In the interpretation of totalitarianism, all laws have become laws of movement. When the Nazis talked about the law of nature or when the Bolsheviks talk about the law of history, neither nature nor history is any longer the stabilizing source of authority for the actions of moral men: they are movements in themselves.

Underlying the Nazis' belief in race laws as the expression of the law of nature in man, is Darwin's idea of man as the product of a natural development which does not necessarily stop with the present species of human beings, just as under the Bolsheviks' belief in class-struggle as the expression of the law of history lies Marx's notion of society as the product of a gigantic historical movement which races according to its own law of motion to the end of historical times when it will abolish itself.[19]

The social system alone does not explain this drive to satisfy the requirements of history or nature by taking the lives of dissidents. Here again, national-cultural differences between Italians and Germans, between Chinese and Russians, loom very large.[20] Cultural traits create their own imperatives: that life is more (or less) important than death; that rehabilitation is always (or never) possible; that rehabilitation is valued and supported by money and effort (or a costly waste of time). The fact that highly genocidal societies cross ideological boundaries like fascism and communism indicates that structural ideological analysis itself does not exhaust the possibilities of understanding social systems.

There is one shadowy area of genocide that permits the state to take lives by indirection, for example by virtue of benign neglect, or death due to demographic causes. The kinds of ecological or environmental events discussed by Josué de Castro[21] or Lester R. Brown[22] cover areas formerly considered as death by natural causes: Malthusian verities of war, famine, floods, plagues, and so on. The efforts of a government to reduce the naturalness of this phenomenon and to harness technology and natural resources to minimize such disasters is itself a central indication of how a society tends to value life.[23] In certain circumstances, specifically in the formation of the Leninist-Stalinist Soviet Union, the state may be working at cross purposes: performing an active role in the cultivation of virgin soil, in hydroelectric dam projects, in reforestation, and so on, while at the same time condemning its own citizens to death in police camps, or sometimes even harnessing manpower in the building of those dams. Thus we must consider the role of even highly genocidal societies in minimizing random death.

Genocidal measurement of the state is to be confined to the area of state power and its attitude toward the sacred or profane nature of the life of its citizenry. As international warfare becomes a decreasing possibility for the settlement of major disputes and as individuals place greater emphasis on the responsibility of society for their economic or social failures, suicide can also be expected to increase. In this technological vacuum, the fundamental unit for taking or preserving life becomes the state. Measurement of the state's achievements must increasingly be made in terms of demographic mortality factors and the social production of goods in society. The central equation of state achievement is the ratio between the arbitrary consumption of people over and against the necessary production of goods.

Time, no less than space, is a crucial element in the characterization of a society as genocidal or pacific. In all social systems, whether in revolutionary or counterrevolutionary causes, moments of great tension lead to a catharsis that often claims many lives. But for a state to earn the appellation of a genocidal society it must conduct the systematic destruction of innocent lives over a relatively brief period of time; often with a planning notion to support such mass murder.[24] Killing must be endemic to the organization of all social life and state activities. On such a scale, one might say that Colombia during the period of *la violencia* and Paraguay under Alfred Stroessner were close to being the apotheosis of genocidal societies in Latin America, in contrast to such nations as Mexico and Peru which experience officially sanctioned violence sporadically and even spasmodically, but nonetheless, randomly and with little notion of a death plan.

A significant task of the state in establishing a genocidal system is its capacity to politically neutralize vast population sectors. This can be achieved in various ways: through careful news leakages of the physical dangers of resistance; rumors about the number of people subject to destruction; delineation of outsider and insider group distinctions to lessen fears of those not targeted for immediate destruction; and finally, rewarding portions of the genocidal society for remaining loyal to the state. (In Nazi Germany, as is not uncommon, such rewards were simplified by the redistribution of Jewish commercial business holdings to a sector of the non-Jewish German population.)

Whatever techniques are employed, the tacit support or quiescence of the larger population is necessary for genocidal practices to prove successful even in short-run terms. The different fates of Jews in nations like Denmark and Poland — in the former they were saved largely through militant support from all social and political sectors, whereas the absence of such broad support in the latter nation markedly contributed to their extermination — indicates that either tacit support or complete demobilization are prerequisites to the success or failure of the genocidal society. The general feeling of collective anomie, or isolation, is a powerful stimulant to the success or failure of a genocidal policy.

A crucial existential distinction should be made between genocide and coercion, between the physical liquidation and cultural stifling of peoples in contrast to bending the will of peoples to a presumed common end. The analysis of genocide does not entail a search for distinctions between good and evil — this is built into the nature of the enterprise as such — but simply the discontinuity between genocidal societies that may indicate a superficial resemblance to one another. Those who widely practice guilt, shame, imprisonment, torture — those malevolent practices with which so many societies are cursed but which, nonetheless, do not cross a psychological or physical threshold involving the taking of lives — are qualitatively different from genocidal societies.

This line of argument does not claim that economic explanations of the nature of genocide are somehow irrelevant. As we have seen, the presumed need for economic growth and the very real economic consequences of genocide in redistributing property and goods have played a considerable part in genocidal practices; and they continue to play a role in the bitter disputes over fiscal settlements and property reparations even a half century after the Holocaust. However, we come upon examples of totalitarian behavior that compel us to go beyond an economic explanation for genocidal practices.

A particular case in point is the utilization of the German railroads (the *Reichsbahn*) in the destruction of European Jewry. The deployment of railroads for such barbaric ends represented an "unprecedented event that was a product of multiple initiative, as well as lengthy negotiations and repeated adjustments among separate power structures."[25] The political use of railroads was real enough. But significantly, the transport of Jews took precedence over the transport of men and materials going to the battle zones; such human cargo also took priority over industrial transport. Hence, purely economic uses were superseded by political uses. As a result, the role of the German railroads in the destruction of Jews does indeed open profound questions about the substance and ramifications of the Nazi Reich. Above all, it becomes apparent that genocide takes place not because of any tremendous peer pressure to conform to the behavior of the actual perpetrators but as a consequence of a widespread, profound, accepted virulent anti-Semitism and racism that led the ordinary German citizen to believe that the Jews were a demonic enemy whose extermination was not only necessary but just.

The implications of this "prioritization," this decision to first eliminate the Jews and then pursue the war effort, indicates more than a choice of the irrational over the rational. It also has to do with the primacy of state over economy with full citizen complicity. For as Anna Pawelczynska has recently noted in her work on Auschwitz: "Concentration camps were state institutions of the Third Reich, operating on the basis of official statutes and a set of strictly secret directive that were

binding on the subordinate levels of government, which acknowledges the right of higher authorities to issue orders and
make laws of this type."[26] The manner in which genocide was
to be conducted was carefully structured: It involved edicts by
the state to paid employees of the camps. Given the nature of
mass murder as work, a special reward system was set up, and
there were even mechanisms for guilt alleviation in the conduct of such work. But the very nature of such state work
involved secrecy, duplicity, and criminal activities, which had
the effect of undermining state authority and lessening any
possibility of it becoming legitimate.

The state character of genocide leads to the conclusion that
it is a drastic oversimplification to identify genocide directly
with the developmental process. Certainly a considerable
amount of invariant correlations between the two might occasion such a general theory. However, the number of instances
in which genocidal practices are used to prevent development
— for instance, civilizations that have employed genocide,
especially racial genocide, to maintain a slave system over and
against an industrial one — clearly indicates that something
other than the necessity for industrial growth is operative as a
stimulant to genocide; that something else, that element which
truly distinguishes genocidal societies from industrial societies
practicing a wide range of coercive procedures to maintain
patterns of economic growth, is essentially political.

When the ruling elites decide that their continuation in
power transcends all other economic and social values, at that
point does the possibility, if not the necessity, for genocide
change qualitatively. For this reason, the chemistry of genocide
involves the fusion of strategies and principles common to
totalitarian regimes. So much is this the case that even when
genocidal practices serve to threaten economic development
— as it did in the irrational expulsion and destruction of Jewish
scientists from Nazi Germany or the mass incarceration of
trained professionals and their reduction to slave labor until
the point of death in the Stalinist experience — they manage

to take priority over "rational" economic goals. Genocide is always a conscious choice and policy. It is never just an accident of history or a necessity imposed by unseen economic growth requirements. Genocide is always and everywhere an essentially political decision.

The purpose then of an authentic political sociology is to provide a theory of the state based on a scale of its preservation and enhancement of life at one end of the continuum and death caused by the will of the state on the other end. There are all sorts of intermediary stages that complicate our task — for example, forms of suffering such as mass starvation that might make death a welcome relief. Yet genocide as an essential measure of the state and its purposes seem to provide an eminently significant break — through in linking the *phenomenon* of imposed death with a *system* of organized repression.

Too often those who make the equation between development and genocide are disguising their own metaphysical malaise. The Stalinists in their justification of the liquidation of the "kulak class," namely nine million or so Ukrainian people, provided a theory of human sacrifice to the gods of growth. Too often developmentalists like the late Paul Baran have not only claimed the necessity of human sacrifice but have gone along to strongly imply that as a private agenda, genocide is worth the price.[27] But what is a satisfactory price for development? Here we get into a type of moral bookkeeping. For example, it is estimated that the human costs of Soviet Communist development were between 20 and 40 million dead.[28] Would a smaller number have made the costs of development more bearable? One gets into a *reductio ad absurdum*. The moment it is argued that no human sacrifice is justified for economic development, the other side immediately comes to the fore, arguing that the consequence of such humanistic absolutism is pure stagnation.

It is virtually impossible to define, much less know, the exact crossover point between the empirical and the ethical. One might welcome research on what constitutes an appropriate number of human losses in the development process. For example: Is the dismemberment of the Indian population, or the emergence of a modern slave system utilizing millions of people and involving an incredible cultural dismemberment and disfiguration, worth the developmental achievement? Whether we pose the issue in historical or contemporary terms, the problem of genocide invites a virtually impossible moral bookkeeping.

Political leaders join a chorus of social scientists in claiming that a certain number of lives are worth a certain amount of development. But when one asks what number or which people, then the issues of genocide are joined. As Solzhenitsyn remarks, there was nothing asked about the disruption of Russian society until 1938 because until then the intelligentsia were not directly involved as victims.

When the victimized group was the peasantry, there was no outcry. When it was the urban proletariat, it was perfectly acceptable that they go to the rack. When it was one ethnic minority after another, it was perfectly rationalized in terms of development and nationalism. But when the intelligentsia felt the lash in 1938, questions about Soviet genocide arose. Genocide becomes a problem only when the intellectuals are affected; until then, they have an incredible capacity for myopic moral bookkeeping.

The intellectuals had no quarrel with Bolshevism in its formative stage. It is only when utopia turned into dystopia, and stories of massacres surfaced, that alarums were sounded. One problem this raises is the selective values of one person or group over another. Genocide is the great leveling device of state terror; it alone equates classes and elites in the name of higher statist goals — quite apart from judgments based on social or even economic contributions to growth. Reversing the history of Western theory, under totalitarian skies, the political system trumped the ethical norm.

It is hardly a matter of fact that genocidal societies achieve higher levels of moral development than democratic ones. Indeed, the record on this is all on the side of consensual societies. As a result, and for a variety of reasons, it is difficult to accept the fatuous communist and fascist arguments that genocide has any organic connection with human development. The presupposition that terror works is a far cry from the notion that terror alone governs the behavior of humans. Indeed, such a cynical reading of impulses and motives is the psychological precondition for the genocidal state.

16

Exclusivity and Inclusivity

of Collective Death

The pervasiveness of activism among Jews, especially in defense of their rights and their existence, derived from the exceptional responsibility that traditional Judaism places on every individual Jew. The obligations to preserve Judaism and the Jewish people have rested not on monarchs or prime ministers, nor on high priests, prophets, or rabbis, but on each Jewish man and each Jewish woman.

— Lucy S. Dawidowicz[1]

THE SUBJECT OF GENOCIDE IN GENERAL AND THE HOLO-CAUST IN PARTICULAR threatens to become a growth industry of the Western cultural apparatus. Books, plays, television dramatizations, and now a spate of museums on the subject pour forth relentlessly. Sometimes they are presented soberly, other times scandalously; but all are aimed at a mass market unfortunately more amazed than disturbed by their implications. There is danger in this massification of Holocaust studies. Western culture is inclined to adopt fads; even Holocaust studies may become a moment in commercial time — interest in them may decline as well as grow, and even peak, leaving in

its wake a void. The residual debris will probably be summarized in musical comedy; we have already seen examples of
this in *The Lieutenant* (Lieutenant Calley) and *Evita* (Eva
Peron) on Broadway. Peter Weiss's play *The Investigation* led
one commentator to suggest that the major character in the
play, in order to elicit shock from the audience, read lines "as
if he were saying: 'Let's hear it for genocide.'"[2] This may be
precursory of things to come.

One of the least attractive features of "post-Holocaust"
studies is the effort of a few to monopolize the field, to make
it the professional preserve of mourners and scholars. As a
consequence, a linguistic battle looms among survivors over
which exterminations even deserve the appellation "holocaust" (the total physical annihilation of a singular people
living in one nation). Such a bizarre struggle over language
remains a grim reminder of how easy it is for victims to
challenge each other and how difficult it is to forge common
links against victimizers.[3] I do not wish to deny Jewish victims
of the Nazi Holocaust the uniqueness of their experience. But
there are strong elements of continuity as well as discontinuity
in the process of genocide, in the evolution of life taking as an
essential dimension by which state power can be measured in
the twentieth century. The risks in reductionist explanations
are to convert the worst case scenario into something exceptional, and in so doing deprive ourselves of working hypotheses that can be utilized in the policy arena to curb if not
eliminate genocide.

Writing with compelling insight, Elie Wiesel personifies the
mystic vision of the Holocaust. Those who lived through it
"lack objectivity," he claims, while those who write on the
subject but did not live through it must "withdraw" from the
analytic challenge "without daring to enter into the heart of
the matter."[4] More recently, it has been suggested that "for
Jews, the Holocaust is a tragedy that cannot be shared" and "it
may be unrealistic or unreasonable or inappropriate to ask
Jews to share the term holocaust. But it is even more unrea-

sonable and inappropriate not to find a new name for what has taken place in Cambodia."[5] Since what took place in both situations is a holocaust from a demographic point of view, we need not invent new terms to explain similar barbaric processes. Those who share a holocaust share a common experience of being victim to the state's ruthless and complete pursuit of human life taking without regard to individual guilt or innocence. They have been punished for identification with a particular group, not for personal demeanor or performance. These are not theological but empirical criteria. To seek exclusivity in death has bizarre implications. The special Jewish triumph is in life. All too many peoples — Jews, Cambodians, Armenians, Paraguayans, Indians, Ugandans — have shared the fate of victims of a mindless taking of life. It is dangerously unbecoming for victims to engage in divisive squabbles about whose holocaust is real or whose genocide is worse.

Those who take an exclusive position on the Holocaust are engaging in moral bookkeeping, in which only those who suffer very large numbers of deaths qualify. Some point out that the 6 million deaths among European Jews is far greater than the estimated 1 million deaths among Armenians. However, the number of Armenian deaths as a percentage of their total population (50 percent) is not much lower than the number of Jewish deaths (60 percent). Others contend that the deaths of Ugandans or Biafrans are too few to compare to the Holocaust; yet here too, tribal deaths in percentage terms rival the European pattern of genocide. In certain instances high death rates (approximately 40 percent of all Cambodians, or 3 million out of 7 million) are indisputable; then one hears that such deaths were only random and a function of total societal disintegration. Yet it has been firmly established that those who were killed were the intellectuals, educators, foreign — born, and literate people — in short, the pattern was hardly random; anyone who could potentially disrupt a system of agrarian slave labor under Communist banners was singled out and eliminated. Even making the definition a matter of percentages risks creating a morality based solely on book-keeping.

There is a need to reaffirm the seriousness of the subject. The problem of genocide must be rescued from mass culture. It must not be returned to academic preserves, but it must be made part and parcel of a general theory of social systems and social structures. The position I oppose has been most vigorously articulated by Emil Fackenheim. I propose to subject its major premises to direct cross-examination.[6] This is no simple task, not the least because Fackenheim speaks with thunderous certitude.

Fackenheim's propositions have come to represent the main trends in the theological or rabbinic school of Holocaust studies. They carry tremendous weight among mass culture figures for whom theological sanction provides legitimation to their endeavors and respite from critics.[7] Professor Fackenheim does not remotely intend his views to become part of mass culture. Quite the contrary; his eight propositions distinguishing the Holocaust in particular from genocide in general represent a tremendous effort to transcend journalistic platitudes, to move beyond an articulation of the banality of evil and into the evil of banality. Nevertheless, it must also be said that an alternative perspective, a social science framework, is warranted.

Fackenheim presents his eight propositions with direction and force. A general theory of genocide and state power, which accounts for the specifics of the Holocaust, can have no better baseline.

▸ *One:* The Holocaust was not a war. Like all wars, the Roman War against the Jews was over conflicting interests — territorial, imperial, religious, other — waged between parties endowed, however unequally, with power. The victims of the Holocaust had no power. And they were a threat to the Third Reich only in the Nazi mind.

The Holocaust *was* a war; but of a modern rather than medieval variety. Earlier wars redistributed power by military means. Genocide redistributes power by technological as well as military means. Robert Lifton stated the issue succinctly:

> The word holocaust, from Greek origins, means total consumption by fire. That definition applies, with literal grotesqueness, to Auschwitz and Buchenwald, and also to Nagasaki and Hiroshima. In Old Testament usage there is the added meaning of the sacrifice, of a burnt offering. That meaning tends to be specifically retained for the deliberate, selective Nazi genocide of six million Jews retained with both bitterness and irony (sacrifice to whom for what?). I will thus speak of the Holocaust and of holocausts — the first to convey the uniqueness of the Nazi project of genocide, the second to suggest certain general principles around the totality of destruction as it affects survivors. From that perspective, the holocaust means total disaster: the physical, social, and spiritual obliteration of a human community.[8]

The precedent for this war against the Jews was the Turkish decimation of the Armenian population. Like the Nazis, the Ottoman Empire did not simply need to win a war and redistribute power; they had an overwhelming amount of power to begin with.[9] A war of annihilation is a war. To deny the warlike character of genocide is to deny its essence: the destruction of human beings for predetermined nationalist or statist goals.

The Holocaust is also modern in that it is an internal war, waged with subterfuge and deception by a majority with power against an internal minority with little power. Here too the Armenian and Jewish cases are roughly comparable. Although one can talk of genocide in relation to the bombing of Hiroshima and Nagasaki, genocidal conflict involves internal rather than external populations. But this is an ambiguous point on the nature of war rather than a denial of the warlike nature of the Holocaust per se.

The victims of the Holocaust did have a certain power: They represented a threat to the Nazi Reich. The Jew as bourgeois and the Jew as proletarian represented the forces of legitimacy and revolution in Weimar Germany. They had modest positions in universities, in labor, and industry. Regarding state power itself, where there were scarcely any Jews, they were powerless. Jews were locked out of the German bureaucratic apparatus much as the Armenians had been locked out of the administrative apparatus — except where they were used in a Quisling-like manner — by the Turkish beys. The Jews posed a threatening challenge to the legitimacy of the Nazi regime.

▸ *Two:* The Holocaust was not part of a war, a war crime. War crimes belong intrinsically to wars, whether they are calculated to further war goals, or are the result of passions that wars unleash. The Holocaust hindered rather than furthered German war aims in World War II. And it was directed, not by passions, but rather by a plan conceived and executed with methodical care, a plan devoid of passion, indeed, unable to afford this luxury.

This argument rests on a peculiar and misanthropic rendition of the Hilberg thesis. The Holocaust did hinder the Nazi war effort in the limited sense that troop transportation took second priority to transporting Jews. But in the longer, larger perspective, there were advantages. Slave labor was itself an advantage; unpaid labor time was useful. The expropriation of goods and materials was an economic gain for the Nazi Reich. People were liquidated at marginal cost to the system. The gold taken from extracted teeth became a proprietary transfer.[10] Fackenheim questions whether war goals were furthered by the Holocaust; this is not simply answered. As a mobilizing device linking military and civil sectors of the population, war ends were enhanced by the conduct of the Holocaust. The Nazi attempt to exterminate the Jews was motivated by passion, as evidenced by the fact that troop movements to the Russian front took second priority.

Hilberg makes clear the direct collusion of the German *Wehrmacht* and the German *Reichsbahn* with respect to the systematic deportation of Jews and the front-line servicing of the armed forces. The management of the German railroad illustrates how irrationality can become rationalized, how a "true system in the modern sense of the term" was employed for the unrelenting destruction of human lives. As Hilberg notes, to the extent that the technification of mass society was exemplified by the transportation network, such human engineering considerations cannot be viewed as ancillary: "It illuminates and defines the very concept of 'totalitarianism.' The Jews could not be destroyed by one Fuhrer on one order. That unprecedented event was a product of multiple initiatives, as well as lengthy negotiations and repeated adjustments among separate power structures, which differed from one another in their traditions and customs but which were united in their unfathomable will to push the Nazi regime to the limits of its destructive potential."[11] The question of passion is a moot point at best; undoubtedly there was a collective passion undergirding the conduct of the Holocaust. It was not simply a methodical event.

Theological arguments over the nature of the Holocaust often overlook parallels in the pursuit of a genocidal state policy following defeat. There are external factors at work converting vicious regimes from pursuing their primary war aims and channeling energies into achieving secondary genocidal aim. After the Turkish defeat at the hands of Bulgaria in 1912, the most massive genocide against Armenians occurred. After the Nazi defeat at Stalingrad in 1943, the most massive destruction of Jews ensued. Whatever the vocabulary of motives — fear of discovery, of reprisal, or of altered policy goals, the use of state-sanctioned murder to snatch victory from the jaws of defeat is evident throughout the century.

The largest part of European Jewry was destroyed after Germany had in effect lost the war. When the major object of the war, defeat of the Allied powers, was no longer feasible, the more proximate aim, destruction of the Jewish people, became the paramount goal. War aims have manifest and latent elements. The manifest aim was victory in the war, the latent aim was defeat of the internal "enemy," the Jews. The decimation and near-total destruction of the Jewish population might be considered the victory of the Third Reich in the face of the greater defeat it faced by the end of Stalingrad.

▶ *Three:* The Holocaust was not a case of racism, although, of course,
the Nazis were racists. But they were racists because they were
anti-Semites, not anti-Semites because they were racists. (The case
of the Japanese as honorary Aryans would suffice to bear this
out.) Racism asserts that some human groups are inferior to
others, destined to slavery. The Holocaust enacted the principle
that the Jews are not of the human race at all but "vermin" to be
"exterminated."

Here Fackenheim represents a considerable body of
thought. But the Holocaust *was* a case of racism. It is not a
question of which comes first, anti-Semitism or racism; that
philosophical dilemma is secondary. Assignment of special
conditions of life and work to Jews implies what racism is all
about: the assumption of intrinsic inferiority or superiority of
people, requiring different forms of treatment, and as deemed
necessary, punishment of those designated as inferior. Ultimately racism is not simply about institutionalizing inferiority
and superiority, but about the denial of the humanity of those
involved. Jewish vis-à-vis Aryan physical characteristics were
studied by German anthropologists to prove that there was
such a thing as race involved. These stereotypes were the
essence of European racism, and with some modification, of
racist practices in the New World as well.

Racism had taken the ideas about man and his world which
we have attempted to analyze and directed them toward the
final solution. Such concepts as middle-class virtue, heroic
morality, honesty, truthfulness, and love of nation had become
involved as over against the Jew; the organs of the efficient
state helped to bring about the final solution; and science itself
continued its corruption through racism. Above all, anthropology, which had been so deeply involved in the rise of racism,
now used racism for its own end through the final solution.
Anthropological studies were undertaken on the helpless inmates of the camps. Just as previously non-racist scientists
became converted by the temptation to aid Nazi eugenic
policies so others could not resist the temptation to use their

power over life and death in order to further their anthropological or ethnographic ambitions.[12]

The fact that U.S. racism has a clear-cut criterion based on skin color does not mean that the physical and emotional characteristics attributed to Jews were less a matter of racism than are the characteristics attributed to U.S. blacks. To deny the racial character of the Holocaust is to reject the special bond that oppressed peoples share, the special unity that can bind blacks and Armenians and Jews. To emphasize distinctions between peoples by arguing for the uniqueness of anti-Semitism is a profound mistake; it reduces any possibility of a unified political and human posture on the meaning of genocide or of the Holocaust. The triumphalism in death implicit in this kind of sectarianism comes close to defeating its own purpose.

> ► *Four:* The Holocaust was not a case of genocide although it was
> in response to this crime that the world invented the term. Geno-
> cide is a modern phenomenon; for the most part in ancient times
> human beings were considered valuable, and were carried off into
> slavery. The genocides of modern history spring from motives,
> human, if evil, such as greed, hatred, or simply blind xenophobic
> passion. This is true even when they masquerade under high-
> flown ideologies. The Nazi genocide of the Jewish people did not
> masquerade under an ideology. The ideology was genuinely be-
> lieved. This was an "idealistic" genocide to which war aims were,
> therefore, sacrificed. The ideal was to rid the world of Jews as one
> rids oneself of lice. It was also, however, to "punish" the Jews for
> their "crime," and the crime in question was existence itself.
> Hitherto, such a charge had been directed only at devils. Jews had
> now become devils as well as vermin. And there is but one thing
> that devils and vermin have in common: neither is human.

Here Fackenheim has a problem of logical contradiction. First we are told the Holocaust is not a case of genocide; and then we are reminded of the Nazi genocide of the Jewish people. But more significant is the contradiction within this framework, an inability to accept the common fate of the victims. Whether they are Japanese, Ugandans, Gypsies, Cambodians, Armenians, or Jews, their common humanity makes possible a common intellectual understanding. Insistence upon separatism, insistence that the crime was *Jewish* existence, different from any other slaughter, whatever its roots, has a dangerous element of mystification. It represents a variation of the belief in chosenness, converting it from chosenness as living God's commandments into chosenness for destruction. This approach is dangerously misanthropic. It misses the point that being chosen for life may be a unique Jewish mission but being selected for death is common to many peoples and societies.

The description of Jews as devils was not the essence of Nazi anti-Semitism; it was only the rhetoric of Nazism. The Ayatollah Khomeini and other Iranian clerics constantly refer to American devils. The essence of the Jewish problem for Nazism was the Jew as a political actor, and beyond that, the Jew as a cosmopolitan, universalistic figure in contrast to fascist concepts based on nationalism, statism, and particularism. The Jewish tradition of social marginality, of reluctance to participate in nationalistic celebrations, makes anti-Semitism a universal phenomenon as characteristic of France as of the Soviet Union. The special character of Jewish living cannot be easily converted into the special nature of Jewish dying. Dying is a universal property of many peoples, cultures, and nations.

▸ *Five:* The Holocaust was not an episode within the Third Reich, a footnote for historians. In all other societies, however brutal, people are *punished for doing*. In the Third Reich, "non-Aryans" were "punished" for being. In all other societies — in pretended or actual principle, if assuredly not always in practice — people are presumed innocent until proved guilty; the Nazi principle presumed everyone guilty until he had proved his "Aryan" innocence. Hence, anyone proving or even prepared to prove such innocence was implicated, however slightly and unwittingly, in the process which led to Auschwitz. The Holocaust is not an accidental by-product of the Reich but rather its inmost essence.

Response to this proposition must acknowledge the basic truths of the first part of this statement. The Holocaust was not merely a passing moment within the Third Reich. It did not occur in other fascist countries, like Italy, for example, where death itself was alien to the Italian culture; where not only the survival of Jews but the survival of Communists was tolerated and even encouraged. Antonio Gramsci's major works were written in a prison that had been converted into a library by his jailers.

The nature of national culture is a specific entity. The Italian people, the Turkish people, the German people each had a distinctive character. Social analysts do not discuss this kind of theme in public. It is not fashionable; we have become even a bit frightened of the concept of national character. Any notion of national character, as that advanced by Fackenheim, carries within itself the danger of stereotypical thought. But how else can we understand these phenomena? How can we understand the character of reaction, rebellion, and revolution in Turkey without understanding Turkish character, especially the continuity of that kind of character in the moral bookkeeping of development?

Ascribing guilt through proving innocence fits the framework of the Nazi ideology. But to construct a general theory of historical guilt may have pernicious consequences in which the sins of the fathers are bequeathed to the children and further offspring. That the Holocaust was an "inmost essence" makes it difficult to get beyond phylogenetic memories, beyond a situation in which a society might be viewed as having overcome its racism. When guilt is generalized, when it no longer is historically specific to social systems and political regimes, then a kind of irreducible psychologism takes intellectual command, and it becomes possible to stipulate conditions for moving beyond a genocidal state. The Holocaust becomes part of a rooted psychic unconsciousness hovering above the permanently contaminated society. To be sure, the Holocaust is the essence of the Third Reich. However, such an observation is not necessarily the core question. Does the destruction of the Jews follow automatically upon a nation that is swallowed by the totalitarian temptation? In which forms of totalitarianism does a holocaust or genocide take place? Was anti-Semitism essential to the Soviet Union as has now been claimed? Does the existence of anti-Semitism prove a theory of totalitarian essence? These are by no means simple questions to answer in a categorical manner.

The uncomfortable fact is that genocide, as has been argued throughout this volume, is the consequence of certain forms of unbridled state power. But whether anti-Semitism or other forms of racism are employed depends on the specific history of oppressor groups no less than oppressed peoples. States that demonstrate their power by exercising their capacity to take lives may be termed totalitarian. Totalitarianism is the essence of the genocidal process. This in itself provides an ample definition. If the Holocaust is unique to the Third Reich, the question of genocide loses any potential for being a general issue common to oppressive regimes. It is parochial to think that the Third Reich somehow uniquely embodied the character of the Holocaust, when we have seen since then many other societies adopt similar positions and policies toward other minorities and peoples.

▸ *Six:* The Holocaust is not part of German history alone. It includes such figures as the Grand Mufti of Jerusalem, Hajj Amin al-Husseini, who successfully urged the Nazi leaders to kill more Jews. It also includes all countries whose niggardly immigration policies prior to World War II cannot be explained in normal terms alone, such as the pressures of the Great Depression or a xenophobic tradition. Hitler did not wish to export national socialism but only anti-Semitism. He was widely successful. He succeeded when the world thought that "the Jews" must have done *something* to arouse the treatment given them by a German government. He also succeeded when the world categorized Jews needing a refuge as "useless people." (In this category would have been Sigmund Freud had he still been in Germany rather than America;

Martin Buber had he not already made his way to the Yishuv.) This was prior to the war. When the war had trapped the Jews of Nazi Europe, the railways to Auschwitz were not bombed. The Holocaust is not a parochial event. It is world-historical.

Curiously, there is no mention of any other kind of history. For example, is the genocide of the Armenian people part of world history or is it simply part of Turkish history? This is a very complicated point; at the risk of sounding impervious to moral claims, one has to be history-specific if anything serious is to emerge. If one blames the whole world for what took place at Auschwitz, or if one wants to blame the whole world for what took place at Vin, one can construct such a theory. But it is more pertinent, more appropriate, more pointed to blame the Turks and not the universe, and to blame the Germans and not the whole world, including the Grand Mufti. The issue is implementation, not rhetoric. The issue is neither the Grand Mufti nor the insecurities of Ambassador Morgenthau.

Fackenheim's idea that Hitler neither exported National Socialism nor wished to do so represents a special reading of events. As Gideon Hausner reminds us,[13] as late as April 1945, when the Soviets were penetrating Berlin for the final assault and when Hitler was imprisoned in his bunker, Hitler's last will and testament concluded by enjoining "the government and the people to uphold the racial laws to the limit and to resist mercilessly the poisoner of all nations, international Jewry." Hausner makes it plain that National Socialism was an international movement, whose linchpin was anti-Semitism.

Fackenheim presumes World War II was all about anti-Semitism, but at a more prosaic level it was about conquest. There was a Nazi government in the Ukraine; there was a Nazi government in Norway; there was a Nazi government in Romania; there was a Nazi government in Yugoslavia — all these regimes were exported. The idea that Hitler was not interested in exporting National Socialism is curious. It would be more appropriate to note that wherever National Socialism was exported, so too did anti-Semitism follow. However, in conditions where the Jewish population was not a factor, Nazism still sought to establish a political foothold either with or without direct military aggression. The relation between National Socialism as an ideology and anti-Semitism as a passion is one that the Nazis themselves were hard put to resolve. The linkage between the ideology and the passion, which seems so close in retrospect, was far less articulated policy than felt need in the earlier stages of the Nazi regime.

Fackenheim slips in a subtle point that the Jews were "trapped" in Europe. But the Jews were not trapped in Europe. They were of Europe and had been of Europe for a thousand years. One of their dilemmas is one rendered in almost every history where those who are to be exploited or annihilated overidentify with their ruling masters. The Jews of Europe were entirely Europeanized. Only a small fragment remained outside the framework of Europeanization. The great divide between German and Russian Jews was the result of participation in European nationalism, of identification with enlightenment. Fackenheim's idea that the Jews were trapped in Europe is a clever misreading of the facts. The added horror of the Holocaust is that it happened to a people who were endemic to that part of the world.

▶ *Seven:* The Jews were no mere scapegoat in the Holocaust. It is true that they were used as such in the early stages of the movement. Thus Hitler was able to unite the "left" and "right" wings of his party by distinguishing, on the left, between "Marxist" (i.e., Jewish) and "national" (i.e., "Aryan") "socialism" and, on the right, between *Raffendes Kapital* (rapacious, i.e., Jewish capital) and *Schaffendes Kapital* (creative, i.e., "Aryan" capital). It is also true that, had the supply of Jewish victims given out, Hitler would have been forced (as he once remarked to Hermann Rauschning) to "invent" new "Jews." But it is not true that the Jew [was] . . . only a pretext for something else. So long as there were actual Jews, it was these actual Jews who were the systematic object of ferreting-out, torture, and murder. Once, at Sinai, Jews had been singled out for life and a task. Now, at Auschwitz, they were singled out for torment and death.

The difficulty with the exclusivist formula is that although Jews were singled out, so too were Gypsies, Poles, and Slavs. Hitler's appeal was to state power, not to unite Left and Right; not to unite bourgeoisie and proletariat, but to make sure that the bourgeoisie and the proletariat of Germany were purified of Jewish elements. If one considers the national aspects of the Third Reich rather than the mystical aspects of Jewish destruction, this becomes a lot easier to fathom. German Jewish concentration points were in the bourgeoisie and proletariat, in leftist socialist politics and in high bourgeois economics. Liquidation of the Jew enabled the German bureaucratic state to manage the bourgeoisie and proletariat of Germany without opposition.[14] The destruction of socialism was attendant to the destruction of the Jews. Without socialist opposition, the German proletariat was an easy mark for Third Reich massification. The first two legislative acts of the Third Reich were bills on labor, on work, and on management. The liquidation of the Jewish population, within both the bourgeoisie and the proletariat, permitted the Nazis to consolidate state power. The Holocaust, from a Nazi standpoint, was an entirely rational process, scarcely a singular act of mystical divination. It was the essential feature of Nazi "domestic" policy in the final stages of the Third Reich.

▸ *Eight:* The Holocaust is not over and done with. Late in the war Goebbels (who, needless to say, knew all) said publicly and with every sign of conviction that, among the peoples of Europe, the Jews alone had neither sacrificed nor suffered in the war but only profited from it. As this was written, an American professor has written a book asserting that the Holocaust never happened, while other Nazis are preparing to march on Skokie, in an assault on Jewish survivors. Like the old Nazis, the new Nazis say two things at once. The Holocaust never happened; and it is necessary to finish the job.

On this point, Fackenheim is on sound ground. Still, the point that he does not make and that requires emphasis is that the Holocaust did happen and could happen again, but it is now more likely to happen to peoples other than Jews or Armenians. It was more likely to happen to Ugandans, and it did; to Cambodians, and it did; to Paraguayans, and it did; to Biafrans, and it did. It is correct to say that the Holocaust is not over and done with. But it is not over and done with because there are other peoples victimized by the very model created by the Armenian and Nazi genocides.

It is important not to fit peoplehood into theories; theories must fit the realities of people. If the restoration of human dignity is to become a theme for social research, it becomes imperative to understand the unified character of genocide, the common characteristics of its victims, and ultimately the need for alliances of victims and potential victims to resist all kinds of genocide. To insist on universalism, triumphalism, or separatist orientations is self-defeating. If there is to be any political consequence of research into genocide, if the victim groups are to do more than pay for annual memorials and remembrances, an understanding of the unity needed to confront state oppression must be made paramount; otherwise little will have been accomplished and nothing will have changed.

Although my analysis has sharply demarcated theological from sociological viewpoints, it should be appreciated that Jewish religious thought is itself far from unanimous on the special nature of the Holocaust. Orthodox segments in particular have cautioned against an overly dramaturgical viewpoint, urging instead a position in which the Nazi Holocaust is but the latest monumental assault on the Jewish people; one that is neither to be ignored nor celebrated, but simply understood as part of the martyrdom of a people.

In discussing his memoir *All Rivers Run to the Sea,* Elie Wiesel caught the spirit of this latest stage in trying to understand the Holocaust in some larger context. "Guilt and innocence are individual descriptions. Only the guilty are guilty. Children of killers are not killers, but children. There are no words. That is the whole problem. The enemy succeeded in opushing his crimes to the outer limits of language, and therefore there are no words. No theory is valid. I have only questions."[15] Still, even to declare that there are no words requires a language to express this metaphysical belief. So the theological vision ends in paradox; or at least leaves open the prospects that social research can add a dimension that can be a factor in understanding if not solving the issue of genocide.

William Helmreich adds a dimension to Wiesel's position in explaining why the orthodox view so often ends in paradox. He maintains that orthodoxy rejects paying special homage by singling out the victims of the Holocaust on both philosophical and practical grounds: "In their view, The Holocaust is not, in any fundamental way, a unique event in Jewish history, but simply the latest in a long chain of anti-Jewish persecutions that began with the destruction of the Temple and which also included the Crusades, the Spanish Inquisition, attacks on Jews led by Chmielnicki, and the hundreds of pogroms to which the Jewish community has been subjected to over the centuries. They do admit that the Holocaust was unique in scale and proportion but this is not considered a distinction justifying its elevation into a separate category."[16] Helmreich goes on to note that the ethical problem, in the view of orthodox believers, is the same whether one Jew or 6 million are murdered. Since Judaism is a *Gemeinschaft*, a community of fate, the sheer volume killed, while awesome, does not in itself transform a quantitative event into a unique qualitative phenomenon.

The significance of this minority theological report is to call attention to the fact that in the problem of the Holocaust, while there are some strong clerical-secular bifurcations, there are also cross-cutting patterns across disciplinary boundaries. For example, certain sociological lessons can be drawn from the Holocaust: the breakdown in egalitarian revolutions of the nineteenth century, the subtle abandonment of the Palestinian mandate after the Balfour Declaration, the lofty assertion followed by a total revocation of Jewish minority rights in the Soviet Union. For orthodoxy, the Holocaust is more a function of the breakdown of Jewish solidarism than of any special evils of the German nation or the Nazi regime.

The sociological view attempts to transcend sectarian or parochial concerns and develop a cross-cultural paradigm that would permit placing the Holocaust into a larger perspective of genocide in the twentieth century rather than seeing the former as entirely distinctive and the latter as some weaker form of mass murder of a different order of magnitude. For example, with the liquidation of roughly 40 percent of the Cambodian population, even the quantitative indicators of the Nazi Holocaust have been approached in at least one other situation.

In the past, it has been argued that genocide of other peoples — Armenians, Ugandans, Paraguayan Indians — has been too random and sporadic to be termed a holocaust. It has also been claimed that the atomic attacks on Hiroshima and Nagasaki were aimed at highly select and refined military targets, and that they were not efforts at the total destruction of a people. Whatever the outcome of such contentions, the Cambodian case would indicate the risks in vesting too much intellectual capital on the sheer numbers involved — although it is clearly a factor to be contended with.

Having argued thus, let me note that qualitative differences do exist that distinguish the Jewish Holocaust from any other genocides. First, there is the systematic rather than random or sporadic nature of the Holocaust: the technological and organizational refinement of the tools of mass slaughter that ultimately reduced all morality to engineering problems. Second, there was an ideological fervor unmatched by any other previous genocides. So intent were the Nazis on their policy of extermination of Jews that they dared contact other nations, especially Axis powers and neutral countries, to repatriate

Jews back to Germany to suffer the ultimate degradation. Third, genocide against the Jewish people represented and rested upon a national model of state power: the purification of the apparatus of repression by a total concentration of the means of destruction in a narrow military police stratum unencumbered by considerations of class, ethnicity, gender, or any other social factors affecting Nazi response to non-Jewish groups. The liquidation of multiple sources of power and authority was made easier, indeed was presupposed, by the total liquidation of the Jewish population.

With all these inner disputations and disagreements accounted for, there were still those who — too guilt-ridden to face the monstrous consequences of the Holocaust against Jews in particular and victims of genocide as a whole — chose the path of evading reality. First isolated voices like that of Arthur R. Butz[17] but then joined in a quasi-intellectual movement with all the paraphernalia of historical scholarship,[18] there was a massive denial of a massive crime. Denials of gas chambers, rejection of photographic evidence, equation of indemnification of the victims with Zionist beneficiaries, are all linked to the rejection that the Holocaust ever occurred. The Nazi "revisionists" dare speak not of Nazism but only of National Socialism; not of Germany under Hitlerism but only of a Third Reich. The Nazi epoch is even spoken of in remorseful terms: "Overwhelming British, American, and Soviet forces finally succeeded in crushing the military resistance of a Germany which they accorded not even the minimum of mercy."[19] Pity the poor victim!

Even the new Nazi "intelligentsia" does not deny mass murder, but only the numbers murdered.[19] It is not supposedly 6 million (then what number is it?). No matter, those massacred were Zionists, Communists, or a hyphenated variety of the two — Jewish-Bolsheviks — any euphemism for Jews other than the admission of a special assassination of Jews as a people. The need for exacting scholarship, the sort that has begun to emerge, with respect to all peoples victimized for their existence is not simply a matter of litanies and recitations but of the very retention of the historical memory itself. The scientific study of genocide is a matter not of morbid fascination or mystic divination but of the need to assert the historical reality of collective crime. Only by such a confrontation can we at least locate moral responsibility for state crimes even if we cannot always prevent future genocides from taking place.[20]

With all due weight given to the different traditions involved in the theological and sociological arguments concerning genocide, they do have a strong shared value commitment to the normative framework in which greater emphasis is placed on the protection of life than on the protection of economic systems or political regimes.[21]

Both traditions are committed, insofar as their dogmas and doctrines permit, to the supreme place of life in the hierarchy of values. This is no small matter. Nazism witnessed the breakdown of religious and scientific institutions alike, and those that could not be broken down, were oftentimes simply corrupted — as in decadent and exotic notions of a Teutonic Church and the equally ludicrous belief in an Aryan Science. In the larger context of world history, in the wider picture of centuries-old barbarisms, we bear witness not to a warfare of science versus theology but, rather, to a shared collapse of any sort of normative structure in which either could function to enhance the quality or sanctity of life.

Treatment of the Holocaust as a dialogue between God and Golem, as ineffable and unspeakable, serves to return death to the antinomic and Manichaean tradition of original sin versus original goodness; or, as it is more fashionably called, historical pessimism versus historical optimism. And while such thought is deeply rooted in western philosophical traditions, it does not quite exhaust the topic at hand. If social science is to make its own serious contribution to Holocaust studies, it must move beyond the mystery of silence or the silence of mysteries. However limited the clinical analysis of collective death may be, we may at least be spared the repetition of some forms of genocide. To incorporate in the Jewish psyche the phrase "never again" requires an antecedent commitment to explain why genocide happened in the first place.

Theologians must not presume an exclusive monopoly on meaning by insisting upon the mystery and irrationality of taking lives. The task of social science remains in this area as in all others, a rationalization of irrationality. Only in this way can victory be denied to Golem and the struggle against evil be understood as a self-assigned task. This is admittedly a far more difficult challenge than standing in silent awe at the tragedies that have befallen our century; or worse yet, await the next coming of a Holocaust.

17

Surviving the Genocidal State

Abstraction is memory's most ardent enemy. It kills because it encourages distance, and often indifference. We must remind ourself that the Holocaust was not six million. It was one, plus one, plus one. Only in understanding that civilized people must defend the one, by one, by one can the Holocaust, the incomprehensible, be given meaning.

— Judith Miller[1]

SOCIAL SCIENCE OFTEN RESORTS TO THE TYRANNY OF IMPERSONAL DETERMINISTIC FORCES to explain major events. The burden of this chapter is to reintroduce the person as a central factor in understanding a phenomenon such as genocide. This is not intended to mechanically reintroduce the individual back into the social order, like some sort of injection to get the machine rolling again, but simply to note that the motives of people should never have been removed from such systematic analysis to begin with. A political psychology must accompany any sound political sociology. For motives of rulers at one end, the behaviors of masses at the other, and the decision makers all along the stratification line, give meaning to terms like "genocide." We have seen that without at least the tacit consent if not active participation of the German people, the twin Nazi drive for extermination and expansion could not have been carried forth. Hence, quite beyond the distinction between life and death, viewing social structures in terms of personal values is of central importance.

The infusion of political psychology into such an analysis may help prompt a better understanding of why some societies generate single-party machineries, powerful secret police, and a war apparatus dedicated to geographic expansion while others do not. We may hypothesize that the higher the level of repression within a society, the greater the need for an apparatus capable of exercising maximum control. Genocidal societies, therefore, usually have either single-party rule or a total absence of competing party machineries.

The genocidal society also reveals a striking similarity between those who have political power and those who exercise administrative and bureaucratic power. And finally, they display a police apparatus far larger than required to simply maintain order. These mechanisms aimed at ensuring obedience are themselves exceedingly costly. They represent a chink in the armor of the genocidal society, a weakness that creates the need for greater repression at higher costs and at the same time the potential and even necessity for more manifest resistance. It might well be that the cost factors for a genocidal society are so exorbitant in economic and human terms that those in charge of government are likely to think most carefully about going that route.

A somewhat different way of arriving at the same outcome is to develop a deep appreciation of the relationships between insiders and outsiders, especially as this distinction manifests itself in assassination societies. The more complete the genocidal nature of a society, the firmer the distinction between who belongs and who does not, between who is human and who is not. The higher the degree of tolerance, the less important is the distinction between belonging and nonbelonging, insiders and outsiders.

When one considers the difference between the Jews of Italy and the Jews of Germany, it becomes painfully apparent that Italian Jews were always known as Italians, and their Jewishness was marginal, hardly understandable to most Italians. For the Germans, the difference between being a German and being a Jew was the paramount distinction at every level: biological, demographic, historical, and all the rest. The society became dedicated to making that distinction; for once made, genocide became easy, even normative. Intense nationalism, in contrast to cosmopolitanism, is itself an essential characteristic of the genocidal society. It instills not only a sense of difference between those who belong and those who do not, but also the inhumanity of those who do not belong and thereby the right of a social order to purge itself of alien influence.

Ralf Dahrendorf offers a new beginning to solving old problems about the nature of equity. Democracy extends from "equal citizenship rights having to be generalized, to conflicts being recognized and regulated rationally, elites reflecting the color and diversity of social interests, and public virtues as the predominant value orientation of the people." He goes on to say that, strictly speaking, we need a theory of human relations as well as organizational frameworks as a precondition for a theory of democracy and social structure.

What can democracy ultimately mean except respect for the lives of people and recognition that one life is as valuable as another? Life itself is a precondition for the democratic social order. It was the breakdown of this sensibility during the Nazi period, and the inculcation of what Durkheim refers to as "the myth of the state," that ultimately made impossible the practice of democracy in a world with German Nazism.

Dahrendorf refers to this peculiar megalomania as a suspension of civil liberties in order to fulfill the imaginary requirements of historical retribution. Such metaphysical predispositions to correct the contours of history lead not just to government with authority but also to an idea of the state as ultimate, irreversible, and untrammeled by individual ideas. Whether it is a matter of German character, German militarization, or German ethics becomes less important than the fact that the society conducted itself in such a way as to violate any notion of a theory of democracy.[2]

The democratic societies of the United States, Great Britain, Italy, France, Japan, and so on have as many differences as similarities. If we were to take systems that have been characterized in some period of their history as fascistic, such as Italy, Germany, and Spain, we would have at least as many differences as similarities. Even the socialists, from the ex-Soviet Union to China and from the East European nations to Cuba, have as many differences as similarities. That is why the analysis of social structure in terms of the formal organization of society may be a necessary condition for explaining the system, but it is not a sufficient condition for explaining the society as a whole.

Just how important differences are between genocidal and nongenocidal societies, and certainly between punitive and permissive societies, is indicated by nations like Turkey and Japan that, almost without parallel, developed revolutions from above far in advance of other nations in the Third World. The cultural component, the belief in the military ethic, permitted the development of elites to mobilize the society toward developmental goals. Unconstrained by democratic norms, these societies were in a position to set the model for Third World development between fifty and a hundred years later.

The most important psychological dilemma in the study of genocide is that it may lead one to exaggerate the grim prospects for the human race. Obviously, for those who take genocide as a serious and central concern, there is already a predisposition to have a grim view toward the subject. Because genocide is so widespread, it is important to recognize the prospects for combatting it; and further, to appreciate how difficult it is to destroy an entire people. Despite relatively low birth rates, the Jewish people, who were the central target of twentieth-century genocidal persecution, now have a larger population than they had at the outbreak of hostilities in 1939. True, the democratic constancy was coupled with massive geographic shifts.

The Armenians too, the unwitting forerunner of the war against the Jews whose decimation at the hands of the Turks certainly rivaled the later treatment of the Jews at the hands of the Nazis, have survived, their numbers have increased, and their culture persists. The Armenians maintained a distinct national identity within the framework of Soviet Russia. They exist as a minority group in Turkey. They represent a considerable element within Greek life. And many of them have made a positive impact on U.S. culture.

Another good illustration of this point is the American Indian. Here is a group that was systematically and diabolically exterminated. Those who were not exterminated were put on tribal lands and subject to elimination through economic atrophy and political delegitimization. Tribalizing a people by placing them within the framework of a permanent compound may be viewed as a prelude to genocide. Yet by 1990 well over a million people claim to be Indians, twice the number who claimed such descent in the 1960 census count. Whether it is demographic shamanism or a resurrection of self-pride, Indians exist as a people.

This does not mean that one should celebrate genocide as a test of the willpower of people. I am not urging the wholesale adoption of Arnold Toynbee's world of challenge and response, testing to the maximum the stress and strain on a people. Yet it is important to emphasize that to study genocide is to examine not simply the successful liquidation of entire peoples but also attempts at liquidation. It is significant to recognize the phenomenon of mass murder, for which genocide is a synonym, as well as the possibilities for existence and survival.

AS ALREADY DISCUSSED IN EARLIER CHAPTERS, A REAL DANGER EXISTS IN EXPANDING a notion of genocide beyond meaningful limits. But there is also a danger posed in diminishing a concept of genocide to collective suicide. Further, if one argues that genocide is merely homicide writ large, then we are dealing with a phenomenon that is more difficult to eradicate, much more difficult to describe in jurisprudential terms as requiring a separate response apart from homicide. There are all kinds of unanswered questions about the relationship of homicide to suicide:

- ▶ Is there a self-destructive impulse in peoples, much as there is an individual impulse to self-destruction? Are there laws of human behavior, or simply historical continuities? Are there frameworks that make collectivities perform in self-destructive ways? Or is that simply another way of using a rhetoric of blaming the system? Is there never such a tendency? Are we always dealing with people who are fighting to the last breath? And if not, when not, no less than why not? When do people fight to the bitter end? When do people submit? What are the conditions of rebellion and retaliation against genocidal patterns? What are the conditions of submission? Is resistance simply a function of raw terror or maximum use of state authority?

All these questions represent a crucial theoretical issue between the psychological and the political. I am in the awkward position of answering a question with other questions. But posing them in this manner moves us beyond conventional ideological postures that rest on the genocide of others and the justifiable homicide of selves. Such a one-sided position distorts, rather than clarifies, the persistence of genocide as the political primal scream of our times.

First comes the act and then comes the word. First a homicide is committed and then someone defines the conditions of murder. First genocide is committed and then a language emerges to describe the phenomenon. The Turkish assassination of the Armenians is a clear case of genocide prior to 1945. Whether such an act is recognized in war crimes trials is a linguistic issue, not a sociological one. There is legal and historical precedent for acts of genocide. The Japanese put Americans on trial who flew the first raid over Tokyo on the same premise, namely that the random destruction of life and property constitutes a pre-condition for systematic decimation that follows. The foundations of the Nuremberg trials, however, were based on actual records of systematic decimation of human life over and above the requirements of wartime struggles.

There are anomalies connected with the widespread usage of the concept of genocide. For example, U.S. Communists were instrumental in introducing a concept of genocide on the docket of world opinion at the very time of the worst postwar Stalinist excesses. William L. Patterson, the foremost Communist black leader of the time, prepared *We Charge Genocide,* the document that contained the basis of the first United Nations resolution on the treatment of blacks in the United States. In the entire document, treatment of the national, religious, and political character of the nation was never established. One can see that there are more than linguistic peculiarities involved. *We Charge Genocide,* which was superfically similar to the statement of principles of Amnesty International, was prepared by those who categorically refused to examine fully documented genocides of minority peoples in the Soviet Union.[3] There are powerful national myopias, sometimes called ideologies, in this area. Diplomats talk about genocide as if referring to someone else. The ability of people to develop myopic visions of their own national performance underscores and underwrites the need for social scientists to involve themselves in this field of research.

The great advantage of "bridge" disciplines such as political psychology or political sociology is that they are able to correct the analytical shortcomings of a vulgar economism. For the most part, the question has been posed: To what degree does the structure of an economic system help explain the nature of genocide? While this is a perfectly valid line of inquiry, it is no less important to ask: To what degree does the practice of genocide help to explain the nature of an economic system? What is the utility of a thing called "social system" if one cannot live to see its benefits or results? The social system is not simply a monetary exchange or a marketplace of ideas. It is a configuration of practices pertaining to life and death. All constitutions read beautifully. If one were to have a discussion about the nature of property relationships in one country vis-à-vis another, one might demonstrate how one or another system encourages a higher mix of public against private ownership.

But the history of twentieth-century political practice shows such definitions often represent an intellectual snare and a delusion leading down a primrose path of self-denial and destruction. System building urges us to worry not about how many people's lives are taken but about the nature of the social system. I am arguing the reverse: that we worry less about the nature of the social system and more about how many lives are taken by each system, state, or nation.

My view is a direct assault against a concept of social systems that starts with a model and ends in death. I start with a person's right to live, and if I can derive a model, so much the better. I do not consider my life consecrated by the creation of models of social order. It is infinitely more important to know what country to travel to in order to prolong one's life than to provide others with an abstract dictionary of social systems. It is not enough to argue the merits of a social system; instead, one should state specifically what brand of say, socialism provides the best life chances. Is it Cuban, Chinese, or Swedish?

Given the differential mix of public and private sectors, it does little good to say that they are all socialist systems. If social science is to provide criteria about where to live and work, one needs a series of criteria, akin to a qualitative Guttman Scale, indicating the social and/or life indicators that show where one's life chances are either maximized or minimized. This is a legitimate and scientific activity of practical use to wider publics.

The basic purpose of my work on genocide is not to add another title to a growing list of horror stories exhibiting a concern over the destruction of human life but, rather, to ventilate and rehabilitate the entire field of social systems analysis. I have no wish to deny the worth of class analysis or race analysis in the study of social systems; only to make it clear that populist and elitist attitudes toward life and death are an independent variable of a profound sort. It is impossible to infer from the class, race, or religious composition of a nation its attitudes toward genocide. The bonds that unite genocidal societies are as overwhelmingly potent as are those that unite permissive or tolerant societies. In this sense the English tradition of political pluralism extending from Locke to Mill has as much to teach us as does the Continental tradition of power and class analysis.

It would be absurd to deny the importance of social structural factors in predicting national systems. But it would be equally absurd to deny the significance of cultural factors. Yet the so-called materialist interpretation of history attempts precisely this sort of reductionist one-sided analysis. And the fact that such a line of analysis came about in intellectual retaliation to the equally one-sided *Geisteswissenschaft* and *Kulturwissenschaft* analysis only means that we inherited polarized theorems that frustrate meaningful social science.

Take the analysis of Japanese development: We ought not to be required to choose between a sociology that argues that the military ensured bourgeois growth in relative isolation from lower-class rebellion, and a culturology that argues that the military ensured a special brand of adventurism and heroism that made Japan preeminent in Asia. Surely one has a right to insist on the equal and joint validity of the economy and culture. It is about time that a multivariate, naturalistic framework replaces older dogmatic expressions of nineteenth-century metaphysics smuggled into social and political analysis. And that is what my work is definitely about.

Our social science must not become so bereft of common sense that it cannot answer the obvious or make choices that almost any reasonable person would make without the aid of high-powered social research. Surely it is not strange, if we take the work of Luigi Barzini[4] on the Italians and Karl Jaspers[5] on the Germans seriously, that despite similarities in economic systems and social structures during the fascist-National Socialist period, the actual behavioral patterns of the two nations were so radically different. Likewise, if adherence to Islamic values were a unique determinant of developmental patterns, how would one explain the entirely different rates of economic growth in countries such as Turkey and Egypt? The mental structure of peoples is certainly as important as their physical structure. Heroic behavior is certainly as important as the size of an armed force. The older dualisms have outlived their intellectual usefulness, and the analysis of genocide dramatically underlines this.

My early interest in social and philosophical ideas and ideologies of war and peace, and the attendant analysis of conflict, consensus, and cooperation, was itself part of a basic commitment to a sociology that takes seriously the right to live as a determinant of other human rights and social alignments. Questions of social structures, cultural orders, and military regimes ultimately reduce to questions of living and dying. It is absurd to believe that transcendental rehabilitation is possible: not by Communists who perform miracles of ideology or by Christians who perform miracles of theology. A naturalistic sociology must take its stand with life and the living. The collective imposition of death by a state must be seen as a common ground at which the needs of sociology and morality interact and intersect. One cannot have a democratic ideology outside the rule of law nor a democratic sociology without the bold assertion of the right to live.

The point of these remarks is not to displace political or military factors: That would be a game of model building. My interest is not to superimpose culturology upon sociology. I am not suggesting that transhistorical concepts of spirit be substituted for historicity of all things. A cultural science would trivialize social science and return us to a condition of *Kulturwissenschaft* of Dilthey and Rickert. It has taken nearly a century to extricate ourselves from this cultural standpoint, and by no means would it be worthwhile to return to it. Cultural values, like economic interests of political systems themselves, all have a common denominator, and that is the attitude toward life within a society and what the state does to a life, or a series of lives, to foster its own general interests. In that way the series of determinisms that plague social science can be reduced to a general theory of society: one that takes seriously not so much cultural phenomena in contrast to economic phenomena, but the obligation of both to deal seriously with the fact of life and death.

We are in the midst of an enormous emotional as well as intellectual upheaval. It extends from questioning the biological meaning of life to the political taking of life. Normative and empirical standards are both being entirely overhauled. Even the most humane are now touched by the matter-of-factness of dying. A clinical view of death is a prelude to a cynical view of the tasks of social systems. In this way, the notion of a political community based on the need to live is being replaced by a vision of pluralism that is nothing more than separated, isolated interest groups tearing at each other's flesh; or at the other end of the political spectrum, demands for authority and order that eat away with equal vigor at the practice of democracy.

To presume obligations to the state is not to assert simply a theory of obedience but, rather, that the state must ensure the right to live without presuming the reasons for living. The management of a society may extend to commands for obedience based on the need for mutual survival, but not beyond that point. Negotiating the rights of individuals and what one does with a life is not a matter of state power. Too much normative theorizing is a subterfuge for reintroducing a doctrine of individual obligations in place of political rights. The record of the twentieth century is soiled by a juridical standpoint that asserts obligations to serve the state without any corresponding sense of right to life within a state. Michael Walzer speaks quite directly to this point: "It is surely not the case that being and feeling obligated are the same. It is not enough that a common life be felt or thought to exist; there must be a common life. I do not mean to defend all those nationalistic or ideological mystifications that lead men to believe they are living in a community when in fact they are not."[6]

One cannot conclude such an examination without at least a brief inquiry into the nature of responsibility for acts of genocide. The efforts of Richard Falk are significant in this connection. Recognizing genocide as the most extreme offense of governments against humankind, he distinguishes between two types of models for its legal punishment:

First, he offers the indictment model "based on the plausibility of indictment and prosecution of individual perpetrators before a duly constituted court of law operating according to due process and adhering to strict rules of evidence." Second, he offers a responsibility model that is based on the community's "obligation to repudiate certain forms of government behavior and the consequent responsibility of individuals and groups to resist politics involving this behavior."

While this distinction is salient, a dilemma of this legal formula is that the genocidal state is the least likely to permit such neat distinctions from being carried into practice. As Falk himself is sadly compelled to admit: "It must be acknowledged, finally, that individual acts of conscience and of resistance may be virtually impossible in a ruthless and efficient totalitarian system."[7] Thus, any efforts to move beyond genocide must again be thrown back upon the political arena, since the relief sought in international law is likely to prove chimeric.

There is a continuing need to establish an authentic socio-biology,[8] one that is grounded in the polity rather than zoology: the social world of the political system in terms of lives taken, years removed from individuals through imprisonment, damages to people through fear of speaking freely. We have moved much too far toward expanding the banality of evil as a necessary component of state existence. One can only hope that such a view of the social order will provide a methodological device for the measurement of social systems, a measurement equal in quantitative power to money for economic science. Quite beyond the methodological aspect is the ideological sense that life is not only worth living, but also that the very task of the social scientist should largely be taken up with an exploration of how to expand such worthiness in life.

One might well inquire as to the feasibility of ever understanding genocide at the empirical level, for example, whether it would not prove more efficacious to search out those aspects of state power and social order that promote equity and well-being rather than to leap to ultimate conclusions and terminations. Such an alternative approach is possible.

In my typology I indicate forms of permissive and open-ended state bureaucratic behavior that discourage genocidal outcomes. Yet one is left with the strong feeling that a wider appreciation of state authority in its efforts to preserve the social order lead to a conclusion not unlike that reached by eighteenth-century utilitarians and nineteenth-century libertarians alike: that the government governs best that governs least. Instead of inventing a new radius of state activities labeled "social welfare," social scientists might well turn their attention to more fundamental issues of the optimum size for sound governance, or how much economic "waste" is worth what sorts of social "values." I am not suggesting that meliorative issues be abandoned by social research, only that basic issues of life and death not be overlooked in the process.

What conclusions can be drawn from this study of the social bases of taking human life? It would be superficial to say that we should bend every effort to expose and prevent any and all forms of genocide. This reflects a rather obvious and basic humanitarian persuasion, one that hardly would be defeated or voted against. Nations that have systematically practiced genocide are not only sponsors of United Nations resolutions against genocide but have also often urged the strengthening of such resolutions: recall the Soviet desire to add to the genocide resolution a concept of any deliberate act having to do with destroying various cultural, racial, or religious beliefs. The very fact that such resolutions could be introduced by a nation that had widely practiced genocide would indicate that something other than polemics is called for.

What can and should be concluded intellectually is that — given the widespread practice of genocide and its virtual autonomy from both economic systems and geographic locations — one should be extremely cautious about the potential for good works of any nation-state. So much fanaticism and rampant chauvinism is generated by mindless adherence to national goals that the use of genocide as a righteous instrument of national and state policy has become highly tempting. Genocide as a technique for achieving national solidarity takes various forms, as we have seen. In the United States, with respect to the Indian question, it is the absorption of "backward tribal nations" into the general nation. In the Soviet Union it was the dissolving of bourgeois nations into a general socialist commonweal. In the former entity of Yugoslavia, it was ethnic cleansing. In short, genocide is a fundamental mechanism for the unification of the national state. That is why it is so widely practiced in "advanced" and "civilized" areas, and why it is so incredibly difficult to eradicate.[9]

The need for faith, trust, and transcendence can be presumed constant. It would be dangerous counsel to assume that nations can properly contain and channel such psychic dispositions. It would be wiser to urge faith in Providence and trust in people.

As for transcendence, an appreciation of the imminence of all existence and the transience of all nations might keep in check those proclivities of the powerful to bend, mutilate, and destroy innocent sections of the human race in order to safeguard a world of order without compassion, and ultimately of law without justice. In the short-run, with regard to grave violations of the right to life, amnesty cannot be readily declared. "Never again" is not a Jewish slogan but a universal human rallying cry.

Part V

STUDYING GENOCIDE

Life, Death, and Sociology

Genocides are a modern phenomenon. They require organiza-
tion and they are likely to become more frequent in the future.

— *Gerard Prunier*[1]

"THE IDEAS FOR WHICH ONE LIVES AND DIES ARE BY THIS
VERY FACT ABSOLUTE, and one cannot at the same time treat
them as relative truths which might be calmly compared with
others and literally criticized."[2] In uttering these words in
Humanism and Terror, Maurice Merleau-Ponty had in mind
not simply the heroic nature of thought, of the martyrs to free
expression of ideas, but the limits to relativism in social theory.
Those who take lives, who see in their ideas a rationalization
for mayhem and carnage, are no less taken with the power of
ideas than are the life givers. Hence, a culture of life taking no
less than life giving is wrapped up with the essential social
institutions and cultural agencies of our age.

The certainty of death is one of the few unchallenged facts
of life. Widely varied are the forms in which any individual will
perish. This is a work on one such form: genocide. It is not an
exercise in the problem of death as such. An individual may
hope for a natural end in old age. People may accept as equally
natural death that occurs as a consequence of sickness or
disease. Accidental death, while hardly to be desired, is not

subject to social condemnation either. Death as a *social* problem in contrast to a *biographical* event begins when life is terminated as an arbitrary action by others.

First, there is death by capital punishment undertaken with the authority of law for specific crimes. Second, there is death brought about through participation in warfare, as a result of a defense of nation or assault upon another sovereign. This too carries with it the force of law and is undertaken not with death as an end but as a consequence of preserving or extending basic human values. Third, there is death by murder, the taking of life, often without official sanction and not infrequently as an "act of passion" performed by one individual against another. These three types of life taking, while subject to critical analysis and a certain inevitable ambiguity, are not the subject of this study of genocide.

This volume is concerned with a special form of murder: state-sanctioned liquidation of a collective group, without regard to whether an individual has committed any specific and punishable transgression. In a larger picture, genocide might be viewed as a special case of mass murder; but at the same time, genocide has come to define that larger picture by becoming an essential and unique expression of our century.

Mass murder and warfare among peoples is an ever-present danger to humankind. Such phenomenon as infanticide, and more circumscribed forms of killing like regicide, have been around for centuries. What makes genocide a particularly malevolent practice in this century, with wide-ranging consequences, is the role of modern technology in the systematic destruction of large numbers of innocents. Just as Hiroshima and Nagasaki moved us beyond the realm of warfare to annihilation, so too Auschwitz, Buchenwald, and other Nazi death camps moved us beyond the realm of sporadic assaults to systematic dismemberment of populations. On this, Hannah Arendt spoke well and wisely, declaring that the current epoch in history is distinguished not by a desire to liquidate total populations but by the actual capacity to do so.[3] This gives the issue of genocide a cogency and urgency it formerly lacked.

The increase in the degree of technological ability to do away with large numbers and the concentration of that efficiency in the hands of small numbers of military or police cadres qualitatively changes the issue of murder from one of random events to systematic policies. Analytical problems remain: To what extent can one describe the liquidation of peoples through such events as ecological and environmental discrimination as genocidal? Are diseases brought to subject peoples a form of systematic liquidation? Is the issue of ethnocide related to genocide (and if so, how), or is all genocide peculiarly geared to the isolation and elimination of an ethnic, national, or racial group? These problems of definition must be placed in an empirical context that takes cognizance of the statist character of genocide and the technological methods that enable us to transform nightmares into realities.

In part, this work is a reflection on the state of a discipline, no less that then state of a society. Why, one must ask, has sociology failed to achieve the status of a fundamental science-not an important or auxiliary discipline, but a fundamental discipline? In the past, I have argued that a forthright distinction needs to be made between basic and secondary sciences. Fundamental disciplines, those that affect a great many if not all people, involve some aspect of life-and-death; or, if not death, then incarceration and illness.

Sociology, either in its relativist or formalist versions, is denied the status of a fundamental applied science, such as medicine or engineering, because it so rarely comes to grips with issues of life-and-death. And ordinary people, whatever else may concern them, are moved to seek the advice of others primarily by root considerations. It is axiomatic that issues of importance are related to living and dying; issues of secondary importance are the quality of life and its purpose. Many sociologists exhibit a studied embarrassment about these larger concerns, a feeling that intellectual issues posed in such a

manner are melodramatic and unfit for scientific discourse. I
am not arguing for a theological view of society or that auxiliary activities are always less important than fundamental
ones, but only that the social status of a science is often
measured by such easy to make but hard to prove distinctions.

This study is an effort to give substance to such a vision and
in so doing to demonstrate that the underlining predicates of
sociology as presently practiced give scant consideration to
basic issues of life-and-death in favor of distinctly derivative
issues of social structure and function. The underlining rationale of this study is a recognition, tragic in its consequences, that
the dominant structural-functional categories of explaining
the social system increasingly hamper the empirical description of systems by reducing the social order to formal labels
or organizational operations. The widespread use of a variety
of formalisms leads to a presumed synergy among societies in
theory that is rarely apparent in fact.

The word "fundamental" is itself value laden and extremely
troublesome. While there is a large literature on the moral
demand for social science to consider fundamental questions
such as mastery and misery or producers and products, the
dilemma persists that there are so many such general concerns
that one is "left with the feeling that the house of social science
is still largely founded on sand."[4] Another view of the sociologically fundamental is contained in the Millsian distinction
between "individual troubles" and "public issues," with those
items of national or international historical meaning being
highest in the rating chart of the fundamental.[5] But while these
are important efforts to establish clear-eyed precepts, they
remain ethical strategies and moral postures rather than sociological efforts to come to grips with the shank of issues.

Life-and-death issues are uniquely fundamental since they
alone serve as a precondition for the examination of all other
issues: public and private, local or historical, products and
producers.[6] Life and death alone move us beyond a relativistic
framework; those works within social science that have most

profoundly gripped our attention over time and through space are linked to problems of life and death. While for the most part our concerns are with life and death as a human, biological fact, we should also consider the life and death of institutions[7] and communities[8] as fundamental social questions. This volume is dedicated to a consideration of genocide within an amplified context of sociology.

Although the entry point in this analysis is sociological, this does not imply either a special meaning or worth to this singular specimen of social science research over others. Each of the social sciences will be compelled, by force of circumstances, to evaluate the structure of genocidal behavior, and more, its involvement in the very process of that terrible phenomenon it seeks to understand. In a sensitive effort, Stephan Chorover has explored how psychology — in particular such areas of the discipline as psychosurgery, mental measurement testing, chemical and drug treatment of patients or prisoners — has traversed the field from genesis to genocide. His study of psychotechnology "is intended to illustrate the interplay between meaning and power that necessarily pervades many areas of contemporary social life." What started out as a study of behavioral control concludes by revealing the "common embeddedness in a larger conceptual, material, and social context."[9] The paradigm of social science is itself transformed under the impact of technological, state-imposed death. The very character of disciplinary boundaries dissolves under the impact of reviewing what has transpired over the course of this century. Advanced societies have indeed shown "the way" to backward societies; and what is revealed is a mixed bag of progress and retrogression. Advanced forms of science such as neurosurgery have shown the darkness behind the light to more macroscopic visions of society. That is why the study of genocide must perforce represent a review and reconsideration of the study of society in general.

It is difficult to avoid comparison between the twentieth century and what Barbara Tuchman referred to as "the calamitous fourteenth century": an era of mad emperors, military plunder, religious persecution, and, of course, the omnipresent and ubiquitous Black Plague. Until the present, at least, it was a common belief that the fourteenth century, with its "cult of death" and "expected end of the world," was the low point in modern history. As Tuchman put it: "Mankind was at one of history's ebbs. At mid-century that Black Death had raised the question of God's hostility to man and events since then had offered little reassurance. To contemporaries the misery of the time reflected sin, and, indeed, sin in the form of greed and inhumanity abounded. On the downward slope of the Middle Ages man had lost confidence in his capacity to construct a good society."[10]

The fourteenth century was particularly vicious in its epidemiological consequences. And this may well have led to the harsh treatment in the next century of the Jews and all other peoples defined as political, economic, or religious out-siders. It has been argued that modern anti-Semitism has its roots in the various inquisitions of the period.[11] But it is also the case that the fifteenth century provided an optimism for those who survived, a continued belief in chivalry that coex-isted side by side with the emergence of a bourgeois class that was not to be denied. Cultural creativity and the potential for mass distribution of its products led to the emergence of the city as the center of modern civilization.

It is hard to say that the twentieth century is any the less ambiguous than the fourteenth or fifteenth centuries; now too we are faced with unparalleled creativity and achievements, standing side by side with the destructive potentials, in nearly all facets of science and technology, if not in art and literature. But the level and technification of the killing system is such as to make the plagues pale by comparison. Numbers are stag-gering at both ends of the societal spectrum, so much so that debates rage precisely in terms of the "warfare" of science and religion.

As Camus reminded us, the plagues at least had the capacity to bring people together since it was humans against elemental nature fighting an entity called the Black Death rather than people fighting each other. This is not to romanticize the plague, since there are all kinds of theories that the Black Death was basically brought about by the effort to undermine Christian civilization. Even the flagellants saw their role as purging the ritual murdering of Christians emanating from a compulsion to reenact Crucifixion. Hence the plague was not without its social consequences. But these were and remain throughout random rather than systemic assaults. The notion of an engineering of death rather than the individuation of death had not yet emerged.

What made possible the engineering of death was a set of value-laden assumptions that the state, whether to purify its racial base or to amplify its economic base, has the right to decide how many sacrifices are required to achieve its goals. As a result, social scientists (along with others) began to raise the issue in terms of how many lives it would take to reach industrialization, political integration, religious hegemony, and so on. In this subtle way, a mutation of values occurred. Decision making hinged on bookkeeping considerations of how many lives, rather than on the more formidable question of the consequence of empowering the state to take lives for any purpose, whatever the ostensible nobility of purpose.

Herein lies the essential difference between the medieval and modern ages: the distinction between the perception of death as unavoidable tragedy willed by Providence and of death, potentially, as manufactured purification of society willed by people. That such purposive behavior was made in the name of biology, history, or science in general pales in importance next to the potentials for making good on theological edicts and ideological agendas of the wildest sorts. Within such a context, the issue of state power and mass murder becomes most sharply focused. Only when death is transformed from a natural, inevitable disaster into a social choice or corporate decision, do concerns over genocide become real and immediate.

Having said this, it remains vital to keep in mind that it is not modernity as some sort of abstract stand-in for technology that is the culprit. Rather, whatever the level of engineering available in any given epoch or system, it is the human beings who command the machinery that define and implement its usages. The idea that we can return to a simpler economy or a return to the land not only ignores patterns of human evolution, but confuses social organization with moral purpose. It is the tortoise like movement of the latter that remains a problem to be examined in depth and without sentimentality.

19

Researching Genocide

What made this immense evil of the genocide possible are two common, altogether ordinary attributes of our daily lives: the fragmentation of the world we live in, and the depersonalization of our relations with others.

— Tzvetan Todorov[1]

IT HAS OFTEN AND PROPERLY BEEN BEMOANED, BY THEIR CHAMPIONS AND CRITICS ALIKE, that the social sciences, unlike the physical sciences, do not travel. By that, I presume, is meant that they lack universal properties that would permit an observer in one place to readily identify the parameters of research and findings from another place halfway around the world. Indeed, if such parochialism is endemic to the social sciences, then the very notion of science as social is itself in dispute.

There is, however, one great and noble exception to this complaint (I should qualify this by saying that there may be others as well, for example, the work done in experimental psychology) in the realm of large-scale analysis of whole societies: namely, the study of life and death and the forms of inflicted nasty behaviors in between. For in the measurement of life-taking propensities of states, societies, and communities, we come upon the universal property that links all humankind.

In this small world of specialized researchers on the arbitrary foreclosure and termination of human life, national boundaries and linguistic differences among the social scientists seem magically to melt. We have the social historian Alex P. Schmid in The Netherlands working on the politics of pain and punishment; famed psychologist Herbert C. Kelman from the United States working on crimes of obedience and authority; Mika Haritos-Fatouros, also a psychologist, in Greece working on the psychology of torture; Israel W. Charny in Israel amassing worldwide studies of comparative genocides with a special emphasis on holocausts directed at the Jewish and Armenian peoples. To be sure, this is a small universe of shared information about the terrible aspects of the large universe.

These names are more illustrative than exhaustive. One could just as well mention scholars of equal rank in Canada, Japan, England, France, and Germany, also hard at work on similar and related subjects. What is important is not disciplinary or national boundaries but human inhumanity writ large — the taking of life, the maiming of life, the deformation of life — not as a morbid preoccupation but as a mechanism by which social science can join the pure and applied fields of science and medicine to heal and repair, and, ultimately, to just leave alone! For those who work in this area have as a common bond a recognition that issues of life and death are critical to social research and that the prolongation of life and the postponement of death is a common meeting ground, not just for people of good will but of researchers of good research habit.

In this specialized world in which the grim side of the twentieth century is explored in depth and with a special poignancy that often defies words — but does not escape numbers — none stand taller than R. J. Rummel, political scientist at the University of Hawaii. In his book *Death by Government*,[2] he has brought to the study of genocide the quantitative — a range of figures that is truly staggering by any scale — and the qualitative, the meaning of all these numbers in the study of the "comparative worth" of civilizations.

What Rummel has done in this book above all others is provide a conceptual map to make future studies easier. He has made the sort of hard distinctions that are data-driven between legal and outlaw states; between genocide and democide, between democratic and authoritarian systems — all anchored firmly in numbers. To be sure, numbers matter. All societies are in their nature imperfect artifacts. But those that hold as their highest value the sanctity of the person are different in their nature and essence from those who see their ultimate mission as obedience and punishment for the transgressors. This easy movement of different types of social scientists converging on the problem of life and death is fueled by the sort of data provided and distinctions made by Rummel. Indeed, we can no longer work in this area without reference to this massive, yet singular effort.

Rummel's work needs no elaboration. But I would like to point to one crucial aspect that stands out above all others: the need to revise our sense of the depth of horrors inculcated by Communist regimes on ordinary humanity. The numbers are so grotesque at this level that we must actually revise our sense and sensibilities about the comparative study of totalitarianisms to appreciate that of the two supreme systemic horrors of the century, the Communist regimes measurably surpass the fascist regimes in their life-taking propensities. For buried in the data on totalitarian death mills as a whole, is the terrible sense that communism is not "Left" and fascism is not "Right" — both are horrors — and the former, by virtue of its capacities for destroying more of its own nationals, holds an unenviable "lead" over the latter in life taking.

One might argue that the fascists had a greater sense of technological modes of destruction, but the Communists utilized the natural hardships of life the better and more effectively to destroy individual capacities for survival. Thus, those for whom the technology of death remains central may still prefer to think of the Nazis as worse offenders, whereas those for whom an elaborate prison system is forever enshrined as the Gulag by Solzhenitsyn will see the Communists as worse offenders. But it is the wisdom of Rummel to urge us beyond such dubious honors into an appreciation of the linkages of totalitarian systems in the murderous pursuit of worthless objectives.

Rummel rarely speaks about morality and virtue. His concerns are not fixated on "normative" concerns of equity and liberty, or the uneven rankings of people in societies. He is not describing the imperfections of democracies or the weakness of Western liberalism. Rather, he is by implication saying that societies in which debate and discussion do not lead to death and decimation will somehow find a means to care for themselves. In that sense, his trilogy *Lethal Politics, Democide,* and *Death by Government* represent by extension a study of the forms of democracy and of the ways in which systems operate to sustain themselves without destroying opposition. This was made perfectly plain in his specialized volume *China's Bloody Century.*

It might be that the study of positive concepts like democracy and freedom will forever remain as spongy as the terms are elusive. But it may also be that we will get a better "fix" on the positive aspects of social systems once we enlist the aid of data to help us arrive at a sense of which societies can truly be called decent. Not all issues are resolved: We are not told whether centralized or decentralized societies are better or worse, whether the impulses to one or another form of societies are driven by external modes of power or internal guides of authority, whether democracy operates best in small or large states, or whether legal or ethical varieties of rule are best. But all these, while important considerations, are secondary, at least in the sense that they presuppose an environment in which life taking is suspended and life giving becomes a widespread norm.

We all walk a little taller by climbing on the shoulders of Rummel's work. He has helped us to redeem the highest aspirations of the founders of social science and yet remain perfectly true to the latest techniques of formal analysis. It is a pleasure to write these words as a fellow laborer in the vineyards of social research. It is no less a pleasure to add that, as president of Transaction, it has been a privilege to serve as publisher of nearly all of Professor Rummel's major works. If we published nothing other than Rummel's works, the justification for the existence of Transaction as a publisher of social science would be confirmed. I can think of no more fitting tribute to this singular scholar in search of collective life.

IN MOVING FROM THE WORK OF RUMMEL TO THAT OF ISRAEL CHARNY, WE ARE ALSO SHIFTING ground from political science to social psychology. And even if sentiments are shared, professional backgrounds do lead to differences in results no less than in emphases. Charny's work is sufficiently unique as to make him a singular figure in the dismal "science" of genocide studies. I should like, in this brief space, to draw attention to three such characteristics: the first theoretical, the second organizational, and the third moral. I do so not to celebrate a colleague — although he merits and has earned such encomiums — but, rather, to highlight what social science can contribute to the course of civilization when done properly and decently.

Charny's opening statement to his edited book *The Widening Circle of Genocide*[3] provides such a pellucid account of the contents of each section that my task here is greatly eased. Clearly, his notion of "the widening circle of genocide" as a concept rather than a title is two-edged: on the one side, there is a growing sense that the numbers of human beings trapped in circles of despair leading to dismemberment continues to exceed our wildest earlier estimates; while on the other, there is an appreciation that this widening circle is one of recognition

— early awareness and early actions that can deter, or at least limit, the practice of genocide.

That our thinking on genocide has progressed to the point of taking the subject to intervention and prevention, and beyond moaning and groaning over what has been, itself raises controversial issues that are being debated daily in policy discourse over Somalia, Bosnia, and Haiti. But this in itself marks a level of consciousness with respect to genocidal practices that did not exist in, say, 1944 — a bare fifty years ago. Indeed, the implication of Charny's work and of that of his colleagues is clear. Had a higher level of political awareness and action been manifest in the Allied powers' response to Nazism, the worst features of that odious system might have been muted, if not averted. In this particular "if /then," we are talking of millions of innocent lives that were consigned to destruction in the fires of the Holocaust.

What then are the special contributions made by Charny and his associates to this painful subject? First, there is the unity of life struggles as such; I refer, that is, to the unitary character of taking lives, whether in Armenia in the past as described by Vahakn Dadrian or in the present in such seemingly exotic places like Rwanda, Afghanistan, East Timor, or Eastern Europe. For the fact is that genocide is an ongoing concern of widening frequency, not a historical remnant. The broad theoretical issue of the distinction between the collective murder of a people, such as befell European Jewry between 1941-1945, and the selective murder of a people, as continues to haunt other peoples, is significant; but it is only of a second order of significance. The theoretical ink spilled over who has claims to higher victim status must surely pale in contrast to the actual blood spilled by real individuals and communities.

Charny's great virtue is that his focus has never wavered from holding in suspension judgments as to who suffers most, while pursuing mechanisms for reducing suffering as such. In this connection, I should like to note the terrible seamless character of genocidal practices; a seamlessness that brings into sharp focus the difference between real theory and nit-picking; or between primary and secondary issues involved in the practice of and, no less important, the prevention of geno-cide.

Let me quote, necessarily at some length, the following from a report filed by Timothy W. Ryback in *The New Yorker* (15 November 1993). It illustrates the unitary character of geno-cide, whatever be its variations. and intensities:

In June, 1940, nine months after the occupation of Poland, the Germans established the *Konzentrationslager* Auschwitz in the brick buildings of a Polish military camp that dated back to the First World War. A former ammunitions depot on the edge of the camp was converted into a crematorium to incinerate the corpses of inmates who had been executed or had perished from disease, exhaustion, or abuse. Poison gas is reported to have first been used in Auschwitz that September, when six hundred Soviet prisoners of war and two hundred and fifty sick prisoners were locked in basement rooms of Block XI and exposed to Zyklon B. Later that month, nine hundred Soviet soldiers were crammed into the morgue of the Auschwitz crematorium and gassed. Rudolf Höss, who observed both operations, recalled the latter one in his memoirs, written in prison after the war: "The Russians were ordered to undress in an anteroom: they then quietly entered the mortuary, for they had been told they were to be deloused. The whole transport exactly filled the mortuary to capacity. The doors were then sealed and the gas shaken down through the holes in the roof. I do not know how long this killing took. For a little while a humming sound could be heard. When the powder was thrown in there were cries of 'Gas!,' then a great bellowing, and the trapped prisoners hurled themselves against both the doors. But the doors held. They were opened several hours later, so that the place might be aired. It was then that I saw, for the first time, gassed bodies in the mass." On January 20, 1942, the Nazi leadership convened a secret meeting at a villa in Wannsee, on the outskirts of Berlin, to discuss plans for the mass extermination of Europe's Jews and other minority groups. Auschwitz, because of its relative isolation and its proximity to major rail links, became the end point for the Nazis' "final solution."

Now the importance of this, beyond its obvious historical interest, is not simply as a search for pedestrian mechanisms of law to preserve artifacts to "prove" that a Holocaust took place but, rather, to note that what was initially tried out on nine hundred Red Army troops, presumably non-Jewish for the most part, became the engineering and chemical prototype for the destruction of 6 million Jews and perhaps an equal number of non-Jews. So whatever be the disputations on the meaning of the Holocaust, the truth of a preemptive genocide cannot be doubted. An early detection system, a rapid deployment of military response, a mass communications participation — any of these might have blunted the blade of the killers. While the deaths of several hundred Red Army troops does not weigh on the same scale as the death of a whole people, the central fact is that they are linked events in history. That, I submit, is a theoretical insight of great importance; and the work of Israel Charny must be seen as central in this regard.

I suspect that Charny would be the last person to deny that problems in this line of argument exist. When should random killing be described as systematic? Is this a matter of counting bodies, or some other form of measurement? When is a rapid deployment of military personnel warranted to prevent or bring to a halt genocidal practices? Whose troops and under whose auspices? And when does mass communication blunt sensibilities rather than spur actions? Do pictures of starving and maimed children provide outrage or sublimate responses in a voyeuristic series of excesses? These issues are now being addressed — perhaps not as fully as one would like. Nonetheless, the lack of awareness is so much higher than a half century ago that we are entitled to salute the pioneering efforts of people like Charny, Leo Kuper, R.J. Rummel, and Yehuda Bauer.

Now let me turn briefly to the organizational efforts involved in Charny's work — or what can best be described as the conspiracy of conscience, or the public representation of private sentiments. For behind the psychological theory is an organizational concept, a belief that issues of life and death frame any realignment of the social sciences. This certainly has been a characteristic of my own work, from *Radicalism and the Revolt against Reason* in the 1960s to *Taking Lives* in its several editions, and finally, to my current interests in linking the reformation of social science to the study of life-taking systems at one end and life-giving societies at the other. For in this shared pursuit, our "conspiracy" shall, nay must, triumph over the furtive efforts in dark corners to hatch new varieties of the murder of innocents. The professional identities of the contributors to *The Widening Circle* tells the story: Charny from psychology, Vahakn Dadrian from sociology, James Dunn from public administration; Leonard Glick and Martin van Bruinessen from anthropology; George Kent and R.J. Rummel from political science; Robert Krell from psychiatry, and Samuel Totten from education.

The key here is transitive: each of these people has had something to say about specific issues or peoples related to genocide. Past professional identities may have helped shape present analyses. But in fact, as a result of such efforts as Charny has launched through his Institute on the Holocaust and Genocide, the professional review of genocide has secured a foothold in the world of social research and, in so doing, helps contribute to what Frances Bacon might well have called the new great instauration of our times.

Now we turn to the final point to note about this collective effort: the moral undertones that help inform the empirical analysis. For without such controlled passions distinguishing right from wrong, life from death, all is lost in a bag of pure relativism. It is the normative standpoint, derived perhaps more from a medical than a social scientific model, that provides the fuel bringing life to these efforts. For while such ethical premises do not of themselves assure high-quality scholarship, without such premises, the work itself could never be conceived, much less carried out.

One does not risk so much for the sake of gaining so little, in personal reward at least, without some Kantian imperative lighting the way. The study of genocide is a value unto itself because life is a good into itself. The "reward" may not be reflected in emoluments or distinctions within traditional departments or societies, but it is surely reflected in the millions of people for whom the Holocaust and the many genocides that stain our century are now part of their *Geist*. Every debate in the *Historikerstreit* in Germany, every trial of an Eichmann in Jerusalem, every archive opened in a Turkish vault gives evidence to the moral fervor that makes possible renewal not only of professional life but of life in general. The work of Israel Charny deserves recognition as a key building block in this effort. *The Widening Circle of Genocide* is but one of several such foundation blocks and deserves, nay commands, our intellectual attention and personal respect as a result.

Following the end of World War II and a realization of the enormity of the death heaped upon millions of innocent victims, studies of the Holocaust fell into four identifiable stages: First, the definition of the issues and the magnitudes involved, as was done by people like Raphael Lemkin and Israel Drapkin. Second was the statistical and eyewitness reconstruction of the full range of the Nazi terror let loose upon the Jews and other "undesirable" ethnic groups like the Gypsies. The works of Lucy Dawidowicz and Raul Hilberg are especially noteworthy in this connection. Third came studies relating the Holocaust to genocide studies as a comparative effort: the efforts of Richard G. Hovannisian, Kurt Jonassohn, and Yehuda Bauer readily come to mind in this area. We are now clearly at a fourth stage, one in which the meaning of genocide as a social, political, and religious phenomenon can be examined in the broad context of established political theory. Among the pioneers in this area are Hannah Arendt, Helen Fein, and Yehuda

Bauer. The work of Robert F. Melson is clearly a product of this approach.

These are by no means neat compartments, and certainly I do not wish to imply that the names given are the only contributors to the newest claimant for a "dismal science." But Robert Melson's *Revolution and Genocide*[4] appears after close to a half century of intensive research efforts, and therefore must be assessed in those terms. Melson's thesis is simple enough: Armenians in the Ottoman Empire and Jews of Imperial Germany survived as ethnic and religious minorities until they suffered mass destruction when the two old regimes were engulfed by revolution and war. Indeed, the burden of the thesis is to prove that there is a direct relationship between revolution and genocide.

His is a bold claim, somewhat oversimplified: to wit, that the revolutionary regimes that embraced Pan-Turkism and National Socialism respectively engaged in genocide as a policy and an ideology. Melson argues further that it was the rise of xenophobic nationalism that fueled the anti-Armenian feelings in Turkey and triggered the anti-Semitism of Germany between 1934-1945. This is a work of contemporary European history no less than political theory. Indeed, the degree to which the theory can be accepted, or considered validated, must be based on the accuracy of the historical claims — the work must be examined in these terms.

Melson's review of the histories of Turkey and Germany contains difficulties of a different sort. The most serious weakness is his assumption that the Kemalist Revolution was a break in attitudes and policies toward the Armenians. It most clearly was not. The Ottoman Empire engaged in massive liquidation of the Armenian peoples between 1894 and 1896; and in 1909, long before Ottomanism and Pan-Islam were abandoned, a second round of massacres took place. The continuation of massacres by the Turkish authorities during and after World War I were just that — a continuation. In addition, Melson has nothing to say about a major power,

Russia, which, after the Bolshevik Revolution no less than
under czarist rule, performed divisive and dangerous roles in
Asia Minor. Indeed, whether in Armenia or Rwanda, one finds
that the interests of major powers and/or colonial powers play
a decisive part in the development of genocidal conditions.

Vahakn Dadrian, in *Genocide as a Problem of National and
International Law*[5], states that "progressive escalation of the
level of genocidal killing of the Armenians in Ottoman Turkey
through episodic and recurrent massacres in the eras of Abdul
Hamit and the Young Turk Ittihadist in particular is a paramount fact." What this suggests is not that the destruction of
nearly half the Armenians living under Turkish rule was trivial
but that the assumption of the existence of some sort of benign
empire in the past contrasted with a present revolutionary
republic simply does not hold water. To resort to an old caveat:
What we have here may be a necessary, but it is hardly a
sufficient, cause of genocide. It is plainly wrong to suggest that
in the case of Armenians at least, the old regime failed to
develop or implement a policy to solve the questions or problems created by the Armenian people.[6] It is the consistency of
Turkish policies over time and change in regime that far
outweighs other factors. This leads one to be skeptical of the
idea that regime shifts are automatically correlated with
changes in policies toward so-called national minorities. It is
more nearly the case that totalitarian regimes can elevate or
dampen certain policies, but they seem incapable of addressing
those cultural formations that lead to genocide in the first
place.

The problem with the thesis of the revolutionary source of
the Nazi Holocaust against the Jewish people is of a different
sort, but equally serious. While it is correct to note that the
Bismarckian system was a "cunning device ensuring the stability and unity of the German state," the seizure of power by
the Nazis proceeded through the Weimar Republic. To speak
of "the German revolution that commenced with the fall of
the *Kaiserreich* in 1918 and ended with the destruction of

Nazism in 1945"[7] is to blur the essential distinctions between two political systems. It might be neat to presume a movement from empire to secular dictatorship, but it does not quite do justice to real history. There is a further problem: While it may be true that there were those who "denied legitimacy" to the Weimar Republic, it was not toppled, as Melson claims by some "concordat" of teachers and bureaucrats, but by a run-away inflation and an economic system in shambles following the depression of 1929.

Whatever the actual course of events in Germany, and however one decides to assess Weimar Germany, as interlude or interregnum, it is indeed the case that the Nazi regime behaved in a way that neither the empire or Weimar period could ever have imagined. Melson's thesis is that a revolutionary seizure of power changed the foundations of society, law, economy, and cultural values and did have a tremendous and direct bearing on the fate of Jewish people — not only the Jews of Germany, but throughout all Europe. It is more nearly the case that Nazism made manifest those latent contradictions in German society already prevalent by the time of the 1933 Nazi seizure of power.

Still, one must wonder whether Melson's thesis is not too simple. It might be argued, as I have done in this book, that it was not the Nazi revolution as such, but the pending doom of Nazism that created the implementation of the Holocaust. The destruction of European Jewry essentially took place between 1942 and 1945; or after the fate of the Hitler regime was sealed in military terms. It was after the Wannsee Conference that the demoniacal plot to destroy the Jewish people took on huge momentum. Between 1933 and 1941 the Jews suffered badly, but the death camps, the systematic engineering of massive destruction, had not gotten underway.

One might argue that nationalist passions deeply embedded in the psyche of the Turkish and German "races" were more directly involved in the massacres than revolutionary forces. Indeed, the forces of political upheaval inspired and made possible massive annihilation, but it was hardly as if the dogs of war were simply a function of voices of revolution.

The question remains as to what kind of revolutions Melson is talking about. Many revolutions have taken place in which anti-Semitism and antiminority feelings have been abated rather than heightened. One need not turn further than the United States for verification. It seems more the case that in this regard, culture looms larger than politics as such. One might say that in revolutions of compassion, racist and anti-Semitic assaults are reduced or at least held in check by a common adhesion to the law. In revolutions of passion, when law and order is itself under attack, genocide, such as that of the Armenians and Jews, becomes possible. One wishes that Melson had taken the next step and looked beyond revolution and war into types of revolutions and wars that produce tranquil rather than destructive outcomes. Still, *Revolution and Genocide* raises important issues in the theory and history of the terrible assaults against the Jewish and Armenian peoples in the twentieth century — for that alone it deserves to be read and pondered.

While in the United States, it has been social scientists like Melson who have carried out the analytic assignments to study genocide, in Europe it has been the historians who have been most active in this enterprise. The subject matter of genocide and the Holocaust is of such enormous and awesome scope that it rightfully can claim to be a field of investigation unto itself. Certainly the volume of work done in this area by the historians of North America, as well as in Europe since the mid-1940s, attests to the seriousness of the study of arbitrary taking of life by political authorities. But their efforts also reveal the deep limitations of German historiography — the strong impulse to apologetics rather than analysis.

George Steiner wrote an essay in 1959 on contemporary Germany called "The Hollow Miracle," in which he notes that "everything forgets. But not a language. When it has been injected with falsehood only the most drastic truth can cleanse it. Instead, the post-war history of the German language has been one of dissimulation and deliberate forgetting. The remembrance of horrors past has been largely uprooted." Steiner probably would have been wiser to say "suppressed" rather than "uprooted," since no phenomenon as devastating and thorough as the Holocaust can be uprooted. That it took until 1986 to open up such a discussion, and in the process, to revitalize what Steiner thought to be dead — the German language — is hardly a wonder. But in this act of consciousness, however clumsy and filled with apologetics, the restoration of not just the German language but the potential of the German nation can be detected. *Forever in the Shadow of Hitler*[8] is a collection without an introduction. It lacks even the semblance of order and is drawn from a variety of authors with diverse (to put it mildly) views. The volume has been published in a physically pedestrian way and was prepared without an editor. Nonetheless, it is must reading, an awful phrase usually reserved for popular novels that hardly last out a publishing season.

The *Historikerstreit,* as the battle over the nature of the Nazi legacy has come to be called, contains the raw texts, and perhaps reveals the raw nerves of current debates by German sociologists and historians of the Nazi epoch. This is not simply a debate between Ernst Nolte and Jürgen Habermas over whether the Holocaust was real; rather, it is a discussion of whether the Holocaust is unique or part of a continuum with genocides the world over, and totalitarian regimes that raged throughout Europe under the flag of international communism in Russia no less than National Socialism in Germany.

German historians and sociologists, in seeming obliviousness to Jewish literature examining the same issues, argue whether the Holocaust committed by the Germans against the Jews is a unique event in history, or one of many afflictions visited upon oppressed peoples. Both Nolte and Habermas treat these issues from the viewpoint of a perpetrating culture; the effort is viewed by both as an attempt to settle accounts with the meaning of German national identity. Habermas's charge of apologetics is complex, stating that the guilt of Germany is being wished way by Nolte in the general upsurge of totalitarianisms of all sorts. Nolte in turn charges Habermas and his followers with emphasizing the Holocaust not so much to remind the German people of the atrocities committed by the Hitler regime but as a mechanism to minimize similar atrocities perpetuated by Stalinists in the name of the Russian people.

The passions that German historians of culture bring to the subject are sufficiently complex to rescue the discussion from banality. Still, in contrast to Jewish historians like Raul Hilberg and Lucy Davidowicz, both sides lack exactitude in describing the Holocaust: There are no discussions of numbers, techniques, or the timing of destruction. The German penchant for "abstract thought" permits the people of Germany to choose sides between the uniqueness of the Holocaust and the universality of totalitarianism without quite coming to terms with concrete history as such.

The bitterness of the debates notwithstanding, and without choosing sides, these are not evil historians or social critics. They are rather people whose craft comes upon issues that cannot be solved simply by appeals to evidence, tradition, or convention. Both Nolte and Habermas face this essential problem, albeit in different ways. Nolte must place the Holocaust in the context of a generalized expression of totalitarianism during the period of 1918 to 1991, with special emphasis on commonalties between Hitler's National Socialism and Stalin's international communism. He does not excuse the crimes of fascism any more than Bullock did in comparing the careers of Hitler and Stalin, but he sees them as part of the crimes of totalitarianism. Habermas for his part seems unable to acknowledge the destruction of many ethnic peoples under Stalin and the continuities of a centrifugal ideology that the Soviet system shared with the Nazi system.

On this point, Habermas scores heavily against Nolte and his formidable associates. He examines the uniqueness of the Nazi assault against the Jews, over and against the more "rational" objectives of the Nazi war machine. For Habermas, the question of moral responsibility inheres precisely in this assault on a people rather than the conduct of a war. For if the destruction of the Jews was simply an extension of a general assault by totalitarians against ordinary people, then we are dealing with a quantitative continuum, not a qualitative break, from the past. And for Habermas, this becomes Nolte's apologetic escape hatch, an opportunity to link Nazism with communism, even in its treatment of Jews and other national minorities.

The essays in this volume shed a great deal of light on the German mentality, especially its capacity for extracting a problem of scholarship from the ashes of its own inspired tragedies. It is less the moral thundering of Habermas and Nolte than the effort to define a national identity (a phrase heard often in these essays) and biological liquidation that is the leitmotiv of the minor figures in particular. Andreas Hillgruber's linkage of the "twofold fall" (the military collapse of the Third Reich and the murder of the European Jews) needs to be examined more closely. He lacks a sense that the murder of the European Jews became an end unto itself for fascism, whether or not the Nazi empire or its advanced posts survived or crumbled.

The best of German scholarship assaulted this cleansing effort, this attempt to relativize National Socialism. The work of Hans Mommsen, Wolfgang J. Mommsen, Jürgen Kocka, Robert Leicht, Kurt Sontheimer, and Martin Broszat take on the challenge. One gets the impression that the democratic historians won the battle, while the revisionists like Nolte won the popular war. The parallels between German defeats and Jewish destruction, and between the unfairness of Nazi guilt as similar to the guilt charged to Jews, are effective. Finally, the wild assumption that the 1939 statement by Chaim Weizmann and the other leaders of the Zionist Movement declaring

Nazism as the enemy of the Jewish people, somehow entitled
a Nazi *response*, in effect reverses cause and effect. Nolte
blames Jews for stimulating the Nazi policies that were crys-
tallized in the Wannsee Declaration and ended in the slaughter
of European Jewry.

Neither side to the debate tries to explain the specific timing
of the Holocaust. Why was the actual slaughter of the Jewish
masses actually undertaken between 1942 and 1945, when all
but the most desperate within the German high command
knew that the war against the Allies had essentially been lost?
The Nazi epoch lasted for thirteen years. But the actual slaughter of the Jews was confined to the last three. The first ten could
be considered a prologue. One might argue that the goals of
war had shifted for the Nazis from the defeat of the Allies to
the slaughter of the Jews. The decade of softening up public
opinion had been sufficiently successful to make possible this
shift of gears in Nazi goals. To the German Right, the shift in
goals makes sense only as a response to the Jewish Menace,
while to the German Left it was part of the reactionary nature
of the regime. Neither side wishes to deal with the consensus
that the Nazis had established to find a victim to blame for the
loss of the war if it could not find a cure to the cause of the war.
If Jewish historians are missing from the analysis, then the
German people are missing from the text altogether.

Both sides are essentially correct in their critique of the
other. Habermas and his colleagues do indeed emphasize the
unique nature of the Holocaust. They do so not just to give the
Jewish people their due but to weaken the sense of their own
culpability in past left-wing totalitarianisms. Nolte and his
supporters suggest the unity of totalitarian systems again, not
so much to excoriate the foundations of such a global phenomenon as to restructure the sense of unique responsibility
of the Nazi regime and the German people for the unscalable
Holocaust. Karl Dietrich Bracher put the matter most succinctly: "The shame about the failure of a cultured civilization,
one that believes itself formed by the values of Christianity,

humanism, and the Enlightenment, can help us to recognize the dangers of totalitarian manipulation. References to similar phenomena in other civilizations should not relativize that experience; rather it should broaden it and make it general. That means not only a remembrance of the past but also a warning for the present and the future."

Unique events in the history of societies can always be linked to historical processes that have taken place elsewhere, while continuities in the tragedy of human destruction clearly reveal unique elements depending on the culture and climate of a people and a place. One suspects that Nolte and Habermas know this. But the question of the uniqueness or universality of German culpability, if it has no empirical content, must have a moral answer, since a people as powerful and central to fin de siècle economy and polity can hardly claim the mantle of victim. The issue rephrased becomes: Do Germans get on with the task of being dominant, admitting the ultimate sin of massive life-taking, or do they get on with the task of remaining dominant by relativizing their sins, linking them to a tradition of twentieth-century tragedies?

In short, for this book, the Holocaust is a German Question, not a Jewish Question. These are essays and articles originally published for the most part in the German newspapers *Frankfurter Allgemeine Zeitung,* and *Die Zeit.* They are not aimed at foreign consumption, nor are they intended to assuage foreign concerns that Nazism haunts the German soul. I suspect that this is not only or even primarily because of what happened to the Jewish people but instead that it is because of what happened to the German people. The discussion will hardly please the Jewish people with the level of understanding shown, nor will it give the remainder of Europe a sense of confidence that Germany is capable of anything other than a highly formalist notion of democratic order. And it is Nolte who senses this better than Habermas, since it is he who appreciates the totalitarian temptation that lurks beneath the views of Habermas. In the very act of condemning the uniqueness of German guilt, there is an implicit denial by Habermas of the Soviet system, a system to which he gave more than lip-service during most of the postwar and Cold War epochs.

Neither Nolte nor Habermas carry the ideological day. Those who took a middle position, such as Immanuel Geiss, sense as much. Only those capable of "walking the tightrope" emerge as rational actors. The crimes of Nazism and the crimes of communism have become melded and blended over time. The moral fervor with which Jürgen Habermas and Rudolf Augstein assault Nolte is contrasted to Nolte's moral obtuseness. Astonishingly enough, we are left with a sense of Christian revival, a "worldwide renaissance with fundamentalist trends in the various religious communities."

What begins with a discussion by professionals of the place of Nazism in German history ends with the place of German history in the revival of, and redemption offered by, Christianity. Little wonder then that the great debates in Germany fizzled out from 1986 to 1993, leaving victimizers and vanquished in essentially the same relationship they had been prior to the entrance into this *kulturkampf* by German men of learning. And it could not end otherwise. For analysis rooted in the tradition of cultural history could hardly be expected to come to terms with less lofty considerations of the machinery as well as the ideology of death.

In this regard, the more recent, empirically oriented studies emanating from the sons and daughters of the victims of genocide have proven far more compelling and long lived. As the young scholar Daniel Jonah Goldhagen, following in the footsteps of Lucy S. Dawidowicz, summarized matters: Genocide is an institutional no less than ideological phenomenon. Indeed, until this conversion from raw animosity for the outsider to a sophisticated apparatus such as the concentration camps take place, the commission of genocide remains a destructive fantasy. The role of the extermination facilities is key "not just because of the enormous number of installations, not just because of the millions of people who suffered within its confines, not just because of the vast numbers of Germans and German minions who worked for and in these camps, but also because it constituted an entirely new sub-system of society."[9]

With German identity rooted in the realm of cultural continuities, Jewish identities have seemingly faded into the background, left to argue the realm of symbolic politics among themselves and their survivors. But at least, in this very bitter debate, some possibilities for the restoration of the German language in its classic form have reemerged. We must be grateful for this small act of contrition performed by contemporary German intellectuals. They provide us with a window of opportunity to understand and penetrate the German academic world — and not so much to learn why the Holocaust happened as to appreciate how it could happen again. Still, this is a small act, one that does not quite come to terms with the perpetrators no less than the victims of genocide. In this regard, social science trumps intellectual history — in both the level of its analytical probe and in its capacity to elicit moral understanding. Whether democracy can trump dictatorship is another, more problematic matter upon which the potentials for an increase or decrease in genocide come to rest.

20

Gauging Genocide

My time, my twentieth century, weighs on me as a host of voices
and the faces of people whom I once knew, or heard about, and
now they no longer exist. Many were famous for something, they
are in encyclopedias, but more of them have been forgotten, and
all they can do is make use of me, the rhythm of my blood, my
hand holding the pen, in order to return among the living for a
brief moment.

— Czeslaw Milosz[1]

THE STUDY OF THE ARBITRARY TAKING OF LIFE IS NOT EX-
ACTLY EQUIVALENT to being a pioneer in the invention of a
new learning field or even the discovery of a new way of
bottling old wine. Indeed, to be a "pioneer" in the study of
collective death says much about the dark side of this extraordinary century, and about the vanity of those who attempt to
make sense of it all. Perhaps it would better if we admitted that
what we "study" is not an "area" but the culmination of a
century in which invention has been matched, discovery by
discovery, by the machinery and technology of death. Genocide is not an area of study that can be bracketed within
well-defined boundaries. Such concerns are the common property of humanity. It is no less a characteristic of our age than
welfare. The twentieth century has mastered the art of destruc-

tion and construction. These are not exactly specific areas of study so much as facts of life that we all share in common.

Still, in the absence of any light side to the subject, I confess to serious concern with the dark arts of mass murder. I came to the study of genocide in an attempt to define a primary social indicator that can help provide sociology with a quantitative equivalent of voting for politics and money for economics. In doing so, in seeking some quantitative, that is numerical, measure for the quality of life unique to our times, I hoped to contribute something positive to the sciences of mass emancipation, and not just the anti-sciences of mass destruction. These remarks are not intended to summarize my *lebenswerke,* only to provide the private undercoating that makes possible a contribution to the public enterprise.

I grew to young manhood in the bowels of World War Two. Because of deep family roots in Russia on both my paternal and maternal side, my first interest was in the fate of the people of the Kiev Basin during the Second World War, where most of my family remained. I followed the course of the war on a daily basis. My room was filled with maps and pins detailing the movement of *Wehrmacht* troops on one side and *Red Army* troops on the other. Seeing the film *Alexander Nevsky*, the great Russian nationalist classic produced by Sergei Eisenstein, formed my imagery. Evil was blue-eyed and blond and adorned in white, Good was etched in darker, Slavic colors of the Russian defenders of the faith. I have never have forgotten this reversal in values between black and white. Having grown up on a diet of Westerns at the Sunset and Luxor theaters in Harlem, New York, where I spent my childhood, violence and death were my constant companions, but so, too, were the wonderful and varied life of a unique and fascinating neighborhood. Living at the edge was the denominator, shared by us all. More of these early experiences were detailed in *Daydreams and Nightmares* and need not be labored further.[2]

My earliest concerns were of war overseas and war in the streets, not of state power and mass murder. Indeed, although

I had a keen sense of being Jewish, having been of the last generation largely educated in the Yiddish culture of the secular socialist Workmen's Circle and Sholom Aleichem schools at the fringes of Harlem, my focus was less on the tragic fate of the Jewish communities of Europe, than on the participation of Jewish communities of American and Russia in the struggle for democracy and anti-fascism. In retrospect, this may appear naïve and even foolish. In the context of the times, 1941-1945, this seemed a natural posture for a very young Jewish teen-ager. My greatest linkage to the Jewish community was a basketball court at the Jewish Center in Flatbush, Brooklyn, where the Horowitz family moved after leaving Harlem.

It was my religious friend from Harlem, Arthur Grumberger, whose family migrated from Budapest, Hungary, who first alerted me to the tragedy that was befalling the Jewish people. Having been reared in Jewish socialist Workman's Circle schools, the emphasis was less on European Jewry than American class wars. It was Arthur who introduced me to religious ritual and observance. He shared with me his Hebrew school texts, and was in fact, my first teacher of the Hebrew language. And while this did not especially "stick", the sense of the Jewish people as a universal people, and the special condition of Jews in the interwar period of 1918-1938 became part of my intellectual arsenal, if such it could be called. My heart was not hardened to my people's suffering, but I was terribly unaware of the magnitude of the war against the Jewish people that was being waged and, alas, won by the Nazi regime at the same time as it was clearly losing the war against the Allied Powers. Genocide does not take place in hot house isolation from other aspects of social life and political struggle. It is a function of legal, ethical and cultural disintegration.

My writings on genocide reflect the circuitous route of an obviously misspent childhood and youth. After two early theses efforts in the history of European thought, specifically on the dialectical tradition in the Italian Renaissance and the

French Enlightenment thought done under the supervision of the great Jewish scholar, Paul Oscar Kristellar in 1952 and 1953 at Columbia University, I wrote my first serious and independent work, *The Idea of War and Peace in Contemporary Philosophy and Social Theory.*[3] The effort had scarcely a word about genocide or the Holocaust. It was the seeming potential for nuclear annihilation that was of paramount concern in that volume. In the mid-1950s, the American nation, indeed the entire world, was gripped by the fear of a nuclear holocaust. Everything from films on the makeup of a post nuclear assault, to books on stages in the processing of such warfare, became common grist. For the first time, the American public came to believe that a third world war would be fought on American shores, as well as European capitals. Despite this, my summary of major figures of our century, from Alfred North Whitehead to John Dewey in philosophy to Vladimir Lenin and Mohandas K. Gandhi in politics, was thought by some to stray too far beyond the path of linguistic philosophy and logical positivist methods that held sway in the Anglo-American world of the 1950s.

With the early 1960s, my work moved from an interest in conflict and its resolution to a more focussed emphasis on anarchism and violence. The heating up of the war in Vietnam seemed the proper time, and still does, a natural extension of my thinking about the metaphysical foundations of war as such. Along with David Riesman, a noted sociologist and author of the acclaimed book *The Lonely Crowd*, I helped found the *Committees on Correspondence*—a monthly bulletin alerting the academic and policy communities about the dangers of the pending expansion of the Southeast Asian conflict. It also was fueled by the academic shift from philosophy to sociology as a career path. It was in such a congruence of practical and academic considerations that the issue of genocide came into any sort of focus. In such works at *Radicalism and the Revolt against Reason,*[4] and a large-scale anthology on *The Anarchists,*[5] I described the issue of genocide as mass murder by state authorities; and saw this as a source of anarchist rationalization of violence against government officials. It also became apparent to me that the anti-statist forms of terrorism cut in multiple ways: some toward radical reconstruction of society, others toward reactionary reconstruction of earlier societies. On either side, the Jewish question became a litmus test for social theory. So whether dealing with one or another variety of radical approaches to the German condition, the situation of the Jewish people became a problematic rather than a given. To study war and conflict in modern times was to look closely at the German contradiction between education and barbarism, rationalism and mysticism. My earliest concerns saw Jews as part of the revolutionary movements within German life, as part of the class structure identified with the "interests" of other radical groups, but not on Jews acting in their own behalf. Hence, everyone from Karl Marx to Werner Sombart and Theodore Herzl came into play by the mid-1960s. To study the Holocaust as concrete expression of human behavior meant to also look at National Socialism as a specific manifestation of German behavior.

By the close of the 1960s, my interests in war, conflict and genocide was given a large boost by an invitation to serve as visiting professor at the Hebrew University in its American Civilization program. That trip had a profound effect on my sense of the magnitude of the Holocaust. I met some survivors, some children of survivors, and realized that Israel as a modern state had itself had risen out of the ashes, the charnel house of a wartime Europe. I met survivors, spoke with people who lived in towns and cities from whence my parents came, and saw first-hand evidence of broken bodies, and even bent spirits that seemed to be a common if subdued inheritance of all Israel. Indeed, some of my closest friends and colleagues were from Hungary and Romania, with untold infirmities that made my own harelip and cleft palate pale in comparison. Some were induced by their concentration camp experiences, others that limited movement or impeded speech. The number of such people on my first visit moved and disturbed me. But more pointedly, these colleagues went about the business of living without self-pity. They nearly all had wives and children—large families at that. The tragic sense of Europe played against the canvas of the liberating sense of Jews reborn in the Old World and new State of Israel. All of that weighed heavily on my mind.

Even before that, a decade earlier as a matter of record, in a demographic study of the Jewish communities in Buenos Aires in 1958-59, I was forced to recognize that the issue of Jewish survival was bundled with the issue of the Holocaust, of the genocide committed against the Jewish people by the fascists in the most obvious sense, and then by the Stalinists in only a slightly more covert sense, i.e., socialism as a struggle against Zionism. But even as backdrop in my book *Israeli Ecstasies and Jewish Agonies*,[6] the sense of genocide remained a distant backdrop to what appeared to me to represent a more urgent set of considerations as exemplified by the title. So it was the actual contact with Israel, remote and transient though it may have appeared at the time, that provided a perspective on genocide in particular and conflict in general, sorely lacking in my earlier work.

On a practical level, I became involved with the struggles of the Jewish people to survive Stalinist and post-Stalinist power in the Soviet Union. I became a fervent advocate of the idea that the struggle of intellectuals was far different than simple identification with political parties and partisan enterprise. Intellectuals in the conduct of their research and work must take a cue from atomic scientists: to struggle against the misuse or abuse of their specific contributions to the century by forming appropriate voluntary associations. Together with a handful of extraordinary people ranging from Hannah Arendt at the New School for Social Research, Daniel Bell and Eli Ginzberg at Columbia University, Andrew Hacker and Milton Konvitz at Cornell University, Ithiel de Sola Pool and George Wald at MIT and Harvard, respectively, to name some of the better-known figures, and with a particular bow to the extraordinary leadership in this effort taken by Hans J. Morgenthau, we formed the Academic Committee on Soviet Jewry—one of several specialist groups mobilized by largely Jewish agencies, to ward off what was felt to be an impending disaster for the Russian Jewish people. Our mission in the late sixties and early seventies, if such were it called, was to assist in the migration of Jewish men and women of letters to Vienna, Rome, Jerusalem, and points west. It was an amazingly successful mission, which combined with other efforts on behalf of Soviet Jewry, paved the way for the massive Jewish migrations from Russia to points West in the 1990s. The support, albeit belated, from the American Jewish Congress, provided an organizational platform that extended our efforts from the university to the political realm. We established contact with important figures in Soviet academic life—linguistics, mathematicians, physicists, musicians—and developed networks for their early emigration and resettlement in Israel and to a lesser extent Europe. It was an effort that extended up to and through the toppling of Communist power in Russia. This is not said in boast, for our committees probably did too little rather than too much. But it was a mechanism by which we translated a concern for a new Holocaust into a practical effort of saving lives. For this chance to participate, I shall be forever grateful.

A strong leitmotif in my work, terrorism, provided an essential piece of the puzzle before I attempted a direct investigation of genocide.[7] In the late 1960s and early 1970s, I conducted a series of seminars for the Council on Foreign Relations on terrorism. Our working group, which included Brian Latell and Paul Wilkinson, two noted theorists on terrorism, developed a variety of scenarios when terrorist acts were likely, and more important, the sources of such acts, that is, from state or anti-state elements in a society. My interest in terrorism derives from the same intellectual background as my interests in genocide—that is, from political sociology as a field for studying the interaction of state and society. Only now, with the publication of my volume *Behemoth,* have I been able to provide a fusion between various strands in the political processes that bring together the story of violence with that of specific assaults on subjugated peoples. And as my work moved from a study of terrorism as a series of actions, to issues of legitimacy and power on one side, and profiling the terrorist and above all, to the victims of terrorism and terrorism's impact on the larger society, the various strands initially seen by myself as separate and distinct, came together. By 1980 I began to see some semblance of a general theory of genocide come into focus. By the close of the millennium, this general theory was completed. It became the grounds for the fourth edition of *Taking Lives*, virtually a new book, and as mentioned above, *Behemoth.* The title, based on the Hebrew word, *Behemah*, meaning huge, unruly, beast, was hardly accidental. It was a shorthand way of bringing together discrete strands in my earlier thinking.

Only when I started work on *Foundations of Political Sociology*[8] at the start of the 1970s did the issue of genocide come into sharp relief. In studying the sources and systems of National Socialism and international communism alike it became apparent that the State, under totalitarian control, exercises its power, not in connection with or on behalf of a social class or strata, and not even with much regard for the nature of the economic system, as is repeatedly claimed from Marx through Lenin, but as an independent actor as Max Weber uniquely understood. My primary evidence became the condition of the Jewish people throughout twentieth-century Germany. Under the Weimar Republic, it was clear that Jews formed a substantial part of the working class in membership and leadership alike. They were active players in the economic expansion of Germany since emancipation. But it was not only that Jews were hence a target from Left and Right perspectives alike, but from the State apparatus, the regulatory mechanisms for the maintenance of social order from the top down. The historic strategy of maintaining a "low profile" in alien environments backfired. Unbridled from considerations of functioning social classes or even economic rationality, the State ferreted out its victims, and "cleansed" the nation of its "enemies." In the process, it satiated the feeding frenzy of its Aryan citizens. The Jews were both victim and explanatory device for the Nazi State. Only the fortuitous death of Stalin and the aborting of the so-called "Doctor's Plot" of Jews against the regime, prevented a similar outcome from evolving in the Soviet Union. The State was the epicenter of genocide because it was the root of terrorism and totalitarianism alike.

What made this a hard lesson to learn was the need to rethink the relationship of fascism to communism, to see them both as "right" and "left" aspects of totalitarianism. With the aid of the classic tradition in political sociology, especially the work of Max Weber and the no less classic, neo-Kantian tradition in legal philosophy as exemplified by Hannah Arendt, it was possible, nay necessary, to rethink fundamental fault lines. The process became simpler once the unitary character of anti-Semitism in Germany and Russia under its dictators became evident to all but the blind. In my case, the strange crossover careers of Hitler and Stalin made it necessary to further understand that these regimes were based on maximum terror, on taking lives.

Here is where I believe I have made a fundamental contribution to the literature on the Holocaust, in the areas of social stratification in which Jews were either absent or poorly represented, most particularly in the bureaucracy and the military. Jews thus became vulnerable as scapegoats for whatever went wrong in the political establishment. The overestimation of the role of economy, combined as it was with the underestimating of the role of the State as an instrument of policy, created a dangerous situation that was to enable demagogues and extremists to lay the blame for whatsoever went wrong at the feet of the Jews. They could be blamed for being bourgeois exploiters of people, and at the very same instance, blamed for being rabble-rousing agitators goading these same masses to anti-government protests and riots. A deep source of genocide in general and of the Holocaust in particular, is the ability of the holders of state power to demonize a group, expose their vulnerabilities, and isolate them from potential allies and supporters. By their estrangement from the levers of state and military power, the Jews, for all of their vaunted historical capacity to survive adversity, found themselves in an impossible situation: without legitimization and without the means to defend themselves. *Taking Lives: State Power and Mass Murder*[9] covering the early 1980s through the mid-1990s, became the basis of the search for sociological and objective, rather than psychological and subjective sources of genocide and a prime mission.

What pushed me in this direction was the twin exaggerations of genocide studies: on one hand, the personal narrative which explained survival techniques and torture better than the systematic destruction of people, and, on the other hand, theological discourse which presumed teleological explanations for Jewish tragedy as something fore ordained by a turn away from *Talmud and* Providence. The personal no less than professional need was to make sense of genocide as part of *Behemoth* itself, that is as a function of the system of governance that not only permitted but mandated racial warfare and religious hatred. The study of the Holocaust also stimulated in me in some as yet undefined way a notion of quantification in the measure of the quality of political and social orders. Thus, my work in this area was self-perceived not simply as an exercise in memory recovery but an exploration in social scientific method and theory.

We have too long taken for granted the nobility of science and social science in and of itself. But it now becomes clear that a vast army of psychologists, physicians, lawyers, demographers, and even anthropologists had maintained their loyalty to the Nazi government. Indeed, a huge and unexplained anomaly is how the Holocaust could be conducted by that nation boasting the highest levels of education, the most advanced institutes of research, and cultural traditions were linked to emancipation and enlightenment. So it becomes evident, to me at least, that the task of social science and social research does not stop with the collation of data or the presentation of theories. It does carry a moral component. But that component can only be exercised by intellectuals and academics acting as a class for and of itself, not as lap dogs for any particular political power or social ideology. To be sure, the perfume of power, the exhilaration of standing in the national limelight defined by others, was and remains itself an element in genocidal practice, no less than critical research. The search for the fine line between science and values is endless. But the pursuit of genocide by totalitarian regimes sharpens that line. I mean by this that the thin line between the taking of life and all other forms of mischief of which statist regimes are capable, even the best of them, thickens the line. My work has increasingly come to rest on distinguishing varieties of anti-democratic regimes from the unique regimes that have practiced genocide. This may not be a pleasant distinction, but it is a useful one—a guideline through the dark voyages into state power.

My primary aim in this field has been to show genocide as part of a general theory of violence; or more broadly, the capacity of unbridled state power to utilize violence against a specific group in order to secure and maximize its own autonomous realm of operations. Once seen in this light, the study of genocide is an extreme end of the continuum involved in war and peace studies. The breakthrough here was made by my dear friend, R.J. Rummel[10] of the University of Hawaii. He has demonstrated in method and theory how anti-democratic states are the unique carriers of the poison of genocide. And conversely, that democratic states are the societies that embody anti-genocide premises and principles.

In my capacity as editorial director at Transaction, we were able to promote his work and indeed publish his final six books. This kind of work, when combined with studies of terrorism and violence of earlier researchers like E. V. Walter,[11] Walter Laqueur,[12] and Robert A. Nisbet[13] provides a framework to bring genocide studies back home, that is back to the world of social science research—where they stand the best chance of being understood and basically overcome. Genocide is not only a problem of power, it is a fact of numbers; and social scientists should know how to count and interpret "raw data."

To permit the study of genocide to become the exclusive domain of theologians and psychoanalysts is to return such studies to self-inflated and not always accurate memoirs of events now considerably long past. This is not to deny the place of a theologically centered and autobiographical witness literature; it is to note that such efforts are starting points, not end points of sound scholarship and social research. It is difficult to speak of matters of death and mean-spirited brutality in clinical and objective terms. But to do otherwise is to remove this enormous characteristic of the century to the realm of the personal, the unspeakable, and ultimately, the mystical.

Whatever else social science is or should be, it must always be in the realm of what one can rationalize and generalize. There are altogether too many social scientists quite pleased to avoid confronting the issue of genocide as a critical test of the very worth of the social sciences. That cannot be permitted, not only as a matter of human responsibility, but as a matter of improving the analytical ground on which we share a common ground. The preservation as well as presentation of human life is a sociological imperative.

In this regard, one of the major efforts I have made in relation to the study of genocide is the publication of outstanding works by others that illumine the field. Transaction Publishers has, in the course of its history of more than 38 years, published a fundamental series of works on the Armenian genocide, including efforts of Ephraim K. Jernazian, Richard G. Hovaniassian, Anny Bakalian, Jacques Derogy, and Vakhan Dadrian. We have published the collective efforts of the aforementioned R.J. Rummel, itself a landmark in the study of genocide and its relationship to contemporary totalitarian regimes from China to Russia, major works by Jewish and Israeli scholars on genocide in comparative geographical as well as ideological contexts, including the work of Israel W. Charny, Donald J. Dietrich, Iwona Irwin-Zarecka, William Helmreich, and Daniel Elazar. More recently, we have published works on the medical and legal aspects of genocide by Kurt Jonassohn, Howard Adelman and Mark Osiel that extend the boundaries of our understanding of the relationship of professional life, moral standards, and legitimizing devices that the State has at its command in the conduct of annihilation. In short, in recent years, my concerns have turned from a personal effort at scientific analysis to publishing the best and the brightest scholars working at the cutting edges in genocide studies. Having said this, I should make clear that my publishing activities were not uniquely published on genocide, but on the social sciences as a whole—of which the study of state power and state terror is a part. But it is precisely that phrase, genocide as part of the fabric of social life, which sets our publishing house as unique and distinct in the field of international social science research.

In the early 1980s, I also became heavily involved in the efforts of the Armenian National Assembly, more directly as a member of the board of the Zoryan Institute did. Although my understanding of the Armenian genocide was relatively weak in the early 1970s, my references to its similarities and antecedents to the Holocaust were evident.[14] And I began to write increasingly on such continuities and discontinuities, especially as issues about the uniqueness of the Holocaust came to the fore. While I recognize the special features of the Nazi assault on the Jewish people, I also felt that it was dangerous to exaggerate the uniqueness of destruction. The rising tide of interest lead to an expansion of victimology as an ideology, one that displaced real analysis with the mantle of self-immolation—a dangerous form that substituted sentimentality for analysis and personal narratives for systematic study.

My later work on the Armenian condition, which was later to involve a trip in the mid-1990s to Yerevan in Armenia and Moscow in Russia provided a comparative framework—one that emphasized prospects for survival and growth of a victimized people without basking in the sunset of defeat. By going to Armenia I was able to appreciate the degree to which the people of that nation and ethnicity had moved considerably beyond reflecting on the past, and were attempting fashion a democratic state in a hostile environment—not entirely unlike the Israeli effort to fashion a Jewish state in a Moslem world. Here too was an ancient civilization coupled with a modern state. And here also was a religious entity surrounded by Islamic theological-political structures. There are, to be sure, profound differences in levels of economic development. It is one thing to have a British mandate, quite another to be of a decaying Soviet empire.

The more I examined the issues, the more it became evident that the business of genocide involved more than professional examination. It entailed a set of personal decisions. Indeed, I say without fear that my three major "passions" of my research in foreign policy—Israel, Armenia, and Cuba—involve a basic struggle for human decency. Small nations are often litmus cases for big issues. Even though the dictatorship of Fidel Castro is in no way commensurate with the horrors inflicted by Nazi secret service agents or Turkish military officers, it is of a piece with the general consideration that to struggle against genocide is to struggle for democracy. I realized through personal involvement that nation-building imposes its own strict rules of survival, and that having been victims of genocide is no sure guarantee of democratic outcomes or error-free political judgments. This is as true of Armenia with respect to Azerbaijan as it is of Israel in relation to Lebanon. This is a hard lesson for all of us working in genocide studies: politics trumps history.

Now that the issue of genocide is on the international docket of ideas, we need studies in a variety of fields to settle old issues and lead the way to new paradigms. Among the highest and thorniest issues that remain to be examined in genocide studies are the following, in no particular order of importance:

- ▸ (1) The relationship of warfare to genocide;

- ▸ (2) The relationship of civil strife and ethnic conflict to genocide, i.e., the systematic elimination of one part of those involved in strife in favor of another;

- ▸ (3) A more exact sense of the distinction between major genocides and whether they can also be described as "Holocausts", i.e., what sort of numbers are involved in each;

- ▸ (4) Why is it that certain forms of totalitarian regimes are non-genocidal and others genocidal, i.e., Italy under Mussolini in relation to Germany under Hitler? Are these differential outcomes the consequence of differential cultural inputs?

- ▸ (5) What price does one place on a life after the fact, namely payments to families of those destroyed in genocidal conditions?

- ▸ (6) What is the degree to which international law is an operational reality or a fiction with respect to the punishment of those who carry out specifically heinous forms of destruction?

- ▸ (7) Does the introduction of notions of cultural genocide enhance or degrade the study of mass physical murder; and

- ▸ (8) And finally, is there is a continuum of means and ends in terminating genocidal regimes, More specifically, can the bombing and decimation of an "evil" regime be viewed as a good, without regard to the damage inflicted on the innocents of the offending nation?

These are just some themes that might lend themselves to social scientific analysis. There are other questions, such as the degree to which it is permissible or impermissible to save oneself at the expense of others in situations of ultimate desperation, the type of issues with which religious and secular law must wrestle. Even framing concerns in these terms makes it evident that the study of genocide entails an examination of the dark side of human nature as well as unbridled State power.

The issues can never be fully resolved or even addressed to universal satisfaction. Even if we can develop a broad consensus at the general level, students of genocide will need to account for specific variations in grounded conditions. Alas, with Cambodia, Rwanda, Bosnia, and most recently, Kosovo, as "case studies" in the present period, we do not lack for confirmation of general propositions or for individual differences in concrete historical settings.[15] But we can move on a variety of fronts: educational, cultural, and analytical to heighten an awareness of the preconditions of genocide. As others have pointed out, we need early warning signals and systems in place, and we need the policy resolve to address and redress such situations. However, by no means, does this imply that every situation will or can admit of solution through direct intervention. Nor can it be asserted that every situation will be resolved in a pacific manner.

To appreciate the limits of analysis is to understand the finite capacities of human nature as such. And that is why the voices of silence will always have their say in the study of genocide. We stand in awe of our staggering accomplishments over the course of the 20th century, and in the abyss of deeper despair over our failures to create a human society. Having said this, we must also deal with quotidian events that do not admit of easy distinctions between good regimes and evil states. At the end of the day is a sense that ours is a tragic century in moral terms and an exhilarating one in technological terms. But we still have yet to learn how to match ethics and engineering. Until we do, the danger of genocide is haunting, while the policy tasks ahead are daunting.

NOTES

Notes

Chapter 1: New Beginnings

1 Norman Cohn, *Warrant for Genocide: The Myth of the Jewish World Conspiracy and the "Protocols of the Elders of Zion"* (New York and Evanston: Harper & Row, 1966).

Chapter 2: Defining Genocide

1 Hannah Arendt. *Eichmann in Jerusalem: A Report on the Banality of Evil* (New York: Viking Press, 1963). 312 pp.

2 Ernst Bloch, *Man on His Own* (New York: Herder and Herder, 1971), p. 43.

3 Ernest Becker, *The Denial of Death* (New York: Free Press/Macmillan, 1974); and, by the same author, *Escape from Evil* (New York: Free Press/Macmillan, 1975). An excellent overview of the sociology of death and dying is the work by Michael C. Kearl, *Endings.* (New York and Oxford: Oxford University Press, 1989), 521 pp.

4 Robert J. Lifton, *Death in Life: Survivors of Hiroshima* (New York: Random House, 1967); also *History and Human Survival: Essays on the Young and Old, Survivors and the Dead, Peace and War, and on Contemporary Psychohistory* (New York: Random House, 1970).

5 Janusz K. Zawodny, *Death in the Forest: The Story of the Katyn Forest Massacre* (South Bend, IN: University of Notre Dame Press, 1962).

6 H. Jon Rosenbaum and Peter C. Sederberg, eds., *Vigilante Politics* (Philadelphia: University of Pennsylvania Press, 1976).

7 Walter Laqueur, "Terrorism — A Balance Sheet," in *The Terrorism Reader,* ed. Walter Laqueur (Philadelphia: Temple University Press, 1978), pp. 251-267 For a more recent (and thoroughly outstanding) compendium on the subject, see Martha Crenshaw, *Terrorism in Context.* (University Park: The Pennsylvania State University Press, 1995), 425 pp.

8 Frank Chalk and Kurt Jonassohn, "A Typology of Genocide," in *The History and Sociology of Genocide,* ed. Frank Chalk and Kurt Jonassohn (New Haven: Yale University Press, 1990), pp. 23, 29-31.

9 William L. Patterson, *We Charge Genocide: The Historic Petition to the United Nations for Relief from a Crime of the United States Government against the Negro People* (New York: International Publishers, 1951 and 1970). See also Patterson's autobiography, *The Man Who Cried Genocide* (New York: International Publishers, 1971), pp. 178-179. The curious myopia of the Communist position was that it viewed the random, sporadic killings of U.S. blacks as genocidal but never mentioned, much less condemned, the systematic and consistent killings of Russian nationals by the Soviet regime. For a balanced account of this, see the compendium, edited by Isidor Walliman and Michael N. Dobkowski, *Genocide and the Modern Age: Etiology and Case Studies of Mass Death.* (Westport, CT, and London: Greenwood Press, 1987), 322 pp.

10 United Nations, *Yearbook of the United Nations, 1947-48* (New York: United Nations, 1949), pp. 595-599; and *Yearbook of the United Nations, 1948-49* (New York: United Nations, 1950), pp. 958-959.

11 Israel Drapkin and Emilio Viano, *Victimology* (Lexington, MA: Lexington Books/D. C. Heath, 1974); and *Victimology: A New Focus-Violence and Its Victims* (Lexington, MA: Lexington Books/D. C. Heath, 1975).

12 Edy Kaufman, *Extra-Judicial Executions: An Insight into the Global Dimension of a Human Rights Violation,* Paper delivered before the International Conference on the Death Penalty, December 1977 (mimeograph).

13 Feliks Gross, *Ethnics in a Borderland: An Inquiry into the Nature of Ethnicity and Reduction of Ethnic Tensions in a One-Time*

Genocide Area (Westport, CT, and London: Greenwood Press, 1978), pp. 70-73, 116-117.

14 Raphael Lemkin, *Axis Rule in Occupied Europe* (New York: Howard Fertig, 1973), pp. x-xii (first published in 1943).

15 Yehuda Bauer, "Against Mystification," in *The Holocaust in Historical Perspective* (Seattle: University of Washington Press, 1978), pp. 30-49.

16 George L. Mosse, *Toward the Final Solution: A History of European Racism* (New York: Howard Fertig, 1978), pp. 232, 234-235.

17 Murray Clark Havens, Carl Leiden, and Karl M. Schmitt, *The Politics of Assassination* (Englewood Cliffs, NJ: Prentice-Hall Publishers).

18 Eugene Victor Walter, *Terror and Resistance: A Study of Political Violence with Case Studies of Some Primitive African Communities* (New York: Oxford University Press, 1969), pp. 109-263

19 Shelton H. Davis, *Victims of the Miracle: Development and the Indians of Brazil* (New York: Cambridge University Press, 1977); and Richard Arens, ed., *Genocide in Paraguay* (Philadelphia: Temple University Press, 1976).

20 Leon Gordenker, "Symbols and Substance in the United Nations," *New Society* 35, No. 697 (12 February 1976): 324-326

21 Doan Van Toai, "The Penitentiary Regime under the Communist Government of Vietnam," in *Documents on Prisons in Vietnam* (Paris: no publisher), pp. 10-16; see also Doan Van Toai and David Chanoff, *The Vietnamese Gulag* (New York: Simon & Schuster, 1986), pp. 312-347.

22 Mark Levene, "Turkey and the Armenian People," *Times Literary Supplement* No. 4845 (9 February 1996): 17.

Chapter 3: Counting Bodies

1 R. J. Rummel, *Death by Government: Genocide and Mass Murder Since 1900* (New Brunswick, NJ, and London: Transaction Publishers, 1994), p. xxi.

2 Irving Louis Horowitz, *Taking Lives: Genocide and State Power,*
   3rd, augmented ed. (New Brunswick, NJ, and London, 1980).

3 R. J. Rummel, "Deadlier than War," *Institute of Public Affairs
   Review* 41, No. 2 (Spring 1985): 24-30; and *Death by Government.*

4 While there has been a substantial body of writings on the
   Holocaust and genocide in general from the social science
   community, comparatively little has been written on how the
   structure of social scientific work changes as a result of such
   fundamental processes of genocidal systems in the technological structures of industrial societies. One such important
   effort is Zygmunt Bauman, "Sociology after the Holocaust,"
   British Journal of Sociology 39, No. 4 (December 1988):
   469-497

5 Robert J. Lifton, *The Nazi Doctors: Medical Killing and the
   Psychology of Genocide* (New York, 1986). For a more detailed and comprehensive effort, see Michael Burleigh, *Death
   and Deliverance*: "Euthanasia" in *Germany, 1900-1945* (New
   York and Cambridge: Cambridge University Press, 1995).

6 Edward F. Maculas, Todd Saddler, and Jean M. Murdock, *International Terrorism in the 1980s: A Chronology of Events,* Vol.
   1: 1980-83 (Ames 1989).

7 Irving Louis Horowitz, "Texture of Terrorism: Socialization,
   Routinization and Integration," in *Political Learning in
   Adulthood: Sourcebook of Theory and Research*, ed. Roberta
   Sigal (Chicago: University of Chicago Press, 1989), pp. 286-
   314.

8 "Silent Bones and Fallen Kingdoms," in *The Lost Notebooks of
   Loren Eiseley*, ed. Kenneth Heuer (Boston: Little Brown,
   1987), pp. 20-23.

9 A political variant of the modernist hypothesis on the Holocaust, most ably propounded by Arno Mayer in *Why Did the
   Heavens Not Darken: The "Final Solution" in History* (New
   York: Alfred A. Knopf, 1988), is that "it was part and parcel
   of a syncretistic ideology combining key tenets of conservatism, reaction and fascism" (p. 449). While such a view has a
   prima facie attractiveness, it tends to wash out the specific role
   of the Jews in history long before there was a final solution,

the uses of anti-Semitism and racism by Communist no less than fascist regimes, and finally, the existence of fascist regimes that did not engage in the final solution. These themes are dealt elsewere in the present volume.

10 Lucy S. Dawidowicz, *The War against the Jews: 1933-1945* (New York: Holt, Rinehart, and Winston, 1975), pp. 150-166.

11 Iwona Irwin Zarecka, *Neutralizing Memory: The Jew in Contemporary Poland* (New Brunswick, NJ, and Oxford: Transaction Publishers, 1988); and Aaron Hass, *The Aftermath: Living with the Holocaust* (New York and Cambridge: Cambridge University Press, 1995).

12 Vahakn N. Dadrian, "The Role of Turkish Physicians in the World War I Genocide of Armenians," *Holocaust and Genocide Studies* 1, No. 2 (1986): 169-192.

13 George Steiner, *No Passion Spent: Essays 1978-1995* (New Havven and London: Yale University Press, 1996), pp.346-347.

14 Dan Jacobs, *The Brutality of Nations* (New York: Alfred A. Knopf, 1987).

15 For a recent update on the conflict between the Hutus and the Tutsis, see "Sin and Confession in Rwanda," in *The Economist* 334, No. 7897 (14 January 1995): 53.

16 Vahakn N. Dadrian, "The Naim-Andonian Documents on the World War I Destruction of Ottoman Armenians: The Anatomy of a Genocide," *International Journal of Middle East Studies* 18, No. 3: 311-359.

17 Vera B. Seedopour, "Iraq Attacks to Destroy the Kurds," *The Institute for the Study of Genocide Newsletter* 1, No. 2 (Autumn 1988): 2-11.

18 Rene Lemarchand, Selective Genocide in Burundi (London 1974). For a more recent and no less poignant account, see Alain Destexhe, "The Third Genocide," *Foreign Policy* No. 97 (Winter 1994-1995): whole issue, pp. 3-17.

19 Barbara Harff and Ted Robert Gurr, "Genocides and Politicides since 1945: Evidence and Anticipation," *Internet on the Holocaust and Genocide No. 13* (December 1987).

20 Ted Robert Gurr, "Persisting Patterns of Repression and Rebellion: Foundations for a General Theory of Political Coercion," in *Persistent Patterns and Emergent Structures in a*

Waning Century, ed. Margaret P. Karns (New York: Columbia University Press, 1988), pp. 149-168

21 Raul Hilberg, "German Railroads/Jewish Souls," *Society* 14, No. 1 (November-December 1976): 60-74.

22 Jane Goodall, "A Plea for Chimps," *New York Times Magazine,* 17 May 1987, pp. 108-121 See also her *The Chimpanzees of Gombe* (Cambridge, MA: Harvard University Press, 1986).

23 Zygmunt Bauman, *Modernity and the Holocaust,* 1st ed. (Cambridge, 1989) p.8.

24 Zygmunt Bauman, *Modernity and the Holocaust,* 2nd ed. (London and New York, 1991); and for a summary of the argument in this book, see "Assimilation and Enlightenment," *Society* 27, No. 6 (September-October 1990): 71-81.

Chapter 4: Collectivizing Death

1 Stanislaw Baranczak, "Always Through," *New Republic* 214, No. 10 (4 March 1996): 41.

2 Tommaso Campanella, *The City of the Sun: A Poetical Dialogue,* trans. Daniel J. Donno (Berkeley and Los Angeles: University of California Press, 1981; first published 1623).

3 Aldous Huxley, *Brave New World* (Garden City, NY: Doubleday, Doran & Co., 1932).

4 George Orwell, *Nineteen Eighty Four* (London: Secker & Warburg, 1987; first published 1949).

5 Saint Augustine, Bishop of Hippo, *The City of God against the Pagans* (Cambridge, MA: Harvard University Press/Loeb Classical Library, 1968-1972). For contrasting views on the political theology of Augustine, see Herbert A. Deane, *The Social and Political Ideas of St. Augustine* (New York: Columbia University Press, 1966); and Peter Dennis Bathory, *Political Theory as Public Confession* (New Brunswick, NJ, and London: Transaction Publishers, 1981).

6 Christoph Schonborn, "The Hope of Heaven, the Hope of Earth," *First Things* No. 52 (April 1995): 32-38.

7 Jean-Jacques Rousseau, "The Social Contract" and "A Discourse on the Origin of Inequality, " in *The Social Contract*

and the Discourses, trans. G. D. H. Cole (New York and Toronto: Knopf/Everyman's Library, 1987), pp. 180-305; also pp. 31-125.

8 Aaron Wildavsky, *Assimilation versus Separation: Joseph the Administrator and the Politics of Religion in Biblical Israel* (New Brunswick, NJ, and London: Transaction Publishers, 1992).

9 Wilhelm Reich, *The Mass Psychology of Fascism* (New York: Farrar, Straus & Giroux, 1970), p. 306

10 Gertrude Himmelfarb, *The De-Moralization of Society: From Victorian Virtues to Modern Values* (New York: Knopf, 1995).

11 Samuel H. Baron, ed., *The Travels of Olearius in Seventeenth Century Russia* (Stanford, CA: Stanford University Press, 1967).

12 Michel Foucault, *Discipline and Punish: The Birth of the Prison* (New York: Pantheon Books, 1977), pp. 3-5. An excellent work that places genocide within a larger context of violence is Daniel Pick's *War Machine: The Rationalization of Slaughter in the Modern Age* (New Haven and London: Yale University Press, 1993), esp. pp. 165-188

13 Thomas Keneally, *Schindler's List* (London: Hodder and Stoughton, 1982).

14 William J. Bennett, *The Book of Virtues* (New York: Simon & Schuster, 1993).

Chapter 5: Individualizing Life

1 John R. Hersey, *The Wall* (New York: Alfred A. Knopf, 1951) pp. 632.

2 Henry Steele Commager, *The American Mind: An Interpretation of American Thought and Character since the 1880s* (New Haven, CT: Yale University Press, 1950), pp. 176-177.

3 Peter M. Glick, "Individualism, Society, and Social Work," *Social Casework* 58, No. 10 (December 1977): 579-584.

4 Hannah Arendt, *Eichmann in Jerusalem: A Report on the Banality of Evil* (New York: Viking Press, 1963), p. 232.

5 Abraham Kisuule-Minge, "Amin's Horror Chamber," *Time* 113, No. 18 (30 April 1979), pp. 45-46.

6 John Lofland, "The Dramaturgy of State Execution," commentary on *State Executions Viewed Historically and Sociologically: The Hangmen of England* by Horace Bleackley (Montclair, NJ: Patterson Smith, 1977), pp. 275-325.

7 George Orwell, "As I Please" (from *The Tribune*, 3 March 1944), *The Collected Essays, Journalism, and Letters of George Orwell*, Vol. 3: 1943-45, ed. Sonia Orwell and Ian Angus (New York: Harcourt, Brace & World, 1968), pp. 103-104.

8 Irving Louis Horowitz, *Foundations of Political Sociology* (New York and London: Harper & Row, 1972), pp. 351-352.

9 Aleksandr I. Solzhenitsyn, *The Gulag Archipelago 1918-1956: An Experiment in Literary Investigation III-IV, Vol. 2* (New York and London: Harper & Row, 1975), pp. 440-445.

10 Erving Goffman, *Asylums: Essays on the Social Situation of Mental Patients and Other Inmates* (Garden City, N.Y.: Doubleday/Anchor Books, 1961), pp. 120-121.

11 David Erdal, "I Work in Mao's China," *Worldview* 20, No. 11 (November 1977): 4-9 For a general analysis, see Amnesty International, *Political Imprisonment in the Peoples' Republic of China* (London: Amnesty International Secretariat, 17 March 1978).

12 Philip E. Devine, *The Ethics of Homocide* (Ithaca, N.Y., and London: Cornell University Press, 1978), pp. 208-209.

Chapter 6: Democracy, Autocracy, and Terrorism

1 Albert Camus. *Resistance, Rebellion, and Death*. (New York: Random House/Modern Library, 196). 209 pp.

2 Maurice Merleau-Ponty, *Humanism and Terror: An Essay on the Communist Problem* (Boston: Beacon Press, 1969; originally published in French, 1947), p. 188.

3 This profile of a terrorist is derived from an earlier essay of mine, "Political Terrorism and State Power," *Journal of Political and Military Sociology* 1, No. 1 (Spring 1973): 147-157 A more

recent effort along these lines provides independent confirmation based on a large sample of 350 presumed terrorists. See Charles A. Russell and Bowman H. Miller, "Profile of a Terrorist," *Terrorism: An International Journal* 1, No. 1 (1977): 17-34.

4 N.N. Sukhanov, *The Russian Revolution: 1917*. Edited and translated by Joel Carmichael. (Princeton, NJ: Princeton University, Press, 1984), pp. 575-576.

5 Frank Kitson, *Low Intensity Operations: Subversion, Insurgency, Peace-Keeping* (London: Faber Publishers, 1972); Robert Jay Lifton, *History and Human Surviual* (New York: Random House, 1970); Martin Oppenheimer, *The Urban Guerrilla* (Chicago: Quadrangle Books, 1969); Milton J. Rosenberg, ed., *Beyond Conflict and Containment: Critical Studies of Military and Foreign Policy* (New Brurswick, NJ: Transaction/E. P. Dutton, 1972); Jerome Skolnick, ed., *The Politics of Protest* (New York: Ballantine Books, 1969); Eugene V. Walter, *Terror and Resistance: A Study of Political Violence* (New York: Oxford University Press, 1969).

6 James J. Weingartner, *Crossroads of Death: The Story of the Malmedy Massacre and Trial* (Berkeley and Los Angeles: University of California Press, 1979), esp. pp. 239-264.

7 See Hannah Arendt, *On Revolution* (New York: Viking Press, 1963); James Chowning Davies, ed., *When Men Revolt and Why* (New York: Free Press, 1971); Harry Eckstein, ed., *Internal War: Problems and Approaches* (New York: Free Press, 1966); Ivo Feierabend, Rosalind L. Feierabend, and Ted R. Gurr, eds., *Anger, Violence and Politics: Theories and Research* (Englewood Cliffs, NJ: Prentice Hall, 1972); Ted Robert Gurr, *Why Men Rebel* (Princeton, NJ: Princeton University Press, 1970).

Chapter 7: Human Rights and Personal Responsibilities

1 Philip Rahv, *Essays on Literature and Politics* (Boston: Houghton-Mifflin, 1978). 366 pp.

2 While genocide as the ultimate crime against human rights was long a relatively well-kept secret, legislative discussion of this linkage began to surface in the late 1970s. See U.S. Congress, Senate Committee on Foreign Relations, *International Convention on the Prevention and Punishment of the Crime of Genocide*, 94th Congress, Second Session, Executive Report 94-23 (Washington, D.C.: U.S. GPO, 1976).

3 Still the most impressive application of social indicators to issues of human rights is contained in *Yearbook on Human Rights for 1993-94* (New York and Paris: United Nations, 1995), pp. 269-317

4 The most innovative recent development in the quantification of human rights is in establishing measures of economic freedom. See, *World Survey of Economic Freedom, 1995-1996*, edited by Richard E. Messick (New Brunswick, NJ, and London: Freedom House/Transaction Publishers, 1996), 219 pp.

Chapter 8: Bureaucracy and State Power

1 Max Weber, *Economy and Society*, in three volumes (New York: Bedminster Press, 1968), 1468 pp.

2 John Archibald Wheeler and Martin Gardner, "Quantum Theory and Quack Theory," *New York Review of Books* 26, No. 8 (17 May 1979): 39-41.

3 Jacob Katz, "Leaving the Ghetto," *Commentary* 101, No. 2 (February 1996): 29-33.

4 The most prescient sources on defining the nature of postindustrialism are both by Daniel Bell, *The Coming of Post-Industrial Society: A Venture in Social Forecasting* (New York: Basic Books, 1973) and *The Cultural Contradictions of Capitalism* (New York: Basic Books, 1976). See also Bell's essay "Is There a Post-Industrial Society?" *Society* 11, No. 4 (May-June 1974): 11, 23-25.

5 For a general introduction to postindustrialism, see Krishan Kumar, *Prophecy and Progress: The Sociology of Industrial and Post-Industrial Society* (New York: Penguin Books, 1978).

6 Harlan Cleveland, "The American Public Executive: New Functions, New Style, New Purpose," in *Theory and Practice of Public Administration: Scope, Objectives, and Methods,* ed. James C. Charlesworth (Philadelphia: American Academy of Political and Social Science, October 1968), pp. 168-178.

7 H.W. Singer, "Multinational Corporations and Technology Transfer," in *The Strategy of International Development: Essays in the Economics of Backwardness* (White Plains, N.Y.: International Arts and Science Press, 1975), pp. 208-233.

8 Seth Kupferberg, "Teaching the Unteachable," *New Republic* 180, No. 15 (14 April 1979), pp. 18-21.

9 John Herbers, "Washington: An Insider's Game," *New York Times Magazine,* 22 April 1979, pp. 33, 84-92.

10 B. Bruce-Briggs, "Enumerating the New Class," in *New Class?* (New Brunswick, NJ: Transaction Books, 1979), pp. 217-225.

11 Max Weber, "Bureaucracy," From *Max Weber: Essays in Sociology,* ed. Hans Gerth and C. Wright Mills (New York: Oxford University Press, 1946), pp. 196-244.

12 See James G. March and Herbert Simon, "The Theory of Organizational Equilibrium," in *Organizations* (New York: Wiley, 1958), pp. 84-108; and also Dorwin Cartwright, "Influence, Leadership, Control," in *Handbook of Organizations,* ed. James G. March (Chicago: Rand McNally & Co. 1963), pp. 1-47.

13 Irving Louis Horowitz, "On the Expansion of New Theories and the Withering Away of Old Classes," *Society* 16, No. 2 (January-February 1979): 55-62.

14 Irving Louis Horowitz, "Methods and Strategies in Evaluating Equity Research," *Social Indicators Research* 16, No. 1 (January 1979): 1-22.

15 Irving Louis Horowitz, "Social Welfare, State Power, and the Limits to Equity," in *Growth in a Finite World,* ed. Joseph Grunfeld (Philadelphia: Franklin Institute Press, 1979), pp. 21-35.

16 Charles E. Lindblom, "The Science of Muddling Through," *Public Administration Review* 19 (Spring 1959): 79-88; and "Policy Analysis," *American Economic Review* 48 (June 1958): 298-299 See also Lindblom's *Politics and Markets: The*

World's Political Economic Systems (New York: Basic Books, 1977), esp. pp. 119-143.

17 Bill G. Schumacher, *Computer Dynamics in Public Administration* (New York: Spartan Books, 1967), pp. 163-171.

18 Dwight Waldo, "Scope of the Theory of Public Administration," in *Theory and Practice of Public Administration* (Philadelphia: American Academy of Political and Social Science, 1968), pp. 1-26.

19 Samuel B. Bacharach, "What"s Public Administration? An Examination of Basic Textbooks," *Administrative Science Quarterly* 21, No. 2 (June 1976): 346-351.

20 Michael Rose, *Servants of Post-Industrial Power? Sociologie du Travail in Modern France* (White Plains, N.Y.: M. E. Sharpe, 1979), pp. 144-173.

21 Michel Crozier, *The Bureaucratic Phenomenon* (London: Tavistock, 1964); and more recently, *The Stalled Society* (New York: Viking Publishers, 1973 first published in French, 1970).

22 Nicos Poulantzas, *State, Power, Socialism*. (London: New Left Books, 1978); and his earlier albeit less decisive enunciation of the same theme, *Political and Social Classes* (London: New Left Books, 1973).

23 Ernest Mandel, *Late Capitalism* (London: New Left Books, 1975), pp. 405-407.

24 Nicos Poulantzas, *State, Power, Socialism*, pp. 127-139.

25 Michel Crozier, *La Société Bloquée* (Paris: Editions du Seuil, 1970), p. 20; see the discussion of this in Rose, *Servants of Post-Industrial Power?* pp. 113-127.

26 Nicos Poulantzas, *State, Power, Socialism*, pp. 251-265.

27 Jean-Jacques Servan-Schreiber, *The Radical Alternative* (New York: W.W. Norton, 1971), pp. 59-61.

28 Aaron Wildavsky, *Budgeting: A Comparatiue Theory of Budgetary Processes* (Boston: Little, Brown, 1975), pp. 155-157.

29 Joseph LaPalombara, *Bureaucracy and Political Development* (Princeton: Princeton University Press, 1963), pp. 48-55.

31 Gordon Tullock, *The Politics of Bureaucracy* (Washington, D.C.: Public Affairs Press, 1965), p. 181.

31 William Howard Gammon and Lowell H. Hattery, "Managing the Impact of Computers on the Federal Government," *The Bureaucrat* 7, No. 2 (Summer 1978): pp. 18-26.

32 Ron Johnson and Philip Gummett, *Directing Technology: Policies for Promotion and Control* (New York: St. Martin"s Press, 1979), pp. 13-14.

33 Alan Peacock, "Public Expenditure Growth in Post Industrial Society," in *Post-Industrial Society*, ed. Bo Gustafsson (New York: St. Martin"s Press, 1979), pp. 91-95.

34 Manfred Stanley, *The Technological Conscience: Survival and Dignity in an Age of Expertise* (New York: Free Press/Macmillan, 1978), pp. 251-253.

35 David Apter, *Choice and the Politics of Allocation* (New Haven, CT, and London: Yale University Press, 1971), pp. 128-154; and Edward R. Tufte, *Political Control of the Economy* (Princeton, NJ: Princeton University Press, 1978), pp. 110-145.

36 For strongly contrasting statements about democracy, which yet manage to appreciate the processual and symbolic nature of the entity, see Dorothy Pickles, *Democracy* (New York: Basic Books, 1970), pp. 9-28 and 169-182; and C. B. Macpherson, *Democratic Theory* (London and New York: Oxford University Press, 1973), esp. pp. 3-23, 29-76.

Chapter 9: Nationalism and Genocidal Systems

1 William Butler Yeats, *A Vision* (A reissue with the author's final revisions). New York: Collier Books, 1965, 205 pp.

2 Claude Levi-Strauss, *A World on the Wane*, trans. John Russell (New York: Criterion, 1961); Stanley Diamond, *In Search of the Primitive: A Critique of Civilization* (New Brunswick, NJ: Transaction Books, 1974); Eric R. Wolf, *Peasant Wars of the Twentieth Century* (New York: Harper & Row, 1969); and Marshall Sahlins, *How "Natives" Think, about Captain Cook, for Example* (Chicago: University of Chicago Press, 1995).

3 Richard W. Wilson, *The Moral State: A Study of the Political Socialization of Chinese and American Children* (New York: Free Press/Macmillan, 1974), pp. 253-254; also Amy Auer-

bacher Wilson, *Deviance and Social Control in Chinese Society* (New York: Praeger, 1977), pp. 1-13.

4 Eduard Spranger, *Types of Men: The Psychology and Ethics of Personality,* trans. Paul J. W. Pigors (Halle: Niemeyer, 1928).

5 Kenneth Fidel, "Social Structure and Military Intervention: The 1960 Turkish Revolution," unpublished dissertation (University Microfilm), Washington University, St. Louis, Mo. 1969; and Ellen Kay Trimberger, *Revolution from Above: Military Bureaucrats and Development in Japan, Turkey, Egypt, and Peru* (New Brunswick, NJ: Transaction Books, 1978).

6 Vahakn N. Dadrian, "Factors of Anger and Aggression in Genocide," *Journal of Human Relations* 19, No. 3: 394-417.

7 Dickran H. Boyajian, *Armenia: The Case for a Forgotten Genocide* (Westwood, NJ: Educational Book Crafters, 1972), pp. 300-314 For a moving personal statement, see Abraham H. Hartunian, *Neither to Laugh nor to Weep: A Memoir of the Armenian Genocide* (Boston: Beacon Press, 1968), esp. pp. 121-205.

8 Vahakn N. Dadrian, *The History of the Armenian Genocide: Ethnic Conflict from the Balkans to Anatolia to the Caucasus* (Providence, Oxford: Berghahn Books, 1995), p. 363.

9 James Bryce, *The Treatment of the Armenians in the Ottoman Empire* (London: Macmillan, 1916); and *Henry Morgenthau, Ambassador Morgenthau's Story* (New York: Doubleday-Page, 1918).

10 Vahakn N. Dadrian, "Factors of Anger and Aggression in Genocide," *Journal of Human Relations* 19, No.3: 414-415.

11 Vahakn N. Dadrian, "The Common Features of the Armenian and Jewish Cases of Genocide: A Comparative Victimological Perspective," in *Victimology: A New Focus on Violence and Its Victims,* ed. Israel Drapkin and Emilio Viano (Lexington, MA: Lexington Books/D. C. Heath, 1975), pp. 106-107.

12 Vahakn Dadrian, "The Structural-Functional Components of Genocide," in Drapkin and Viano (eds.), *loc. cit.,* pp. 123-135.

13 Cf. Emilio C. Viano, ed., *Victims and Society* (Washington, D.C.: Visage Press Inc., 1976), pp. 541-592.

14 R. Albert Berry, Ronald G. Hellman, and Mauricio Solaun, *The Politics of Compromise: Coalition Government in Colombia*

(New Brunswick, NJ: Transaction Books, in cooperation with The Center for Inter-American Relations, 1979).

15 William S. Stokes, "Violence as a Power Factor in Latin American Politics," in *Conflict and Violence in Latin American Politics*, ed. Francisco José Moreno and Barbara Mitrani (New York: Thomas Y. Crowell, 1971), pp. 446-469.

16 Darcy Ribeiro, *The Americas and Civilization,* trans. Linton L. Barrett and Marie Barrett (New York: E. P. Dutton, 1971), pp. 295-296.

17 German Guzman Campos, Orlando Fals Borda, and Eduardo *Umàa Luna, La Violencia en Colombia: Estudio de un Proceso Social* (Bogota, 1964), pp. 407-411.

18 Ribeiro, *The Americas and Civilization*, p. 296.

19 Martin Carney, "Amin's Uganda," *The Nation*, 12 April 1975, pp. 430-435.

20 Whitney Ellsworth, "The Structure of Repression in Uganda," *Amnesty International Release,* 15 June 1978.

21 Geoffrey Fairbairn, *Revolutionary Guerrilla Warfare: The Countryside Version* (Harmondsworth, Middlesex, Eng.: Penguin Books, 1974), pp. 125-174.

22 Michael Schultheis, "The Ugandan Economy and General Amin, 1971-1974," *Studies in Comparative International Development* 10, No. 3 (Fall 1975): 3-34.

23 Robert G. Weisbord, *Genocide? Birth Control and the Black American* (Westport, CT: Greenwood Press, 1975).

24 William Lerner, *Statistical Abstract of the United States,* 97th annual edition, U.S. Department of Commerce (Washington, D.C.: U.S. GPO, 1976).

25 William L. Patterson, *We Charge Genocide: The Historic Petition to the United Nations for Relief from a Crime of the United States Government against the Negro People* (New York: International Publishers, 1951 and 1970), pp. 125-132.

26 Hugo Adam Bedau, "Genocide in Vietnam?" in *Philosophy, Morality, and International Affairs,* ed. Virginia Held, Sidney Morgenbesser, and Thomas Nagel (New York: Oxford University Press, 1974), pp. 5-46.

27 Guenter Lewy, *America in Vietnam* (New York: Oxford University Press, 1978), p. 576.

28 Philip Gourevitch, "After the Genocide," *New Yorker,* 71, No. 41 (18 December 1995). Gourevitch reports that "although the killing (in Rwanda) was low tech, it was carried out at dazzling speed: of an original population of seven million seven hundred thousand, at least eight hundred thousands were killed in just a hundred days. Pol Pot's slaughter of a million Cambodians in four years looks amateurish, and the bloodletting in the former Yugoslavia measures up as little more than a neighborhood riot" (pp. 78-95).

29 Theodore Jacqueney, "Castro's Political Prisoners," *AFL-CIO Free Trade Union News* 32, No. 5 (May 1977): 1-2, 7-10; and Edward Tonat, "Castro's Captive Unions," *AFL-CIO Free Trade Union News* 33, No. 7 (July 1978): 1-5.

30 E. K. Bramstedt, *Dictatorship and Political Police: The Technique of Control by Fear* (London: Kegan Paul, Trench Trubner, and Co., 1945), p. 39.

31 Ralph Della Cava, "Brazil: The Struggle for Human Rights," *Commonweal* 102, No. 20 (1975): 623-626.

32 Norman Lewis, "Genocide," in *A Documentary Report on the Conditions of Indian Peoples in Brazil* (Berkeley, CA: Indigena, and American Friends of Brazil, 1974), pp. 9-11.

33 Margaret Jones and Gero Ruge, "Crime and Punishment in China," *Atlas: World Press Review* 22, No. 9 (September 1975): 19-22.

34 Amnesty International, *Political Imprisonment in the People's Republic of China* (London: Author, 1978), p. 27.

35 Richard Slotkin, *Regeneration through Violence: The Mythology of the American Frontier, 1600-1860* (Middletown, CT: Wesleyan University Press, 1973), pp. 14-15.

Chapter 10: Totalitarianism as a Penal Colony

1 Milovan Djilas, *Land without Justice.* (New York: Harcourt Brace, 1958). 287 pp.

2 Aleksandr I. Solzhenitsyn, *Nobel Lecture,* trans. F. D. Reeve (New York: Farrar, Straus, & Giroux, 1972).

3 Aleksandr I. Solzhenitsyn, *The Gulag Archipelago, 1918-1956: An Experiment in Literary Investigation (I: The Prisons Industry; and II: Perpetual Motion),* trans. Thomas P. Whitney (New York and London: Harper & Row, 1973).

4 Aleksandr I. Solzhenitsyn, *The Gulag Archipelago, 1918-1956: An Experiment in Literary Investigation (III: The Destructive Labor Camps; and IV: The Soul and Barbed Wire),* trans. Thomas P. Whitney (New York and London: Harper & Row, 1975).

5 Aleksandr I. Solzhenitsyn, *The Gulag Archipelago, 1918-1956: An Experiment in Literary Investigation (V: Katorga; VI: Exile; and VII: Stalin Is No More),* trans. Harry Willets (New York and London: Harper & Row, 1978).

6 John and Carol Garrard, *The Bones of Berdichev: The Life and Fate of Vasily Grossman.* (New York: Free Press, 1996), 437 pp. See Walter Laqueur's review, "A Life and a Fate," *New Republic* (June 3, 1996), Whole Number 4246, pp. 44-45.

7 Gennadi Kostyrchenko, *Out of the Red Shadows: Anti-Semitism in Stalin's Russia.* (Buffalo: Prometheus Books, 1996), 333 pp. Archival research on this subject is now underway. For a report, see Robert Conquest, "Stalin and the Jews," *New York Review* (Vol. XLIII, No. 12, July 11, 1996). Pp. 46-52.

Chapter 11: Memory as History

1 Michael Ignatieff, Lecture for the Committee on Conscience of the U.S. Holocaust Memorial Museum, December, 2000.

2 Paul Johnson, *A History of the Jews*, (New York: HarperCollins, 1998), 644 pp.

3 Peter Gay, *My German Question: Growing Up in Nazi Berlin,* (New Haven: Yale University Press, 1998), 240 pp.

4 Victor Klemperer, *I Will Bear Witness: A Diary of the Nazi Years, 1933-1941,* (New York: Random House, 1998), 502 pp.

5 Daniel Jonah Goldhagen, *Hitler's Willing Executioners: Ordinary Germans and the Holocaust,* (New York: Knopf Publishers, 1996), 634 pp.

6 Hagen Schulze, *Germany: A New History,* (Cambridge, MA: Harvard University Press, 1998), 356 pp.

7 George Steiner, *Language and Silence: Essays on Language, Literature, and the Inhuman,* (New Haven: Yale University Press, 1999), 444 pp.

8 *Forever in the Shadow of Hitler, Original Documents of the Historikerstreit: The Controversy Concerning the Singularity of the Holocaust,* trans. by James Knowlton and Truett Cates. (Atlantic Highlands, New Jersey: Humanities Press, 1993), 282 pp.

9 Ernst Nolte, *Three Faces of Fascism: Action Francaise, Italian Fascism, National Socialism*, (New York: Columbia University Press, 1967), 424 pp.

10 Jürgen Habermas, *Observations on "The Spiritual Situation of the Age": Contemporary German Perspectives,* (Cambridge, MA: MIT Press, 1985), 324 pp.

Chapter 12: Banality of State Power

1 R.J. Rummel, *Death By Government*, (New Brunswick and London: Transaction Publishers, 1994), Preface. 496 pp.

2 Amos Elon, "The Case of Hannah Arendt," in *The New York Review of Books*, November 6, 1997. pp.25-29.

3 Hannah Arendt, *The Origins of Totalitarianism*, (New York: Harcourt. Brace & World, 1951, new edition, 1966). 526 pp.

4 Hannah Arendt, *Eichmann in Jerusalem: A Report of the Banality of Evil,* revised edition, (New York: Penguin Books, 1997).

5 Hannah Arendt, *The Human Condition,* (Chicago: University of Chicago Press, 1950), 332 pp.

6 Hannah Arendt, *On Revolution.,* (New York: The Viking Press, 1963), 363 pp.

7 Hannah Arendt, *Between Past and Future: Eight Exercises in Political Thought,* (New York: Penguin Books, 1968), 306 pp.

8 Hannah Arendt, *Love and Saint Augustine,* edited by Joanna Vecchiarelli-Scott and Judith Chelius Stark, (Chicago: University of Chicago Press, 1996).

9 Lucy S. Dawidowicz, *The War Against the Jews, 1933-1945,* (New York: Holt, Rinehart & Winston, 1975).

10 Raul Hilberg, *The Destruction of the European Jews,* (New York: Quadrangle Books-New York Times Book Co., 1961).

11 Hannah Arendt, *Lectures on Kant's Political Philosophy,* edited by Ronald Beiner, (Chicago: University of Chicago Press, 1982).

12 Nora Levin, *The Holocaust: The Destruction of European Jewry, 1933-1945,* (New York: Schocken Books, 1973); and Isaiah Trunk, *Judenrat: The Jewish Councils in Eastern Europe Under Nazi Occupation,* (New York: Stein & Day, Publishers, 1972).

13 Hannah Arendt, *The Life of the Mind, Volume One: Thinking,* edited with a Postface by Mary McCarthy, (New York: Harcourt Brace Jovanovich, 1978), pp. 258.

14 Hannah Arendt, *The Life of the Mind, Volume Two: Willing,* edited with a Postface by Mary McCarthy, (New York: Harcourt Brace Jovanovich, 1978), pp. 277.

15 Steven E. Aschheim, *Culture and Catastrophe: German and Jewish Confrontations with National Socialism and Other Crises,* (London: Macmillan, 1997), 210 pp.

16 Karl Dietrich Bracher, *The German Dictatorship: Origins, Structure, and Effects of National Socialism,* (New York: Praeger Publishers, 1970).

17 Yechaim Weitz, "The Holocaust on Trial: The Impact of the Kasztner and Eichmann Trials on Israeli Society," in *Israel Studies.* Volume 1, Number 2 (Fall 1996), pp. 1"26.

Chapter 13: A Natural History of the Holocaust

1 Yehuda Bauer, *Rethinking the Holocaust.* (New Haven: Yale University Press, 2001), 335 pp.

2 Lucy S. Dawidowicz, *The War against the Jews: 1933-1945,* (New York: Holt, Rinehart & Winston, 1975).

3 Raul Hilberg, *Destruction of the European Jews,* (New York: Holmes & Meier Publishers, 1985).

4 Nora Levin, *The Holocaust: The Destruction of European Jewry, 1933-1945*, (New York: Thomas Y. Crowell Co., 1968), 768 pp.

5 Fortunately we have several remarkable new reference works that will serve to rationalize and update the record. See Walter Laqueur, ed., *The Encyclopedia of the Holocaust,* (New Haven: Yale University Press, 2001), 848 pp.; Israel W. Charny, ed., *Encyclopedia of Genocide,* (Santa Barbara: ABC Clio Publishers, 2000), 1128 pp.; and Martin Gilbert, *Never Again: A History of the Holocaust,* (New York: Rizzoli International Publications, 2000), 192 pp.

6 Steven T. Katz, *The Holocaust in Historical Context: The Holocaust and Mass Death Before the Modern Age,* (New York and London: Oxford University Press, 1994), 657 pp.

7 Evgeny Grossman and Ilya Ehrenberg, *The Black Book of Russian Jewry,* (New Brunswick and London: Transaction Publishers, 2001), 890 pp.

8 Christopher R. Browning, *Nazi Policy, Jewish Workers, German Killers,* (New York: Cambridge University Press, 2000), pp. 32-34, 174-175.

9 Georg Simmel, *The Philosophy of Money*, 2nd edition, (London: Routledge & Kegan Paul, 1990), 537 pp.

10 Viviana Zelizer, *The Social Meaning of Money,* (Princeton, NJ: Princeton University Press, 1997), 304 pp.

11 Gabriel Schoenfield, "Holocaust Reparations: A Growing Scandal," *Commentary,* September 2000, pp. 25-34; and also various exchanges on the subject in *Commentary,* January 2001, esp. pp. 10-21.

12 See Jan T. Gross, "Neighbors: The Destruction of the Jewish Community in Jedwabne," *The New Yorker* (March 12, 2001), pp. 64-71, and his *Neighbors: The Destruction of the Jewish Community in Jedwabne, Poland* (Princeton, NJ: Princeton University Press, 2001), 216 pp. See also Adam Michnik, "Poles and the Jews: How Deep the Guilt?" *New York Times* (March 17, 2001), Arts Section, and Associated Press, "Experts Look for Jewish Burial Site," *New York Times* (March 17, 2001), World Section.

Chapter 14: Jewish Survival in a Post-Holocaust World

1 Elie Wiesel, "The Holocaust as Literary Inspiration," in *Dimensions of the Holocaust.* (Evanston, IL: Northwestern University Press, 1977), pp.5-19.

2 Compare and contrast such quite different efforts as that of H.H. Ben-Sasson, *A History of the Jewish People.* (Cambridge: Harvard University Press, 1985); and Robert M. Seltzer, *Jewish People, Jewish Thought.* (New York: Macmillan, London: Collier Macmillan, 1980).

3 Shlomo Deshen, Charles S. Liebman and Moshe Shokeid, T*he Sociology of Religion in Israel: Israeli Judaism.* (New York and London: Transaction Publishers, 1995).

4 Irving Louis Horowitz, *Israeli Ecstasies—Jewish Agonies.* (New York and London: Oxford University Press, 1974). Another work that pursues these same dialectical themes is Allon Gal's edited volume, *Envisioning Israel: The Changing Ideals and Images of North American Jews.* (Detroit: Wayne State University, 1996), 444 pp.

5 Irving Louis Horowitz, *Taking Lives: Genocide and State Power,* fourth edition, (New Brunswick and London: Transaction Publishers, 1997).

6 Richard L. Rubenstein, *After Auschwitz: History, Theology and Contemporary Judaism,* (Baltimore: Johns Hopkins Press, 1992), 38 pp.

7 Abba Eban, *Heritage: Civilization and the Jews,* (New York: Random House, 1984); and his earlier *Autobiography.* (New York: Random House, 1977), 628 pp., provide a pragmatic type of minimalism that typifies liberal Judaism in both the United States and Israel.

8 David Ben-Gurion, "How is Israel Different?"*Jewish Frontier,* Vol. 21 (August 1962). Cited in Howard M. Sachar,*A History of Israel: From the Rise of Zionism to Our Time,* (New York: Alfred A. Knopf, 1976), pp.718-719.

9 Geoffrey Wheatcroft, *The Controversy of Zion,* (London: Sinclair-Stevenson Publishers, 1996), pp.342-43.

10 David Vital, The *Future of the Jews*. (Cambridge, MA.: Harvard University Press, 1990), 161 pp.

11 Marshall Sklare Jonathan D. Sarna, eds., *Observing America's Jews*, (Waltham, MA.: Brandeis University, 1993), 623 pp., and the earlier volume by Marshall Sklare on *America's Jews*. (New York: Random House, 1971).

12 Melvin I. Urofsky, "Do American Jews Want Democracy in Jewish Life?" *Inter-Change*. Vol. I, No. 7, 1976. pp. 1-7; and Chaim I. Waxman, "The Centrality of Israel in American Jewish Life: A Sociological Analysis." *Judaism*. Vol. 25, No. 2, 1976.

13 B.Z. Sobel, Hebrew Christianity: *The Thirteenth Tribe*. (New York: John Wiley & Sons, 1974) and Robert Eisen, "Jewish Mysticism: Seeking Inner Light," *Moment*. Vol. 22, No. 1, 1997, pp. 38-43.

14 Shmuel N. Eisenstadt, *Jewish Civilization: The Jewish Historical Experience in a Comparative Perspective*, (Albany: State University of New York Press, 1992); and Amos Elon, *The Israelis: Founders and Sons*, (New York: Holt, Rinehart, and Winston, 1971).

15 Charles Liebman and Steven M. Cohen, *Two Worlds of Judaism: Israeli and American Experiences*, (New Haven: Yale University Press, 1990).

Chapter 15: Functional and Existential Visions of Genocide

1 Heinrich Böll, *Missing Persons* (New York: McGraw-Hill, 1977). 281 pp.

2 Talcott Parsons, "Some Sociological Aspects of the Fascist Movements," in *Essays on Sociological Theory* (Glencoe, Ill.: Free Press/Macmillan, 1949), pp. 124-141 It should be noted, in all fairness to Parsons, that his later writings on social systems have tended to emphasize their "evolutionary" characteristics and not just their "structural" components. See, for example, "Polity and Society: Some General Considerations," in *Politics and Social Structure* (New York: Free Press/Macmillan, 1969), pp. 473-522.

3 S. J. Woolf, *The Nature of Fascism* (New York: Random House, 1968); see in this connection Renzo De Felice, *Fascism: An Informal Introduction to Its Theory and Practice* (New Brunswick, NJ: Transaction Books, 1977). A major corrective to the rather undifferentiated past accounts of fascism is the outstanding reader, drawn from largely original sources, prepared by Roger Griffin, ed., *Fascism* (Oxford and New York: Oxford University Press, 1995).

4 Martyrs and Heroes Remembrance Authority, *The Holocaust* (Jerusalem: Yad Vashem, 1975), pp. 46-63.

5 The most authoritative figure available is 5,820,960 Jews who perished during the Holocaust; see "The Holocaust" in *Encyclopedia Judaica* (Jerusalem: Keter Publishing House Ltd., 1971), Vol. 8, pp. 827-915.

6 Raul Hilberg, *The Destruction of the European Jews* (Chicago: Quadrangle Books, 1961), pp. 766-767; and Lucy S. Dawidowicz, *The War against the Jews: 1933-1945* (New York: Holt, Rinehart, and Winston, 1975), pp. 150-166.

7 Henry L. Feingold, *The Politics of Rescue: The Roosevelt Administration and the Holocaust* (New Brunswick, NJ: Rutgers University Press, 1970), p. 304.

8 William Korey, *The Soviet Cage: Anti-Semitism in Russia* (New York: Viking Press, 1973), pp. 125-163.

9 Aleksandr I. Solzhenitsyn, *The Gulag Archipelago 1918-1956* (New York and London: Harper & Row, 1973), Vol. 1, pp. 24-25 For a fuller treatment of this point, Chapter 10, "Totalitarianism as a Penal Colony" is central.

10 Wilhelm Reich, *The Mass Psychology of Fascism*, trans. Vincent Carfagno (New York: Farrar, Straus & Giroux, 1970), p. 281. To this day, no one has exceeded Reich's effort to link fascist and communist systems as a sub-set of totalitarianism. In this, the title of Reich's book is more confined than the message of the book as such.

11 Antonio Gramsci, *Letters from Prison*, selected, trans., and introduced by Lynne Lawner (New York and London: Harper & Row, 1973), pp. 131-132 Perhaps no single research effort equals that of Renzo De Felice in understanding the crucial elements of *conciliazione* and *consenso* in Mussolini's Italy.

See especially *Mussolini il fascista: L'organizzazione dello state fascista — 1925-1929* and *Mussoloni il duce: Gli anni del consenso, 1929-1936* (Turin: Giulio Einaudi Editore, 1968 and 1974).

12 Federico Chabod, *L'Italia Contemporanea, 1918-1948* (Turin: Giulio Einaudi Editore, 1961), pp. 91-101.

13 Michael A. Ledeen, "Italian Jews and Fascism," *Judaism* (Summer 1968): 278-281; "The Jewish Question in Fascist Italy," paper delivered at the American Historical Association, December 1973; and "Fascist Social Policy" (section on Fascism and the Jews), in *The Use and Abuse of Social Policy: Behavioral Science and National Policy Making,* edited by Irving Louis Horowitz (New Brunswick, NJ: Transaction Books, 1971), pp. 90-108.

14 Zeev Sternhell, "Fascist Ideology," in *Fascism: A Reader's Guide,* ed. Walter Laqueur (Berkeley and Los Angeles: University of California Press, 1976), pp. 360-362.

15 John M. Steiner, *Power Politics and Social Change in National Socialist Germany* (The Hague: Mouton, 1976).

16 R. J. Rummel, "Dimensions of Foreign and Domestic Conflict Behavior: A Review of Empirical Findings," in *Theory and Research on the Causes of War*, ed. D. G. Pruitt and R. C. Snyder (Englewood Cliffs, NJ: Prentice-Hall, 1969), pp. 226-227.

17 Emile Durkheim, *Suicide: A Study in Sociology* (New York: Free Press/Macmillan, 1951), p. 39.

18 Hannah Arendt, *The Origins of Totalitarianism*, new edition. (New York: Harcourt, Brace, and World, 1966), p. 462.

19 Ibid., p. 463.

20 Contrast for example, Luigi Barzini, *The Italians,* with Ralf Dahrendorf, *Society and Democracy in Germany* (Garden City, NY: Doubleday, 1967).

21 Josué de Castro, *The Geography of Hunger* (Boston: Little, Brown, & Co., 1952).

22 Lester R. Brown, *World without Borders* (New York: Random House, 1972).

23 Don F. Hadwiger and William P. Browne, *New Politics of Food* (Lexington, MA: D. C. Heath, 1978).

24 Richard Arens, "Death Camps in Paraguay," *American Indian Journal* 4, No. 2 (July 1978): 3-12.

25 Daniel Jonah Goldhagen, *Hitler's Willing Executioners: Ordinary Germans and the Holocaust* (New York: Knopf, 1996). This is, by far, the most compelling work yet to appear arguing the full complicity of German citizens and civilians in the Nazi Holocaust. For an empirical confirmation of broad mass support for the Nazi extermination policy, see Raul Hilberg, "German Railroads/Jewish Souls," *Society* 14, No. 1 (November-December 1976): 60-74.

26 Anna Pawelczynska, *Values and Violence in Auschwitz* (Berkeley and Los Angeles: University of California Press, 1979), pp. 15-23.

27 Paul Baran, *The Political Economy of Growth* (New York: Monthly Review Press, 1957), p. 3 et passim. See my critique of the orthodox Communist position in *Three Worlds of Development: The Theory and Practice of International Stratification* (New York and Oxford: Oxford Unviersity Press, 1972), pp. 284-314.

28 R. J. Rummel, *Death by Government: Genocide and Mass Murder Since 1900* (New Brunswick, NJ, and London: Transaction Publishers, 1994). This contains the best brief account of the actual numbers of lives taken in the name of development (by the Soviets) and in the name of racial purity (by the Nazis).

Chapter 16: Exclusivity and Inclusivity of Collective Death

1 Lucy S. Dawidowicz, *The War Against the Jews: 1933-1945* (New York: Holt, Rinehart, and Winston, 1975).

2 John Vinocur, "In West Berlin: A New Curtain Rises on Auschwitz," *New York Times,* 7 April 1980, p. 2.

3 Yehuda Bauer, *The Holocaust in Historical Perspective* (Seattle: University of Washington Press, 1978), pp. 30-49.

4 Elie Wiesel, *Legends of Our Time* (New York: Holt, Rinehart, & Winston, 1968), p. 6. For an analysis of this vision, see Terrence Des Pres, "The Authority of Silence in Elie Wiesel"s Art," in *Confronting The Holocaust: The Impact of Elie Wiesel,* ed.

Alvin H. Rosenfeld and Irving Greenberg (Bloomington: Indiana University Press, 1978), pp. 49-57.

5 Peter J. Donaldson, "In Cambodia, A Holocaust," *New York Times,* 22 April 1980, p. 17. More recent information has not only confirmed, but deepened a realization of the magnitude of the Cambodian genocide. See Seth Mydans, "Cambodian Killers' Careful Records Used Against Them," *New York Times.* 7 June 1996, pp.1, 8. Estimates now range that the Communist Khmer Rouge murdered two million out of an estimated seven million Cambodian people.

6 Emil L. Fackenheim, "What the Holocaust Was Not," *Face to Face,* an interreligious Bulletin issued by the Anti-Defamation League of B'nai B'rith, 7 (Winter 1980): 8-9. This set of propositions is derived from Fackenheim"s Foreword to Yehuda Bauer's *The Jewish Emergence from Powerlessness* (Toronto: University of Toronto Press, 1979).

7 For a full version of what has become a dominant and widely accepted Jewish viewpoint on the Holocaust, see Emil L. Fackenheim, *God's Presence in History* (New York: Harper Torchbooks/Harper & Row, 1972), pp. 70-73.

8 Robert J. Lifton, "The Concept of the Survivor," in *Survivors, Victims, and Perpetrators: Essays on the Nazi Holocaust,* ed. Joel E. Dimsdale (Washington, D.C.: Hemisphere, 1980), pp. 113-126

9 Literature on the Armenian subjugation is uneven, and only now facing up to the herculean research tasks involved. An excellent compendium of available materials for 1915-1923 is contained in Richard G. Hovannisian, *The Armenian Holocaust,* rev. ed. (Cambridge, MA: Armenian Heritage Press, 1980).

10 Anna Pawelczynska, *Values and Violence in Auschwitz* (Berkeley and Los Angeles: University of California Press, 1979), pp. 101-105.

11 Raul Hilberg, "German Railroads/Jewish Souls," *Society* 14, No. 1 (November-December 1976): 60-74 For a general introduction to this subject, see *Captured German and Related Records: A National Archives Conference,* ed. Robert Wolfe (Athens: Ohio University Press, 1974).

12 George L. Mosse, *Toward the Final Solution: A History of European Racism* (New York: Howard Fertig Publishers, 1978), pp. 226-227.

13 Gideon Hausner, "Six Million Accusers," in *The Jew in the Modern World: A Documentary History,* ed. Paul R. Mendes-Flohr and Jehuda Reinharz (New York: Oxford University Press, 1980), pp. 521-523.

14 D. L. Niewyk, *Socialist, Anti-Semite, and Jew: German Social Democracy Confronts the Problems of Anti-Semitism* (Baton Rouge: Louisiana State University Press, 1971).

15 Elie Wiesel, "The Struggle of the Survivor" (an interview with Christian Tyler based on *All Rivers Run to the Sea*) in *The Financial Times* (16 June, 1996) p.18 (weekend segment).

16 For a full discussion of the orthodox (minority) viewpoint on the Holocaust in the context of Yeshiva life, see William Helmreich, "Making the Awful Meaningful," *Society* 19, No. 6 (September-October 1982): 62-66.

17 Arthur R. Butz, *The Hoax of the Twentieth Century* (Torrance, CA: Noontide Press, 1976).

18 See Austin J. App, "The 'Holocaust' Put in Perspective," *Journal of Historical Review* (Spring 1980): 43-58.

19 Charles E. Weber, "German History from a New Perspective," *Journal of Historical Review* (Spring 1980): 81-82.

20 The most authoritative estimate of the number of European Jews killed by the Nazis — 5,978,000 out of a prewar population of 8,301,000, or 72 percent — is contained in Leon Poliakov and Josef Wulf, eds., *Das Dritte Reich und die Juden: Dokumente und Aufsaetze* (Berlin: Arani-Verlag, 1955), p. 229.

21 For an articulate statement of legal and social issues at an individual level that have direct relevance to our discussion at the collective level, see George Z. F. Bereday, "The Right to Live and the Right to Die: Some Considerations of Law and Society in America," *Man and Medicine* 4, No. 4 (1979): 233-256.

Chapter 17: Surviving the Genocidal State

1 Judith Miller, *One by One, by One: Facing the Holocaust* (New York: Simon & Schuster, 1990), p. 287.

2 Ralf Dahrendorf, *Society and Democracy in Germany* (Garden City, N.Y.: Doubleday, 1967), pp. 205-209. This remains the best single volume effort at understanding German society throughout the century.

3 William L. Patterson, *We Charge Genocide: The Historic Petition to the United Nations for Relief from a Crime of the United States Government against the Negro People* (New York: International Publishers, 1951, 1970).

4 Luigi G. Barzini, *The Italians* (New York: Atheneum, 1964).

5 Karl Jaspers, *The Future of Germany,* trans. and ed. E. B. Ashton (Chicago: University of Chicago Press, 1967).

6 Michael Walzer, *Obligations: Essays on Disobedience, War and Citizenship* (New York: Simon & Schuster, 1970), p. 98.

7 Richard A. Falk, "Ecocide, Genocide, and the Nuremberg Tradition of Individual Responsibility," *in Philosophy, Morality, International Affairs,* ed. Virginia Held, Sidney Morgenbesser, and Thomas Nagel (New York: Oxford University Press, 1974), pp. 136-137.

8 Albert Somit, *Biology and Politics: Recent Explorations* (The Hague and Paris: Mouton, 1976), pp. 3-11.

9 Christian Tomuschat, "International Criminal Prosecution: The Precedent of Nuremberg Confirmed," in *The Prosecution of International Crimes,* edited by Roger S. Clark and Madeleine Sann. (New Brunswick and London: Transaction Publishers, 1996), pp. 17-28.

Chapter 18: Life, Death, and Sociology

1 Gerard Prunier, *The Rwanda Crisis: History of a Genocide* (New York: Columbia University Press, 1996). 326 pp.

2 Maurice Merleau-Ponty, *Humanism and Terror: An Essay on the Communist Problem* (Boston: Beacon Press, 1969; originally published in French, 1947), p. 88.

3 Hannah Arendt, *The Origins of Totalitarianism*, new edition (New York: Harcourt, Brace, & World, 1966), pp. 460-463.

4 John R. Seeley, "Social Science: Some Probative Problems," in *Sociology on Trial*, ed. Maurice Stein and Arthur Vidich (Englewood Cliffs, NJ: Prentice-Hall, 1963), pp. 64-65.

5 C. Wright Mills, *The Sociological Imagination* (New York: Oxford University Press, 1959), pp. 3-13.

6 Irving Louis Horowitz, *War and Peace in Contemporary Social and Philosophical Theory* (London: Souvenir Press; New York: Humanities Publishers, 1973; originally published in 1957), pp. 192-203.

7 W. F. Cottrell, "Death by Dieselization: A Case Study in the Reaction to Technological Change,"*American Sociological Review* 16, No. 3 (June 1951): 358-365.

8 Harry M. Caudill, *Night Comes to the Cumberlands: A Biography of a Depressed Area* (Boston: Little, Brown/Atlantic Monthly Press, 1963), pp. 305-324.

9 Stephan L. Chorover, *From Genesis to Genocide: The Meaning of Human Nature and the Power of Behavior Control* (Cambridge and London: MIT Press, 1979), esp. pp. 1-10, 77-111.

10 Barbara W. Tuchman, *A Distant Mirror: The Calamitous 14th Century* (New York: Knopf, 1978), pp. 509-511.

11 Benzion Netanyahu, *The Origins of the Inquisition in Fifteenth Century Spain* (New York: Random House, 1995), p. 1348.

Chapter 19: Researching Genocide

1 Tzvetan Todorov,*Facing the Extreme: Moral Life in the Concentration Camps* (New York: Henry Holt, 1996), pp. 289-291.

2 R. J. Rummel, *Death by Government: Genocide and Mass Murder since 1900* (New Brunswick and London: Transaction Publishers, 1994).

3 Israel Charny, ed., *The Widening Circle of Genocide* (New Brunswick and London: Transaction Publishers, 1994). Charny's work merits attention in bibliographic no less than intellectual terms. Indeed, his four volumes on *Genocide: A Critical Bibliographic Review* (of which the aforementioned is the third in the series) has become the standard for any serious literature review on the subject.

4 Robert F. Melson, *Revolution and Genocide: On the Origins of the Armenian Genocide and the Holocaust* (Chicago: University of Chicago Press, 1992).

5 Vahakn Dadrian, Genocide as a Problem of National and International Law, in *Yale Journal of International Law*, volume 14, number 2 (summer 1989) p. 333. For a fuller discussion of these themes by the same author, see "The Armenian Genocide in Relation to the Holocaust and the Nuremberg Trials", in *The History of the Armenian Genocide,* Providence and Oxford: Berghahn Books, 1995 pp.394-419.

6 Ibid., p. 247.

7 Ibid., p. 173 See also, Leo Kuper, *Genocide: Its Political Use in the Twentieth Century.* New Haven and London: Yale University Press, 1982 pp.256.

8 *Forever in the Shadow of Hitler? Original Documents of the "Historikerstreit," the Controversy Concerning the Singularity of the Holocaust,* trans. James Knowlton and Truett Cates (Atlantic Highlands, NJ: Humanities Press, 1993), pp. 282.

9 Daniel Jonah Goldhagen, *Hitler's Willing Executioners: Ordinary Germans and the Holocaust* (New York: Alfred A. Knopf, 1996). See also, John Weiss, *Ideology of Death: Why the Holocaust Happened in Germany* (Chicago: Ivan R. Dee, Publisher, 1996). It is only fit and proper that the final reference in this chapter be to the work of Lucy S. Dawidowicz, *The War Against the Jews: 1933-45* (New York: Holt, Rinehart, Winston, 1975).

Chapter 20: Gauging Genocide

1 Czeslaw Milosz, *Milosz's ABCs*, trans. by Madel G. Levine (New York: Farrar, Straus & Giroux, 2001), 313 pp.

2 Irving Louis Horowitz, *Daydreams and Nightmares: Reflections of a Harlem Childhood*, (Jackson and London: University Press of Mississippi, 1990), 114 pp.

3 Irving Louis Horowitz, *War and Peace in Contemporary Social and Philosophical Theory*, (New York: Paine-Whitman Publishers, 1956; London: Souvenir Press. 1973), 220 pp.

4 Irving Louis Horowitz, *Radicalism and the Revolt Against Reason* (London: Routledge & Kegan Paul, 1961; New York: Humanities Press, Inc. 1962); Expanded edition (Carbondale: Southern Illinois University Press, 1968), 338 pp.

5 Irving Louis Horowitz, ed., *The Anarchists*, (New York: Dell/Delta Publishing (Laurel Original), 1964), 640 pp.

6 Irving Louis Horowitz, *Israeli Ecstasies and Jewish Agonies*, (New York and London: Oxford University Press, 1974), 244 pp.

7 Irving Louis Horowitz, "The Texture of Terrorism: Socialization, Routinization, and Integration," in *Political Learning in Adulthood: A Sourcebook of Theory and Research,* edited by Roberta S. Sigel, (Chicago and London: The University of Chicago Press, 1989), pp.386-414.

8 Irving Louis Horowitz, *Foundations of Political Sociology,* (New York and London: Harper & Row, 1972), 590 pp.

9 Irving Louis Horowitz, *Taking Lives: Genocide and State Power,* fourth edition, (New Brunswick and London: Transaction Publishers, 1997), 325 pp.

10 R.J. Rummel, *Death by Government*, (New Brunswick and London: Transaction Publishers), 1994.

11 Eugene V. Walter, *Terror and Resistance: A Study of Political Violence*, (New York: Oxford University Press), 1959.

12 Walter Laqueur, *Origins of Terrorism*, (Washington, DC: Woodrow Wilson Center Press), 1998.

13 Robert A. Nisbet, *Tradition and Revolt,* (New York: Random House), 1968.

14 Irving Louis Horowitz, "Genocide and the Reconstruction of Social Theory," in a special issue of *The Armenian Review on Genocide and Crimes Against Humanity.* Vol.37, No.1 (Spring 1984), pp. 1-22.

15 Irving Louis Horowitz, "The Vietnamization of Yugoslavia." *Society.* Volume 36, Number 5, July-August 1999, pp. 3-10.

INDEX

Index of Names and Topics

1984, 50, 76

Adelman, Howard, 401
Adenauer, Konrad, 220
al-Husseini, Hajj Amin, 330
Alexander Nevsky, 390
All Rivers Run to the Sea, 335
Allende, Salvador, 97
Amin, Idi, 71, 164-166
Anarchists, The, 392
Arendt, Hannah, 12, 70, 185, 229-253, 309, 360, 376, 394, 397
Aristotle, 199, 246
Asylums, 75, 187
Atatürk, Kemal, 157, 158, 377
Augstein, Rudolf, 226
Axis Rule in Occupied Europe, 20

Bacon, Francis, 375
Bakalian, Anny, 400
Balfour, Arthur James, 336
Bamm, Peter, 70
Baran, Paul, 315
Baranczak, Stanislaw, 49
Barzini, Luigi, 349
Bauer, Yehuda, 255, 374, 377
Bauman, Zygmunt, 46
Behemoth, 396, 398
Bell, Daniel, 394
Ben-Gurion, David, 279

Bennett, William J., 64
Bernstein, Eduard, 215
Biondich, Mark, 264
Bismarck, Otto von, 378
Black Book of Russian Jewry, The, 263
Bleackley, Horace, 71
Bloch, Ernst, 12
Böll, Heinrich, 297
Bonaparte, Louis, 171
Bones of Berdichev, The, 205
Book of Virtues, The, 64
Bracher, Karl Dietrich, 225
Brave New World, 50
Brezhnev, Leonid, 185
Broszat, Martin, 224
Brown, Lester R., 310
Browning, Christopher, 263, 264
Buber, Martin, 331
Bullock, Alan, 223
Burke, Edmund, 231, 234
Butz, Arthur R., 337

Calley, William J., 320
Campanella, Tomasso, 50
Camus, Albert, 89, 365
Cancer Ward, The, 183
Castro, Fidel, 171, 401
Castro, Josue de, 310
Chalk, Frank, 14, 15

Charny, Israel W., 368, 371, 372, 374-376, 401
Chessman, Caryl, 78
China's Bloody Century, 370
Chmielnicki, Bogdan, 335
Chorover, Stephan, 363
City of God, 53
City of Sun, 50, 53
Cohn, Norman, 3
Commanger, Henry Steele, 67
Commentary, 268
Committees on Correspondence, 392
Condillac, Etienne Bonnot de, 217
Controversy of Zion, The, 280
Critique of Judgment, 250
Critique of Practical Reason, 250
Critique of Pure Reason, 250
Crozier, Michel, 141, 142

Dadrian, Vahakn, 16, 17, 158, 372, 375, 378, 400
Dahrendorf, Ralf, 343
Damiens, 58, 69, 70
Darwin, Charles, 33, 161, 204, 309
Dawidowicz, Lucy, 36, 222, 241, 257, 284, 319, 376
Daydreams and Nightmares, 390
De-Moralization of Society, 57
Death by Government, 368, 370
Death in Life, 185
Debray, Regis, 97
Democide, 370
Derogy, Jacques, 400
Der Stürmer, 216
Destruction of the European Jews, The, 185
Devine, Philip E., 84

Dewey, John, 95, 392
Diary of the Nazi Years, A, 216
Dickens, Charles, 215
Die Zeit, 226
Dietrich, Donald J., 401
Dilthey, Wilhelm, 350
Dimensions: A Journal of Holocaust Studies, 4
Discipline and Punish, 58
Discourses on Inequality, 53
Djilas, Milovan, 181
Dostoyevsky, Feodor, 185
Drapkin, Israel, 16, 376
Dunn, James, 375
Durkheim, Emile, 251, 308, 343

Eban, Abba, 279
Ehrenberg, Ilya, 263
Eichmann, Adolf, 70, 240-243, 259, 262, 376
Eichmann in Jerusalem, 231, 240-244
Eiseley, Loren, 35
Eisenstein, Sergei, 390
Elazar, Daniel, 401
Elon, Amos, 229
Engels, Friedrich, 192
Enver Pasha, 158
Ethics of Homocide, The, 84
Evita, 320

Fackenheim, Emil, 322, 324, 326, 327, 329, 331, 332, 334
Falk, Richard, 352
Federalist Papers, The, 239
Fein, Helen, 376
Feingold, Henry, 301
First Circle, The, 183
Fleming, Peter, 173

Ford, Gerald, 103
Forever in the Shadow of Hitler, 221
Foucault, Michel, 58, 69
Foundations of the Metaphysics of Morals, 250
Foundations of Political Sociology, 396
Frankfurter Allgemeine Zeitung, 226
Freud, Sigmund, 331
Future of Mankind, The, 233, 238

Gandhi, Mohandas K., 62, 392
Garrad, Carol, 205
Garrad, John, 205
Gay, Peter, 211-219, 221
Geiss, Immanuel, 226
Genocide as a Problem of National and International Law, 378
Gilmore, Gary, 78
Ginzberg, Eli, 394
Glick, Leonard, 375
Goebbels, Joseph, 216, 333
Goethe, Johann Wolfgang von, 41, 194
Goffman, Erving, 75, 187
Goldhagen, Daniel Jonah, 217, 227
Goodall, Jane, 45
Gorbachev, Mikhail, 207
Gordenkener, Leon, 25
Göring, Hermann, 299
Gramsci, Antonio, 304, 329
Gross, Feliks, 17-20
Gross, Jan T., 268
Grossman, Evgeny, 263
Guevara, Ernesto (Che), 106

Gulag Archipelago, The, 74, 182-208, 302, 370

Habermas, Jürgen, 222-227
Hacker, Andrew, 394
Hamit, Abdul, 378
Haritos-Fatouros, Mika, 368
Hausner, Gideon, 331
Hegel, Georg Wilhelm Friedrich, 144, 217, 244, 250, 252
Heidegger, Martin, 244, 250, 251, 264
Heine, Heinrich, 212
Helmreich, William, 335, 401
Helvètius, Claude Adrien, 217
Hersey, John, 67
Herzen, Aleksandr Ivanovitch, 253
Herzl, Theodor, 282, 393
Herzog, Vladimir, 83
Hess, Rudolf, 373
Hilberg, Raul, 44, 185, 187, 222, 223, 241, 257, 324, 325, 376
Hillgruber, Andreas, 224
Himmelfarb, Gertrude, 57
Himmler, Heinrich, 262
Historikerstreit, 222
History and Memory, 4
History of the Jews, A, 211
Hitler, Adolf, 8, 22, 102, 130, 167, 217, 220, 223, 230, 301, 302, 331, 333, 337, 397
Hobbes, Thomas, 10, 40, 77, 134, 135
Hollow Miracle, The, 221, 380
Holocaust and Genocide Studies, 4
Hope of Earth, The, 53
Hope of Heaven, The, 53

Hovannisian, Richard G., 376, 400

Human Condition, The, 233, 235, 244, 245

Humanism and Terror, 359

Huxley, Aldous, 50

I Speak for the Silent, 206

I Will Bear Witness, 214

Idea of War and Peace in Contemporary Social and Philosophical Theory, 7, 392

Ignatieff, Michael, 211

Investigation, The, 320

Irving, David, 266

Irwin-Zarecka, Iwona, 401

Israeli Ecstasies, Jewish Agonies, 275, 279, 394

Jaspers, Karl, 233, 238, 349

Jernazian, Ephraim K., 400

Jesus Christ, 208

Johnson, Lyndon, 100

Johnson, Paul, 211

Jonassohn, Kurt, 14, 15, 376, 401

Jones, Reverend Jim, 23

Jung, Carl Gustav, 177, 178

Kant, Immanuel, 51, 244, 247, 249, 250, 252, 376

Katz, Jacob, 130

Kaufman, Edy, 17, 18

Kelman, Herbert C., 368

Kennedy, John F., 103

Kennedy, Robert, 103

Kent, George, 375

Kevorkian, Jack, 5, 6

Khomeini, Ayatollah, 328

King, Martin Luther, Jr., 103

Kisuule-Minge, Abraham, 71

Klemperer, Victor, 211-219, 221, 265

Kocka, Jürgen, 224

Konvitz, Milton, 394

Kosygin, Alexi N., 185

Krell, Robert, 375

Krikorian, Y.H., 245

Kristellar, Paul Oscar, 392

Krushchev, Nikita, 189

Kuper, Leo, 374

Lamarck, Jean Baptiste, 63

Laqueur, Walter, 205

Latell, Brian, 395

Leaves from a Russian Diary, 206

Leicht, Robert, 224

Lemkin, Raphael, 20, 376

Lenin, Vladimir, 96, 142, 184, 187, 189-193, 198, 199, 205, 302, 310, 392, 396

Letelier, Orlando, 83

Lethal Politics, 370

Levene, Mark, 26

Leviathan, The, 10

Levi-Strauss, Claude, 173

Levin, Nora, 257

Liebman, Charles, 292

Lieutenant, The, 320

Life of the Mind, 244, 245, 247, 249

Lifton, Robert J., 185, 187, 323

Lipstadt, Deborah, 266

Locke, John, 95, 178, 250, 349

Lofland, John, 71

Lonely Crowd, The, 392

Machiavelli, Niccolo, 134, 135

Malthus, Thomas, 310

Mandel, Ernest, 141, 142
Mann, Thomas, 212
Mao, Tse-tung, 77, 96
Marx, Karl, 64, 95, 96, 141, 142, 184, 187, 191-192, 198, 205, 251, 252, 306, 310, 393, 396
Mead, H.G., 245
Melson, Robert F., 308, 376, 377, 379
Merleau-Ponty, Maurice, 89, 359
Metternich, Klemens Wenzel Nepomuk Lothar von, 98
Michnik, Adam, 268
Mill, John Stuart, 95, 349, 362
Miller, Judith, 341
Milosz, Czeslaw, 389
Minawa, Farouk, 71
Mommsen, Hans, 224
Mommsen, Wolfgang J., 224
Montesquieu, Charles de Secondat (Baron), 95
Morgenthau, Hans, 244, 395
Morgenthau, Henry, 331
Moses, 54
Mosse, George, 21, 22, 177, 265
Mussolini, Benito, 217
My German Question, 216

Napoleon III, 171
Nazi Policy, Jewish Workers, German Killers, 263
Neumann, Franz, 214
New York Times, The, 185
New Yorker, The, 244, 373
Niemoller, Martin, 264
Nietzsche, Friedrich, 57, 244
Noelle-Neumann, Elizabeth, 215
Nolte, Ernst, 222-224, 226, 227
Nomad, Max, 190

Obote, Milton, 162
On Revolution, 233, 235, 237, 244
One Day in the Life of Ivan Denisovich, 183
Origins of Totalitarianism, The, 230-232, 234, 235, 244
Orwell, George, 50, 76
Osiel, Mark, 401

Parsons, Talcott, 298, 299
Patterson, William L., 347
Pavlov, Ivan, 187
Pawelczynska, Anna, 313
Peron, Eva, 320
Pinochet, Augusto, 172
Pipes, Richard, 189
Pius XI, 265
Pius XII, 265
Plato, 199, 250, 297
Politics of Rescue, The, 301
Pollard, Jonathan, 291
Pool, Ithiel de Sola, 394
Popper, Karl, 250
Poulantzas, Nicos, 141
Proudhon, Pierre, 96
Prunier, Gerard, 359

Radicalism and the Revolt Against Reason, 375, 392
Rahv, Philip, 111
Rauschning, Hermann, 332
Reagan, Ronald, 103
Reich, Wilhelm, 56, 303
Report on the Evil of Banality, A, 241
Revolution and Genocide, 377, 380
Ribeiro, Darcy, 164

Rickert, Heinrich, 350
Riefenstahl, Leni, 49
Riesman, David, 392
Robespierre, Maximilien
    François Marie Isidore de,
    113, 233, 239
Roosevelt, Franklin Delano, 301
Rousseau, Jean Jacques, 52-54
Rummel, R.J., 29, 229, 368-371,
    374, 375, 399, 401
Russia in Chains, 206
Ryback, Timothy W., 373

Saint Augustine, 52, 54
Sakharov, Andrei, 83
Schindler, Oskar, 242
Schindler's List, 4, 63
Schmid, Alex P., 368
Schonborn, Christoph, 53
Schulze, Hagen, 219, 220
Servan-Schreiber, Jean-Jacques,
    142
Shah of Iran, The (Muhammad
    Riza Pahlevi), 174
Shoah, 215
Sholokhov, Mikhail, 49
Simmel, Georg, 268
Slotkin, Richard, 177
Smith, Adam, 68
Social Contract, The, 53
*Social Deviance and Political
    Marginality*, 74
Solonevich, Ivan, 206
Solzhenitsyn, Aleksandr, 74, 182-
    208, 229, 253, 302, 316, 370
Sombart, Werner, 393
Sontheimer, Kurt, 224
Sorel, Georges, 97
Sorokin, Pitirim, 206

Spender, Stephen, 244
Spranger, Eduard, 154
Stalin, Joseph, 17, 38, 64, 96, 102,
    130, 165, 167, 185, 188-193,
    197, 230, 263, 302, 303, 310,
    347, 397
Stanley, Manfred, 148
Stannard, David E., 266
*State Executions Viewed Histori-
    cally and Sociologically*, 71
State, Power, Socialism, 142
Steiner, George, 37, 221, 380
Sternhell, Zeev, 306
Stokes, William, 163
Stroessner, Alfred, 311

Taking Lives, 7-11, 275-278, 375,
    396, 398
Talmon, Jacob, 234
Tchernavi, Vladimir, 206
Thermidor, 239
Thinking, 244, 246
Tocqueville, Alexis de, 234
Todorov, Tzvetan, 367
Totten, Samuel, 375
Toynbee, Arnold, 345
*Travels of Olearius in Seven-
    teenth Century Russia*, 58
Tuchman, Barbara, 215, 216
Tullock, Gordon, 145
Types of Men, 154

Ulam, Adam, 189
Urofsky, Melvin, 286

van Bruinessen, Martin, 375
Viano, Emilio, 16
Voegelin, Eric, 234

Voltaire, François Marie Arouet de, 212

Wald, George, 394
Wallace, George, 103
Walzer, Michael, 351
War Game, The, 7
We Charge Genocide, 347
Weber, Max, 129, 137, 251, 397
Weingartner, James, 108
Weiss, Peter, 320
Weizmann, Chaim, 224
Wheatcroft, Geoffrey, 280

Wheeler, John Archibald, 129
Whitehead, Alfred North, 392
Wilkinson, Paul, 395
Widening Circle of Genocide, The, 371, 375, 376
Wiesel, Elie, 273, 320, 335

Yeats, William Butler, 153
Yeltsin, Boris, 207

Zelizer, Viviana, 268

THIS WORK WAS COMPUTER-TYPESET using Ventura Publisher, Version 8. Text was set in 11-point Times Ten, developed by Linotype as a soft-type version of Times Eurpoa, itself a derivative of the classic Times Roman designed by the Monotype Corporation for the *Times* of London in 1931. Chapter headers were set in Maryland, a soft-type face designed in 1993 by Brother International.